FRANCES E. WILLARD

Frances E Willard
LONDON, 1893.

THE BEAUTIFUL LIFE
OF
FRANCES E. WILLARD

A MEMORIAL VOLUME

BY

ANNA A. GORDON

For twenty-one years her private secretary

INTRODUCTION BY

LADY HENRY SOMERSET

With Character Sketches and Memorial Tributes

BY

THE GENERAL OFFICERS OF THE WORLD'S AND THE NATIONAL W. C. T. U., ENGLISH LEADERS, DR. EDWARD EVERETT HALE, DR. FRANK W. GUNSAULUS, DR. NEWELL DWIGHT HILLIS, PRESIDENT HENRY WADE ROGERS, DR. MILTON S. TERRY, DR. C. J. LITTLE, DR. CHARLES F. BRADLEY, JOSEPH COOK, JOHN G. WOOLLEY, COL. GEO. W. BAIN, MARY LOWE DICKINSON, MARY A. LATHBURY, ELIZABETH STUART PHELPS WARD, MARY A. LIVERMORE, SUSAN B. ANTHONY, LILLIAN WHITING, BISHOP VINCENT, BOOKER T. WASHINGTON, ELIZABETH CADY STANTON, FRANCIS E. CLARK, CONSUL BOOTH-TUCKER, MAUD BALLINGTON BOOTH, HON. JOHN D. LONG, DWIGHT L. MOODY, DR. THEODORE L. CUYLER, RABBI HIRSCH, PUNDITA RAMABAI, AND OTHER DISTINGUISHED PERSONS.

PUBLISHED BY THE
WOMAN'S TEMPERANCE PUBLISHING ASSOCIATION
CHICAGO, ILL.

COPYRIGHT, 1898, BY
THE WOMAN'S TEMPERANCE PUBLISHING ASSOCIATION
All rights reserved

"O young Mariner,
  You from the haven
  Under the sea-cliff,
  You that are watching
  The gray Magician
  With eyes of wonder,
  I am Merlin,
  And *I* am dying,
  I am Merlin
  Who follow The Gleam.
  . . . . .

"And so to the land's
  Last limit I came——
  And can no longer,
  But die rejoicing,
  For thro' the Magic
  Of Him the Mighty,
  Who taught me in childhood,
  There on the border
  Of boundless Ocean,
  And all but in Heaven
  Hovers The Gleam.

"Not of the sunlight,
  Not of the moonlight,
  Not of the starlight!
  O young Mariner,
  Down to the haven,
  Call your companions,
  Launch your vessel,
  And crowd your canvas,
  And, ere it vanishes
  Over the margin,
  After it, follow it,
  Follow The Gleam."
                    — *Tennyson.*

CONTENTS

PART I
BIOGRAPHY

CHAPTER		PAGE
I.	Ancestral Gifts	17
II.	Childhood	22
III.	Student Life	35
IV.	Religious Development	46
V.	Teacher — Preceptress — Dean	54
VI.	A Traveler Abroad	67
VII.	The Choice of a Career	92
VIII.	Organizer and Leader of the Woman's Christian Temperance Union	98
IX.	Founder of the World's Woman's Christian Temperance Union	147
X.	A Great Mother	204
XI.	In the Mother Country	216
XII.	Answering Armenia's Cry	258
XIII.	Old Haunts and Homes Revisited	270
XIV.	Nearing the Heavenly Home	282
XV.	Translation	292

PART II
IN MEMORIAM

The Commemorative Services — New York City; Churchville, N. Y.; Willard Hall, Chicago; Evanston; Rose Hill Cemetery 299

Character Sketches — Tributes 334

ILLUSTRATIONS

Frances E. Willard.
Photograph — Miss Willard, London, 1893.
Rev. Samuel Willard.
Miss Willard's Birthplace, Oberlin Residence, Forest Home.
School Buildings and Woman's College.
Churches — Churchville — Ogden — Janesville — Evanston.
Katharine A. Jackson.
"My Four."
Anna A. Gordon.
General Offices of the National W. C. T. U.
The Temple.
Willard Fountain.
Marble Bust, by Anne Whitney.
The General Officers of the World's W. C. T. U.
Miss Willard in Her "Den."
The Polyglot Petition.
Lady Henry Somerset, 1890.
St. Courageous, Her Daughter Frances and Anna A. Gordon.
Miss Willard, London.
Interior Views, Eastnor Castle, England.
Miss Willard in "The Cottage," Reigate, England.
Group Photograph — Rest Cottage, Catskills Cottage, Eastnor Castle, Reigate Cottage.
A Group of Armenians, Marseilles, France, 1896.
Hill Homestead — Willard Home.
Photograph Group — From Childhood to Present Time.
The Empire Hotel, New York City.
Katharine Willard Baldwin.
Miss Willard's Successor as President of the National W. C. T. U.
Miss Willard's Successor as President of the World's W. C. T. U.
Platform of Willard Hall, February 23, 1898.
Mrs. Mary B. Willard and Her Daughter, Mary.
Namesakes.

PREFACE

THE sending forth of a Memorial Volume at the loving insistence of the General Officers of the National Woman's Christian Temperance Union is a sad and sacred privilege intrusted to me because for twenty-one years God gave me that which was my highest joy, the opportunity to share the most toilsome period of Frances E. Willard's sublime and heroic life. It is brought out thus early to meet an immediate demand and is published by the Woman's Temperance Publishing Association, the official Publishing House of the National Woman's Christian Temperance Union.

I could not have undertaken the work without the approval and sympathetic co-operation of Lady Henry Somerset, that loyal and great-hearted friend, who by the law of kinship among great souls was closely united to Miss Willard in endeavor, achievement and ideals. The generous assistance of two of Chicago's leading clergymen, Dr. Frank W. Gunsaulus and Dr. Newell Dwight Hillis, is also gratefully acknowledged, together with suggestions and contributions from many valued friends.

Since the volume must be devoted in large part to character sketches, tributes, and a description of the commemorative services, it is evident that anything beyond an outline biography would be impossible; but we believe this picture of Miss Willard's remarkable and winsome personality will deepen in the hearts of the people she loved, the desire to hold aloft her white banner of purity and peace, patriotism and prohibition, the protection of the home and the redemption of humanity.

Among Miss Willard's treasures long and carefully guarded, I have found a little book bearing the title, "Memoir of Nathan Dickerman," probably the first memorial biography on which her childish eyes rested. On the fly leaf is written: "Read on the long, lonesome Sundays at Forest Home in my childhood. I remember a delicate, exquisite odor that adhered to the book from its relation somewhere with a sweet and pervasive perfume so that I early got the notion of fragrance and religion as inseparable."

Truly, "pure religion and undefiled" is inseparable from the fragrance of Frances Willard's life. Strong, courageous, indomitable, yet a fair sweet flower "whose petals and whose perfume expand so far that we are all enfolded and sheltered in its tenderness and beauty."

Anna A. Gordon

CHICAGO, March 10, 1898.

INTRODUCTORY

BY

Lady Henry Somerset

A CABLE has come asking me to send an introduction to the memorial biography that is being prepared of the greatest woman philanthropist of our generation. I do not hesitate at the use of this word "greatest." I *know* that time alone can prove the worth of any work, and that only down the perspective of the years are we able to gauge the comparative importance of the human lives that have made history; but I am persuaded that, when the annals of the nineteenth century are written, when the record of the modern movement that has metamorphosed the position of woman comes to be told, Frances Willard's name will stand pre-eminent as the one who saw with a keen prophetic eye ahead of her time, who realized the dangers, who steered clear of the rocks and shoals that beset any great change, and who furnished the women, not only of a great continent but the world over, with a just realization of their rightful position, and with that safe-guarding gospel, "Womanliness first —afterward what you will." The Temperance cause was the open door through which she entered into her service for the world. The defense of woman, her uplift, her education for the widening way, was the task she set herself to accomplish. But to no special Cause did Frances Willard belong, her life was the property of Humanity; and I believe that there was not one single cry that could rise from the world, not one single wrong that could be redressed, not one "wail of weakness" of any kind that did not find an immediate echo in her heart, that did not call her to rise and go forth in that chivalric strength and gentleness which have clad her as with a holy panoply in the battle of life. To us who knew her childlike simple spirit, her keen intellect, her power of sympathy, the hospitable width of her mind, her unerring vision of the truth, it seems as though no words could ever paint the woman as she was, and only time will tell the world all she has accomplished. But this I dare to prophesy, that as the years go by, and the history of the New World comes to be read by those who desire to know the builders that reared a civilization so great and so strong, the name of Frances Willard will stand by the side of Lincoln, Wendell Phillips and Garrison.

The personal grief of her going is as yet too deep and the wound too sore to make it possible for me at this early date to write all that is in my mind about the woman who was so near and dear a friend; but as she has done me the honor of leaving me her literary executor in conjunction with her faithful and loved Anna Gordon, I send these few words of introduction to a memorial of the inspired life that has meant so much to the women of the world.

For years her name has been a household word among all those who work for the uplift of Humanity in England; and I well remember the day when I first received a letter of encouragement and cheer from her, words so sisterly and sympathetic that it seemed as though a new light had shined in the darkness and difficulty of our Temperance reform. In that letter she sent me a little knot of white ribbon, and all these years that little bow has been pinned into my Bible. It came as a promise of the most beautiful friendship that ever blessed any life.

In 1891 I saw her in the fullness of her power at the great Boston Convention, and as I think of her then, it seems to me that no other will ever fill the place that she has left vacant, for to no other could be given that rare combination of power and perfect gentleness, of playful humor and tender pathos, that strange mixture of reserve with an almost childlike confidence, and above all that sublime spirituality that always made you feel how near she was to the invisible, how lightly the mantle of the material lay upon her.

She came to us in England in the summer of 1892, bowed with grief at the loss of the mother who had been the strong staff of her life, who had upheld her through her work, cheered her in her discouragements, pointed her onward in her days of weariness. I think I have never known a human soul feel sorrow so acutely as did this daughter, when for a while a cloud hid that mother from her sight. It was like the grieving of a little child that holds out its hands in the dark and feels in vain for the accustomed clasp that sent it happily to sleep. She was welcomed in this country as I suppose no philanthropist has been welcomed in our time. The vast meeting that was organized to greet her at Exeter Hall was the most representative that has ever assembled in that historic building; and certainly no more varied gathering of philanthropists could be brought together with one object than met there that day. On the platform sat members of parliament, dignitaries of our own church, and temperance leaders from the Roman Catholic Church, leaders of the Labor movement and of the Salvation Army, and delegations from the Methodist, Baptist and Congregational Churches and the Society of Friends. The chief Jewish rabbi sent a congratulatory letter and signed the address of welcome, which was also signed by hundreds of local branches of the British Women's Temperance Association.

"What went ye out for to see?" was the question that one asked one's self as that frail form stood in the midst of the vast assembly. A woman called of God, a woman who preached Christ in politics, Christ in the home, the equality of the purity of men and women, the liberation of the oppressed, the destruction of legalized wrong, the upbuilding of all that was great in home, in government, and in the nation. And she who had gone forth without money and without influence, but with an untarnished name, a clear brain, an indomitable will, and a God-given inspiration, had in her twenty years of work gathered round her, not the sympathies of her own land only, but the admiration and good will of the whole English-speaking race. The time she spent in England was a triumphal procession, and greetings awaited her in every city of importance throughout the whole of Great Britain and Ireland. The Synod Hall in Edinburgh, the historic temperance town of Preston, Dublin and Glasgow, vast assemblies in the Free Trade Hall in Manchester, packed audiences in Liverpool and Birmingham — all vied to do her honor; and wherever she went, her clear, incisive thought, the pathos and power of her words, and perhaps most of all the sweet, gentle woman won the heart as well as the intellect of all who met to greet her and assembled to hear her. There was no trait in Miss Willard's character that was more prominent than her generous power of help. If an idea came to her, she had no thought but to share it with her fellow-workers. Anything that she had said was common property, anything that she could write might bear another's signature; to help, to help — this was her only thought; for she was inspired by a love which "seeketh not her own," but that gave of the treasure that had been poured into her life as freely as the sunshine ripens and blesses the world.

"I saw a saint — how cans't thou tell that he
    Thou sawest was a saint?
I saw one like to Christ so luminously
By patient deeds of love, his mortal taint
Seemed made his groundwork for humility.

"And when he marked me downcast utterly,
    Where foul I sat and faint,
Then more than ever Christ-like kindled he;
And welcomed me as I had been a saint,
Tenderly stooping low to comfort me.

"Christ bade him, 'Do thou likewise.' Wherefore he
    Waxed zealous to acquaint
His soul with sin and sorrow, if so be
He might retrieve some latent saint:
'Lo, I, with the child God hath given to me!'"

— *Christina Rossetti.*

REV. SAMUEL WILLARD
PASTOR OF THE OLD SOUTH CHURCH, BOSTON. BORN, 1639

THE WILLARD RESIDENCE.
Oberlin, Ohio.

MISS WILLARD'S BIRTHPLACE.
Churchville, N. Y.

"FOREST HOME."
Janesville, Wis.

CHAPTER I

ANCESTRAL GIFTS

WHEN Macaulay was shown the vast clustering vines in Hampton Court, with trunk like unto a tree, he expressed a wish to behold the mother root in Spain from which the scion was cut. Similarly, we confess to an eager desire to trace the ancestral forces that are united in every son and daughter of genius. No great soul appears suddenly. The foothills slope upward toward the mountain-minded man. Mental and moral capital are treasures invested for us by our forefathers. Nature takes the grandsire's ability and puts it out at compound interest for the grandson. Plato says: "The child is a charioteer, driving two steeds up the long, ripe hill; one steed is white, representing our best impulses; one steed is dark, standing for our worst passions." Who gave these steeds their colors? "Our fathers," Plato replies, and the child may not change one hair white or black. Oliver Wendell Holmes would have us think that the child's value to society is determined one hundred years before its birth. Back of Harriet Beecher Stowe was a father who was at once a moral hero and an intellectual giant, and a mother who gave to the strong Beecher type its rich, warm, glowing tones. Ralph Waldo Emerson had back of him seven generations of scholars. A great river like the Nile or Mississippi has power to bear up fleets of war and fleets of peace, because the storms of a thousand summers and the snows of a thousand winters have lent it depth and power. And the measure of greatness in a man or woman is determined by the intellectual streams and the moral tides flowing down from the ancestral hills and emptying into the human soul.

In every great soul, however, there is an unexplored remainder that must be referred to God alone. The secret of greatness is in part ancestral, but chiefly divine. God breathes it. When the explorer has traced the river Nile back to the initial lakes, he has still fallen short of the sources of that mighty stream. Above him, in the distant clouds, are the secret and invisible sources that fill the springs and crowd the water on in massy flow. And having traced every great soul back to the traits of distant ancestors, we find that the source of genius is in that holy of holies where dwell clouds and thick darkness. For in the last analysis genius is an unread riddle. It is God who baptizes the hero or heroine with a divine afflatus, girds the man and woman for the life task, and sends them forth with faculties like unto the prophet's sword, "all dipped in heaven."

Miss Willard's father, Josiah Flint Willard, born in Wheelock, Vermont, and her mother, Mary Thompson Hill Willard, a native of Danville in the same State, fell heir to all the best qualities that have ripened upon the rich soil of New England, and they in turn bequeathed their united treasure to the daughter, whom they trained for her career as teacher, author, orator, philanthropist and social reformer.

Major Simon Willard, of Horsmonden, Kent, the first Willard to settle in the New World in 1634, was one of the founders of Concord, Massachusetts, afterward famous as the home of Emerson, Hawthorne, Thoreau and the Alcotts, and as the literary center of New England. Major Willard was a Puritan who took for his intellectual motto, "Truth for authority, not authority for truth." The early history of Massachusetts is full of allusions to his many and varied services in an official capacity, all reflecting high honor upon his character as a man of integrity, ability and energy. "He was early called into positions of public trust, disciplined by the teachings of toil, deprivation and varied experience, and had the confidence and affection of an enlightened community throughout all the emergencies of a new State." Among the immediate descendants of this rugged and righteous ancestor are two presidents of Harvard University, also Rev. Samuel Willard, pastor of the Old South Church, Boston, who opposed the hanging of the witches, and Solomon Willard, of Quincy, Massachusetts, the architect of Bunker Hill Monument, who refused pay for his services, of whom Edward Everett said, "His chief characteristic was that he wanted to do everything for everybody for nothing."

Miss Willard's great grandfather, Rev. Elijah Willard, was for forty years pastor of a church in Dublin, near Keene, New Hampshire, and served as chaplain throughout the Revolutionary War. Miss Willard loved to tell the following droll story of his powers as a peacemaker. A member of his church had called another "an old skinflint," whereupon accusation was brought by the offended party. When the authorities of the church were sitting in council on this grave piece of indecorum, Elder Willard suggested, in his character of presiding officer, that they should look in the dictionary and see what a "skinflint" was. This met with great favor. But lo, and behold! there was no such word in the book referred to. The Elder then said, that inasmuch as there was no definition there given, he would appeal to the brother who had used the word to give the definition. This was done, the brother replying, "Why, Elder, what I meant was that Brother —— is a downright clever sort of a man." It is shrewdly suspected that Elder Willard prearranged this reconciliation, dictionary and all.

Miss Willard's father was a man elegant in person, of charming manners, devoutly religious, gifted with a fine mind, an inflexible will, and unusual powers of thought and speech. His daughter Frances further describes him as "thoroughly intellectual, an insatiable reader, and a man possessing exceedingly fine taste."

Miss Willard's mother, Mary Thompson Hill, came of a singularly gifted family and one greatly blessed of God. Her grandfather Hill was a man of self-sacrificing integrity. "When, early in his career, he had become security for a friend who failed, men of good conscience came to him, urging that a man's family was 'a preferred creditor' in all business relations, and that he should refuse to give up all he had to satisfy another man's creditors. But he was a man of clean hands — swearing to his own hurt and changing not. He only answered, 'It is the nature of a bondsman when the principal fails to stand in the gap.' And he stood in the gap, losing all his fortune rather than fail to be true to the implied promise of his bond."

In Mrs. Willard's maternal grandfather, Nathaniel Thompson, of Durham, New Hampshire, we find the moral courage that characterized our fearless reformer. He was once a guest at a dinner where everyone drank the health of the tyrant whom Americans were fighting, each saying as glasses were clinked, "King George's health and it shall go round," when the young hero, Nathaniel, startled the disloyal Tories by crying out, "*Washington's health and it* shall go round," and was nothing daunted, though driven from the room and in danger of his life. Her father, John Hill, was a kind of moral Hercules. Long before Garrison and Phillips, Channing and Beecher had meditated their attack through voice and pen upon slavery, this youth made himself known in his community as an uncompromising foe of the slave market and the horrors of the cotton field. Oft in hours of retrospection did Miss Willard relate to her listening friends an incident in her grandfather's career that interprets the quality of his mind and heart. One spring he employed a colored youth to help in the task of sheep-shearing. The young African was the first of his people to find his way into that neighborhood, and his appearance at church or upon the streets of the village created a profound sensation. But John Hill took the young man to his home and brought him to his table. Just before the family assembled for the evening meal one of his daughters went to her father with a private request. "Sister Abigail," she said, "has a very poor appetite and cannot relish her food at the table with that colored man; can he wait?" "No," replied the father, "but *she* can." John Hill was a man of great courage and decision, widely known for his democratic principles and his deep interest in all those agencies that were fitted to develop the intellectual and moral forces of the community, while his wife, gentle Polly Thompson, possessing a character described as "almost angelic," was equally well known for her zeal for school, college and church.

Scientists tell us that climate affects character; that the children of ease and abundance in the tropics are the children of lassitude and laziness, without tools, without books, without home, church or school; while civilization follows the belt of the snow-drift, and in the rigorous warfare with those elements named winter, adversity, poverty, struggle, man develops self-reliance, hardihood, courage — develops instruments also for intellectual culture and moral wealth. And certain it is that the oak and rock of the New England hills seem to have repeated themselves in the iron will and the unyielding courage of the Willard family. Their very name means "one who wills," and this doubtless explains the family motto, "Gaudet patientia duris" (patience rejoices in hardships).

Born of such parents, blessed with such gifts of nature and nurture, God trained Frances Willard for her life-task and made her ready to help the pilgrim hosts with their sorrows, sufferings and sins.

CHAPTER II

CHILDHOOD

IT was a rarely endowed home into which Frances Elizabeth Willard was born September 28th, 1839, in Churchville, New York; a home sheltered from adverse chance to soul or body by the father's strength of heart and arm and will; with the mother-climate warm within, winning out and fostering all wholesome developments — a richly nurtured child-garden, where the sturdy small plants struck deep root and spread wide leafage to the air, catching every drop of pure knowledge and every beam of home-love falling within its rays. Here the "rosy-white flower of the child's consciousness unfolded its five-starred cup to the bending blue above."

Baby Frances talked before she could walk, "speaking quite wisely at fourteen months," but not until she was two years of age did her little feet begin their pilgrimage in obedience to the dictates of that electric brain and humanity-loving heart.

Sixty years ago was almost the time of the hegira from the East. The rough line of the pioneers, the sappers and miners of civilization, had finished their task, and made clear paths through the wilderness and the woods. Then everywhere, from cultured and thoughtful homes in the East, the exodus began, no longer going forth by individuals, man by man, each fighting for his own hand, but by families, friendly and allied. The future would bring new outward conditions, but they carried with them the means and appliances. Indeed they were in themselves, in aptitude and skill of heart, mind and hand, the mature human harvest of all the fullness of the past — that human harvest which is at once the summing up of the old and the seed of the new.

In this onward march it was fitting that the Willards should have their place. Reared amid the loveliest surroundings, royal Americans in heart and mind, members of the old stone church, which bore the simple name, "The church of God in Ogden," and recognized no lines of doctrinal difference in worship and life, but united on the ground of acknowledgment of the Lord and His Word and a life of loving obedience thereto, it was no wonder that in the providence of God these two were sent out as choice and chosen seed for the new lands of the West.

Their first journey overland from Churchville, New York, terminated at Oberlin, Ohio, where five years of student life at the college were invested by these discerning parents, who had both been successful teachers in the Empire State.

Here the beloved sister Mary was born, and here the older children, Oliver and Frances, received in awe and love the early impress of the ideas of religion and scholarship. The ardent desire for learning which had hitherto led the parents on as by a pillar of fire changed to the threatening cloud of the father's failing health, which imperatively demanded, so the physicians said, the free air of the open West and the simplest farming exercise.

In the spring of 1846 we find them again following westward. Three of the quaint, roomy, white-hooded prairie schooners, which were then the common feature of Western highways, carried the intrepid family. The father led the way. The little son, ambitious of manhood, with gravely assumed responsibility guided the strong and gentle horses which pulled the second vehicle over the smooth prairie miles or the jouncing corduroy lengths that bridged inconvenient morasses. The mother, with her baby girls perched safely beside her in the fine seat father's old-fashioned desk made when it was properly pillowed, brought up the rear.

They passed through Chicago, then chiefly notable as a place in vast need of improvement, and continuing their three weeks' journey, save the Sunday "rests," which were strictly observed, came at length to the banks of the beautiful Rock River, near Janesville, Wisconsin, about fourteen miles from Beloit. Here they stopped. To the west was the winding river, serene and broad, with its spacious outlook to the setting sun. To the east, the illimitable prairie, to be for ages green with the springing wheat, yellow with the ripening grain, and every morning glorified in all its level miles by the streaming light and abundant promise of the sun at its rising. To right and left the wooded hills, like softly sheltering arms, gathered protectingly around. What more perfect place for a home-nest to be?

Miss Willard has often pictured to us the simple dwelling that was soon erected on this charming site, "Forest Home," a picturesque cottage, with rambling roof, gables, dormer-windows, little porches, crannies, and out-of-the-way nooks. "The bluffs, so characteristic of Wisconsin, rose about it on the right and left. Groves of oak and hickory were on either hand; a miniature forest of evergreens almost concealed the cottage from the view of passers-by; the Virginia creeper twined at will around the pillars of the piazza and over the parlor windows, while its rival, the Michigan rose, clambered over the trellis and balustrade to the roof. The air was laden with the perfume of flowers. Through the thick and luxuriant growth of shrubbery were paths which strayed off aimlessly, tempting the feet of the curious down their mysterious aisles." Here for twelve happy years these three children lived an idyllic life of love and labor, play and study and prayer.

Happy the mother who could say of her child, she was "affectionate, confiding, intuitive, precocious, original. She early manifested an exceeding fondness for books. She believed in herself and in her teachers. Her bias toward certain studies and pursuits was very marked. Even in the privacy of her own room she was often in an ecstasy of aspiration. She strongly repelled occupations not to her taste, but was eager to grapple with principles, philosophies and philanthropies, and unwearyingly industrious along her favorite lines."

Happy the daughter who could say of her mother: "My mother held that nature's standard ought to be restored, and that the measure of each human being's endowment was the only reasonable measure of that human being's sphere. She had small patience with artificial diagrams placed before women by the dictates of society in which the boundaries of their especial 'sphere' were marked out for them, and one of her favorite phrases was, 'Let a girl grow as a tree grows — according to its own sweet will.' She looked at the mysteries of human progress from the angle of vision made by the eyes of both the man and the woman, and foresaw that the mingling of justice and mercy in the great decisions that affected society would give deliverance from political corruption and governmental one-sidedness."

The opportunities that came to the children at Forest Home were opportunities to be useful; to read, to study, to work with their hands, to love each other, to reverence nature and nature's God. The visitors at first were chiefly the chipmunks and birds, change of season and turn of day. Before the days when Froebel's name became familiar to the tongue, this mother, as good mothers always have done, lived with her children. "I had many ambitions," she said, "but I disappeared from the world that I might reappear at some future day in my children." They made believe the country was a city; they organized a club with as many rules as a parliamentary manual and printed a newspaper of which Frances was the editor, to say nothing of "breaking the calf" to circus antics. In all this childish activity the mother was aider and abettor, and we have never learned that she discouraged that marvelous novel of adventure, four hundred pages long, written by the aspiring Frances as she sat in the top of her favorite old oak, where she guarded herself from all intruders (!) by fastening to the tree a board with these words printed upon it in large letters:

> THE EAGLE'S NEST — BEWARE.

While the mother certainly fostered every characteristic impulse of the more daring, firmer-handed Frances, she did not fail to note, encourage and assist the growth of Mary's quieter genius, and reward its achievements also with love and approbation. "I do not know which of us she loved the more. I do not think the question ever occurred to us. Each had her own heaven in our mother's heart," said Frances, years afterward, when the name of Mary and the life motto she gave to Frances with her latest breath, "Tell everybody to be good," had been carved for many a year on the headstone at Rose Hill. "We were content, and oh, how we loved one another!"

Amid all their fun and frolic and endless experiment in activity there was much solid and systematic study. Before the time when the little brown schoolhouse was built in the woods, the father arranged a study room in the house, with desks and benches made by his own hands. The mother gathered in some neighbors' children, themselves without other advantages, to be all together with her own brood, under her own eyes. A bright, charming, accomplished young woman, Miss Anna Burdick, just from the East and Eastern schools, came daily, and was a loved and delightful teacher. The Institute for the Blind, located not far away, gave them additional opportunities for musical training, while they themselves, in the establishment of various outdoor clubs, the "Rustic" and others, continued to study afield what they had learned in books of botany and natural history, while the exercises of the "Studio," with the consequent sketching trips, carried the art instruction Miss Burdick began quite a little way further. In art, however, Mary was easily first. Frances liked better to dream, philosophize and plan in the presence of a beautiful scene, than to patiently draw it. Her part consisted chiefly in stating the "objects," arranging the routes and drafting the rules. These rules were very practical. "If one member goes off alone, he shall let Margaret Ryan know of it, so the folks needn't be scared." This also is practical: "There shall always be something good to eat"; and the following is excellent: "We, the members of this club, hereby choose Fred as our dog, although once in a while we may take Carlo. Carlo can go when he has sense enough." This club was doubtless the one having for its object "to tell what great things we have done ourselves, or what Oliver and Loren or the Hodge boys have, or Daniel Boone, or anybody else."

Great frolics were enjoyed in Forest Home, and it is no reflection on the "Peace" principles dominating her later life that here Frances was the ringleader in the exciting "Indian fights" when mother and girls tried to "hold the fort" against the invading enemy — two boys and a dog! Then it was that Frances as Commanding-General, issued her famous order to "have ready a piece of sparerib to entice the dog away from those two dreadful Indians!" and so weaken the forces to be encountered — a piece of strategy she remembered in after days as possibly applicable to politics.

Forest Home always had its "Fourth of July," celebrated with intense enthusiasm; "Thanksgiving was passed lightly over in that new country where there were no absent members of the family to come home; Christmas made them hang up their stockings and find but little there, next morning; New Year hardly counted at all; birthdays cut no great figure, even Washington's going for almost nothing, but the Fourth of July! — *that* came in, went on and passed out in a blaze of patriotic glory. This does not mean fireworks, though, and a big noise, for never a cracker or torpedo snapped off their Yankee Doodle 'sentiments' on the old farm in all the years. The children had no money to spend, and if they had it would not have been allowed to pass away in smoke. So much had their mother talked to them about America that their native land was to them a cherishing mother, like their own in gentleness and strength, only having so many more children, grateful and glad, under her thoughtful care. They loved to give her praises, and half believed that some time, when they grew big enough and got out into the wide, wide world, they should find her and kneel to offer her their loving service and to ask her blessing." Nothing could be more interesting than Miss Willard's graphic description of those glorious "Fourths," prophetic of the temperance reform, the independence of women and the bringing of the home spirit into all the world's affairs; "for when temperance triumphs," she was wont to say, "there will be no drinking on the Fourth; when women march in the procession there will be no powder; when father, mother and the children have equal part in the great celebration it will be very peaceable and more an affair of the heart than of the lungs."

We are told on the best authority that the only piece of sewing Frances Willard ever attempted without complaint was when she helped make a flag for the patriotic procession the children had planned for one of these great days. To be sure, this flag was only an old pillow case with red calico stripes sewed on and gilt paper stars pinned in the corner, and they lifted it up upon a broomstick (again a bit of prophecy, mayhap), but it was their country's flag, and Oliver, who marched proudly at the head of the procession, flag in hand, was gallant enough to say to Frances when half the distance agreed upon had been traversed, "Wouldn't you like to carry the flag half the time?" Frances tells us she was not at all backward about coming forward in that kind of business, and her father and mother laughed heartily when she changed the order of exercises by saying, "That 'Yankee Doodle' we were playing (nobody had dreamed before that it had professed to be a tune) does not go very well; let us try 'Forever Float'!" so they all joined in singing as she held the flag:

> "Forever float that standard sheet
> Where breathes the foe but falls before us,
> With freedom's soil beneath our feet,
> And freedom's banner streaming o'er us."

Frances slyly whispered to her sister Mary, "That's a clear case of *We*, *Us* and *Company;* why can't it always stay so?"

Just a peep into the girlish journals of those halcyon days will delight the children who love and reverence Miss Willard, and will reveal the first pledge that long ago she administered for the peace of the community and the good of the parties concerned, and to which her small sister set her signature. This extract is taken from Mary's neatly written book:

Frank said we might as well have a ship if we did live on shore; so we took a hencoop pointed at the top, put a big plank across it and stood up, one at each end, with an old rake handle apiece to steer with; up and down we went, slow when it was a calm sea and fast when there was a storm, until the old hen clucked and the chickens all ran in, and we had a lively time. Frank was captain and I was mate. We made out charts of the sea and rules about how to navigate when it was good weather, and how when it was bad. We put up a sail made of an old sheet and had great fun, until I fell off and hurt me.

Today Frank gave me half her dog Frisk, that she bought lately, and for her pay I made a promise which mother witnessed and here it is:

"I, Mary Willard, promise never to touch anything lying or being upon Frank Willard's writing desk which father gave her. I promise never to ask, either by speaking, writing or signing, or in any other way, any person or body to take off or put on anything on said stand and desk without special permission from said F. W. I promise never to touch anything which may be in something upon her stand and desk; I promise never to put anything on it or in anything on it; I promise if I am writing or doing anything else at her desk to go away the minute she tells me. If I break this promise I will let the said F. W. come into my room and go to my trunk or go into any place where I keep my things and take anything of mine she likes. All this I promise unless entirely different arrangements are made. These things I promise upon my most sacred honor."

From "Frank's" journal of the same period we quote her first poem, composed in her tenth year, which proves afresh that the thoughts of youth "are long, long thoughts":

> "Am I almost of age, am I almost of age?
> Said a poor little girl, as she glanced from her cage.
> How long will it be
> Before I shall be free
> And not fear friend or foe?
> If I somewhere could go
> And I some folks could know,
> I'd not want to 'be of age'
> But remain in my cage."

In the last winter of her free life we find her still singing of "captivity" in a dainty bit of verse addressed to a snowbird:

* * * * *

> " Dear little bird with glancing wing,
> Did you but know I long to fly,

> Perhaps you'd sit quite near and sing
> To me in my captivity.
>
> "Dear human heart be not afraid,
> Thy need of food, thy dream of flight
> He knows, by whom the worlds were made;
> To speed thee on is His delight."

They were kind to "every harmless living creature," those "out-doorsy" little people; as the same journal tells us:

One day when we girls were having our good times down by the river the three Hodge boys came along hunting for birds' nests. "But you mustn't carry any away," said Mary, greatly stirred; "You may climb the trees and look, if you want to see the eggs or little ones, but you can't hurt a birdie, big or little, in *our* pasture." The boys said their mother told them the same thing and they only wanted to look. So Mary and I showed them under the leafy covert some of the brown thrushes housekeeping, and the robins, too, and told them they were nice, kind boys.

Brotherhood and sisterhood meant much in the Willard household. The liveliest stories are told about the comradeship of Frances and Oliver. They were up to no end of jolly times together. If he liked better to play "Fort," and she to play "City," that was no reason they should be divided in their play. She played "Fort" with him, entering into his imagination of it with cordiality and swing, and played it gloriously. He played "City" with her, assisting her "in consideration of the resources of the corporation." Brother and sister thus mutually annexed each other's land, and became richer by the resources in liking and faculty of both.

"A boy whose sister knows everything he does will be far more modest, genial and pleasant to have about," Frances once said; then, smiling quietly, she added, "and it will be a great improvement to the sister also." I believe she regarded this commerce between the lands of brother and sister, of man and woman; the association, not of bodily presence only, such as takes place around every breakfast table, but a true association of minds; this unselfish and unstinted entrance of one nature into the feeling, thought and activity of another for a little space, like a journey into a neighboring country, from which a wise traveler comes back laden with riches for his own — all this she doubtless regarded soberly as a "wider education" for women. It was certainly one of the powerful and enlarging influences which made Frances Willard a great woman.

Brother and sister, father and daughter, friend and friend — all her life long this woman's heart and mind was going out toward the labors, the thoughts, the aims of men, with hearty sympathy, quick intelligence, large helpfulness. She was great enough to see clearly and proclaim firmly that fundamental truth, that it takes both a man-angel and a woman-angel to make the heavenly human in God's sight. This beautiful and helpful association of brother and sister, beginning as merrily and sweetly as that of George Eliot and her brother in early years, did not cease with those years, but continued as long as both lived, a wholesome, uplifting friendship, full of grace and strength.

Yet all these after-riches and fullness and power of life were folded away in those beginnings, so heavenly simple and true. In those years, when through home and the fair country around, father and mother, brother and sister, and God's Fatherhood over all, ministered to the child, there was implanted and nourished in her the "sweet skill" of loving much, of trust and truth, obedience and endeavor. It is a fascinating study to see how in that early day many of our leader's after-greatnesses put forth their first leaves. She was a born organizer, which only means she was magnificently a woman, for woman is the born organizer of creation. She early discovered the "usefulness of association," and in numerous preambles drawn up when she could scarcely write "straight" she called attention to it. In the self-derived charter of "Fort City" we find announced: "We will have no saloons or billiard halls, and then we will not need any jails"— a somewhat rash and girlish generalization, for the devil can sow tares in human nature, even though whisky-soaked ground should fail him. It looks in the right direction, so far as municipal order and cleanliness go, for there is scarcely any other sin so much of a nuisance to the neighbor or so obviously a loss to the country as is drunkenness.

She learned to read from "The Slave's Friend," thus early imbibing from her Abolition parents the sentiments that swept through her soul in the succeeding years, making her more than any other modern reformer the friend of the negro race, and giving birth to a phrase in one of her prophetic mottoes: "No sect in religion, no sex in citizenship, no sectionalism in politics."

The children early signed the total abstinence pledge inscribed in the old family Bible, where the names of the father and the mother preceded the childish autographs. This was the pledge, and we hope that many a child-reader of this old-fashioned, iron-clad promise will here and now affix his name to the same noble resolution:

> "A pledge we make, no wine to take,
> Nor brandy red that turns the head,
> Nor fiery rum that ruins home,
> Nor whisky hot that makes the sot,
> Nor brewers' beer, for that we fear,
> And cider, too, will never do;
> To quench our thirst we'll always bring
> Cold water from the well or spring.
> So here we pledge perpetual hate
> To all that can intoxicate."

Fifty years after Miss Willard had signed this pledge, she composed one especially for her boy friends, which I here transcribe in sacred memory of their elder sister's love and prayerful expectation for the boys and girls of this and future generations:

PLEDGE FOR BOYS.

> "I pledge my brain God's thoughts to think,
> My lips no fire or foam to drink
> From alcoholic cup,
> Nor link with my pure breath tobacco's taint.
> For have I not a right to be

THE SCHOOL HOUSE.
Near Forest Home, Janesville, Wis.
First school attended by Miss Willard.

THE SCHOOL HOUSE AT HARLEM.
Near River Forest, Ill.
First school taught by Miss Willard.

EVANSTON COLLEGE FOR LADIES.
Evanston, Ill.

CONGREGATIONAL CHURCH
CHURCHVILLE N.Y.

OLD M.E. CHURCH EVANSTON

NEW M.E. CHURCH EVANSTON

THE OLD STONE CHURCH, OGDEN N.Y.
BUILT 1832

FIRST M.E. CHURCH,
JANESVILLE, WIS.

As wholesome, pure and free as she
Who through the years so glad and free
Moves gently onward to meet me?
A knight of the new chivalry
For Christ and Temperance I would be —
In nineteen hundred; come and see."

The home Frances Willard was to find in millions of hearts was wistfully foreshadowed when she stood in the doorway of the old barn at Forest Home "that lonesome day in early spring." She tells us it was gray with fog and moist with rain. It was Sunday and there was no church to attend, and the time stretched out before her long and desolate. "She cried out in querulous tones to the two who shared her every thought, 'I wonder if we shall ever know anything, see anybody or go anywhere?' 'Why do you wish to go away?' said sweet little Mary, with her reassuring smile. 'Oh, we must learn — must grow, and must achieve; it is such a big world that if we don't begin at it we shall never catch up with the rest.'"

Dear little eagles in their "eagle's nest," they were growing their wings for future flights all through those lovely years. The seed of the after-harvest of mature love and wisdom, God first sows in the garden plot of childhood by means of every innocent activity and delight, every simple and reverential knowledge. Our very helplessness, as we lie in the arms of our mothers, brooded over by the mother-angel which is at the heart of every true woman, gives the Lord and the angelic host their first way with us. And the long period of our ignorance and immaturity furnishes only so much more time to shape the human organism during its growth to a wide range of choice, of love, of understanding and activity.

"It was a beautiful childhood," Miss Willard said, sitting on the porch in the twilight one quiet evening, watching a far star across the lake; "I do not know how it could have been more beautiful, or how there could have been a truer beginning of many things. To me it has often seemed as if those earlier years were 'seed to all my after good.'" A little later, she repeated softly to herself:

> "'Long years have left their writing on my brow,
> But yet the freshness and the dew-fed beam
> Of those young mornings are about me now.'

I thank Thee, O bountiful God, that I have so much of happiness, of quiet enjoyment to remember. *I thank Thee that I have not forgotten, cannot forget.* I thank Thee that wherever I may dwell, no place can be so dear, so completely embalmed in my heart, so truly the best beloved of all to me as 'Forest Home.'"

CHAPTER III

STUDENT LIFE

WHEN Frances Willard was fourteen, her father and a neighbor bestirred themselves for their children's sake, and the little brown schoolhouse was built in the wood, about a mile away. It was the simplest of district schoolhouses, plain and inviting, Frances says, "a bit of a building under the trees on the river bank. It looked like a natural growth, a sort of big ground-nut. The pine desks were ranged around the wall, the boys on one side, the girls on the other, and a real live graduate from Yale was teacher." "There will be lots of rules," said Oliver to his sisters, the evening before their first real school day opened. "Never mind," said Frances, "It will be a pleasant change to have some rules and live up to them."

In this school the sisters had ten months of bright inspiring instruction keyed to high ideals for heart and head. We can hear the ardent child Frances leading in rich contralto tones the favorite song with which they made "the rafters ring":

> "Now to heaven our prayer ascending,
>   God speed the right!
> In a noble cause contending,
>   God speed the right!"

With these school days began an enlarged social outlook for the young recluses whose home playmates heretofore had scarcely been other than brother and sister, father and mother. The storing and unfolding of mind was continuous and an unending series of beautiful experiences was laid away for future consideration. In addition to some odd volumes of travel and biography the books they had thus far studied were the Bible, "Pilgrim's Progress" and Shakespeare. Shakespeare was a "most wise instructor," and certain it is that before she was fifteen the eager girl had read, reread and commented upon all his plays, this giving her an immense advantage when she entered school.

But now the brother at college came into his library. Great was the revelry when he brought home the Bohn translation of the classics — Plato, Epictetus, Marcus Aurelius, "Don Quixote," which the young folks read aloud; the "Imitation of Christ," which grew dear to Frances' heart, and many other treasures. The vacations became, in their new occupation with books, scarcely less stimulating intellectually than were the school days.

In Frances' fifteenth year, after a trip to the old homestead in the East, where they saw their father's witty old mother and their mother's father powerful in prayer, and compared views on subjects profound and simple with the conservative young cousins, the girls Frances and Mary attended a "select school" in Janesville, where Frances especially enjoyed Cutler's physiology and awakened astonishment by the way she edited the school paper when it came her turn.

A great gift to the girls' lives was a summer visit in the home of Southern friends who had driven from Georgia to Wisconsin in their own carriage for the sake of pleasure and health. Owners and teachers of a ladies' school at home, elegant and cultured people, it was the greatest event thus far in the lives of these forest nymphs to go six miles from home to spend several weeks studying with these friends in their rural retreat, and for the first time to sleep out from under the old home roof. "The all-overish feeling of loneliness" was conquered by the thought of how much they should *know* when the separation was over, and they were soon devoted to their gifted teachers. Here Frances made her first acquaintance with the Bronte novels — at least through to the middle of "Villette." Her father coming upon her with it in her hands shut the book and briefly remarked to her instructor, "Never let my daughter see that book again, if you please,

Madam." The daughter religiously respected her father's prohibition regarding the book, and as years passed learned how much she owed to "the firm hand that held her impetuous nature from a too early knowledge of the unreal world of romance."

At Forest Home Frances won her first spurs as a writer. The *Prairie Farmer* having offered a prize for the best essay on the embellishment of a country home, Mrs. Willard, who forbade her children no harmless thing along the line of their impulses, encouraged her daughter to compete; her father contributed a suggestion about the planting of evergreens, and the fateful manuscript was dispatched. Great was the glee when in return for the effort came a beautiful cup and a note of congratulation.

In 1857, Frances and Mary were students in the Milwaukee Female College, where their aunt, Miss Sarah Hill (Mrs. Willard's youngest sister) was Professor of History. Frances, then seventeen, found in this aunt her greatest intellectual guide. The moral atmosphere of the school was excellent; there was the finest honor among the girls; they were expected, and expected themselves, to be ladies, careful scholars and obedient to the rules. Here the young girl found a charming circle of friends, true companions, with whom she stood in the heartiest, healthiest, most helpful relation. Here she found also the beautiful "Marion," bright particular star of those years, whom she so loved that she writes: "I never rested until, like her, I also heard 'ten — ten,' meaning perfect in conduct and scholarship, read out after my name each week." As McDonald says, "Love loves to wear the livery of the beloved."

On "Examination Day" Frances read an essay on "Originality of Thought and Action," to the applause of the audience, including father and mother, the exercises receiving an additional flavor for this young author when a charming poem of hers, almost her first effort in that line, was read by a young girl friend, and, writes truthful Frances, "I was downright sorry to go home."

The speedy popularity of the Willard girls with both teachers and pupils rested upon no less sound a basis than what they were in themselves and what they could do. Certainly none of it depended upon the possession of what people called "means." Absolutely all the spending money they had for three months was the fifty cents which Irish Mike, the farm hand, sent the two girls himself. After careful consultation, Frances invested hers in a ticket to the menagerie, a blank book to write essays in, and peppermint candy, which list of expenditures makes us love her for the unspoiled humanness of it. It was this same Irish Mike who, years after, when Miss Willard was struggling in the political prohibition arena, sent word: "That lady and her folks were good to me when I was a green boy from the old country, and now the lady hasn't a vote to bless herself with; but me and my boys will put in three for her. And I thought I would write and tell you. Respect. Mike Carey." The little blank book lies on the table before me. It bears a dashing autograph on the first page, and above it, written by that rememberful hand many years later, is this explanatory note: "Mike Carey sent Mary and me fifty cents between us when we were pupils at Milwaukee, and out of mine this book was bought — all the money of that sort we had in the three months' term."

Frances celebrated the arrival of her eighteenth birthday by writing the following:

"I am eighteen.
I have been obedient.
Not that the yoke was heavy to be borne,
For lighter ne'er did parents fond
Impose on child.
It was a silver chain,
But the bright adjective
Takes not away the clanking sound!
The clock has struck!
I'm free! Come joy profound!
I'm alone and free —
Free to obey Jehovah only,
Accountable but to the powers above!"

Then she took Ivanhoe, seated herself on the porch and began to read with calm satisfaction. Her father chanced up the steps.

"What have you there?" "One of Scott's novels." "Have I not forbidden you to read any novels?" "You forget what day it is, father." "What difference does the day make in the deed?" "A great deal. I am eighteen today, and I do not have to obey any laws but those of God hereafter. In my judgment, Ivanhoe is good to be read." The amazed father was for half an instant minded to take away the book by force. Then he laughed, called her mother, and the two contemplated this woman-child of theirs. At length he said, seriously: "She is evidently a chip of the Puritan block." That was an old-fashioned Protestant declaration of independence. "Well, we will try to learn God's laws and obey them together, my child."

The two sisters had been looking forward to further study in Milwaukee, but their Methodist father desired a more strictly sectarian school for his children, and selected the Northwestern Female College at Evanston, Illinois, where, at the beginning of the spring term in 1858, when Frances was in her nineteenth year, they entered as pupils. At Evanston, as at Milwaukee, "Frank" (as she was always called) was soon an acknowledged leader in scholarship and school activities. But at Evanston the girls were smiled at for the first time because of their simple dress, this giving occasion to the last overt manifestation of Frank's fighting powers in the incident which still lives in Evanston tradition. Their father always had the whim of giving his personal care to the purchase of his daughters' wardrobe, taking counsel only of his own taste. So he sent the girls a couple of red worsted hoods for their winter wear. Now, a red worsted hood might be charming on the head of Mary, but to Frances it was far from becoming. She hated it with a "hatred and a half," she says, and the girls guyed her unmercifully about the plain homespun thing. One of them, a tall, handsome creature, guyed her once too often as she was putting it on. Frank turned on her, threw her down, crumpled her up under a desk, and walked off defiantly tying the strings of that despised hood. Hood or no hood, there was no discounting the position she soon acquired in school. She was a power, rejoicing in nothing so much as taking the initiative. A reckless spirit full of adventure, does some one say? This was not true. The great woman to be was just now coming into a great girlhood, and girlhood in a time of ferment. Only in the light of the woman she was to be and the work she was to do can we justly estimate the passing phases of that preparatory growth under God's providence and His guiding will. It was a great nature unfolding itself, finding and testing its own powers. A strong will, full both of audacities and self-controls, yet with such a beautiful habit of confidence toward her mother that she says, "I could scarcely tell where her thought ended and mine began."

In spite of the revelations of her all-producing journal during her student life, Frances Willard as a young woman must have possessed a rare and exquisite beauty. One who first met her at the Evanston College writes: "My interest was excited by the golden-haired young woman, Frank Willard. I saw she was younger than any of the women about her and then looked far younger than she was. I was attracted by her apparent youth and by the vivid expression of her absorbed and attentive face." Speaking forty years later, this friend says of her: "The same vivid indescribable light was in her face, grown more delicate and illusive; it was as if all the years had subtly refined and enriched that precious and fragrant substance, the oil of the life lamp."

Sundry notes in Miss Willard's journal during her college days are significant of the girl's self. "Dr. Foster closed the Bible, after his discourse at the University chapel yesterday with these words: 'Brothers, with most men life is a failure.' The words impressed me deeply; there is sorrow in the thought, tears and agony are wrapped up in it. O Thou who rulest above, help me that my life may be valuable, that some human being shall yet thank Thee that I have lived and toiled!' . . . ." Of the hero of a book she remarks: "He is a noble character but he weeps too much, and I do not like his ideas about a wife obeying her husband — that I scout wherever I see it." In those days she often had almost a cramp of self-consciousness in company at all strange to her, or under unaccustomed conditions, and in her journal likens herself to Charles Lamb, who, outside his immediate circle was not himself, neither natural nor at ease. "Perhaps," she says, "that is why I like books so much; they never frighten me. However," she continues, addressing herself, "as you have begun to think much on this subject, probably by and by your manner will assume of itself that half-cordial, half-dignified character that accords best with your nature."

Her ambitions grew definite: "I thought that, next to a wish I had to be a saint some day, I really would like to be a politician."

. . . . . .

"Professor detained me after devotions this morning, and with his most 'engaging' smile made this announcement: 'By vote of your teachers you are appointed valedictorian.' I was glad, of course; 'tis like human nature. To others it will seem a small thing; it is not so to me."

. . . . .

"I am more interested in the 'Memoirs of Margaret Fuller Ossoli,' than in any other book I have read for years. Here we see what a woman achieved for herself. Not so much fame or honor, these are of minor importance, but a whole character, a cultivated intellect, right judgment, self-knowledge, self-happiness. If she, why not we, by steady toil?"

. . . . .

"Everything humbles me, but two things in the highest degree. One is to stand in a large library, the other to study astronomy. In both cases I not only see how much there is to be known, how insignificant my knowledge is, but I see how atomic I am, compared with other human beings. Astronomers 'think God's thoughts after him.' Alas, I can hardly think their thoughts after them, when all is clearly represented!"

Mrs. Mary Bannister Willard, her closest heart-friend among college mates and later her beloved sister-in-law, paints this charming picture of Miss Willard's wit and wisdom during her schoolgirl days: "None of the pupils who attended the Northwestern Female College in the spring term of 1858 will fail to recall the impressions made by two young girls from Wisconsin on their entrance upon this new school life. Mary, with her sweet, delicate face, winning, almost confidential manner, and earnest, honest purpose, conquered the hearts of teachers and pupils at once. Schoolgirls are a conservative body, reserving favorable judgment till beauty, kindliness or fine scholarship compels their admiration. Frances was at first thought proud, haughty, independent — all cardinal sins in schoolgirl codes. The shyness or timidity which she concealed only too successfully under a mask of indifference gave the impression that she really wished to stand aloof from her mates. When it came to recitations, however, all shyness and apparent indifference melted away. The enthusiasm for knowledge and excellence shone from the young girl's face on all these occasions. After 'class' her schoolmates gathered in groups in corridor and chapel, and discussed her *perforce* favorably. 'My! can't she recite? Look out for *your* laurels now, Kate!' 'The new girl beats us all,'— these were the ejaculations that testified of honest schoolgirl opinion, and prophesied her speedy and sure success. It was but a few weeks till she was editor of the College paper, and leader of all the intellectual forces among the students. She was in no sense, however, an intellectual 'prig.' None of us was more given over to a safe kind of fun and frolic; she was an inventor of sport, and her ingenuity devised many an amusement which was not all amusement, but which involved considerable exercise of wit and intelligence — and our beloved 'Professor' (William P. Jones) soon found that he could always rely upon her influence in the school to counteract the tendency to silly escapades and moonlight walks with the 'University boys.' A young man would have been temerity itself who would have suggested such a thing to her. In fact, she came to be something of a 'beau' herself — a certain dashing recklessness about her having as much fascination for the average schoolgirl as if she had been a senior in the University, instead of the carefully dressed, neatly gloved young lady who took the highest credit marks in recitation, but was known in the privacy of one or two of the girls' rooms to assume the 'airs' of a bandit, flourish an imaginary sword, and converse in a daring, slashing way supposed to be known only among pirates with their fellows.   .   .   .   .   .

"Study did not end with the abandonment of the classroom, but, as she had planned, went on in new forms, and with the intent and intensity of original research. Her schoolmates when they visited her in her quiet little room, with its bright south and east windows brimming the cosy nook with warm sunshine, found her always at her desk with books, paper and pen, for with her independent mind, the thoughts and investigations of others were not properly her own until she had fixed them in the mold of personal judgment, and phrased them in the forceful language of her own opinions.

"While society, or the superficial intercourse known by this name, had little charm for this studious young woman, whose keen spirit soon pierced its disguises and rated it at its real value, to her journal she philosophized about it in this wise:

"As I gain in experience, I see more and more distinctly that a young lady must have accomplishments to be of value in society. That august tyrant asks every candidate for preferment in its ranks: 'What can you do for me? Can you tell me a story, make me a joke or sing me a song? I am to be amused!' Society is not for scholarly discipline. Study is for private life. Benefactions, loves, hates, emoluments, business — all these go on behind the scenes. Men grow learned, and good, and great otherwhere than in society. They ponder, and delve, and discover in secret places. Women suffer and grow uncomplaining in toil and sacrifice, and learn that life's grandest lesson is summed up in four simple words — 'Let us be patient' — in the nooks and corners of the earth. Into society they may bring not their labors but the fruit of their labors. Public opinion, which is the mouthpiece of society, asks not of any man: 'When did you do this, where did you accomplish it?' but, 'What have you done? we do not care for the process, give us the results.'

"Society is to everyday life what recess is to the schoolboy. If it has been crowded from this, its right relation, then it is for every right-thinking member to aid in the restoration to its true position. Let no cynical philosopher inveigh against society. Let none say its fruits are simply heartlessness and hypocrisy. Man is a creature of habits; when among his fellows, he does his best studiously at first, unthinkingly afterward. I will venture to assert that the man who was greater than any other who walked the earth was the kindest, the best bred, the most polite. Society is not an incidental, unimportant affair; it is the outward sign of an inward grace. Let us, then, if we can, be graceful; cultivate conversational ability, musical talent ; improve our manners — and our beauty, if we are blessed with it. Harmonious sounds cheer the heart. Fitness is admirable. All these are means of happiness to us who have sorrow enough at best. It is no light thing to perform the duties we owe to society, and it is better to approximate than to ignore them."

"Scattered all along through this year the journal shows many a deep longing for the best and most symmetrical of all lives — that of the Christian.

"In the vacation summer of 1858, on returning from Evanston, Frances took possession of the little schoolhouse near Forest Home, and for six weeks carried on the school herself, with great comfort and pleasure. Early in the autumn the Willard family removed to Evanston. Tenants were placed in charge of their beloved Forest Home, and 'Swampscott' became their residence— a pleasant place near the lake, the large grounds of which were Mr. Willard's pride and pleasure, as he saw them, under his skillful management, growing constantly more beautiful. Nearly every tree and vine was set with his own hands, often assisted by Frank, and all were imported from Forest Home.

. . . . . .

"The life of the home was a very bright and merry one at this time, for the three children were all together, all earnestly at work, but all as uniquely bent on enjoyment as ever they had been in the old delightful days of Forest Home. Oliver having finished his college studies, was preparing for the ministry; Mary was joyfully nearing her own graduation day — full of enthusiasm for knowledge, for happiness, for all the real values of life. Frances alone at home, deep in a young girl's philosophy of existence, was nevertheless as fond of a romp, a joke and a good time, as any girl today of the particular fun and frolic that young people nowadays engage in. Deeply envious of the brothers and friends who were so fond of their college fraternity, and so tantalizing with their half-displayed secrets, the girls of 1859 and 1860, an exceptionally bright and clever company, organized a secret society of their own, in which Frances and Mary were among the deepest plotters. Since Greek letters were in order, ours was the Iota Omega fraternity, or sorority; dark and dreadful were its ceremonies, grave and momentous its secrets. It was not allowed to degenerate, however, into anything worse than autograph hunting, and even in these early days of that nuisance, we received some sharp reprimands for our importunity. Horace Greeley particularly berated us in a long letter, which, fortunately, we could not entirely decipher, and which was so wretchedly illegible that we could exhibit it to envious Sigma Chi brothers without fear of taunt or ridicule. Abraham Lincoln gave his friendly 'sign manual,' Longfellow wrote out a verse of 'Excelsior' for the collection, but Queen Victoria, alas! to whom we had applied in a letter addressed,

'Victoria,
    Buckingham Palace,
        London,
            England, The World,'

never deigned us a reply.

"We had a department of 'Notes and Queries' also, that was given to Frank's especial charge, and she was never more herself than when setting all of us at work with slender clues upon the hunt for some valuable bits of information more than she or we knew at the time. She was our instructor and leader."

Taking Miss Willard's student life all in all, we find her brave and modest, merry and wise, winsome, gentle, generous and good, gracious in her dignity, dainty in attire, superb in her friendliness, remarkable in scholarship and valedictorian of her class.

The school days, she has told us, were a blessed time, full of happiness and aspiration, having in them the charm of success and the witchery of friendship, deepening in her heart the love of humanity and exalting her spirit to the worship of God.

CHAPTER IV

RELIGIOUS DEVELOPMENT

AS a lisping child the little Frances learned the mighty first chapter of St. John's Gospel from her mother's lips. It was the first lesson she ever learned by heart. Then came the rocking-chair lullaby in her father's deep tones:

"A charge to keep I have,
　A God to glorify,
A never-dying soul to save
　And fit it for the sky.

"To serve the present age,
　My calling to fulfill,
Oh, may it all my powers engage
　To do my Master's will."

A prophetic hymn — this first one ever taught the young warrior soul, whose "charge" and whose "calling" far outran the boundary of her father's conserving thought. Then followed the old Bible stories delightful to a child, yet stored with the sacred history of the soul. Somewhat later, "Pilgrim's Progress" became the *vade mecum* and "Greatheart" her chosen knight.

The Forest Home trio were early trained to "deeds of weekday holiness," but Sundays were ideal days of praise and aspiration. How they loved the drives to church in the democrat wagon, or when there was no service to which they could go, how humanly sweet, simple and sacred the Sabbath of the home was made. In the morning the stately father walked to the riverside among the sentinel trees, his little girls stepping proudly beside him, and his grave voice carrying to their young minds and hearts the vibrations of the great and devout thoughts of the race. In the afternoon, as Miss Willard's hallowed memory pictures it to us, there were walks with mother, when she clipped a sprig of caraway or fennel for the girls or a bunch of sweet-smelling pinks for Oliver from the pretty little beds in the heart of the orchard, where no one was privileged to go except with mother. "Here she talked to us of God's great beauty in the thoughts He works out for us; she taught us tenderness toward every little sweet-faced flower and piping bird; she showed us the shapes of clouds and what resemblances they bore to things upon the earth; she made us love the Heart that is at Nature's heart. When one of us was afraid of the dark and came to mother with the question 'Why,' she replied, 'Because you do not know and trust God enough yet; just once get it into your heart as well as your head that the world lies in God's arms like a babe on its mother's breast, and you will never be afraid of anything.'"

A loving aunt, long years a teacher, visited the home, and leading the children out under the far-off stars at night, made them forevermore familiar with the flaming belt of Orion and the clustering Pleiades, quoting reverently lofty passages from the Bible about the starry heavens; while Frances, looking upward from the vantage ground of the wide prairie, would repeat, almost with tears, the lines from Addison taught her by her mother:

> "The spacious firmament on high
> And all the blue ethereal sky,
> With spangled heavens, a shining frame,
> Their Great Original proclaim;
> The unwearied sun, from day to day
> Doth his Creator's power display,
> And publishes to every land
> The work of an Almighty hand."

"Oh, sacred Sabbaths of our childhood! Oh, early mornings in the spring, when we ran together through the dewy grass or laid our ears to the brown bosom of the earth to hear her vibrant breathing, to thrill at her pulsing heart! Oh, birds that sang for me, and flowers that bloomed, and mother-love that brooded and father-love that held! And **God**'s sky over all, and Himself near unto us everywhere; yea, nearer than near! Surely heavenly and without end are the blessings of the Lord to children! Verily, His goodness and His mercy are with us all our days." So sang the heart of Frances Willard in its ripe womanhood when moved by the recurring touch of those years.

Miss Willard's enjoyment of the Sunday twilight hour of song dated back to Forest Home when "Guide me, O Thou Great Jehovah," or Kirke White's "Star of Bethlehem" used to melt the heart of the child, even then conscious of the struggle between natural resistance to religious influence and the love that yields itself in submission to God.

If she was slow in growing to the simplicities of adult womanhood, when heart, mind and life are all in harmony, she grew toward them continually, the fact of her being the powerful and effective woman that she was proving this, although perhaps she could not have been this publicly effective woman without her positive turbulent temper. "If I stubbed my toe against anything it was prompt instinct within me to turn again and rend that thing." "If I remember rightly," she said, "our ancient brother Xerxes furnished several entertaining incidents to history." But even in her warlike moods she was like a wholesome spring day. Its breeze may get things disarranged a trifle, but there is plenty of oxygen.

As the first flame of youth began to kindle in the cheeks and eyes of this reticent yet ambitious girl, she coveted such wealth of beauty as she saw in other faces and wept with discontent at what she considered her own modest competence of loveliness. Her mother tenderly comforted her in motherfashion, but added: "Grandfather Hill was the noblest looking man I ever saw, and you are very like him, my dear." Thereupon the active little girl instantly resolved to be very "noble looking," and that she might be quite complete and admirable, resolved to be very noble feeling also, a resolution she certainly lived up to, although not until the

KATE JACKSON

MY FOUR.

impulse from which it sprang was tempered by many years of God's grace.

"I am afraid it almost turned a rather innocent outward vanity into an inward pride, much more difficult to get rid of," she afterward said. "As for my brother's kindly speech, 'Never mind, Frank, if you are not the handsomest girl in school, you are the smartest,' I nearly made a prig of myself over it, because as 'Watson's' Dr. Johnson would say, 'I was not without a modest consciousness that it was true.' It was the old story of the rag doll over again. 'She's a rag doll — only she's good, and not proud like a wax doll.' And it makes me laugh even now to think how simply and naturally in all our play 'organizations' the chief incentive, reward and honor of the leading officer's position was a right to have the 'say so.'"

It made one smile tenderly sometimes to note the way in which, in quiet hours, she was inclined to deplore, as a half-sin, all this development of the "selfhood," which yet gives edge, strength, practical force to all our abilities in this wicked and workaday world.

How blessed she was in her mother-confidant, that wise woman who knew that the storm and stress period of youth is normally inevitable, that the natural will must get its natural growth and training before there is any truly individual will to be submitted to God or bend its force to God's service. She was not a woman of fears. If she had any she did not tell her daughter. She only told the Lord, knowing He was in the heart of her child, to will and to do of His good pleasure even as He is at the heart of His universe.

A passage from Miss Willard's journal when a teacher at twenty-four reveals the questioning soul seeking after the truth of an eternal existence.

"Two letters have been received from two poet-souled women in obscure life, and for the time they have transfigured me. Full of insight they were, for these women love much and read the significance of destiny by clear burning tapers lighted at the altar of consecration to their homes. I have read of the French Revolution and Charlotte Corday, and the Unknown and Invisible has risen before me, misty and dark, as I wonder what vision burst on the freed soul of that marvelous girl as she lay on the plank of the scaffold and 'the beam dropped, the blade glided, the head fell.' I have listened to the Bible reading at our quiet chapel prayers, and have pondered much over Job's words, 'Why should a man contend against God?' and as I thought, my soul went out after Him, this awful, overwhelming Power that holds all things in equilibrium, and has come back again with some dim, shuddering consciousness that He is, and some sweet faith that 'He is a rewarder of all such as diligently seek him.' I have looked at my pliant, active fingers and wondered over this strange imparted force that is ordained to live a while in me, that joins itself in some weird way to muscle, sinew, tissue and bone; that filters through my nerves and makes all things alive, among them the organic shape that is called me. I wish I could talk tonight with some one who would say, with quick, emphatic gesture, 'Yes, I understand; I have felt so too.' 'Be Cæsar to thyself.' The words are brave, but tonight I am too tired to say them truly, and so I will pray to God and go to sleep."

It was during the leisure of convalescence from the serious illness that prevented her presence at the graduating exercises of her class that Frances Willard's first affirmative turning toward a religious life began, and it began very simply. These "hidden things of the heart" are best told by herself, and happy are we in their priceless possession.

"GOD AND MY HEART"

"It was one night in June, 1859. I was nineteen years old and was lying on my bed in my home at Evanston, Illinois, ill with typhoid fever. The doctor had said that the crisis would soon arrive, and I had overheard his words. Mother was watching in the next room. My whole soul was intent as two voices seemed to speak within me, one of them saying, 'My child, give me thy heart. I called thee long by joy, I call thee now by chastisement; but I have called thee always and only because I love thee with an everlasting love.' The other said, 'Surely, you who are so resolute and strong will not break down now because of physical feebleness. You are a reasoner and never yet were you convinced of the reasonableness of Christianity. Hold out now and you will feel when you get well just as you used to feel.'

"One presence was to me warm, sunny, safe, with an impression as of snowy wings; the other cold, dismal, dark, with the flutter of a bat. The controversy did not seem brief; in my weakness such a strain would doubtless appear longer than it was. But at last, solemnly, and with my whole heart, I said, not in spoken words, but in the deeper language of consciousness, 'If God lets me get well I'll try to be a Christian girl.' But this resolve did not bring peace. 'You must at once declare this resolution,' said the inward voice.

"Strange as it seems, and complete as had always been my frankness toward my dear mother, far beyond what is usual even between mother and child, it cost me a greater humbling of my pride to tell her than the resolution had cost of self-surrender, or than any other utterance of my whole life has involved. After a hard battle, in which I lifted up my soul to God for strength, I faintly called to her from the next room and said: 'Mother, I wish to tell you that if God lets me get well I'll try to be a Christian girl.'

"She took my hand, knelt beside my bed, and softly wept and prayed. I then turned my face to the wall and sweetly slept.

"That winter we had revival services in the old Methodist church at Evanston. Doctor (now Bishop) Foster was president of the university, and his sermons, with those of Doctors Dempster, Bannister and others, deeply stirred my heart. I had convalesced slowly and spent several weeks at Forest Home, so these meetings seemed to be my first public opportunity of declaring my new allegiance. The very earliest invitation to go forward, kneel at the altar and be prayed for was heeded by me. Waiting for no one, counseling with no one, I went alone along the aisle with my heart beating so loud that I thought I could see as well as hear it beat as I moved forward. One of the most timid, shrinking and sensitive of natures, what it meant to me to go forward thus, with my student friends gazing upon me, can never be told. I had been known as 'skeptical,' and prayers (of which I then spoke lightly) had been asked for me in the church the year before. For fourteen nights in succession I thus knelt at the altar, expecting some utter transformation — some portion of heaven to be placed in my inmost heart, as I have seen the box of valuables placed in the corner-stone of a building and firmly set, plastered over and fixed in its place forever. This is what I had determined must be done, and was loath to give it up. I prayed and agonized, but what I sought did not occur.

"One night when I returned to my room baffled, weary and discouraged, and knelt beside my bed, it came to me quietly that this was not the way; that my 'conversion,' my 'turning about,' my 'religious experience' (re-ligare, to bind again), had reached its crisis on that summer night when I said 'yes' to God. A quiet certitude of this pervaded my consciousness, and the next night I told the public congregation so, gave my name to the church as a probationer, and after holding this relation for a year — waiting for my sister Mary, who joined later, to pass her six months' probation, I was baptized and joined the church, May 5, 1861, 'in full connection.' Meanwhile I had regularly led, since that memorable June, a prayerful life — which I had not done for some months previous to that time; studied my Bible, and, as I believe, evinced by my daily life that I was taking counsel of the heavenly powers. Prayer meeting, class meeting and church services were most pleasant to me, and I became an active worker, seeking to lead others to Christ. I had learned to think of and believe in God in terms of Christ Jesus. This had always been my difficulty, as I believe it is that of so many. It seems to me that by nature all spiritually disposed people (and with the exception of about six months of my life, I was always strongly that) are Unitarians, and my chief mental difficulty has always been, and is today after all these years, to adjust myself to the idea of 'Three in one' and 'One in three.' But while I will not judge others there is for me no final rest, except as I translate the concept of God into the nomenclature and personality of the New Testament. What Paul says of Christ, is what I say; the love John felt, it is my dearest wish to cherish."

In her ripest years she wrote from the rich fullness of knowledge and experience: "The Life of God flowing into the soul of man is the only Life, and all my being sets toward Him as the rivers to the sea. Celestial things grow dearer to me every day and I grow poorer in my own eyes save as God gives to me. I still care a little too much for the good words of the good, but God helps me even in that."

How Christlike she became the whole world knows. How great she grew in gentleness, how simple in prayer, how trustfully she waited upon the Lord, whose grace all her childhood through was touching her fine spirit to the finest issues of her future life! How much of that inner peace, rest, candor and simplicity radiated out in the abundant warmth, sweetness, serenity and power of her life and her life's high aim and great endeavor! And at the last, when God for many years had had His will and way with her, how the whole self-nature became the obedient servant of her inward humility toward Him, and her outgoing helpfulness to men. The "good words of the good" are forever abundantly hers.

CHAPTER V

TEACHER — PRECEPTRESS — DEAN

IT was at Forest Home where all her young ambitions were born that Frances, recuperating from the illness of her graduation year, determined to teach. Few other paths were then open to adventurous spirits among women, and even this course was strongly deprecated by Miss Willard's father, while he must have admired his own force of character as shown in his child's outcry for independence at whatever cost. "I have not yet been out in the world to do and dare for myself," she argued. "Single handed and alone I should like to try my powers, for I have remained in the nest a full-grown bird long enough, and too long. It is an anomaly in natural history."

Through the Superintendent of Cook County Public Schools a primitive red schoolhouse away out on the prairie, ten miles from Chicago, was discovered minus a teacher, and this plucky young woman as usual won the day and in her twenty-first year found at "Harlem" a surplus of isolation and a sufficient field for the cultivation of her powers.

While packing her trunk for this first new departure Miss Willard philosophized thus:

"If I become a teacher in some school that I do not like, if I go away alone and try what I myself can do and suffer, and am tired and lonesome; if I am in a position where I must have all the responsibility myself and must be alternately the hammer that strikes and the anvil that bears, I think I may grow to be strong and earnest in practice, as I have always tried to be in theory. So here goes for a fine character. If I were not intent upon it, I could live contented here at Swampscott all my days."

Well for her that of good humor and stoutness of heart she had a plentiful supply, for on her arrival at Harlem she found her savage little pupils had broken the windows and were engaged in "sundry forms of controversy emphasized with fisticuffs." Imagine the wonder of these twenty pupils, most of whom were foreigners of different nationalities, when on the opening morning this frank-souled, sweet-voiced young schoolmistress read a few verses from her little pocket Testament and suggested they should sing a hymn. We are inclined to differ from Miss Willard's afterthought that the hymn selected was "incongruous though familiar," and heartily wish we might have heard the aspiring little company's attempt to sing "I want to be an angel."

Happy little hoodlums! No doubt their angelic qualities speedily developed under an alert-minded teacher who could pray like a seraph, but could also manage the boy taller than herself who needed a bit of trouncing in the good old-fashioned way.

Miss Willard's voluminous records of this first period of teaching would make a valuable handbook of the art, summed up in her prescient observation, "When you get them all to think alike and act alike by your command, you can do with them what you will."

The hammer blows were not lacking, the metal rang true, the brave young spirit got more discipline than her pupils, the teacher's head was often bowed in prayer.

She found a generous-hearted girl-friend in the home that sheltered her during these days when life was a serious business and the two girls started a Sunday school in the forlorn little schoolhouse, out of which grew a well-ordered Methodist church in what is now the charming Chicago suburb of River Forest.

As an assistant in the Academy at Kankakee, forty miles from Chicago, Miss Willard spent only one term, her brother Oliver meanwhile succeeding her on the Harlem prairie, going thither with his father's blessing and his sensible reminder, "If you do as well with that school as Frank has done I shall be perfectly satisfied."

One of the first beautiful outgrowths of the independent life this young teacher had longed for was seen when the County Bible Association met in Kankakee, and Miss Willard wrote her mother, "When they took up a collection and I wrote 'F. E. W., $1,' I felt a new thanksgiving that I could earn and use money according to my own judgment. I have promised myself that I will give as much as I can from all my earnings to promote the doing of good in the world."

After a home vacation Miss Willard again taught the Harlem school for a few weeks in the spring of 1861, and on her return to Evanston, as she has chronicled the story, "for three-quarters of a year she wore a ring and acknowledged an allegiance based on the supposition that an intellectual comradeship was sure to deepen into unity of heart."

In 1862 we find her, in company with Mary Bannister, battling with youthful Evanstonians in the public school; a typical American specimen of that institution where demure and well-bred children brought bouquets and beaming smiles to "teacher," and where two overgrown boys, alarmed at Miss Willard's approach, stick in hand, vaulted out of an open window and never dared return.

Into these bright days, when teaching and the charm of home joys made a composite wellnigh perfect, there came the first great grief of Miss Willard's life. She lost her sister Mary, the gentle girl with sensitive ethical standards, keen love of the beautiful and the good, whose going changed all the world to her sister Frances and in an age of skepticism gave her "an anchor that would hold."

Other changes rapidly followed. The sweet home by the lake, every tree and shrub surrounding it beloved by Frances, was sold; Forest Home passed out of the hands that had builded and blessed it; Oliver, the young theologian, and Mary Bannister, his wife, were soon to go to their new home in Denver, Colorado, when in August of this year, 1862, Frances was elected Preceptress of Natural Sciences in her alma mater. Until the close of the year she taught nine and ten classes per day, while the keynote of all her underlying thought and spirit's yearning was set to the pitiful refrain, "Mary didn't get well."

Two years of teaching in the Pittsburg Female College opened a wider circle of life to Miss Willard. A friend then closely associated with her writes: "We all recognized in the brilliant, genial, warm-hearted girl a genius which was rare and which seemed to give promise of much in the future, and yet none of us dreamed of the career that was before her and of the grand achievements of her life. She was always bubbling over with wit and humor, and at the same time full of pathos and sentiment. She had already been touched by the subduing power of a great sorrow which had not embittered her but made her more tender and loving toward all. She seemed to have a vocabulary of her own and often used words and phrases of her own coining, and with a *sang froid* which no other person could ever imitate. I can see her now as I often saw her then, sitting on the steps of the old college of a summer evening, surrounded by a bevy of teachers and students, holding them spellbound by the power of her vivid imagination, and ofttimes convulsed with laughter at her sallies of genuine wit. She had a wonderfully magnetic influence over young girls, believed in them, trusted them, stood by them, often when others condemned, and sought out those who were shy and retiring and had little confidence in themselves, praised them for their smallest efforts, and sought ever to inspire them with her own high ideals of life and character."

While in Pittsburg, Miss Willard's strange new sense of loss and loneliness was solaced as she sang herself into the pages of "Nineteen Beautiful Years," that blessed biography of her heavenly human sister Mary, that tells everybody to be good.

On Miss Willard's return to Evanston she was one of a talented trio who taught the Grove School, a private enterprise where Miss Willard found an opportunity of putting many of her unique pedagogic inventions to a successful practical test among "the best-born and best-mannered children in Evanston." In the summer vacation of that year Miss Willard, as Corresponding

Secretary of the American Methodist Ladies' Centenary Association, helped to build Heck Hall in Evanston, a home building for the students of the Garrett Biblical Institute.

When her parents were established in Rest Cottage, their new home, in the autumn of 1866, Miss Willard taught for a year as preceptress in the Genessee Wesleyan Seminary (the oldest seminary of the Methodist Church) in the historic village of Lima, New York, only thirty miles from her birthplace.

In January, 1868, another severance in the sacred home circle brought its vigils and its sorrow — Miss Willard's honored father, after a lingering illness, the last weeks of which were spent in Churchville, "going triumphantly home to God."

When, in the spring, Miss Kate A. Jackson, a loved and sympathetic friend who for several years had lived and taught with Miss Willard, proposed a "tour of Europe," it was a joy that lost nothing for its complete and fresh surprise. What more natural than for Miss Jackson to gain her generous father's consent to meet every expense of the extended journey these enthusiasts planned, the keen and kindly gentleman telling Miss Willard she must believe that it was to him the fulfillment of an earnest desire that his daughter should go abroad, but never until now had he found one with whom he felt inclined to send her.

Could Miss Willard's mother bear the loneliness of another separation? Yes, Spartan that she was, with her child's good ever forming the horizon of her own hopes and happiness, she would go to Oliver and Mary in Appleton, Wisconsin, while Frances and Kate studied Europe and themselves.

Miss Willard returned from that wonderful trip abroad with a human picture gallery in her heart far exceeding in its riches and realities the galleries of Europe whose masterpieces crowded her brain. "What can be done to make the world a wider place for women?" was the question that surged through her soul.

In Paris came the prophetic inspiration which, if courageously carried out, she felt would best satisfy her resolute ideals. This brave plan was "to study by reading, personal observation and acquaintance the *woman question* in Europe, and, after returning to America, study it further in relation to her own land; *talk in public* on the subject and cast herself with what weight or weakness she possessed against the only foe of what she conceived to be the justice of the subject — unenlightened public opinion." "It is to be a word-and-idea battle," she wrote, "that will only deepen with years and must at last have a result that will delight all who have helped to hasten it."

It was "the human question" rather than the woman question, as Miss Willard has eloquently affirmed, that was shaping itself in her mind and winning her heart's loyalty, when on St. Valentine's day, 1871, she was elected President of the Evanston College for Ladies, the first woman to whom such a title was ever accorded.

The history of the relation of this college to its neighbor University, the Northwestern, has more than once repeated itself in the evolution of the higher education of women during the last thirty years. Mrs. Mary F. Haskin and other thoughtful women of Evanston, anxious to secure for their daughters the advantages for study they themselves had missed, founded a woman's college with a board of women trustees, a woman president who should confer diplomas and be recognized and proved as the peer of men in administrative power.

Coincident with the transfer of Miss Willard's alma mater, the Northwestern Female College, with its list of alumnæ, to the trusteeship of the Evanston College for Ladies, Rev. Dr. (afterward Bishop) E. O. Haven accepted the presidency of the Northwestern University on condition that "every door should be flung wide to humanity's gentler half." Doctor Haven possessed sufficient skill and diplomacy to meet the problem of this triangle of educational interests — the old college, the new college and the university — and under his presidency the two institutions moved on in the utmost harmony.

The new president of the college threw herself with great zest into this endeavor. A better building was needed; the "Woman's

Fourth of July" was planned, and for three months Miss Willard waked and slept in a combined atmosphere of education and patriotism. The Educational Association, with Mrs. A. H. Hoge as president, sent out countless circulars; Miss Willard's ingenious brain and busy hand were back of many of the original plans that resulted in a "Woman's Fourth," with no suggestion of cannon or torpedo, but with a subscription list that aggregated $30,000, and a sale of $3,000 worth of dinners to the hungry participants in the fun and frolic of the day. Everybody helped in most generous fashion; the village authorities presented the Committee with one of its parks as the building site of the college, and on that Fourth the corner stone of the new building was laid, women's hands assisting in the ceremony amid great rejoicings of heart.

The first catalogue of the Evanston College for Ladies contains a statement from the president, Miss Willard, regarding her plan for "self-government," a question of such vital interest to her then and throughout her life, and to the cause of education as well, that we record it briefly here.

"The general basis of government in this institution is, that merit shall be distinguished by privilege. Any young lady who establishes for herself a trustworthy character will be trusted accordingly. After a probation of one term, anyone who, during this time, has been loyal to the regulations of the school, and has not once required reproof, will have her name inscribed upon the 'Roll of Honor' and will be invested with certain powers and responsibilities usually restricted to the 'Faculty.' The 'Roll of Honor' has its constitution, officers and regular meetings, and sends reports to the teachers relative to the trusts of which it is made the depository. A single reproof 'conditions,' and two reproofs remove any of its members, who can regain their places by the same process through which they were first attained. Those who, during one entire term, have not been 'conditioned' upon the roll of honor, are promoted to the 'Self-Governed List' and give this pledge: 'I will try so to act that, if all others followed my example, our school would need no rules whatever. In manners and in punctuality I will try to be a model, and in all my intercourse with my teachers and schoolmates I will seek, above all else, the things that make for peace.'

"Thenceforward these young ladies 'do as they please,' so long as they 'please' to do right. Every pupil in school is eligible, first, to the roll of honor; next, to a place among the 'self-governed'; hence there is no ground of jealousy. Scholarship does not enter into the requirements of admission — character is placed above all competition here.

"It is believed that this system may develop a true sentiment of 'honor' among pupils, one that shall favor the school rather than the delinquent. The false ideas of honor that still prevail to an absurd extent among young people at school are the last relics of the mediæval system of oppression, and of espionage, its sworn ally. As a democratic form of government inspires the sentiment of loyalty to itself, and implies the duty of all patriotic citizens to bring to justice those whose conduct threatens the public welfare, so in an institution where the pupils are intrusted with a part of the responsibility, and where the possibility of self-government is set before them, it is a logical inference that they will stand by the government of which they form a part."

In the same catalogue Miss Willard adds:

"While it is true that many universities and colleges are now nominally open to women, it is equally true that, without special provision for convenient and economical residence, and for such studies as they may wish to undertake not found in the university curriculum, the advantage is often more nominal than real. Aside from this, young ladies coming to a university with none of their own sex among the instructors to counsel them, sympathize with and help them, cannot be said to enjoy advantages equal to those which are offered to young men. The Evanston College for Ladies, under the direction and control of a board of lady trustees, seeks to make these special provisions and to aid the Northwestern to accomplish its nobly undertaken task — the higher education of women."

Miss Willard was facing one of the gravest problems of the educator, "How can I make school discipline most conducive to the formation of noble, self-reliant character?" For a proof of her own plan, tested for two years at the Evanston College for Ladies, I have asked one of her warm-hearted, quick-brained pupils of that history-making period, and Mrs. Isabella Webb Parks, a leading Roll of Honor girl, now the mother-teacher of a large fireside circle of her own, contributes the following sketch:

"I met Miss Willard for the first time in the fall of 1871. The Northwestern University, at Evanston, Illinois, had just opened its doors to women. The women of Evanston, anxious to make the experiment of co-education a success in their town, had organized the 'Evanston College for Ladies,' an institution designed to provide the young ladies who should attend the University with home surroundings, with women for their counselors and friends. Of this institution Miss Willard was the Dean, and it was my happy lot to be one of those whom she always lovingly designated as 'my girls.' What it was for girls to be closely associated with Miss Willard in the formative period of their life, only those who knew her well can at all appreciate. Such broad views of life and destiny as she opened to our sight; such high ideals of character as she set before us; such visions of the heights to which we might climb, of the noble deeds we might achieve, and, with it all, such a deep and weighty sense of responsibility for the use we made of life with its gifts and opportunities, I have never seen nor felt through the inspiration of anyone else. It was like living upon Alpine heights to be associated with her.

"Her first Friday afternoon talk to us struck the keynote of her influence. In those days co-education was still looked upon as very much of an experiment, and, though I doubt if it has been tried in more friendly and congenial surroundings than at Evanston, there were many there who looked doubtfully upon it and were ready to seize upon the slightest indications of evil. Before Miss Willard was gathered in that old chapel a company of average girls. None of them wanted to do anything very bad. Many were inspired with a more or less earnest purpose to make the most of themselves and had, therefore, sought these opportunities for higher education. But the majority had no clearer understanding of life's meaning, no deeper appreciation of its responsibilities than is usual among girls of their age. They possessed, moreover, quite the average amount of animal spirits and love of fun. Had they been placed in a regulation female seminary with its multitude of inconsequential rules, they would have acted as girls usually do under such circumstances — set at naught the exasperating and trivial restrictions which implied a lack of good sense and self-respect on their part. To my knowledge there were girls there who only waited the occasion to rebel against such strictures. But in that first talk Miss Willard disarmed all such incipient rebellion. She gave us briefly the history of the opening of the University to women, told of President E. O. Haven's generous, brotherly interest and faith in us; of the anxiety with which the women of Evanston had planned for our coming and had sought to make the way plain and easy before us; of how ready they were to help us in any way we needed and with what interest they were watching us. Though we saw only unfamiliar faces about us, yet, she said, 'Friendly eyes are upon you as you walk our streets and the kind hands of strangers are ready to clasp yours.' Then she reminded us that this was a new movement, a step forward in woman's advancement, and its success must depend chiefly upon those in whose interest it was made. With the impressive tone and manner which only those who have heard her can appreciate, she said, 'Your feet and mine are treading ground untrod before. I am speaking to those whose intellects must be active and keen, whose hearts must be loyal and true, else the new experiment is a failure.' By the time she had finished, every girl in her presence felt that the eyes of all Evanston were fixed upon our little band with anxious but sympathetic and kindly interest; that the cause of co-education depended very largely upon our success as students and our loyalty to right; that even the larger cause of woman's advancement was involved in the use we made of the opportunities now placed within our reach. I do not believe there was a girl there who would not have despised herself if she had knowingly been false to the responsibilities resting upon her.

"It was not long after this that an incident occurred, small in itself, yet very significant of the effect of Miss Willard's influence. The old Seminary grounds, which we occupied temporarily in the hope of entering a year later the beautiful new college then building, were very near the railroad track. One afternoon a train passed loaded with young men students. There were twenty or more girls in the yard or on the porch, and the young men on the train gave the 'Fem. Sem.' the 'Chautauqua salute.' Not a handkerchief waved in return. On the contrary, the demonstration was regarded in the light of an insult and called forth some indignant remarks. Yet there were girls in that group who, under other circumstances, would have considered it great sport to answer the salute, principally because it was a defiance of a command which implied lack of sense and self-respect in those upon whom it was laid. Miss Willard had given no specific directions how her girls should deport themselves toward young men or anyone else. She had simply inspired them with a sense of their individual responsibility, had made them feel that greater interests than they had dreamed of depended upon their conduct. An 'arrest of thought' was always, in her view, a far more effectual way of reaching the desired end than rules and monitors, for she believed that the only true government is self-government. It was on this idea that she founded her self-governed system, which was a perfect success.

"Never before had I lived under such a keen sense of personal responsibility, nor has it been exceeded in later years. One must have been callous indeed to have resisted it who lived under her influence, for she appealed always to the highest motives. 'Help us always to be what in her best moments each of us wants to be,' was the frequently recurring petition in her prayer at our evening devotions. To that ideal self she always appealed. She seemed to ignore the possibility of our allowing any lower self to have a voice in making up our decisions, and the self to which she thus appealed responded. It was the same years after when, instead of half a hundred school girls, she gathered as her pupils 'the women of two hemispheres.' And very seldom did those appealed to disappoint her. It could not be expected that there should be no exceptions; Judas became a thief and a traitor under the constant influence of the Master himself, and there were a few who did not measure up to Miss Willard's faith and trust. But by far the most have been lifted up to higher planes of life and thought by her generous confidence.

"It was not strange that warm-hearted girls, their affections unchilled by experience with the world's coldness and their faith unshaken by its deceptions, should have idolized her. Some onlookers, beholding the devoted loyalty and passionate affection which she inspired in us, declared that her influence was inexplicable on natural grounds; that it actually bordered on the uncanny; that she possessed a kind of occult magnetism not to be resisted by those who came within its reach. But it was not so. Her power was only that which a great soul, full of the spirit of Christ, must ever wield over its fellows. It is the power which has made Miss Willard the organizer and leader of the womanhood of her time, and the commanding figure of this century."

The story of Miss Willard's withdrawal from her work as Dean of the Woman's College and of Professor of Æsthetics in the Northwestern University is recorded in her own words in full detail. The spirit in which she took this step is commented upon in the address of President Henry Wade Rogers, now at the head of the University, on the occasion of the Commemorative Service in Evanston, and tribute has been paid in this address to the wisdom of her course, the thoughtfulness and sincerity of her motives and the sensitive conscientiousness of her attitude toward her colleagues from whom she was compelled to differ in regard to matters of administration.

Dr. Frank M. Bristol, pastor of Miss Willard's home church, in his farewell address to his congregation on March 27, said:

"Frances Willard taught me in the University, and she made the classroom seem like a flower bed."

When Miss Willard introduced her self-government plan to her college girls, she tells us she felt "that she was going into a garden planted out with beautiful maiden flowers." Is not this the perfection of teaching, that to both teacher and pupils the recitation room should have the orderliness, life and fragrance of a flower bed?

Glad and grateful acclaim must fill the hearts of the two thousand pupils whose young lives received the impress of such a teacher: their beloved Miss Willard whose boundless faith and prophetic insight taught them in the wide fields of character and destiny "How to Win." Let her name be loved and remembered in every schoolroom in the land.

Roll of Honor
If thou doest ill, the joy fades, not the pain;
If well, the pain doth fade, the joy remains.

CHAPTER VI

A TRAVELER ABROAD

IN the days of the Guilds no man could write himself "Master" until, as "journeyman," he had traveled from city to city, from land to land, learning whatever might be new and serviceable to him in the customs of his craft. When the time of his wandering was over, if he had been diligent and wise, he returned to his own land, no longer a mere workman provincial in his art, but a master, with a world-wide training.

Frances E. Willard, who was to be both mistress and teacher of the art of life, having already passed her apprenticeship of instruction and experimental practice, was now to wander in other lands, see life under other conditions, with other customs, studying its advantages and disadvantages, its helps and its hindrances, as thus expressed.

All the gathered gain and fruitage of the past, the results of the ripe culture of its ages in art, music, literature, architecture, history — all this she strove to make her own. She worked and studied in every capital in Europe but one; she traveled north into Finland, east to the banks of the Volga; she lived in Damascus, and spent some time in Palestine in the company of eminent scholars; she climbed the Pyramids, and went south till she could look over into Nubia and see the Southern Cross in the sky.

In the course of this trip few of the fine flavors of the earth escaped her discerning taste. Give such a woman, with such capabilities, such an opportunity, and she will naturally make more of it than a regiment of smaller people could. As the friend who was her daily companion through these years, herself a woman of more than ordinary perception, used to say: "I never knew how much we saw, or how much there was in what we saw, until Frank began to tell about it. Sometimes I likened her mind to the philosopher's stone. Common clay turned to gold at its touch."

It was a great change in circumstances for the young woman who, not so many years before, stood in the barn door at old Forest Home and wailed: "Shall we ever go anywhere, or know anything, or see anybody!" but all seems to have come about as gently, each thing in its time, as if it were nothing uncommon. As George MacDonald has said: "Not only is the impossible possible with God, but it is *verra* possible."

Throughout this period Frances flung herself into the stream of its labors and enjoyments with that ardor and abandon to the moment, that concentration of purpose upon the precise matter in hand, which was her happy characteristic all her life. She got out of each stage, as it came, all she was capable of at the time. She was just as brave, as bright, and as half-shy, during this trip to Europe as she had been at home. She gives a diverting account of the "benumbing effect" upon her of the stately, black-coated array of waiters at the Lakes of Killarney. But the "benumbing effect" manifestly did not extend to her brain, for she accompanies it with one of the most charming and graceful accounts of the beauty of the place ever penned.

The itinerary of these two pilgrims, Miss Willard and her friend Miss Kate A. Jackson, is fascinating reading. Ireland, Scotland, England, France, Switzerland, Denmark, Sweden, Finland, Russia, Poland, Germany, Belgium, Holland, the Rhine, Italy, Egypt, Palestine, Greece, Constantinople, the Danube, Hungary, Vienna, Paris, London, Paris again, are some of the headings. No wonder they had a good time. Think of it! They had all the great sculpture, the perfect paintings of the world to study till the soul made their largeness of line, fitness of composition, right harmonies of color, its own.

Miss Willard had always been responsive to the spontaneous music of nature. Now she had the great music of ages of human life also, to vibrate over heart and nerves. What must this have meant to one who, as a child, had kissed the old melodeon good-by, and who eight years before had written: "Five minutes of beautiful singing or playing will change my entire mental attitude."

The two women went everywhere. The stage and the stage-setting of the drama of history for centuries was before them, and they were deeply versed in history, not as a dry study held in memory alone, but as students who, in learning it, were so sympathetically disposed that they almost experienced it as they read. For this perfect preparation Frances had to thank her aunt Sarah, one of the greatest and most dramatic teachers of history this country has known.

Nor did the tourists confine themselves to the beaten paths which led by the great historical landmarks only. They loved the people and the places for their present selves. Both the human oddity and the human identity, as differing circumstance and custom set them forth, were dear to them. Bicycle girls today scarcely search more diligently for delightful and unspoiled corners.

They climbed the Alps to study the serenity and poise of monastic life, and loved the human-eyed St. Bernard dogs of the friendly hospice. At London they tried athletic feats in the globe of St. Paul's Cathedral, at least Frances did; Kate had more good sense! They went up the Nile in a steamer borrowed of the Pasha for the occasion. Certain insects — not locusts — of Egypt demanded first attention, and a half-page of journal comment settles them as probably lineal descendants of the historical plagues. But even the fleas, engaging from their very activity, were forgotten when "in the frame of the violet sky hung constellations." They perched on the broken columns of ancient temples, they faced with questioning woman-eyes the eternal woman, the Sphinx, themselves part of her mystery, most unknown to themselves.

In Palestine they took no joy in pretended tombs and places, alien with the mixed breath of crowds, although they tried to "do" them dutifully. But as the day shut its doors they went out to the Mount of Olives, where our Lord prayed in the deepening silence, and the same stars looked down on them which looked on Him that night so long gone by, the same stars He had created. And they went to Bethany, the Lord's "home of rest," where lived those He loved, who loved Him; Jordan, and Jericho, and the Dead Sea, where by some mischance of travel they found themselves with just ten minutes to stay; but why add to the list? each place lived again in that clear-cut, imaginative life.

In Greece their time was far too limited for their limitless desires. It was sufficiently long for them, however, not only to see the usual sights, but to search out a shallow, pebbly brook, perhaps the very brook through the cool stream of which Socrates walked barefoot that bright Athenian day, and following along its course to a solitary turn where the grass bank sloped gently and a single tall tree grew, there sit down together in its shade and read their Phædrus to the hum of the cicadæ, and the stirring of the breeze, and the lisp of the brook around its stones; just as at Jerusalem they looked for a sight of the valley, now covered with gardens, where was the great single-arched bridge across which the Queen of Sheba advanced to meet King Solomon, and drawing out their Bible read the story over.

In Italy Frances wrote: "I never dreamed in those lethargic years at home what a wide world it is, how full of misery." The swarming wretchedness of it nearly broke her heart. In this grief also she turned to God, that omnipotent Love and Wisdom that had a right to create, and created; that Lord of Life "in Whom we live and move and have our being"; He who knows the end from the beginning, and had inexorably made us. "Let my soul calm itself, O God, in Thee!" she cries, again and again.

But the maladministration, the love of dominion she found aroused her soul to revolt and abhorrence. While her whole European trip seemed on the surface to be given up to culture for culture's sake, Miss Willard's journal indicates the constant trend of the deeper currents of her nature toward helping poor old humanity that must be lifted toward God. In Paris they studied in the College de France and at the Sorbonne, attended the lectures of Laboulaye and Guizot, Legouve Chasles, Franck, the historian, Chevalier, the political economist, and others, and were there for the last time when the German armies began to gather their hostile lines closer about the great city. Before they left they made a last pilgrimage to bid farewell to Our Lady of Milo, before whom Heine poured out the heart-break of endless separation. After two years and a half of absence they were ready, even eager, to go home. Everywhere they had been welcomed. Everywhere their hearts and minds had received profit.

To the freedom and pleasure of their movements Miss Jackson's knowledge of French had contributed much. Great store they had laid by for future years of growth and activity, and in the fall of 1870 they embarked for their own dear land.

From Miss Willard's journals, faithfully kept throughout this eventful trip, we quote a section on "Egypt," and add "The New Chivalry," Miss Willard's first public lecture, of which she has said: "It is chiefly made up of observations upon women in Europe — whose sorrowful estate, as I studied it, had much to do with giving me the courage to become a public speaker."

EGYPT

FROM A YANKEE SCHOOL-MA'AM'S POINT OF VIEW

. . . . . .

I rode on, all alone, a mile or more, to Memnon's statue. You know the story — that in the magic days of old, when the rays of the rising sun struck the statue, it gave forth sweetest music. But perhaps you do not know that the heroic name of Memnon does not rightfully belong to it, antiquarians having agreed that it is the statue of Amenophis, one of Egypt's ancient kings. But apart from these pitiless, prosaic facts, this is the most poetic piece of sculpture in existence, except the sphinx. And here was I, riding alone and free over the plain of Thebes, and yonder sat the vocal statue on his solemn throne, just as he was sitting at this same hour — under these heavens — four thousand years ago. Another statue, twin to this, but probably some centuries less venerable, and not endowed with vocal gifts, is close beside it. It is a near relative (some say the uncle of its nephew, the vocal statue), and the profane Britishers christened the twain "Lord Dundreary and his brother Sam." My donkey galloped nimbly around this dignified pair, while I measured with long glances the awful height of Memnon, quite oblivious of his less celebrated relative. Mindful of the explanation some scientific men have given of the musical tradition, namely, that certain stones by a rearrangement of their particles under the influence of blows have been known to give forth harmonious sounds, I pelted the old patriarch with stones, but waked no such response as fancy's ear had often caught when I was far from Thebes. A lithe Arab, seeing my endeavor, climbed the statue's side and rapped away with some vigor upon the stone that lies across its knee, producing some faint show of resonance, but exigent imagination sneered at this attempt, as is its malicious custom. I picked up some cubes of rich brown Nile mud, crystallized here since last the river shrank away from Memnon's feet, and the dozen Arabs who had crowded around me gathered leaves and blades of grass from the pedestal's base to offer me. Two really pretty girls of twelve smoothed my hand with their hard, slim fingers, and looked me over curiously — my broad-brimmed hat with its long white scarf, and my traveling dress of navy blue, being as strange to them as their ocher-stained fingers, grease-plastered hair, and three rings in each ear, were to myself. Another girl passed by as I sat there in reverie, with a mud tray upon her head containing cakes of mingled straw and manure — the only fuel of these poor people, and generator of the vermin which swarm in their miserable villages.

This sight brought me back through two-thirds of the world's lifetime, and set me thinking about the present of the Egyptian race — a subject the most painful I have ever contemplated. Especially does the awful degradation and oppression of women, which is its cause, here distress me. When will the stronger member of the human family in every land discover that if he uses his more muscular arm to hold down to the earth the weaker member, he is putting the knife to his own breast — signing the death-warrant of his own manhood? That two and two make four is not more capable of demonstration than that in every age and country woman has been the stone around man's neck to sink him to the lowest depths, or the winged angel to help him to the purest heights that he has ever won. And away there toward the sunset, beyond the mystic Nile, the yellow sand, the wash of blue waves, is the land where man has grown free enough, wise enough, brave enough, to let woman be just what she can become without his uninspired restriction — the land where man has withdrawn his own in favor of his Maker's "thus far, and no farther." Involuntarily I turned toward the inspiring west, and rode around full of thoughts and hopes and purposes.

How can I give some idea of the Temple of Jupiter Ammon, at Karnak? Suffice it for my modest pages to relate, concerning the most stupendous ruins in the world, that they quite "fill the eye of fancy"— nay, even oppress that airy orb, such is their ponderous magnitude. Tracing their plan like that of all Egyptian temples (for these people, more than any other, believed in the virtue of what the wisest of all critics called "vain repetition"), we passed in one afternoon through nearly three thousand years of human history and toil — for such is the gulf that separated Ousertesen, the projector, from Ptolemy-Alexander, the last restorer of the temple. Under such a weight of time and beneath such masses of architecture as these, the mind feels oppressed, and struggles vainly to grapple with the abstract idea of duration, and the concrete idea of columns, capitals and crumbling walls, that seem as if the Titans only could have reared them.

We looked from the lofty masses of architecture to the slim-legged Arabs crouched on fragments of rock below, and felt more than ever that they belonged to a degenerate race. If not, then a single despot soul like that of Rameses II. must have wielded a million bodies like these as we control the members of our own.

A horrid thought this, heavier upon the heart than all these piled-up stones. Never does one get the impression of "man's inhumanity to man" so deeply graven on his spirit as in this land, the tyranny of whose kings have made it accursed of God.

The king is the one figure of supreme prominence, carved upon all these noble columns and minutely sculptured walls. He stands proudly erect, in his chariot; he draws his bow victoriously against his foes, and tramples them down under his chariot wheels; contemplates with serene triumph their severed heads and hands piled up before him by his warriors, and offers as chief among equals such trophies, human or otherwise, as please him, to the gods. A sweet-smelling savor are these to the hawk-headed, jackal-headed, and crocodile-headed monsters whom the Egyptians worshiped, and who alone dispute pictorial honors with the sovereign. Not a touch of pity, not a hand of helpfulness, not a hint of charity, relieves the bitter gloom that broods over these splendid carvings of the greatest temple ever reared by man, and the heart turns wearily away while the eye seeks those smiling heavens that bend in changeless love over our poor world in its stormful career, and comfort comes from thought of Him who reigns there, and, late or early, blots out the very memory of the vile oppressors of our race.

> "The mills of God grind slowly,
> But they grind exceeding small,"

I murmured with deep satisfaction, as my donkey trotted homeward over the pavement of stones, crumbled to powder, but which once had helped to make Sesostris' pride.

I will close this paper by a description of Karnak by moonlight.

Our kind friend, the interpreter, who had taken us lately, by a sort of tacit consent, under his care, produced for me the very cream of all donkeys for this evening's excursion, borrowing him from his especial friend, the "chief of police" at Luxor. So it fell out, that while Semiramis ambled along tranquilly, attended by her unfailing escort, the interpreter, I galloped on alone, my swift-footed lad of the previous excursions dancing attendance behind me. That half-hour's ride from Luxor over the plain to Karnak — most stupendous of all the Theban ruins — I shall never forget. It was the culmination of all the East can yield.

Above me were new heavens. In the frame of a violet sky hung constellations I had never seen before — their palpitating globes of gold recalled the fruit-waving trees of the Hesperides. And dear, familiar stars were there, only in places very different from those they occupied "in the infinite meadows of heaven," that bent above my home. The Dipper lay on the horizon's rim, tipped wrong side up; the Pleiades had climbed far up toward the zenith; and the changeless face of the North Star was hard to recognize amid surroundings so unusual.

Around me was a new earth. The sandy plain stretched away into the purple darkness, full of attractive mystery. Far off gleamed the firefly lamps of a straggling Arab village, and on the cool, invigorating breeze, which had succeeded to the day's stifling heat, came the lonesome bark of dogs and jackals, so characteristic of the East.

I rode beneath a grove of palm trees, magnificent in stature, and of a symmetry unequaled by any others ever seen. The shadows that they cast, like mosaics in the moonlight, I could compare to nothing but an emblazoned shield. The white wall and graceful dome of a sheik's tomb gleamed through the trees and for a moment deepened the lacework of their shadows. I rode along the ruined avenue of sphinxes that once extended over the mile that separates the temple at Luxor from that of Zamah. How still it was, and how significant that stillness in the highway through which, for two thousand years and more, all that was rarest and most royal in the wide earth had proudly passed — processions of kings and priests and captives, compared with which those of the Greeks were as the sport of children; and this ere Romulus laid the first stone of his far-famed wall, or Æneas fretted the blue waves of the Ægean with his adventurous prow. The pride and glory of a world had here its center, ere Cadmus brought letters into Greece or Jacob saw his wondrous vision on the Judean plains. How insignificant is that dramatic justice which lends the charm to romance, compared with the visible hand of vengeance with which a merciful God who loves the creatures He has made has smitten this stronghold of cruelty — wrenched from their lofty places the statues of bloodthirsty tyrants, and sent the balm of moonlight drifting through the shattered walls, and mellowing the fallen columns where once "power dwelt among her passions."

We sat upon a broken pedestal in the great court of the temple, Semiramis and I, and let the wondrous lesson of the place fall on our hearts. One isolated column, the last remaining fragment of a stately colonnade, outlined itself against the liquid sky. Its white shaft was brilliant in the moonlight, and its broad capital, corolla-shaped like the lotus flower, held far aloft, like a lily's cup, uplifted for the dew. Beyond was the shattered propylon, once gay with the banners of Isis and Osiris, but frowning now like the bastion of a fortress; while still beyond, an avalanche of fallen rocks showed where ruin had struck the Temple of Jupiter-Ammon its blow of doom.

More distant still was the forest of columns which has been the wonder of all travelers — unequaled in its kind by any work of man. It numbers 134 pillars, 70 feet in height and 35 in circumference (or about 11 feet thick), covered from base to abacus with carefully wrought sculptures, brilliantly colored in their palmy days. A single one among these massive pillars had been wrested from the foundation, and leaned heavily, with its huge architecture, against its neighbor, perhaps the most mournfully significant column that human hands had ever carved from stone and left to the slow canceration of time and ruin.

Last of all, at the end of this long vista which comprises twenty-eight centuries of human history, gleamed the tapering finger of the largest obelisk in Egypt, as fresh and clear-cut in its outline as on the day the chisel left it — the chisel held by a nameless artisan who had become a mummy before Phidias had reared the Parthenon or Zeuxis and Appelles commenced their rivalries. Against this obelisk leaned an old Arab in voluminous white turban, and at its base were seated several others, all by their costumes and their bearing as perfectly in harmony with the scene as human accessories could be, and lending to it a strange charm as the mind reverts to those who reared this temple, and contrasts with theirs the insignificant achievements of their descendants.

In that far-off realm of our endless life shall we some day meet these mighty builders whose work we contemplate under these moonlit heavens? What a thought is that, that in this changeful round of being we shall encounter somewhere, some day, the awful king Sesostris, the witching Cleopatra, the Pharaoh overwhelmed in the revengeful sea.

But hark! They have arrived, the four and forty whom we call "the others." In phalanx close they ride through the vast courts, among the hundred pillars; some with cigars in mouth, others in lively conversation, and all at a brisk trot. One jolly young Englishman fires off a pistol two paces from us, at the base of the lone pillar with the capital of lotus flower.

Our donkey boys accumulate; their shrill voices pierce the ruined temple through and through; their offers of a porcelain scarabæus, a glass sphinx, a scrap of papyrus, a chip of mummy case, become vociferous. We climb with much alacrity upon our donkeys and hurriedly gallop back across the wide and pleasant plain to our steamer at Luxor.

THE NEW CHIVALRY; OR, THE SCHOOLMISTRESS ABROAD

Bayard Taylor, Du Chaillu, Dr. Hayes and Paul picture for us the inhospitable climes in whose exploration they hazarded their lives; Emily Faithful comes across seas to tell us of her work among the toiling masses of Great Britain; the Sage of Concord, founder of our lecture system, comes from his meditations to tell us that he heard a voice saying unto him, "Write."

A humbler duty lies upon my heart. I have no poem to recite, no marvelous discovery to herald. I come to you in the modest character of the schoolmistress abroad; in the capacity of friend-in-general to our girls.

Gail Hamilton, in that most racy of her essays, entitled "Men and Women," exclaims with a burst of enthusiasm: "I love women, I adore them!" But, by way of compensation, she declares in the next sentence that "There's nothing so splendid as a splendid man."

Now, I have no disposition to deny either of Gail's statements, but I would repeat and emphasize the first.

And by "women," be it distinctly understood, I always and invariably mean girls. The largest part of my life, thus far, has been spent in their service. I claim to have coaxed and reproved, caressed and scolded, corrected the compositions and read the love-letters of more girls than almost any other schoolma'am in the Northwest. I began with them before I was eighteen, in my "Forest Home" on the banks of Wisconsin river, the noblest river in the world to me, though since last I floated on its breast I have wandered as far as the Volga, the Jordan and the Nile.

In district schools, academies, and ladies' colleges, both East and West, I have pursued their fortunes. In schools where they were marshalled, two by two, when taking daily exercise, and when it was my happy lot to be their guardian on shopping expeditions; and anon in easy-going schools, where in the recitation rooms black coats were numerous as basques, and opposite each demure young lady at the dinner table sat a being with a bass voice and hair parted on one side. Then I wandered away from the merry-faced girls of America, and for two years and a half studied their sisters in Europe and the East. Coming home full of new thoughts and more earnest purposes, I gathered them around me once again — the fortunate daughters of the dear Home Land — and understood, as I could not have done before, what maketh them to differ from the sad-faced multitudes beyond the seas.

Let me then invoke your patience while together we review the argument from real life which has placed me on the affirmative side of the tremendous "Woman Question"—while we consider the lot of woman beyond the seas, and then contrast this with her position, present and prospective, here in America, and while we seek the reasons of this amazing difference. Or, as I like better to express it, let me try to picture the position taken by the New Chivalry of our native land in contrast with that of the Old Chivalry in the old world. And by this term, "New Chivalry," for I do not use it as a dictionary word, I mean to denote, sometimes sincerely, and sometimes sarcastically, the sex now dominant upon this planet.

I shall ask you, first of all, to take a glance with me at the saddest of destinies in whose presence I have deduced conclusions, the destiny of an Egyptian woman. It is a June day in the month of February. We are floating lazily along the balmy Nile, reclining on the crimson cushions of our gay dahabeah. As we gaze upon the plumy palm trees and away over the desert's yellow sands, a tall, slight form comes between us and the dreamy horizon, passes rapidly along the bank and looks weird and strange in its flowing robe of black. If we come near enough, the sight of that dusky face, into which the misery of centuries seems crowded, will smite us like a blow; and as the child shares always in the mother's degradation — as in her joy — we shall find the baby on this sad woman's shoulder the most wretched little being ever victimized into existence. This woman is perhaps seventeen years old, and has already passed the noonday of her strength. Into this fate of marriage was she sold before the age of ten, by her own father's hand. If she should prove unfaithful to its vow, honor would call upon him, with imperious voice, to cut her into pieces and consign her to the Nile. The history of this silent, uncomplaining woman is a brief one. She asserts her "rights" in no "convention"; she flings no gauntlet of defiance in the face of her "manifest destiny." She is the zero-mark upon the scale of being, and her symbol is a tear. But upon a fate so dire as this

I will not ask you to look longer. Let us turn our eyes westward — the Star of Bethlehem moves thither evermore, and the next illustration of old-world chivalry, though sad enough, will be far less painful than the last.

La Signora Sopranzi is a Roman matron of the period, with all Italia's romance stifled in her heart. She was once celebrated for her beauty, but she is already thirty-four years old. Her hair is gray, her gentle eyes are dim, and of the glory, long ago departed, only those "traces" remain on which the novelist lingers with so much pathos. Her father was a Roman lawyer, but he was also Garibaldi's friend, and so the Pope shut him up in the ample dungeons of St. Angelo's. Her husband, the veriest ne'er-do-well who joined the beauty of Adonis to the wiles of Mephistopheles, has gallantly left her to solve the problem of a maintenance for himself, herself, and her little ones. The only "genteel" vocations suited to her "sphere" are to keep a fashionable boarding-house and give Italian lessons. I have reason to congratulate myself upon the remarkable enterprise she thus displayed, for in her capacity of hostess and instructor, she introduced me to an extensive circle of acquaintances among the more intelligent of her countrywomen, and all I learned of them gave me a stronger purpose of helpfulness toward women. They were not innovators, I promise you! They had never heard about a "college education"; no taint of the new world's unrest had ever reached their placid souls. Indeed, their average wisdom as to a great republic is well illustrated by this question, propounded gravely to me on more than one occasion:

"When our Christoforo Colombo discovered your America did he find many Indians there as light-complexioned as yourself?" They knew they were not very wise, poor things! and often said, shrugging their shoulders most expressively:

"We marry so early, you know, there is really very little need that we should study much. Indeed, in Italy it hurts a woman's prospects to be *troppo istrutta* ('too well instructed'), and you see this is a point we cannot guard too carefully, for out of marriage there is no place for us except the cloister."

My landlady's daughter, Bianca, was the most beautiful girl in Rome, chief city of fair women. Although but twelve years old, she was a woman in her words and ways. I was very fond of her, and used often to wish I could lift her out of that lifeless atmosphere — breathed by so many generations that almost all the oxygen is gone — and electrify her with the air that blows across our Illinois prairies. In one of our frequent conversations she thus stated her ideas upon a theme to which she had evidently given no casual thought. Remember I give her precise language — that of a young lady of twelve — for my practice when abroad illustrated that line of Burns', "A chiel's amang ye takin' notes":

"We are too tender-hearted, we women of Italia. Why, I have a cousin who is dying of grief because her lover seems cold of late. I laugh at her and say, 'Ah, bella Margherita, you are a little idiot! You should not waste yourself thus upon that silly Antonio.' You shall see how I'll behave! I will never marry in this world. I have seen too much unhappiness among these husbands and wives. And yet, you see, 'twill not be easy for me to escape," she said with a charming naivete. "Why, the other evening I went to see the sunset from the Pincian hill with my naughty, handsome papa, and a foolish boy, not so tall as I am, a mere child, indeed, but dressed up like a young gentleman, with white vest, gold chain, and carrying a silly little cane, whispered to me, while papa smoked his cigar upon the terrace and I sat near the fountain, that he should come this very night and play the mandolino under my window. But I turned my face away, and when he persisted I scowled at him from under my black eyebrows and just dared him to come! I tell you, Signorina, that I will not fall in love for a long, long time yet, if ever, for in our country it kills women or else it drives them mad. I'm going to give Italian lessons, like my poor mamma, and in character singing, to be a real Americana — calm as the broad Campagna, cold as the Catacombs. For I am very sad over the women of my country. Life begins with them at twelve, and at twenty-five they are already old; the lights are out, the play is over."

And yet when I have sung the praises of my native land to beautiful Bianca, her eyes have gleamed with a new splendor as she stood erect and said: "Ah! but I am a Roman, and still to be a Roman were greater than a king." (But, mind you, some bright American had taught the little magpie that!)

Somewhat to the same purpose as dark-eyed Bianca's words were those her pale-faced mother had spoken to me that very morning: "Men cannot be as good as we are," she said, in her voice, most musical, most melancholy. "I'm sure that they are not so dear to God. We suffer so—our lives call down the pity of all the saints in heaven. Life gives us just one choice—to be wives or to be nuns—and society sneers at us so cruelly if we neither wear the marriage-ring nor the consecrating crucifix, that we are never happy unless we are miserable—and so we marry! You of the North have a thousand defences," she continued, mournfully, "the intellect yields you so many pleasures, and your manner of life renders you brave—so that you are seldom at the mercy of your hearts. Sometimes I think there must be a sort of magic, though, about it all, and I have asked many of your countrywomen to let me have their talisman, for my daughter's sake."

One of my nicest little friends in Rome was Greca Caveri, of Genoa, who had come with her father to witness the opening of the Æcumenical Council. She was seventeen years old, and evinced so much delight when I offered to give her English lessons that, struck with her youth, I asked why she did not go to school. She looked at me in much surprise, saying, "Does not the Signorina know that I am superior in education to my countrywomen generally? My father is one of King Victor Emmanuel's own lawyers, and a learned man. Moreover, he has very advanced ideas about what a lady should be permitted to know, and so he placed me in the best school for girls at Turin. I completed my education there on my sixteenth birthday, one year ago. This is what has kept me unsettled until I am so old. But, then, I have learned music, French, drawing and dancing — not to speak of the Catechism and the lives of the Saints."

She went on to tell me that her dear mamma, whose loss her dear papa so much deplored, had been three years married at her age, and then it dawned on my dull wits that she was one among that vast and noble army of martyrs who, with sad face and lifted glance, await the Coming Man.

Poor Greca's sad dilemma gave me long, long thoughts about a brave young country far away, whose institutions each year more generously endeavor to take sides with homely women in the tug of life, and to compensate thus for nature's wayward negligence. I tried to talk of this to sweet-voiced Greca, and she listened with a flush of pleased surprise, but soon relapsed into her normal way of thinking, saying as she shook her little head: "But then, dear friend, you know we women have but one vocation — there's no denying it."

A few days later, on New Year's morning, she ran to my room, saying: "Now, I'm going to try a sign! As I go to the Vatican with papa, on this first day of the year 1870, I'm going to notice whom I meet first. If it's a *giovinotto* (young man), I shall surely be married this year; if it's a priest, why, I shall die, and there will be an end of it; but misericordia! if it should be an old man, I must *restore in casa* another year still."

"What's that?" I asked. The idiom was new; literally translated it meant, "Stay in the house."

"Why, don't you understand?" the girl explained, "in my country, if a girl isn't married, she stays in the house, and oh! I do so long to get out into the world!"

"You say, Signorina, that the women are so crazy as to set up for doctors in your country? It is a folly and a crime. I wonder that the priests don't interfere. Whatever will become of the buttons and the general housework?"

Thus spake an elderly Italian dame, the thinning ranks of

whose own buttons I was even then contemplating with a somewhat startled glance!

"And you tell me there are fifty thousand lady teachers in the United States? It is alarming! What will you come to, at last, in a country where women are permitted thus to usurp authority over the men?"

I told her what a wag has called "the horrible statistics." How that two millions of men had been killed in our late war, and that hence there were in many of our States thousands more women than men; that in England there are three millions of unmarried women, of whom two millions had a choice different from the fair Italians, namely, to be their own breadwinners, or starve. Indeed, my figures grew conclusive, whereupon she stopped her ears and exclaimed, with a charming grimace, "For love of Heaven, don't go up any higher! Don't you know that I can't add more figures than I have fingers on this hand?"

I should regret to weary you with my Italians, but am tempted to give you a glimpse into the life of a Roman old maid; because I fancy I have here that single aspect of human life in Rome which neither poet nor historian has ever treated — and because the reverse of the medal has a lesson for us also.

She was a *rara avis*. I did not see another of her species in all Italy, and if she had not been a little unbeliever she would long ago have sought the shelter of a convent, and borrowed the name of some woman-saint, since she could not otherwise get rid of her own. And yet hers was a pretty one, I thought — Alessandrina Paradisi. She was one of those against whom nature seems to have a pique; yet often, as I looked at her puny, humpbacked figure and heavy features, it seemed to me that, after all, Nature had treated her very much as legend tells us Jupiter did the Poet, who came to him complaining that to Tellus had been assigned the earth, and to Neptune the sea, while to him nothing whatever had been offered, whereupon Jupiter said: "For thee, O Poet, I have reserved the key of Heaven, that thou mayst come and go at will, and be my guest." For a spirit looked from the intense dark eyes of Alessandrina, which had no peer among her sisters; an eloquent voice kept silence behind those mournful lips; a brain that harbored noble thoughts was lying half asleep under the mass of shadowy hair.

Permit this record of an evening's talk with my favorite, Alessandrina:

January 10, 1870. She has been to see me again, "*la povera piccola sorella*" ("the poor little sister"), as they all call her. It is really marvelous, the faculty this little creature has of making me understand the rich, soft utterance of her mother-tongue. Tonight she gave me, without intending it, perhaps, a peep into a place I had greatly wished, but dared not hope to see — *her heart*. It was on this wise. She was describing a representation she had witnessed, recently, at the theater in Naples. As the climax approached she became animated. It was as it ought to be always, the triumph of virtue and punishment of vice, or, to employ her words — "So, at last, the husband confessed his fault to his forgiving wife, and they lived in peace ever after, while the hateful woman who had caused the mischief was sent off to parts unknown." And here the little narrator clapped her hands, saying — "Don't you see, *cara amica*, that it was a beautiful play?" When I asked if, after witnessing the pageants of the stage, everyday life did not seem doubly tame, she scowled, shrugged her poor shoulders, and *presto* came my peep at hearts:

"Yes, signorina, what you say is true. But look at me! Life cannot yield me much at best. Indeed, it is so somber, that it doesn't matter if these brilliant contrasts the theater affords make that look a shade darker, which is always dark. I frankly tell you that if the good God had asked me I would have begged him not to trust me into this world. But he did not, and here I am, and there is nothing left me but to make the best of it. I am twenty-nine years old, and by this time, you see, I am accustomed to my lot. I quarreled with it sadly, though, when I was younger. Ah, I have passed some bitter years! But I've grown wiser now, and try to bring what happiness I can to others, and to forget myself.

Only I dread lest I must grow old, with nobody to take care of me. But I try to keep a young heart, and so I give my thoughts to God's fair world, and to hopes of a future life. Is not God kind, who gives me sweet sleep, always, and dreams more fair than anything that I have seen in any play or read in any poem? And He lets me sleep ten hours in every twenty-four, and dream right through them all! I would never dare to care for anyone, you know, and nobody could be expected to find any charm in me — besides, in Italy, people like me never go into society. And so Rome, my native city, has the love I might have given in ties more tender. Ah, shall I live, I wonder, to see Rome free? What would I not do for her, if I dared?"

But here her tone changed to the mocking spirit that is more pitiful than tears: "Women are nothing in Italy, you know! Think of it! I am twenty-nine years old! my brother Romana is eighteen, but on my father's death, this boy became my guardian, and I take from his hand whatever he chooses to give me from the estate for my support, and do not murmur. For him there is that independence which I count one of the noblest elements of character, for him there is brave work to do; for me there is — *to twirl my thumbs* and wait to see if the *next life can possibly atone for this.*"

Poor child! Let me hasten to deliver her from the limbo to which by some she may have been consigned. She never heard about a college education, and a wider work with better pay for women who must earn their bread, and those frightful words "strong minded" have never been translated into her sweet, Italian tongue.

In our quest for illustrations of what Chivalry has wrought beyond the seas, the most ancient and the most poetic civilizations have yielded us their lessons; let us pass on to interrogate the most luxurious. We shall soon see how differently they do these things in France. In Egypt, as we have observed, the husband buys his wife; in Paris, by strange condition, it is the wife who buys her husband, and he knows his value, be assured! In proof of this, let me give a conversation I chanced to have with an intelligent Parisian lady, who, starting out in life without sufficient capital, had made no matrimonial investment up to the ripe age of forty-four.

"I am much concerned," she said, "for my friend, Madame D., who is just now doing her best to marry off her daughter; and it is high time, too, for the girl is already eighteen. But it will not be an easy task, I fear, for she has not a tempting dowry, and but few personal charms."

"How will they begin their operations?" I inquired.

"Oh, the parents will say *tout franchement* (quite frankly) to their friends, 'find me a husband for my daughter,' and the friends, knowing that one good turn deserves another, will beat up for recruits, and will, perhaps, find a young man who is deemed suitable, and who is willing 'to consider the project,' at least. Then, as if by chance — for we are a people of quite too much delicacy to give a business air to proceedings of this nature" — she explained with true French vivacity, "then, as if by chance, the parties will meet in the picture gallery of the Luxembourg, or at an open-air concert in the Champs Elysees. The young people are now introduced, while the old ones look on sharply, to witness the effect. After several minutes of casual conversation, they separate. The young man says to his friends, 'She pleases me,' or 'She pleases me not,' and upon this turns the decision."

"But what about the girl?" I pursued innocently.

"Oh, the girl? She is charmingly submissive. She simpers and makes a courtesy, and says: 'As you please, dear parents, you know what is for my good far better than I'— so glad is she to marry upon any terms, it is *such a release*." The lady then went on to say, "If the girl has been so fortunate as to 'please' the young man, and if his friends pronounce her adequate, the necessary papers are made out; she receives half-a-dozen calls from her *fiance* in the presence of her mother; he sends her a huge bouquet daily for about three weeks, and 'like the swell of some sweet tune,' the courtship merges in the wedding day."

Will you believe it? I was stupid enough (but then 'twas

because of the interest I take in girls) after all this to ask: "*And what about love?*" How she laughed! — that "lady of a certain age"— as the French say, avoiding harsher epithets.

"Dear Mademoiselle," was her voluble reply, "that question tells the whole story! You are *Americaine*, you have read those pretty fictions of Miss Dinah Mulock, and you have not lived very long abroad."

Then she explained to me how, established in her new home, the young wife tastes her first liberty. Her husband goes his way to theater and club, and she goes hers, often learning what love is (since you insist) from another than he. Her children she puts away from her at an early age; the girls in a convent, the boys in a Lycee, and when they emerge from there, they repeat the scene of their parents' courtship and marriage — the sons, after several years of profligate life; the daughters, after a brief period of espionage at home. And so the drama goes from age to age.

In the good old Fatherland the relations of men and women are hardly less irrational than in France. Young gentlemen never visit young ladies, and the latter are rigidly prohibited from all social intercourse with them except in presence of their parents and guardians and at the public balls. How they ever arrive at an engagement is one of the mysteries that the uninitiated desire to look into; but, strange to say, that stupendous crisis does at last occur. Whereupon the friends of the parties are promptly notified, and it is customary to call upon the fortunate maiden who has staked her all upon a throw, and won. With the young gentleman — a gallant knight of the old chivalry — it is quite a different matter. His good fortune consists principally in the amount of very hard cash that rewards the sacrifice of his liberty. He has paid the sex a great compliment in the person of his betrothed, which she will appropriately acknowledge on her own and their behalf. Not that he means to be exacting — oh, no! He is a downright good-natured fellow, and will require in return nothing more than — unconditional surrender to his will from this time forth "until death do us part."

A friend, long a resident in Berlin, writes me as follows:

"In Germany, girls exist so exclusively for marriage, that the linen for her bridal *trousseau* is collected from the time a girl is born. At family Christmas festivals contributions to this outfit form the prominent feature of the gifts to girls, and being questioned, they will reply without the least embarrassment: 'Oh, that's for my *ausstener* — wedding outfit.' German girls marry principally for greater social freedom. Those of the upper classes care less for this, and are slower to change their estate in life."

In "Merrie England" there is more freedom, but Thackeray's incomparable satires, which denounce, "more in sadness than in anger," the customs that preside over marriages in high life, are as true today as when he wrote them. To my delight I found Thackeray reverenced in England as we reverence Bryant, and loved as we love Whittier; but to my grief they told me the shades in his sad pictures are not dark enough. You remember the episode in that noblest of his books "The Newcomes," about the queenly Ethel, whose aristocratic grandmamma is bound to marry her to Lord Farintosh, in spite of her repugnance and her protestations, and how Ethel is made to pursue the noble lord through every lane of life until he lays his coronet before her? You remember how this compromised young woman, visiting an art collection and seeing a green card with the word "Sold" attached to a picture there, slyly carries it off, fastens it in front of her white muslin frock, and thus appears at dinner. When asked what this queer fancy means, she makes the old dowager a profound courtesy, saying, "Why, grandmamma, I am a *tableau vivant* — living picture." "Whereupon," says Thackeray, "the old lady, jumping up on her crooked stick with immense agility, tore the card out of Ethel's bosom, and very likely would have boxed her ears, but that just then the Marquis of Farintosh, himself, came in. 'But, after his departure, there was, I promise you, a pretty row in the building,' relates Ethel afterward."

Going to Hyde Park at the fashionable hour, one sees many a poor Ethel who needs no green ticket on her dress to tell the story of her barter. One's heart aches at the thought of "sweet bells jangling," whose music might have filled so many lives with soothing melody. For Hyde Park is the scene — as an English gentlemen express it in language that grates harshly on our ears — "of the richest and most shameful marriage market in the world." "Men stand by the rails," he says, "criticising with perfect impartiality and equal freedom, while women drive slowly past, *for sale in marriage*, with their careful mothers at their side, to reckon the value of biddings and prevent the lots from going off below the reserved price. Instinctively you listen for the auctioneer with his 'going — going — gone!'"

Listen to the moral drawn by the same Christian Englishman under his frightful picture:

"Such is the pitch at which we have arrived by teaching women *that marriage is their whole duty*."

I turn with grateful pride from these sad pictures of the Old World, to the glowing colors of the New. The difference between them has been often figured to my fancy by that between the mystic, melancholy sunsets behind Rome's sad Campagna, and their brilliant pageantry, as they light up the west from the prairies of my own Illinois. I see what is noblest in the manhood of America rallying like St. George of old, to fight the Dragon, while firm and brave rings out their manly war cry, claiming "Fair play for the weaker" in life's solemn fight. Do you wonder if this contrast set me thinking about the New World's Chivalry? or if, the more I studied the movements of this matchless age, the more clearly I saw that it can give a Roland for an Oliver, till History calls off its last heroic name.

The Knights of the Old Chivalry gave woman the empty husk of flattery; those of the New offer, instead, the wholesome kernel of just criticism; the Knights of the Old Chivalry drank our health in flowing bumpers; those of the New invite us to sit down beside them at the banquet of truth.

"By my lady's bright eyes," was the watchword of the Old; "Fair play for the weaker," is the manly war cry of the New!

Talk about the chivalry of ancient days! Go to, ye mediæval ages, and learn what the word meaneth! Behold the sunny afternoon of this nineteenth century of grace, wherein we have the spectacle, not of lances tilted to defend the *prestige* of "my lady's beauty," by swaggering knights who could not write their names, but the noblest men of the world's foremost race, placing upon the brows of those most dear to them, above the wreath of Venus, the helmet of Minerva, and leading into broader paths of knowledge and achievement, the fair divinities who preside over their homes!

CHAPTER VII

THE CHOICE OF A CAREER

UPON the summits of lofty mountain ranges which serve as the great watersheds of our country, the merest apparent accident — as a puff of wind or the encountering of a chance resistant force in tree or shrub — determines whether a particular raindrop shall lend itself to the streams which flow eastward, or whether it shall become a part of the mighty waters which sweep toward west or south. It is an old figure and yet one which comes continually to mind in considering the crowning epoch in the life of Frances E. Willard. So little do we comprehend those mysterious forces which shape human destiny that even now, after the lapse of twenty-five years, we find ourselves praising God as we think how slight a thing might seemingly have affected her decision, and changed the trend of her entire life. "Had she accepted the educational position a few would today bless the memory of a gifted teacher; the other was accepted, and today a world blesses God for Frances Willard." Truly a Hand was on the helm other than hers; the eternal forces had her life plan in their mighty onward sweep. The raindrop of the individual life gave itself gladly to that side of the mountain range whence issue the streams of beneficent reform, and so surely was the gift of God's ordering that almost immediately the stream itself took on the character of her living, and her whole after-life became to unnumbered thousands like "a spring of water whose waters fail not."

Who could have prophesied in 1874 that Miss Willard was to be the leader of the temperance movement in America? Dean of the Northwestern Female College and Professor of Æsthetics in the Northwestern University, in her were embodied much of nineteenth century civilization and culture.

The Shakespeare and the musical clubs knew her, as did meetings for the discussion of Oriental and Greek thought and all the delightful dominating external culture of the mind of the day. She was admired by the great, loved where love was a pride, leading, active, regnant, and may have seemed in danger of being forever bound by outward success and applause. But God had long before planted in her soul in abundant measure a store of vital, childlike love and worship to remain there as a germ capable of responding to the loving warmth of His own radiant energy whenever the hour of the heart's springtime should come. She herself has quoted George Meredith's saying, "A check to the pride of a boy will frequently divert him to the paths where lie his subtlest powers," adding with winsome humor, "and girls are sometimes very boyish."

God had larger purposes for her than she knew, and as she approached the widening yet lonely path of philanthropy up which she was to toil, He gently and wisely prepared her for the change by opening in her thoughts new channels of interest in which all the currents of her life were soon to flow with a deeper, purer, stronger tide than the old channels had ever known. It was the year of the Woman's Temperance Crusade; there had been no unusual activity in temperance circles, but suddenly, without warning, the crusade began. As if by magic armies of women — delicate, cultured, home women — filled the streets of the cities and towns of Ohio, going in pathetic procession from the door of the home to that of the saloon, singing, praying, pleading with the rumsellers with all the eloquence of their mother-hearts. The movement ran like wildfire over the land, breaking out here, there and everywhere without known concert of action. "It was like the fires we used to kindle on the western prairies," Miss Willard said; "a match and a wisp of dry grass were all that were needed, and behold the magnificent spectacle of a prairie on fire sweeping across the landscape, swift as a thousand untrained steeds and no more to be captured than a hurricane." All this could not fail to arouse Miss Willard's attention. She was moved to help them, although she might not leave her own place to do it. All through this battle of Home versus Saloon she read every word she could find about "that whirlwind of the Lord which in fifty days swept the liquor traffic out of two hundred and fifty towns and villages." She took pains to let her sentiments and her sympathies be widely known, giving to her pupils in rhetoric such novel composition subjects as "John B. Gough," "Neal Dow" and "Does Prohibition Prohibit?"

Her brother, Oliver A. Willard, then editor of the Chicago Evening *Mail*, gave favorable and full reports of the Crusading bands, saying privately to his sister, "I shall speak just as well of the women as I dare to"—"a most characteristic editorial remark, though more frequently acted out than uttered!" And to the young Dean came this illumination: "It occurred to me, strange to say, for the *first time*, that I ought to work for the good cause *just where I was*—that everybody ought. Thus I first received 'the arrest of thought' concerning which, in a thousand different towns, I have since then tried to speak, and I believe that in this simple change of personal attitude, from passive to aggressive, lies the only force that can free this land from the drink habit and the liquor traffic. It would be like dynamite under the saloon if, *just where he is*, the minister would begin active work against it; if, *just where he is*, the teacher would instruct his pupils; if, *just where he is*, the voter would dedicate his ballot to this movement; and so on, through the shining ranks of the great powers that make for righteousness, from father and mother to kindergarten toddlers, if each were this day doing what each could, *just where he is*."

The wave of the Crusade struck Chicago; a band of women visited the City Council to petition for enforcement of the Sunday-closing law. They were treated with mocking slight and rudely jostled on the street by a band of rough men, half out for a lark, half ugly. This was in March, 1874. Miss Willard was thoroughly aroused. "Treat any woman with contumely, and as soon as she hears of it every other woman in the world worth anything feels as if she also were hurt." Busy as she was, it was not many days before she found time publicly to declare this as "everybody's war," and to assure the temperance women she was with them heart and mind and hand. She made a second speech, and a third, so successfully that she was in demand at temperance gatherings. Her heart warmed to the work. "To serve such a cause would be utterly enthralling," she exclaimed, "if I only had more time — if I were more free!" Within three months she was free, perfectly free, to choose, to do, or to leave undone, to continue work along her own lines or to go into the new temperance field, differences of opinion between herself and the President of the University on matters of government having led to her resignation from the position of Dean of the Woman's College. In the sleepless night that followed there came a *heavenly vision* to which she was not disobedient, bringing to her soul the tranquil knowledge that "the Lord is *real*, His whole nature is Love."

Miss Willard's interest in the Crusade soon carried her to the East to study the temperance movement and to confer with its leaders in New York City, Boston and Portland. She went down into the slums of New York, saw its mission temperance work, and there the fire of pity that never left her was kindled in her soul for the physical and mental misery that intemperance causes among the poor. She attended the first Gospel temperance camp meeting known in temperance annals, at Old Orchard, Maine, listened to the story of the "Maine Law" from the lips of Gen. Neal Dow, and first met Mrs. L. M. N. Stevens, of Portland, ever after to be her strong and dependable coadjutor. It was in a Portland hotel, while she wondered where money was to come from to meet her own and her mother's expenses, that she opened the Bible lying on the table and read the verse that "clinched her faith for this difficult emergency": "Trust in the Lord and do good; so shalt thou dwell in the land, and verily thou shalt be fed."

Going to Boston for further counsel and bending all her energies to find "where to stand within the charmed circle of the temperance reform," she waited and watched for providential intimations. Meanwhile many and varied offers came from the educational field, tempting in respect to their wide outlook and large promise of financial relief. "In this dilemma," so we read her record, "I consulted my friends as to their sense of my duty. Every one of them, including my dear mother and my revered counsellor, Bishop S———, united in the decision that he thus expressed: "If you were not dependent on your own exertions for the supply of current needs I would say be a philanthropist, but of all work the temperance work pays least and you cannot afford to take it up. I therefore counsel you to remain in your chosen and successful field of the higher education." "No one," she continues, "stood by me in the preference I freely expressed to join the crusade women except Mrs. Mary A. Livermore, who sent me a letter full of enthusiasm for the new line of work and predicted success for me therein."

While visiting in Cambridge, Massachusetts, Miss Willard received two letters on the same day. The first was from Rev. Dr. Van Norman, of New York City, offering her the position of Lady Principal of his elegant school for young women with a salary of $2,400 and such duties as she might choose. The other was from Mrs. Louise S. Rounds, of Chicago, begging her to take the presidency of the Chicago branch of the Woman's Christian Temperance Union, while she confessed its present weakness of organization and its financial inadequacy. "It has come to me," said Mrs. Rounds, "as I believe from the Lord, that you ought to be our president." Our temperance Greatheart did not hesitate; the offer of Dr. Van Norman was declined, that of Mrs. Rounds accepted. This was the real election of Frances E. Willard's life — this was her choice of a career.

"No words can adequately characterize the change wrought in my life by this decision," wrote our leader. "Instead of peace, I was to participate in war; instead of the sweetness of home,

ANNA A. GORDON

THE GENERAL OFFICERS OF THE NATIONAL W. C. T. U.

LILLIAN M. N. STEVENS, Vice-President-at-large. FRANCES E. WILLARD, President. KATHARINE LENTE STEVENSON, Cor. Sec'y.
HELEN M. BARKER, Treasurer. FRANCES E. BEAUCHAMP, Ass't Rec. Sec. CLARA C. HOFFMAN, Rec. Sec'y.

never more dearly loved than I had loved it, I was to become a wanderer on the face of the earth; instead of libraries, I was to frequent public halls and railway cars; instead of scholarly and cultured men, I was to see the dregs of saloon and gambling house and haunt of shame. But women who were among the fittest Gospel survivals were to be my comrades; little children were to be gathered from near and from far in the Loyal Temperance Legion, and whoever keeps such company should sing a psalm of joy, solemn as it is sweet. Hence I have felt that great promotion came to me when I was counted worthy to be a worker in the organized Crusade for 'God and Home and Native Land.' Temporary differences may seem to separate some of us for awhile, but I believe with all my heart that farther on we shall be found walking once more side by side."

CHAPTER VIII

ORGANIZER AND LEADER OF THE WOMAN'S CHRISTIAN TEMPERANCE UNION

ON her homeward journey the heaven-born leader of the Woman's Christian Temperance Union was to receive her Crusade baptism. It was in Pittsburg. Miss Willard's vivid description of the scene tells us —

"The Crusade had lingered in this dim-colored city well nigh a year, and when I visited my old friends at the Female College I spoke of it with enthusiasm, and of the women who were, as I judged from a morning paper, still engaged in it here. They looked upon me with astonishment when I proposed to seek out those women and go with them to the saloons; but, too polite to disappoint me, they had me piloted by some of the factotums of the place to the headquarters of the Crusade. Here I was warmly welcomed, and soon found myself walking down street arm in arm with a young teacher from the public school, who said she had a habit of coming in to add one to the procession when her day's duties were over.

"We paused in front of Sheffner's saloon, on Market street. The ladies ranged themselves along the curbstone, for they had been forbidden in anywise to incommode the passers-by, being dealt with much more strictly than a drunken man or a heap of dry-goods boxes would be. At a signal from our gray-haired leader, a sweet-voiced woman began to sing, 'Jesus the water of life will give,' all our voices soon blending in the song. I think it was the most novel spectacle that I recall. There stood women of undoubted religious devotion and the highest character, most of them crowned with the glory of gray hairs. Along the stony pavement of that stoniest of cities rumbled the heavy wagons, many of them carriers of beer; between us and the saloon in front of which we were drawn up in line, passed the motley throng, almost every man lifting his hat, and even little newsboys doing the same. It was American manhood's tribute to Christianity and to womanhood, and it was significant and full of pathos. The leader had already asked the saloonkeeper if we might enter, and he had declined, else the prayer meeting would have occurred inside his door. A sorrowful old lady, whose only son had gone to ruin through that very death-trap, knelt on the cold, moist pavement and offered a broken-hearted prayer, while all our heads were bowed.

'At a signal we moved on, and the next saloonkeeper permitted us to enter. I had no more idea of the inward appearance of a saloon than if there had been no such place on earth. I knew nothing of its high, heavily corniced bar, its barrels with the ends all pointed toward the looker-on, each barrel being furnished with a faucet; its shelves glittering with decanters and cut glass, its floors thickly strewn with sawdust, and here and there a table with chairs — nor of its abundant fumes, sickening to healthful nostrils. The tall, stately lady who led us, placed her Bible on the bar and read a psalm, whether hortatory or imprecatory I do not remember, but the spirit of these crusaders was so gentle I think it must have been the former. Then we sang 'Rock of Ages' as I thought I had never heard it sung before, with a tender confidence to the height of which one does not rise in the easy-going, regulation prayer meeting, and then one of the older women whispered to me softly that the leader wished to know if I would pray. It was strange, perhaps, but I felt not the least reluctance as I knet on the sawdust floor, with a group of earnest hearts around me, and behind them, filling every corner and extending out into the street, a crowd of unwashed, unkempt, hard-looking drinking men. I was conscious that perhaps never in my life, save beside my sister Mary's dying bed, had I prayed as truly as I did then. This was my Crusade baptism. The next day I went on to the West, and within a week had been made president of the Chicago W. C. T. U."

The story of Miss Willard's early Chicago work reads like a romance. Into it she flung herself with the ardor of a St. Francis d'Assisi. She made the little great, the weak a power. She who had studied books, now studied humanity. Delighting in music and in art, she gave herself with abandon to scenes the world would consider the reverse of artistic. For music she now had Gospel hymns, not always rendered effectively from the standpoint of the musical critic, but no grand oratorio could have thrilled her soul as did those hymns sung by men upon whose lips the praises of God were like the unaccustomed lispings of babes. Nor was it ease or the promptings of cultured taste alone which Frances Willard sacrificed; she endured real hardship, the prosaic hardship of poverty, and even at times of hunger. So determined was she in her heroic soul to be led of God alone that she would not suffer the women of the Union to speak of compensation, and they, thinking that in some unknown way abundant means were supplied her, accepted her service all unmindful of the fact that the slender figure which stood before them day after day had often walked many miles because she did not possess the "prerequisite nickel for car fare," or that she came to them hungry because she had no money with which to buy bread.

When Madam Willard's common sense prevailed and the situation was revealed, their regret partook almost of the nature of remorse and a modest but adequate salary was immediately provided. When persuaded that her position was no longer tenable, Miss Willard did not regret the experience of those months, which gave her an insight into human hearts and a revelation of human needs. Often as she went about the great city, searching for the friendless and forgotten, she had said to herself, "I am a better friend than you dream, I know more about you than you think, for, bless God, I am hungry too." Thus early in her temperance career we catch the blended strains of tender sympathy and resolute determination, the strong notes of the harmony that rang through all her after life.

From the outset of her Chicago work it was apparent that a wider sphere was awaiting her, and when the organizing convention of the Illinois W.C.T.U. was held in Springfield in October, 1874, she was elected to the office of corresponding secretary. In August of the same year there had gone forth from Chautauqua, New York, a call to the women who had been interested in the Woman's Temperance Crusade to meet at Cleveland, Ohio, November 18-20, for the purpose of effecting a permanent national organization. Thither went Frances Willard to clasp hands with those whose very names had thrilled her heart as she had read of their brave warfare for the protection of the home. They recognized in her a most valuable ally and she was placed upon the Committee on Resolutions, one of the most important positions within the gift of the convention. In this capacity she wrote the famous resolution which was in its essence her own spirit and the ruling principle of her life:

Resolved, That, recognizing that our cause is and will be combated by mighty, determined and relentless foes, we will, trusting in Him who is Prince of Peace, meet argument with argument, misjudgment with patience, denunciation with kindness, and all our difficulties and dangers with prayer.

Although Miss Willard had been elected to the office of corresponding secretary, she might without doubt have been made president had she not promptly refused to have her name used, saying that she preferred to learn of those who were veterans in this warfare rather than assume for herself a position of such responsibility.

Within a few brief months after her choice of a career we find Miss Willard's guiding hand upon three distinctively important positions in local, State and national Unions. Her history in those days made itself with startling rapidity. When once the hour had found the woman it was as if she had been from the beginning of her life filling the place, her fitness for which was so universally recognized. Five years later, in 1879, she was elected to the presidency of the National Union and her every heart-beat was from that day given to the best interests of the organization which was far dearer to her than life itself. Indeed, the National Union was bounded by the compass of her great thought, warmed by the sunshine of her all-embracing love and nourished by her very life-blood. Rarely has the world seen so complete a death of self, so far as personal aims are concerned, or so glorious a resurrection of the true self in the lives of countless others.

While corresponding secretary of the National Woman's Christian Temperance Union in the winter of 1877, Miss Willard went to Boston by invitation of Dwight L. Moody, to conduct daily meetings for women in connection with his revival services, and for three memorable months the Gospel according to "Saint Frances" was the magnet for mother-hearted women, young and old, who crowded Berkeley street, Park street and Clarendon street churches, giving sisterly help to the young leader, and learning as never before the meaning of the Love that never faileth and of "that light which lighteth every man that cometh into the world." And not alone were women's hearts warmed and uplifted by the glow and enthusiasm fresh from the spirit of this woman evangel, for to many a manly heart was revealed through her the truth that there is neither male nor female in Christ Jesus.

On the fly leaf of the Bible Miss Willard studied during these "Boston days," presented to her by the Central W. C. T. U., of Chicago, at a farewell reception in Farwell Hall, we find this entry: "My first *whole* day of real, spiritual, joyful, loving study of the kernel of God's word, simply desirous to learn my Father's will, is this *17th of February, 1877*, with the Boston work just begun. And on this sweet, eventful day, in which, with every hour of study, the Bible has grown dearer, I take as my life-motto henceforth, humbly asking God's grace that I may measure up to it, this wonderful passage from Paul: 'And whatsoever ye do, in word or deed, do all in the name of the Lord Jesus, giving thanks to God and the Father by Him.' Col. 3:17."

"Sweet, eventful day" to her, and its anniversary, twenty-one years later, was to witness "the sad hour selected from all years"—nay, the glad hour when her soul

> " Began to beckon like a star
> From the abode where the eternal are."

In March, 1878, her brother Oliver, of whose great gifts and genial nature Miss Willard could never say enough, suddenly passed away, and the editorship of his paper, the Chicago *Evening Post*, was for many weeks bravely carried by Miss Willard and her intrepid sister-in-law.

A multitude of memories grave and gay overwhelm one who attempts to chronicle Miss Willard's life in its years of white-ribbon leadership; the pioneer work in the far West, the visits to every province of Canada, the campaigns for constitutional amendments in various States, constructive work for the International Council of Women, the writing of six or eight books in addition to an autobiography, the editorship of the *Union Signal*, the presentation of Mrs. Hayes' portrait to the White House, heroic work for the Temple, the National Temperance Hospital, and the Woman's Temperance Publishing Association. Yet these are not a tithe of the interests that, in addition to continuous public speaking and incessant correspondence, pressed their claims upon a heart that was always "at leisure from itself, to soothe and sympathize."

The Temple was always in Miss Willard's thought our "House Beautiful," the *Home* of the W. C. T. U. At the National Convention in Buffalo, when there were cross-currents of opinion on this vital subject and Miss Willard was interviewed by a journalist sent to her from Chicago, she replied to his question, "What do you believe the Temple means to the future of the W. C. T. U.?" by saying: "Perhaps I can best answer that question by an illustration. A Swedish woman arrived in the city; she was an utter stranger, but she wore the white ribbon and she knew about the Temple. She said to the first policeman she met, 'Vimmin's Temple,' and he pointed in a certain direction, and she walked on. She repeated her question to the next one and reached the building in peace and quiet, appeared in the offices of the World's W. C. T. U., sat down in a big rocking chair and uttered the word 'Home.' There is a light in the window of the Temple that throws its beams to the uttermost parts of the earth. We have received gifts from every civilized land; not large amounts, but pathetic sums given by the heart as well as the hand. For one I will never live to see those true and honest hearts fail of their expectation."

"I see that you attach great value to the sympathetic side of the enterprise," said the newspaper man.

"Yea, verily, you cannot overestimate its meaning. The mind loves to see great and beautiful ideas incarnated; the struggle of the soul is toward expression. This is the explanation of the arts. Every statue, every painting, every musical composition, every poem, was once a thought. Architecture has been called 'frozen music.' The mind of man goes out with delight and inspiration toward the masterpieces of architecture. No poet has a greater fame than that of the sculptor who built the Parthenon; the fame of Michael Angelo as a sculptor is outrun by his fame as the architect of St. Peter's Cathedral. Now this Temple of the White Ribbon women is in itself an æsthetic object to behold. One of our most gifted Chicago editors has said that it is like a lady drawing about her shoulders a beautiful lace shawl; there is a grace combined with dignity, a symmetry combined with amplitude, such as I certainly have never seen in a business block before, and I have beheld the finest architecture in the great cities of the continent. We all remember the sense of tranquillity mingled with exaltation that comes to the spirit in one of those great cathedrals that man's faith has reared for the worship of God. Now, I say it reverently, but I doubt if any building in the world that has stood for so few years has ever had wafted toward it so much of tender hope, of beautiful faith, of love for humanity. That Temple stands among the buildings of Chicago, and the careless or sordid passer-by thinks nothing of it; but it is so different from any other business building in Chicago, or on the face of the earth, that if built out of the whitest of marble from turret to foundation stone we could not thus symbolize its meaning in tens of thousands of hallowed Christian homes."

Another affiliated interest of the National Woman's Christian Temperance Union which commanded Miss Willard's unabated sympathy was the National Temperance Hospital and Training School for Nurses, in Chicago, formally opened in May, 1886. In April, 1896, she wrote "A Clarion Call" for the Hospital, from which the following paragraphs are quoted:

"The National Temperance Hospital was founded ten years ago for the purpose of demonstrating the practicability of the successful treatment of disease without the use of alcoholic liquors. At that time it was the only institution of its kind, except the famous London Temperance Hospital, of which that celebrated expert in hygiene, Sir Benjamin Ward Richardson, is chief. It has now a medical staff made up of first-class practitioners representing different schools of medicine, and it has also a training school for nurses.

"We are glad to have had so many testimonies in bygone years that the National Temperance Hospital has taken a deep hold on the thought and affection of a large proportion of our most intelligent and devoted members, and that its name and fame have become established in temperance circles throughout the world. To our ever-widening circle of devoted men and women we now appeal for funds to erect a permanent building. . . . . . . 'No great deeds are wrought by falterers who work for certainties.'"

Her faith in the principle upon which this hospital is erected was unswerving. She believed science and morality clasped hands in declaring alcohol an evil, and it is to be doubted if any other W. C. T. U. enterprise appealed more strongly to her heart and brain alike.

As an organizer Miss Willard possessed rare powers of discernment, and a still more rare magnetism. Like the "Ancient Mariner" she could have said:

"Whenever that his face I see,
I know the man who must hear me—
To him I tell my tale";

only the message was primarily to woman, because she saw that the interests of the home, of childhood, of a purer manhood, were bound up in the elevation of women, not because she made the mistake of which she accused the author of "Getting On in the World," namely, "squinting at humanity and seeing only half of it." She saw the real significance of the Woman's Christian Temperance Union.

In the new, despised society she saw the first attempt to unite women into an organization which should make the influence of womanhood an appreciable power in the world. She saw that the army called into existence by the ravages of the saloon upon the home, could, with proper leadership, be arrayed likewise against every other evil which threatens the home and strikes at our civilization. She saw in it, too, a great educational agency for women, and this ideal gave strength and courage for the ceaseless journeyings, difficult and distant, which were to mark the next ten years of her life. Almost immediately upon her election to the national presidency she began that wonderful tour which was not to end until she had spoken in every city and town of ten thousand inhabitants in the United States, and in many of smaller size. In 1883 she traveled 30,000 miles, visiting every State and Territory, speaking in the capital cities of all save Idaho and Arizona. During a dozen years she averaged one meeting a day, and only six weeks in a year for mother-love and home. Such toil seems superhuman when one takes into account the fact that the weary journeys were never allowed to interrupt the constant flow of thought and work. To Miss Willard a railway train became for the time being only another Rest Cottage workshop, and the busy fingers were constantly flying over her writing tablet as the train sped on its swift way. Some of her most inspired and inspiring utterances were given to the world under these conditions, for nothing was able to keep her from the accomplishment of her great purpose.

She seldom turned aside for sight-seeing. A trip to Yellowstone Park was relinquished because she found that thus one more point could be visited and one more Union organized. The goal of her consecrated ambition was a universal sisterhood united in a common cause, and she was deaf to all sounds and blind to all sights which might lure her from that goal. She aroused in the women who rallied to her call not alone a deep love and devotion to herself, but a new faith in their own possibilities and a new hope for the race of which she was a part. One cultured Southern woman, who later occupied a prominent position in national work, has said: "The first time I heard her I lay awake all night for sheer gladness. It was such a wonderful revelation to me that a woman like Miss Willard could exist. I thanked God and took courage for humanity." That same courage has been breathed into unnumbered lives. Women, "seeing her faith," have had a like faith kindled in their own hearts — a faith not alone in their individual ability, but in the power of an organized womanhood. No wonder that Unions, State and local, sprang up like magic wherever her feet trod. She brought to each woman that most mighty of cohesive forces, mingled faith and love.

By far the larger number of State and Territorial Unions in the South and in the far West call Miss Willard mother. Her first trip through the Southern States marks an epoch in history. "It was the first ray of hope that had come into our lives since the war," said one gentle woman of the "solid South." "We had been sitting dumb and crushed amid the wreckage of our past, and it seemed as if there were no future for us; but Miss Willard came and held out to us that little white hand, and its clasp gave us new heart and new hope. She made the white ribbon God's olive branch of peace."

Bishop Stevens, who, as Colonel Stevens, commanded the battery that fired the first shot on Fort Sumter, introduced Miss Willard to her first Southern audience in Charleston, saying, "This woman, this Northern woman, this Northern temperance woman, brings us the magic initials W. C. T. U. Shall we not interpret them in our case to mean, We come to unite the North and the South, and we come to upset the liquor traffic?" The truth of this prophetic utterance was seen at the next National Convention, in Washington, D. C., when Southern women for the first time sat side by side with their Northern sisters, saying to the beloved president of them all, "We have enlisted with you to wage a peaceful war for God and Home and Native Land."

Miss Willard was essentially a harmonizer, loving peace with a love so deep that she would make any concession, except one of principle, to maintain it. Her power to organize was pre-eminent, for the organizer, the constructionist, must always be a man or woman of peace. Yet her love of peace was never cowardly inertia. She could wage most vigorous warfare and prove herself a sternly uncompromising foe whenever war seemed necessary. With a nature strong yet gentle, uncompromising yet pliable, we understand why she effected the largest organization of women the world has ever known.

Miss Willard disproved Goethe's statement that "women are ever isolated, ever work alone," and, as a suffrage leader in Massachusetts has said, "She has shown how they may be brought together into a mighty force which, wisely directed, may revolutionize the world." Whittier well summed up her lifework in the lines written for the marble bust of Miss Willard presented to Willard Hall by Lady Henry Somerset:

> " She knew the power of banded ill,
> But felt that love was stronger still,
> And organized for doing good,
> The world's united womanhood."

Miss Willard's genius for organizing individuals is written upon every page of the history of the Women's Christian Temperance Union. How often has she said:

"Alone we can do little. Separated, we are the units of weakness; but aggregated we become batteries of power. Agitate, educate, organize — these are the deathless watchwords of success. The fingers of the hands can do little alone, but correlated into a fist they become formidable. The plank borne here and there by the sport of the wave is an image of imbecility, but frame a thousand planks of heart of oak into a hull, put in your engine with its heart of fire, fit out your ship, and it shall cross at a right angle those same waves to the port it has purposed to attain. We want all those like-minded with us, who would put down the dramshop, exalt the home, redeem manhood, and uplift womanhood, to join hands with us for organized work according to a plan. It took the allied armies to win at Waterloo, and the alcohol Napoleon will capitulate to a no less mighty army.

"It is the way commerce has marched across the continents and captured them for civilization — one by one; it is the way an army is recruited — one by one; it is the way Christ's Church is built up into power, and heaven adds to its souls redeemed — just one by one.

"Women of the Church, the Home, the School, will you not rally to the holy call of individual responsibility and systematically united effort?

"'For the cause that lacks assistance,
For the wrong that needs resistance,
For the future in the distance,
And the good that you can do!'

"The human biped is a timid creature, who loves to march in platoons rather than to strike out swiftly and alone; but he carries a jewel behind the forehead, and is, therefore, the single sentient creature concerning whom there is hope. You can change his opinions though they are bone of his bone, flesh of his flesh, and dearer to him than his own right eye. There are forces that can disintegrate from the igneous rocks of his prejudice the broader stratifications of kindlier custom and more righteous law. What with 'line upon line, precept upon precept, here a little and there a little' of persuasion founded upon justice, the work is done.

"In the morning of its life every movement for man's elevation shines out with a light like that of Rembrandt's pictures, narrow, but intense. As the day deepens, the light becomes like that in Raphael's pictures, broad and all-comprehending. So it is with Christianity, and so, as White Ribboners steadfastly believe, it will be with that great Temperance Reform which was born of the Gospel, and has been designated by that intrepid leader, Lady Henry Somerset, as 'an embodied prayer.'

"He who climbs, sees. Poets tell us of

> 'The one far-off, divine event,
> Toward which the whole creation moves,'

and in this mighty movement toward the power that organization only can bestow, what end have we in view? Is it fame, fortune, leadership? Not as I read women's hearts, who have known them long and well. It is for love's sake — for the bringing in of peace on earth, good will to men. The two supreme attractions in nature are gravitation and cohesion. That of cohesion attracts atom to atom, that of gravitation attracts all atoms to a common center. We find in this the most conclusive figure of the supremacy of love to God over any human love, the true relation of human to the love divine, and the conclusive proof that in organizing for the greatest number's greatest good, we do but 'think God's thoughts after Him.'

"White Ribbon women distinctly disavow any banding together of women as malcontents or hostiles toward the correlated other half of the human race. Brute force, to our mind, means custom as opposed to reason, prejudice as the antagonist to fair play, and precedent as the foe of common sense.

"It was a beautiful saying of the earlier Methodists, when they avowed a holy life, 'I feel nothing contrary to love.' But the widening march of Christianity has given a wonderfully practical sense to such words, and we actually mean here today that whatever in custom or law is contrary to that love of one's neighbor which would give to him or her all the rights and privileges that one's self enjoys, is but a relic of brute force, and is to be cast out as evil.

"And because woman in our most civilized nation is still so related to the law that the father can will away an unborn child, and that a girl of seven or ten years old is held to be the equal partner in a crime where another and a stronger is principal; because she is in so many ways hampered and harmed by laws and customs pertaining to the past, we reach out hands of help especially to her that she may overtake the swift marching procession of progress, for its sake, that it may not slacken its speed on her account, as much as for hers that she be not left behind. We thus represent the human rather than the woman question, and our voices unite to do that which the President of the New York Woman's Club beautifully said in a late letter to the Club of Bombay:

"'Tell them the world was made for woman, too.'

"It has been well said[*] no other association of philanthropic workers has touched so many springs of praise and blame, of love and hate, and become equally distinguished for the friends it has won and the enemies it has made, and the proof of the effectiveness of the mission undertaken is easy to find on the very surface of things. Cursed at the bar of the legalized dramshop; hissed on the floor of the Beer Brewers' Congress; scorned by conventions of political parties; misrepresented by the all-powerful press; denied its prayer in the halls of legislation; sneered at in places of fashion, where the wineglass tempts to destroy; criticised by conservative pulpits; and unwelcome often in the Christian church, it has been left to this organization of ballotless women to arouse all classes of opposers and find for themselves the hate of hate. But, on the other hand, blessed by the fevered lips of the drunkard ready to perish; sought by the wandering feet of the boy or girl who went astray; hallowed by loving thoughts at thousands of firesides; baptized with holy tears by the mothers whose battle it wages; perfumed by the stainless prayers of little children; indorsed by the expressed principles of organized Christianity; sustained by the highest and freshest authorities in the scientific world; praised by lips grown careful through statesmanlike speech;

---

[*] Mrs. Mary T. Lathrap, of Michigan, before the National Council of Women, Washington, D. C., 1890.

believed in by the best, trusted by the most needy, it has been granted us also to find the 'love of love.'

"As a working hypothesis, no age and no race of men can ever go beyond Christ's simple dictum, 'The kingdom of heaven is within you.' It cometh not by observation; that is, it cometh not suddenly, but little by little, imperceptibly as one particle after another is added to one's stature, so by every thought, word and deed, that kingdom has woven its warp and woof, wrought out its wonderful beauty in our own breasts. All pure habits, all health and sanity of brain, make for the kingdom of heaven. The steady pulse, the calm and quiet thought, the splendid equipoise of will, the patient industry that forges right straight on and cannot be abashed or turned aside, these make for the kingdom of heaven. The helpful hand outstretched to whatsoever beside us may crawl or creep, or cling or climb, is a hand whose very motion is part of the dynamic forces of the kingdom of heaven. The spirit of God, by its divine alchemy, works in us to transform, to recreate, to vivify our entire being, in spirit, soul and body, until we ourselves incarnate a little section of the kingdom of heaven.

"The deepest billows are away out at sea; they never come in sight of shore. These waves are like the years of God. Upon the shore line of our earthly life come the waves of the swift years; they bound and break and are no more. But far out upon eternity's bosom are the great, wide, endless waves that make the years of God; they never strike upon the shore of time. In all the flurry and the foam about us, let us bend our heads to listen to the great anthem of that far-off sea, for our life barks shall soon be cradled there; we are but building here, the launch is not far off, and then the boundless ocean of the years of God."

Miss Willard's magnificent conception of the necessary correlation of reform forces, her influence in allying so many other moral forces with the original purpose of the Crusade, has made the Woman's Christian Temperance Union the most broadly comprehensive organization the world has ever known. This "Do Everything Policy" Miss Willard thus defines:

THE TEMPLE

Sculptor, Geo. E. Wade, London.

WILLARD FOUNTAIN IN BRONZE, AT ENTRANCE TO WILLARD HALL
PRESENTED TO CHICAGO BY BOYS AND GIRLS OF THE LOYAL TEMPERANCE LEGION—1893.

"When we began the delicate, difficult and dangerous operation of dissecting out the alcohol nerve from the body politic, we did not realize the intricacy of the undertaking, nor the distances that must be traversed by the scalpel of investigation and research. More than twenty years have elapsed since the call to battle sounded its bugle note among the homes and hearts of Hillsboro, Ohio. One thought, sentiment and purpose animated those saintly 'Praying Bands,' whose name will never die out from human history: 'Brothers, we beg of you not to drink, and not to sell!' This was the single wailing note of these moral Paganinis, playing on one string. It caught the universal ear, and set the key of that mighty orchestra, organized with so much toil and hardship, in which the tender and exalted strain of the Crusade violin still soars aloft, but upborne now by the clanging cornets of science, the deep trombones of legislation, and the thunderous drums of politics and parties. The 'Do Everything Policy' was not of our choosing, but is an evolution, as inevitable as any traced by the naturalist, or described by the historian. Woman's genius for details, and her patient steadfastness in following the enemies of those she loves 'through every lane of life,' have led her to antagonize the alcohol habit, and the liquor traffic, just where they are, wherever that may be. If she does this, since they are everywhere, her policy will be, 'Do Everything.'

"A one-sided movement makes one-sided advocates. Virtues, like hounds, hunt in packs. Total abstinence is not the crucial virtue in life that excuses financial crookedness, defamation of character, or habits of impurity. The fact that one's father was, and one's self is, a bright and shining light in the total abstinence galaxy, does not give one a vantage ground for high-handed behavior toward those who have not been trained to the special virtue that forms the central idea of the Temperance Movement. We have known persons who, because they had 'never touched a drop of liquor,' set themselves up as if they belonged to a royal line, but whose tongues were as biting as alcohol itself, and whose narrowness had no competitor, save a straight line. An all-round movement can only be carried forward by all-round advocates ; a scientific age requires the study of every subject in its correlations. It was once supposed that light, heat and electricity were wholly separate entities; it is now believed, and practically proved, that they are but different modes of motion. Standing in the valley, we look up and think we see an isolated mountain; climbing to its top, we see that it is but one member of a range of mountains, many of them of well-nigh equal altitude.

"Some bright women who have opposed the 'Do Everything Policy,' used as their favorite illustration a flowing river, and expatiated on the ruin that would follow if that river (which represents their Do One Thing Policy) were diverted into many channels; but it should be remembered that the most useful of all rivers is the Nile, and that the agricultural economy of Egypt consists in the effort to spread its waters upon as many fields as possible. It is not for the river's sake that it flows through the country, but for the sake of the fertility it can bring upon the adjoining fields, and this is pre-eminently true of the Temperance Reform.

"Let us not be disconcerted, but stand bravely by that blessed trinity of movements, Prohibition, Woman's Liberation and Labor's Uplift.

"Everything is not in the Temperance Reform, but the Temperance Reform should be in everything.

"'Organized Mother-Love' is the best definition of the White Ribbon Movement, and it can have no better motto than: 'Make a chain, for the land is full of bloody crimes and the city of violence.'

"If we can remember this simple rule, it will do much to unravel the mystery of the much-controverted 'Do Everything Policy,' namely, that every question of practical philanthropy or reform has its temperance aspect, and with that we are to deal."

Miss Willard's conviction of the essential right and justice of the principle of woman's suffrage, with a twin conviction that she must be its public advocate, came to her in the capital of the

Crusade State in 1876, while she was upon her knees in prayer, lifting her heart to God with the cry, "What wouldst Thou have me to do?" She felt that all the power of God would be at her disposal in her advocacy of the views she felt constrained to declare, and at once asked permission to present the subject at the projected Centennial temperance meeting, in the Academy of Music, Philadelphia, but the request was declined. Even at Chautauqua, a few weeks later, she felt the conservative influence and refrained from speaking out her deepest thought. This dauntless pioneer next visited Old Orchard Beach, and tells us that in the "fragrant air of Maine's dear piney woods, with the great free ocean's salt spray to invigorate lungs and soul, I first avowed the faith that was within me. All around, my good friends looked so much surprised and some of them so sorry." Miss Willard found a strong friend in Maria Mitchell, who gave her a "home-protection audience," at the Woman's Congress. Her first avowal of this theme, dear to her heart, before the National Woman's Christian Temperance Union, was made in the year 1876 before the annual convention, held in Newark, New Jersey. Miss Willard's own pen picture is the best delineation of that now historic scene:

"By this time my soul had come to 'woe is me if I declare not this gospel.' Welcome or not, the words must come. In a great crowded church, with smiles on some faces and frowns on others, I came forward. Our gifted Mary Lathrap had told a war story in one of her addresses about a colored man who saw a boat bearing down upon the skiff drawn up to shore, in which he and three white men were concealed. If he could only push off instantly they would be saved, but to show himself was fatal. But he did not hesitate; calling out, 'Somebody's got to be killed, and it might as well be me,' he launched the boat and fell with a bullet in his heart. In that difficult hour this story came to me, and as I told it some of my good friends wept at the thought of ostracism which, from that day to this, has been its sequel — not as a rule, but a painful exception. When I had finished the argument, a lady from New York, gray-haired and dignified, who was presiding, said to the audience: 'The National Woman's Christian Temperance Union is not responsible for the utterances of this evening. We have no mind to trail our skirts in the mire of politics.' She doubtless felt it her duty to speak, and I had no thought of blame, only regret. As we left the church, one of our chief women said: 'You might have been a leader in our national councils, but you have deliberately chosen to be only a scout.'"

Miss Willard had no way of knowing, unless by divine intuition, that this prophecy was false; yet a scout she dared and chose to become. Three years later, at the very Convention which elected her its President, the Woman's Christian Temperance Union declared for the ballot in the hands of woman, and during the years which have followed it is universally acknowledged to have accomplished more in molding the public opinion of the home and the church in favor of this reform than has any other one agency.

THE "HOME PROTECTION" ADDRESS.

The whisky power looms like a Chimborazo among the mountains of difficulty over which our native land must climb to reach the future of our dreams. The problem of the rum power's overthrow may well engage our thoughts as women and as patriots. Tonight I ask you to consider it in the light of a truth which Frederick Douglass has embodied in these words: "We can in the long run trust all the knowledge in the community to take care of all the ignorance of the community, and all of its virtue to take care of all of its vice." The difficulty in the application of this principle lies in the fact that vice is always in the active, virtue often in the passive. Vice is aggressive. It deals swift, sure blows, delights in keen-edged weapons, and prefers a hand-to-hand conflict, while virtue instinctively fights its unsavory antagonist at arm's length; its great guns are unwieldy and slow to swing into range.

Vice is the tiger, with keen eyes, alert ears and cat-like tread, while virtue is the slow-paced, complacent, easy-going elephant, whose greatest danger lies in its ponderous weight and consciousness of power. So the great question narrows down to one of methods. It is not, when we look carefully into the conditions of the problem, How shall we develop more virtue in the community to offset the tropical growth of vice by which we find ourselves environed, but rather, how the tremendous force we have may best be brought to bear, how we may unlimber the huge cannon now pointing into vacancy, and direct their full charge at short range upon our nimble, wily, vigilant foe?

As bearing upon a consideration of that question, I lay down this proposition: All pure and Christian sentiment concerning any line of conduct which vitally affects humanity will, sooner or later, crystallize into law. But the keystone of law can only be firm and secure when it is held in place by the arch of that keystone, which is public sentiment.

I make another statement not so often reiterated, but just as true, namely: The more thoroughly you can enlist in favor of your law the natural instincts of those who have the power to make that law, and to select the officers who shall enforce it, the more securely stands the law. And still another: First among the powerful and controlling instincts in our nature stands that of self-preservation, and next after this, if it does not claim superior rank, comes that of a mother's love. You can count upon that every time; it is sure and resistless as the tides of the sea, for it is founded in the changeless nature given to her from God.

Now, the stronghold of the rum power lies in the fact that it has upon its side two deeply-rooted appetites, namely: in the dealer, the appetite for gain, and in the drinker, the appetite for stimulants. We have dolorously said in times gone by that on the human plane we have nothing adequate to match against this frightful pair. But let us think more carefully and we shall find that, as in nature, God has given us an antidote to every poison, and in grace a compensation for every loss, so in human society He has prepared against alcohol, that worst foe of the social state, an enemy under whose weapons it is to bite the dust.

Think of it! There is a class in every one of our communities— in many of them far the most numerous class — which (I speak not vauntingly, I but name it as a fact) has not in all the centuries of wine, beer and brandy drinking, developed, as a class, an appetite for alcohol, but whose instincts, on the contrary, set so strongly against intoxicants that if the liquor traffic were dependent on their patronage alone it would collapse this night as if all the nitro-glycerine of Hell Gate reef had exploded under it.

There is a class whose instinct of self-preservation must forever be opposed to a stimulant which nerves with dangerous strength arms already so much stronger than their own, and so maddens the brain God meant to guide those arms that they strike down the wives men love, and the little children for whom, when sober, they would die. The wife, largely dependent for the support of herself and little ones upon the brain which strong drink paralyzes, the arm it masters and the skill it renders futile, will, in the nature of the case, prove herself unfriendly to the actual or potential source of so much misery. But besides this primal instinct of self-preservation, we have in the same class of which I speak, another far more high and sacred — I mean the instinct of a mother's love, a wife's devotion, a sister's faithfulness, a daughter's loyalty. And now I ask you to consider earnestly the fact that none of these blessed rays of light and power from woman's heart are as yet brought to bear upon the rum shop at the focus of power. They are, I know, the sweet and pleasant sunshine of our homes; they are the beams which light the larger home of social life and send their gentle radiance out even into the great and busy world.

But I know, and as the knowledge has grown clearer, my heart has thrilled with gratitude and hope too deep for words, that in a republic all these now divergent beams of light can, through that magic lens, that powerful sun-glass which we name the ballot, be made to converge upon the rum shop in a blaze of light that shall reveal its full abominations, and a white flame of heat which, like a pitiless moxa, shall burn this cancerous excrescence from America's fair form. Yes, for there is nothing in the universe so sure, so strong, as love; and love shall do all this — the love of maid for sweetheart, wife for husband, of a sister for her brother, of a mother for her son. And I call upon you who are here today, good men and brave — you who have welcomed us to other fields in the great fight of the angel against the dragon in society — I call upon you thus to match force with force, to set over against the liquor-dealer's avarice our instinct of self-preservation; and to match the drinker's love of liquor with our love of him! When you can center all this power in that small bit of paper which falls

"As silently as snowflakes fall upon the sod,
But executes a freeman's will as lightnings do the will of God,"

the rum power will be as much doomed as was the slave power when you gave the ballot to the slaves.

In our argument it has been claimed that by the changeless instincts of her nature and through the most sacred relationships of which that nature has been rendered capable, God has indicated woman, who is the born conservator of home, to be the Nemesis of home's arch enemy, King Alcohol. And, further, that in a republic, this power of hers may be most effectively exercised by giving her a voice in the decision by which the rum-shop door shall be opened or closed beside her home.

This position is strongly supported by evidence. About the year 1850, petitions were extensively circulated in Cincinnati (later the fiercest battleground of the Woman's Crusade), asking that the liquor traffic be put under the ban of law. Bishop Simpson — one of the noblest and most discerning minds of his century — was deeply interested in this movement. It was decided to ask for the names of women, as well as those of men, and it was found that the former signed the petition more readily and in much larger numbers than the latter. Another fact was ascertained which rebuts the hackneyed assertion that women of the lower class will not be on the temperance side in this great war. For it was found — as might, indeed, have been most reasonably predicted — that the ignorant, the poor (many of them wives, mothers and daughters of intemperate men), were among the most eager to sign the petition.

Many a hand was taken from the washtub to hold the pencil and affix the signature of women of this class, and many another, which could only make the sign of the cross, did that with tears, and a hearty "God bless you." "That was a wonderful lesson to me," said the good Bishop, and he has always believed since then that God will give our enemy into our hands by giving to us an ally still more powerful — woman with the ballot against rum-shops in our land. It has been said so often that the very frequency of reiteration has in some minds induced belief, that women of the better class will never consent to declare themselves at the polls. But tens of thousands from the most tenderly sheltered homes have gone day after day to the saloons, and have spent hour after hour upon their sanded floors, and in their reeking air — places in which not the worst politician would dare to locate the ballot box of freemen, though they but stay a moment at the window, slip in their votes, and go their way.

Nothing worse can ever happen to women at the polls than has been endured by the hour on the part of conservative women of the churches in this land, as they, in scores of towns, have plead with rough, half-drunken men to vote the temperance tickets they have handed them, and which, with vastly more of propriety and fitness, they might have dropped into the box themselves. They could have done this in a moment, and returned to their homes, instead of spending the whole day in the often futile endeavor to beg from men like these the votes which should preserve their homes from the whisky serpent's breath for one uncertain year. I spent last May in Ohio, traveling constantly, and seeking on every side to learn the views of the noble women of the Crusade. They put their opinions in words like these: "We believe that as God led us into this work by way of the saloons, He will lead us out by way of the ballot. We have never prayed more earnestly over the one than we will over the other. One was the Wilderness, the other is the Promised Land."

A Presbyterian lady, rigidly conservative, said: "For my part, I never wanted to vote until our gentlemen passed a prohibition ordinance so as to get us to stop visiting saloons, and a month later repealed it and chose a saloon-keeper for mayor."

Said a granddaughter of Jonathan Edwards, a woman with no toleration toward the Suffrage Movement, a woman crowned with the glory of gray hairs, a central figure in her native town — and as she spoke the courage and faith of the Puritans thrilled her voice: "If, with the ballot in our hands, we can, as I firmly believe, put down this awful traffic, I am ready to lead the women of my town to the polls, as I have often led them to the rum shops."

We must not forget that for every woman who joins the Temperance Unions that have sprung up all through the world, there are at least a score who sympathize, but do not join. Home influence and cares prevent them, ignorance of our aims and methods, lack of consecration to Christian work — a thousand reasons, sufficient in their estimation, though not in ours, hold them away from us. And yet they have this Temperance cause warmly at heart; the logic of events has shown them that there is but one side on which a woman may safely stand in this great battle, and on that side they would indubitably range themselves in the quick, decisive battle of election day, nor would they give their voice a second time in favor of the man who had once betrayed his pledge to enforce the most stringent law for the protection of their homes. There are many noble women, too, who, though they do not think as do the Temperance Unions about the deep things of religion, and are not as yet decided in their total abstinence sentiments, nor ready for the blessed work of prayer, are nevertheless decided in their views of Woman Suffrage, and ready to vote a temperance ticket side by side with us. And there are the drunkard's wife and daughters, who from very shame will not come with us, or who dare not, yet who could freely vote with us upon this question; for the folded ballot tells no tales.

Among other cumulative proofs in this argument from experience, let us consider, briefly, the attitude of the Catholic Church toward the Temperance Reform. It is friendly, at least. Father Matthew's spirit lives today in many a faithful parish priest. In our processions on the Centennial Fourth of July, the banners of Catholic Total Abstinence Societies were often the only reminders that the Republic has any temperance people within its borders, as they were the only offset to brewers' wagons and distillers' casks; while among the monuments of our cause, by which this memorable year is signalized, their fountain in Fairmount Park — standing in the midst of eighty drinking places licensed by our Government — is chief. Catholic women would vote with Protestant women upon this issue for the protection of their homes.

Again, among the thousand churches of America, with their million members, two-thirds are women. Thus, only one-third of this trustworthy and thoughtful class has any voice in the laws by which, between the church and the public school, the rum shop nestles in this Christian land. Surely all this must change before the Government shall be upon His shoulders "who shall one day reign King of Nations as He now reigns King of Saints."

Furthermore, four-fifths of the teachers in this land are women, whose thoughtful judgment, expressed with the authority of which I speak, would greatly help forward the victory of our cause. And finally, by those who fear the effect of the foreign element in our country, let it be remembered that we have six native women for every one who is foreign born, for it is men who emigrate in largest numbers to our shores.

When all these facts (and many more that might be added) are marshaled into line, how illogical it seems for good men to harangue us as they do about our "duty to educate public sentiment to the level of better law," and to exhort true-hearted American mothers to "train their sons to vote aright." As said Mrs. Governor Wallace, of Indiana — until the Crusade an opponent of the franchise —"What a bitter sarcasm you utter, gentlemen, to us who have the public sentiment of which you speak, all burning in our hearts, and yet are not permitted to turn it to account."

Let us, then, each one of us offer our earnest prayer to God, and speak our honest word to man in favor of this added weapon in woman's hands, remembering that every petition in the ear of God, and every utterance in the ears of men, swells the dimensions of that resistless tide of influence which shall yet float within our reach all that we ask or need. Good and true women who have crusaded in rum shops, I urge that you begin crusading in halls of legislation, in primary meetings, and the offices of excise commissioners. Roll in your petitions, burnish your arguments, multiply your prayers. Go to the voters in your town — procure the official list and see them one by one — and get them pledged to a local ordinance requiring the votes of men and women before a license can be issued to open rum-shop doors beside your homes; go to the legislature with the same; remember this may be just as really Christian work as praying in saloons was in those other glorious days. Let us not limit God, whose modes of operation are so infinitely varied in nature and in grace. I believe in the correlation of spiritual forces, and that the heat which melted hearts to tenderness in the Crusade is soon to be the light which shall reveal our opportunity and duty as the Republic's daughters.

Longer ago than I shall tell, my father returned one night to the far-off Wisconsin home where I was reared; sitting by my mother's chair, with a child's attentive ear, I listened to their words. He told us of the news that day had brought about Neal Dow and the great fight for prohibition down in Maine, and then he said: "I wonder if poor, rum-cursed Wisconsin will ever get a law like that?" And mother rocked a while in silence in the dear old chair I love, and then she gently said: "Yes, Josiah; there'll be such a law all over the land some day, when women vote."

My father had never heard her say so much before. He was a great conservative; so he looked tremendously astonished, and replied in his keen, sarcastic voice: "And pray how will you arrange it so that women shall vote?" Mother's chair went to and fro a little faster for a minute, and then, looking not into his face, but into the flickering flames of the grate, she slowly answered: "Well, I say to you, as the apostle Paul said to his jailer, 'You have put us into prison, we being Romans, and you must come and take us out.'"

That was a seed-thought in a girl's brain and heart. Years passed on, in which nothing more was said upon this dangerous theme. My brother grew to manhood, and soon after he was twenty-one years old he went with his father to vote. Standing by the window, a girl of sixteen years, a girl of simple, homely fancies, not at all strong-minded, and altogether ignorant of the world, I looked out as they drove away, my father and my brother, and as I looked I felt a strange ache in my heart, and tears sprang to my eyes. Turning to my sister Mary, who stood beside me, I saw that the dear little innocent seemed wonderfully sober, too. I said: "Don't you wish we could go with them when we are old enough? Don't we love our country just as well as they do?" and her little frightened voice piped out: "Yes, of course we ought. Don't I know that? but you mustn't tell a soul — not mother, even; we should be called strong-minded."

In all the years since then I have kept these things, and many others like them, and pondered them in my heart; but two years of struggle in this temperance reform have shown me my duty, as they have ten thousand other women, so clearly and so impressively, that I long ago passed the Rubicon of silence, and am ready for any battle that shall be involved in this honest declaration of the faith that is within me. "Fight behind masked batteries a little longer," whisper good friends and true. So I have been fighting hitherto; but it is a style of warfare altogether foreign to my temperament and mode of life. Reared on the prairies, I seemed predetermined to join the cavalry forces in this great spiritual war, and I must tilt a free lance henceforth on the splendid battlefield of this reform; where the earth shall soon be shaken by the onset of contending hosts; where legions of valiant soldiers are deploying; where to the grand encounter marches today a great army, gentle of mien and mild of utterance, but with hearts for any fate; where there are trumpets and bugles calling strong souls onward to a victory that heaven might envy, and

> "Where, behind the dim Unknown,
> Standeth God within the shadow,
> Keeping watch above His own."

I thought that women ought to have the ballot as I paid the hard-earned taxes upon my mother's cottage home — but I never said as much — somehow the motive did not command my heart. For my own sake, I had not courage, but I have for thy sake, dear native land, for thy necessity is as much greater than mine as thy transcendent hope is greater than the personal interest of thy humble child. For love of you, heartbroken wives, whose tremulous lips have blessed me; for love of you, sweet mothers, who, in the cradle's shadow, kneel this night beside your infant sons; and you, sorrowful little children, who listen at this hour, with faces strangely old, for him whose footsteps frighten you; for love of you have I thus spoken.

Ah, it is women who have given the costliest hostages to fortune. Out into the battle of life they have sent their best beloved, with fearful odds against them, with snares that men have legalized and set for them on every hand. Beyond the arms that held them long, their boys have gone forever. Oh! by the danger they have dared; by the hours of patient watching over beds where helpless children lay; by the incense of ten thousand prayers wafted from their gentle lips to heaven, I charge you give them power to protect, along life's treacherous highway, those whom they have so loved. Let it no longer be that they must sit back among the shadows, hopelessly mourning over their strong staff broken, and their beautiful rod; but when the sons they love shall go forth to life's battle, still let their mothers walk beside them, sweet and serious, and clad in the garments of power.

The same calm and, to a superficial observer, reckless disregard of consequences, marked her policy in the later struggle for affiliation with that political party which, in her judgment, alone breathed the spirit of the Crusade. When convinced by the resistless logic of events, and the equally resistless logic of her own mind, that woman's ballot could be an effective agency for the preservation of the home only as a proper channel should be supplied through which it might express itself, she at once set out to find that channel. When she believed she had found it, she did not hesitate to throw the whole weight of her influence in favor of that party which seemed to her the best embodiment of home protection. It was not an easy thing to do. Party feeling ran far higher in those years than, please God, it is likely to do again. It took courage to go against those with whom for years she had been in perfect accord, courage to be branded as a fanatic and an iconoclast; but just that splendid courage was hers, and having once set her hand to the plow, there was for her no looking back. Her first utterance in favor of party prohibition was made at the Boston Convention in 1880; her last at Buffalo, when, the report of the Committee on Resolutions having been presented during her absence from the hall, she arose in the great public meeting at night and, in her quaintly humorous way, announced that it had been "moved, seconded and unanimously carried in her own mind" that the differing factions existing among her beloved brethren should once more come together, should insert a woman's suffrage plank in their platform, and under the glorious name of the "Home Protection Party" march on to victory. During those intervening years no faction, no schism, no ridicule, no persecution, had turned her from her purpose. She still believed a party might and should exist which would embody in its name, and in its platform, all that the term "Home Protection" meant to her home-loving heart! Having "done all," she stood!

Hers was the genius which not only sees new light and invents new methods, but which recognizes all that is true in the old light and uses old methods in such a way as to make them seem perennially new. This was especially true of her use of the time-honored custom of petitioning. She believed with all her heart in the petition as a medium for the expression of opinion and as a means for educating public sentiment, but she took the old form and made it wholly new by her skillful manipulation. Witness the famous "Home Protection Petition" of Illinois, which was her first work as President of her adopted State:

THE HOME PROTECTION PETITION.

To the Senate and House of Representatives of the State of Illinois:

WHEREAS, In these years of temperance work the argument of defeat in our contest with the saloons has taught us that our efforts are merely palliative of a disease in the body politic, which can never be cured until law and moral suasion go hand in hand in our beloved State; and

WHEREAS, The instincts of self-protection and of apprehension for the safety of her children, her tempted loved ones, and her home, render woman the natural enemy of the saloon;

Therefore, Your petitioners, men and women of the State of Illinois, having at heart the protection of our homes from their worst enemy, the legalized traffic in strong drink, do hereby most earnestly pray your honorable body that by suitable legislation it may be provided that in the State of Illinois, the question of licensing at any time, in any locality, the sale of any and all intoxicating drinks shall be submitted to and determined by ballot, in which women of lawful age shall be privileged to take part, in the same manner as men, when voting on the question of license.

To this Petition were secured in ninety days two hundred thousand names. The State House in Springfield was draped with the petition which was pasted upon white cloth, one edge of which was bound with red and the other with blue, and its presentation was made a genuine gala-day.

Her Memorial presented before the various political conventions in the year 1884 is another example of the skillful use to which she could put "the right of a sovereign people to petition," while her Purity Petition, which served largely as the basis of the White Cross and White Shield work in the National W. C. T. U. has been presented before the legislatures of nearly every State in the Union with blessed results.

PETITION OF THE WOMAN'S CHRISTIAN TEMPERANCE UNION
FOR FURTHER PROVISION FOR THE PROTECTION OF WOMEN AND CHILDREN.

To the Honorable, the Senate and House of Representatives of the State of ———:

The increasing and alarming frequency of assaults upon women, the frightful indignities to which even little girls are subject, and the corrupting of boys, have become the shame of our boasted civilization.

We believe that the statutes of ——— do not meet the demands of that newly awakened public sentiment which requires better legal protection for womanhood and childhood;

Therefore, we, the undersigned citizens of ———, County of ———, and State of ———, pray you to enact further provision for the protection of women and children. And we call attention to the disgraceful fact that protection of the person is not placed by our laws upon so high a plane as protection of the purse.

As a presiding officer Miss Willard was without a peer. It was an education in itself to see her marshal the hosts at one of the great conventions of the National W. C. T. U. However skeptical a visitor might be of "women's meetings"— however prejudiced against this particular woman as the embodiment of "white-ribbon fanaticism"— he was not proof against the magic spell of the gavel in her firm little hand and the inspiration of her exquisite face. How much he might have gone "to scoff," he remained— if not "to pray," to marvel at the power of the woman whom he had seen before him perhaps for days. Her graceful tact, her quickness of repartee, her wondrous grace and graciousness, her felicity of word and phrase, her comprehensive mind and her all-embracing heart were never more clearly seen than in one of those home-gatherings of the white-ribbon clans. She was not an uncrowned but a crowned queen in those days, and her loyal, devoted subjects delighted to bow to her mandate and to do her glad homage. For nineteen years "her banner over us was love"; love like the mighty waves of the ocean from her heart to ours— an answering love, the chorus of many waters— from our hearts to hers.

The best definition of the Woman's Christian Temperance Union and its multiplied activities must be given by our leader her-

FRANCES E. WILLARD
MARBLE BUST BY ANNE WHITNEY, IN WILLARD HALL, THE TEMPLE.

THE GENERAL OFFICERS OF THE WORLD'S W. C. T. U.

FRANCES E. WILLARD,
President.

AGNES E. SLACK,
Secretary.

LADY HENRY SOMERSET,
Vice-President-at-large.

ANNA A. GORDON,
Assistant Secretary.

MARY E. SANDERSON,
Treasurer.

self, and we quote from one of her matchless annual addresses before the National Convention:

"More than any other society ever formed, the Woman's Christian Temperance Union is the exponent of what is best in this latter-day civilization. Its scope is the broadest, its aims are the kindest, its history is the most heroic. I yield to none in admiration of woman's splendid achievements in church work and in the Foreign Missionary Society, which was my first love as a philanthropist, but in both instances the denominational character of that work interferes with its unity and breadth. The same is true of woman's educational undertakings, glorious as they are. Her many-sided charities, in homes for the orphaned and the indigent, hospitals for the sick and asylums for the old, are the admiration of all generous hearts, but these are local in their interest and result from the loving labors of isolated groups. The same is true of the women's prisons and industrial schools, which are now multiplying with such beneficent rapidity. Nor do I forget the sanitary work of women, which gleamed like a heavenly rainbow on the horrid front of war; but noble *men* shared the labor as they did the honor on that memorable field. Neither am I unmindful of the Woman's Christian Association, strongly intrenched in most of our great cities, and doing valiant battle for the Prince of Peace; but it admits to its sacramental host only members of the churches known as 'Evangelical.' Far be it from me to seem indifferent to that electric intellectual movement from which have resulted the societies, literary and æsthetic, in which women have combined to study classic history, philosophy and art, but these have no national unity; or to forget the 'Woman's Congress,' with its annual meeting and wide outlook, but lack of local auxiliaries; or the 'Exchanges,' where women too poor or proud to bring their wares before the public, are helped to put money in their purse, but which lack cohesion; or the state and associated charities, where women do much of the work and men most of the superintendence. But when all is said, the Woman's Christian Temperance Union, local, state and national, in the order of its growth, with its unique and heavenly origin, its steady march, its multiplied auxiliaries, its blessed out-reaching to the generous South and the far frontier, its broad sympathies and its "abundant entrance" ministered to all good and true women who are willing to clasp hands in one common effort to protect their homes and loved ones from the ravages of drink, is an organization without a pattern save that seen in heavenly vision upon the mount of faith, and without a peer among the sisterhoods that have grouped themselves around the cross of Christ.

"In the fullness of time this mighty work has been given us. Preceding ages would not have understood the end in view and would have spurned the means, but the nineteenth century, standing on the shoulders of its predecessors, has a wider outlook and a keener vision. It has studied science and discovered that the tumult of the whirlwind is less powerful than the silence of the dew. It has ransacked history and learned that the banner and the sword were never yet the symbols of man's grandest victories, and it begins at last to listen to the voice of that inspired philosophy, which through all ages has been gently saying: 'The race is not always to the swift, neither the battle to the strong.'

. . . . . .

"The W. C. T. U. stands as the exponent, not alone of that return to physical sanity which will follow the downfall of the drink habit, but of the reign of a religion of the body which for the first time in history shall correlate with Christ's wholesome, practical, yet blessedly spiritual religion of the soul. 'The kingdom of heaven is within you' shall have a new meaning to the clear-eyed, steady-limbed Christians of the future, from whose brain and blood the taint of alcohol and nicotine has been eliminated by ages of pure habits and noble heredity. 'The body is the temple of the Holy Ghost' will not then seem so mystical a statement, nor one indicative of a temple so insalubrious as now. 'He that destroyeth this temple, him shall God destroy,' will be seen to involve no element of vengeance, but instead to be the declaration of such boundless love and pity for our race, as would not suffer its deterioration to reach the point of absolute failure and irremediable loss.

"The women of this land have never had before such training as is furnished by the topical studies of our society, in the laws by which childhood shall set out upon its endless journey with a priceless heritage of powers laid up in store by the tender, sacred foresight of those by whom the young immortal's being was invoked. The laws of health were never studied by so many mothers, or with such immediate results for good on their own lives and those of their children. The deformed waist and foot of the average fashionable American never seemed so hideous and wicked, nor the cumbrous dress of the period so unendurable as now, when from studying one 'poison habit,' our minds by the inevitable laws of thought reach out to wider researches and more varied deductions than we had dreamed at first. The economies of co-operative housekeeping never looked so attractive or so feasible as since the homemakers have learned something about the priceless worth of time and money for the purposes of a Christ-like benevolence. The value of a trained intellect never had such significance as since we have learned what an incalculable saving of words there is in a direct style, what value in the power of classification of fact, what boundless resources for illustrating and enforcing truth come as the sequel of a well-stored memory and a cultivated imagination. The puerility of mere talk for the sake of talk, the unworthiness of 'idle words,' and vacuous, purposeless gossip, the waste of long and aimless letter-writing, never looked so egregious as to the workers who find every day too short for the glorious and gracious deeds which lie waiting for them on every hand.

"But to help forward the coming of Christ into all departments of life is, in its last analysis, the purpose and aim of the W. C. T. U. For we believe this correlation of New Testament religion with philanthropy, and of the Church with civilization, is the perpetual miracle which furnishes the only sufficient antidote to current skepticism. Higher toward the zenith climbs the Sun of Righteousness, making circle after circle of human endeavor and achievement warm and radiant with the healing of its beams. First of all, in our gospel temperance work, this heavenly light penetrated the gloom of the individual, tempted heart (that smallest circle, in which all others are involved), illumined its darkness, melted its hardness, made it a sweet and sunny place — a temple filled with the Holy Ghost.

"Having thus come to the heart of the drinking man in the plenitude of His redeeming power, Christ entered the next wider circle, in which two human hearts unite to form a home, and here, by the revelation of her place in His kingdom, He lifted to an equal level with her husband the gentle companion who had supposed herself happy in being the favorite vassal of her liege lord. 'There is neither male nor female in Christ Jesus'; this was the 'open sesame,' a declaration utterly opposed to all custom and tradition; but so steadily the light has shown, and so kindly has it made the heart of man, that without strife of tongues, or edict of sovereigns, it is coming now to pass that in proportion as any home is really Christian, the husband and the wife are peers in dignity and power. There are no homes on earth where woman is 'revered, beloved' and individualized in character and work so thoroughly as the fifty thousand in America, where 'her children rise up and call her blessed; her husband also, and he praiseth her,' because of her part in the work of our W. C. T. U.

"Beyond this sweet and sacred circle where two hearts grow to be one, where the mystery of birth and the hallowed face of child and mother work their perpetual charm, comes that outer court of home, that third great circle which we call society. Surely and steadily the light of Christ is coming here, through the loving temperance Pentecost, to replace the empty phrase of punctilio by earnest words of cheer and inspiration; to banish the unhealthful tyranny of fashion by enthroning wholesome taste and common sense; to drive out questionable amusements and introduce innocent and delightful pastimes; to exorcise the evil spirit of gossip and domesticate helpful and tolerant speech; nay, more, to banish from the social board those false emblems of hospitality and good-will — intoxicating drinks.

"Sweep a wider circle still, and behold in that ecclesiastical invention called 'denominationalism,' Christ coming by the union of His handmaids in work for Him; coming to put away the form outward and visible that He may shed abroad the grace inward and spiritual; to close the theological disquisition of the learned pundit, and open the Bible of the humble saint; to draw away men's thoughts from theories of right living, and center them upon right living itself; to usher in the priesthood of the people, by pressing upon the conscience of each believer the individual commission, 'Go, disciple all nations,' and emphasizing the individual promise, 'Lo, I am with thee always.'

"But the modern temperance movement, born of Christ's Gospel and cradled at His altars, is rapidly filling one more circle of influence wide as the widest zone of earthly weal or woe, and that is government. 'The government shall be upon His shoulder.' 'Unto us a King is given.' 'He shall reign whose right it is.' 'He shall not fail, nor be discouraged until he hath set judgment in the earth.' 'That at the name of Jesus every knee should bow, and every tongue confess that Jesus Christ is Lord, to the glory of God the Father.' 'Thy kingdom come, thy will be done *on earth*.' Christ shall reign — not visibly, but invisibly; not in form, but in fact; not in substance, but in essence, and the day draws nigh! Then surely the traffic in intoxicating liquors as a drink will no longer be protected by the statute book, the lawyer's plea, the affirmation of the witness, and decision of the judge. And since the government is, after all, a circle that includes all hearts, all homes, all churches, all societies, does it not seem as if intelligent loyalty to Christ the King would cause each heart that loves Him to feel in duty bound to use all the power it could gather to itself in helping choose the framers of these more righteous laws? But let it be remembered that for every Christian man who has a voice in making and enforcing laws there are at least two Christian women who have no voice at all! Hence, under such circumstances as now exist, His militant army must ever be powerless to win those legislative battles which, more than any others, affect the happiness of aggregate humanity. But the light gleams already along the sunny hilltops of the nineteenth century of grace. Upon those who in largest numbers love Him who has filled their hearts with peace and their homes with blessing, slowly dawns the consciousness that they may — nay, better still, *they ought* to — ask for power to help forward the coming of their Lord in government; to throw the safeguard of their prohibition ballots around those who have left the shelter of their arms only to be entrapped by the saloons that bad men legalize and set along the streets.

" 'But some doubted.'

"This was in our earlier National Conventions. Almost none disputed the value of this added weapon in woman's hand — indeed, all deemed it 'sure to come.' It was only the old, old question of expediency; of 'frightening away our sisters among the more conservative.' But later on we asked these questions: Has the policy of silence caused a great rallying to our camp from the ranks of the conservative? Do you know an instance in which it has augmented your working force? Are not all the women upon whose help we can confidently count, favorable to the '*Do Everything Policy*,' as the only one broad enough to meet our hydra-headed foe? Have not the men of the liquor traffic said in platform, resolution, and secret circular, 'The ballot in woman's hand will be the death knell of our trade?'

"And so today, while each State *is free to adopt or disavow* the ballot as a home protection weapon, and although the white-winged fleet of the W. C. T. U. in a score of States crowds all sail for constitutional prohibition, to be followed up by 'Home Protection,' still though 'the silver sails are all out in the West,' every ship in the gleaming line is all the same a Gospel ship — an '*old ship Zion — Hallelujah!*'"

. . . .

No setting forth of the departmental system of the Woman's Christian Temperance Union would do it justice as does Miss Willard's practical, as well as spiritual, exposition of "The Crusade Psalm," the first Scripture read in connection with the Ohio Women's Whisky War.

THE CRUSADE PSALM.
(Psalm cxlvi.)

FOUNDATION TEXT:

"*In the name of our God we will set up our banners.*"— Psalm xx, 3.

ORIGIN

Every great movement has some one historic document on which it is based, and which forms the foundation of its "Evidences." The Christian Church has the Bible, the British Government has the Magna Charta, the American Republic has the Declaration of Independence, the colored race has the Emancipation Proclamation, the temperance world in general has the Total Abstinence Pledge, the Women's Crusade has the Crusade Psalm.

The Crusade Psalm has in it but ten verses, and yet it gives us the keynote, the rallying cry, the prophetic exhortation, the plan of work, and the song of victory in our holy war.

KEYNOTE:

"*Praise ye the Lord. Praise the Lord, O my soul.*"— Psalm cxlvi, 1.

This is the keynote. The word praise is translated in the margin by that magnificent marching word of the Hebrews, Hallelujah; so that the more correct rendering would be,

"Hallelujah to the Lord; Hallelujah to the Lord, O my soul; while I live will I sing Hallelujah to the Lord, I will sing Hallelujah unto my God while I have any being."

A more jubilant strain never clashed its golden cymbals on the ear of the triumphant host in the midst of the great day of rejoicing at the dedication of the temple; a more jubilant strain was not sung by Miriam and her maidens when the people of God had escaped forever out of the hands of their oppressors; nay, verily, the Crusade Psalm utters a higher note because its *Laus Deo* came before a single stroke of work had been wrought, or a single victory achieved. It was the keynote. It set the minds and hearts of the White Ribbon women at concert pitch. It claimed by faith that which was to be slowly and patiently wrought out in deeds. It was the Jericho shout over again, only here the voices were soprano rather than bass; nay, these were the musical tones of the home rather than the discordant blast of the ram's horn, or the clash of broken pitchers in the darkness.

It is a principle of Psychology no less than of Philosophy and Religion that the mental and spiritual attitudes of good cheer and heavenly expectation are the only ones that will ever claim, promote and capture victory. All leaders have been optimists — if there are lions in the way they do not see them, for their eyes are lifted "to the hills, whence cometh their help."

In the Woman's Christian Temperance Union it has been a custom in many of the conventions to urge upon the workers the adoption of this pledge: "I hereby solemnly promise, by the help of God, that I will seek to make it a rule of my life not to speak discouraging words about the work, or disparaging words about the workers."

It is only by preserving this mental and moral attitude toward those about us that we can ever hope to win, for God's laws written in our constitution have put an everlasting ban upon those who hold lugubrious views of life or disheartening opinions about the holy war in which they are enlisted soldiers. Whether we realize it or not, to do this is to be a traitor. We are in an army where "to doubt would be disloyalty, to falter would be sin." Let us not, then, pipe on our own little reed the discontent that the devil may whisper because it is his tune, but let us join our voices in the Hallelujah Chorus which calls bravely out: "In the name of our God we have set up our banners."

EXHORTATION.

"Put not your trust in princes, nor in the son of man, in whom there is no help.

"His breath goeth forth; he returneth to his earth; in that very day his thoughts perish.

"Happy is he that hath the God of Jacob for his help, whose hope is in the Lord his God;

"Which made heaven and earth, the sea and all that therein is; which keepeth truth forever."—Psalm cxlvi., 3-6.

This is the Exhortation, and some have said that it is in direct opposition to the genius of the Woman's Christian Temperance Union, which seeks to the utmost to enlist the "princes" in Church and State, and the "son of man" who forms the rank and file of that procession of political power which we expect some day to see added to the procession of the White Ribbon. But from one end of the good Book to the other we are taught that God works by means. Incarnation is the unchanging method of that progressive revelation by which we study Him in the Bible of revelation, the Bible of nature and the Bible of humanity.

To illustrate this in a homely fashion, consider the telegraph poles that perpetually run and race with the railroad train. How inconsequent, even grotesque, are these tall posts until one knows that across their tapering tops is laid a wire, in itself equally inconsequent, but which is connected with an electric battery so that the dull wire transmits messages of incalculable importance to the world. We believe that in like manner society and government are but the connecting wires of God's great telegraphic system, along which He sends the shock of power from His own heart. They are but the channels, conduits and conductors of His thought, purpose and affection.

If we put our trust in God, happy are we, for "He made heaven and earth, the sea and all that therein is ; He keepeth truth forever ;" and the "princes," and the "son of man" shall yet do His will, so that His kingdom shall come upon the earth.

He made the earth, and He will not always suffer it to be unredeemed. He made the earth just as truly as He made the heavens, and because these things are so we may well take for our keynote, "Hallelujah to the Lord." "Every plant that my Heavenly Father hath not planted shall be rooted up," says Christ. We have a "sure word of testimony," so we fight "not as one that beateth the air." "We know in whom we have believed."

The word "help" (in the third verse, "in whom there is not help,") is more literally translated in the margin as "salvation," and as the keynote of the Crusade army is Hallelujah, so is its keyword Salvation. It is not help alone we seek to give, for help is often both inadequate and temporary, but salvation saves; salvation knows no palliatives; salvation is thorough-going out and out; it is indeed ideal; it is the word of faith; it is the central thought of revelation. We must use that magic word in no diminished sense, but spread it to the utmost of its scope, and that makes it wide as the world, high as the hope of a saint, and deep as the depths of a drunkard's despair.

A famous minister once said to me, "If you would confine your ministrations to the reformation of drunkards, I could go with you, for I believe that is according to the Gospel plan; but when you take up such side issues as prohibition and the woman's ballot, my conscience obliges me to withdraw from the movement."

From the White Ribbon point of view this good man was wofully deluded. He took that great word "salvation," broad enough to flash across the whole heavens, and shut it up in the cell of his own preconceived notions.

But what does salvation mean to us? We believe in salvation first of all for the individual through a change of heart, "repentance toward God and faith in our Lord Jesus Christ"; but we believe that the drunkard might have been saved from drinking if he had been wisely drilled and disciplined when he was a little fellow. We believe that this salvation might have come to him in the quiet temple of the schoolhouse where the scientific temperance text-book taught him a "thus saith Nature, thus saith Reason, thus saith the Lord" for total abstinence.

We believe there is salvation for society from drink through the total abstinence propaganda and the Pauline doctrine of not making "my brother to offend."

We believe there is the salvation of God for the government in universal prohibition of the liquor traffic, the gambling house, the haunt of shame.

We believe there is the salvation of God for politics in the home vote for two which shall conduct to a white life for two, for we believe that "two heads in counsel" are the best working forces in the world for God and Home and Every Land.

PLAN OF WORK:

"*The Lord executeth judgment for the oppressed; the Lord giveth food to the hungry. The Lord looseth the prisoners:*

"*The Lord openeth the eyes of the blind; the Lord raiseth them that are bowed down: The Lord loveth the righteous:*

"*The Lord preserveth the strangers: He relieveth the fatherless and widow: but the way of the wicked He turneth upside down.*" Psalm cxlvi, 7-9.

Now comes the plan of work of the Woman's Christian Temperance Union.

More frequently than I have ever uttered any other single exhortation to my comrades, except that they should seek to be given up to the indwelling of the Spirit, has been the exhortation that they should give their best and keenest thought to the three verses given above, for if its members would do this no local union need ever be at a loss as to "the next thing" that it ought to undertake.

In the reading and study of these verses, freighted like a boat carried to the water's edge by the greatness of its cargo, we should emphasize in every instance those words, "The Lord." I have heard the psalm read innumerable times with this Name of names hurried over in the most casual manner, but it is the key to the position. "The Lord executeth judgment for the oppressed," but He does so through courts and customs and through intervention of those who have His love in their hearts.

For instance: In the first year of my Temperance work I remember reaching home late in the evening from a trip, and saying to mother as I bade her goodnight, "I am going to Niles, Michigan, tomorrow, and must be up and off early, so do not try to see me in the morning." Whereupon with that wise smile I so tenderly recall, she replied, "You will be off early, indeed, if you get ahead of me, for I take the five o'clock train to ——— where several of the officers of our Evanston W. C. T. U. (she was then president) are going to stand by a poor woman whose husband whipped her when he was drunk, and who said if we would rally around her she would then have the courage to testify against him under the Civil Damage Act." That was mother's practical interpretation of the plan of work in our Crusade Psalm where it says "The Lord executeth judgment for the oppressed." To my mind, whatever relates to the protection of the defenseless who come within the circle of our knowledge is a part of our plan of work under its first specification. The families of those who drink are the most likely to suffer from the conduct of those who "are not themselves," but are "crazy on purpose," and I have always felt that we should regard them as our special charge. In many States, homes for the children of the drunkard have been established by our societies, and our department of "Homes for Homeless Children" is meant to help cover this ground. The "Department of Mercy" (for the prevention of cruelty to animals) comes under the same general classification.

The Lord giveth food to the hungry.

I once heard a stirring exposition of this verse from a famous Crusader who said, "We women were so hungry for this Temperance work that God gave it to us in His own good time!" but the larger scope of the passage includes every form of service that we can render to those who are hungry in body or soul. The Saxon word "Lady" means "Giver of bread"; we must be that, but we ought to be much more. "Giver of the bread of life" should be a definition including the loaf in one hand and the New Testament and Total Abstinence pledge in the other.

The Lord looseth the prisoners.

The great work for the reformation of drinking men and women comes in here; the Blue Ribbon movement, the Red Ribbon movement, the Good Templars, Sons of Temperance, and other societies, the Homes for inebriates, the various "Cures" founded for the reformation of the drunkard, but most of all that "loosing of the prisoners," which comes from the "expulsive power of a Divine affection," so that a New Testament replaces the flask in the side pocket of the drinking man, and he bends upon his knees in prayer instead of bowing hopelessly over the bar. No society ever did more for the reformation of the drunkard than the W. C. T. U. We have tried all means; we must ignore none, but let us always exalt "the power of God unto salvation to everyone that believeth," remembering Him who said, "And I, if I be lifted up, will draw all men unto me."

Our work for the prisoners includes not only those who are under the bond of drink, but those who are prisoners of the tobacco habit, the habit of personal impurity, the gambling passion, or any of those curses of life which center in the dramshop; nor must we forget that there is now hardly a prison, jail or penitentiary between the oceans that is not visited by the White Ribbon women with the Gospel in their hands, the helpful Bible-reading, the leaflet, *The Union Signal* and *The Young Crusader*, and the little bunch of posies with its Scripture text, through which we often find the heart we should otherwise have missed. Our Flower Mission department fits into this niche of our "plan" more fully, perhaps, than any other.

The Lord openeth the eyes of the blind.

When we read the Scripture we are inclined to give it away with a liberal hand to those about us; indeed there is nothing with which we are so generous. We hope that Mr. —— will take note of that passage, "he is a stingy man and needs to listen to it." We hope that Mrs. —— will "take heed to her gabbling tongue," and so on and so on. But for myself I have always felt that the plan of work set forth in this passage, "The Lord openeth the eyes of the blind," applied very particularly to my own case, for though I early became a member of the church of God, and was brought up a teetotaler, my blind eyes had not been opened to see the duty and privilege of a Christian woman to be an active worker in the temperance reform until the great Crusade in the West, wheeling onward in its mighty course, caught me up in one of its outermost eddies on an Illinois prairie, and brought me forevermore to the goodly fellowship of those whose eyes were opened to see that "Christianity applied" is the only thing that will bring salvation and set the Hallelujah Chorus rolling around the world. To open the eyes of the blind we needed the Woman's Temperance Publishing Association, with its great weekly newspaper, its books and pamphlets, its leaflets and responsive readings, its prohibition literature of every sort and kind, its social purity department, its woman suffrage leaflets, its well filled and fitted arsenal of temperance weapons. If the local unions did nothing else but exploit these leaves, saturated through and through as they have been by the spirit of the Gospel, that would be work enough to make their record hallowed. The press department, seeking to reach and utilize the plant of the newspaper, both religious and secular, in every town and village, is one of our mightiest engines of power. The Scientific Temperance Instruction for the children and the youth in colleges has no peer in power, but it rests largely with the local union to make that department a success or a failure. The Young Women's Work, the Loyal Temperance Legion, and the Department of Mercy are skillful openers of "the eyes of the blind." What is the local union doing to build up these departments into beautiful allies? The study of hygiene, physical culture and sanitary cookery, the splendid outlook of the Sunday-school work, the circulation of literature among foreigners, the presentation of our cause to influential bodies, and its relation to capital and labor; the school of parliamentary usage, all these come under the head of "opening the eyes of the blind."

Here, too, belong our great affiliated interests. The Woman's Temple, that object lesson in brick and mortar of woman's faith and prayer; the Woman's Temperance Publishing Association, that prophecy of her future power; and the National Temperance Hospital, which is proving daily to a gainsaying world that alcohol is not an essential remedy for all the ills that flesh is heir to. What has so fully opened the blind eyes of the world to woman's work and worth as these great enterprises?

The "opening of the eyes of the blind," comes not only through the varied channels of which an outline has been given, but the printed page is strongly reinforced by means of the earnest, logical and persuasive voice.

The Lord raiseth them that are bowed down.

This includes our work for the defective, dependent and delinquent classes. The departments are so numerous that I will not undertake to name them all. In our Annual Leaflet all may read the list of those blessed endeavors grouped under the head of evangelistic and social work.

The Lord loveth the righteous.

It seems as if this declaration were interpolated as a note of affectionate encouragement to those who, notwithstanding their failures and faults, nevertheless feel in their inmost souls that they do seek righteousness. Let any among us who are downcast remember that the will is the king-bolt of the faculties, and if the will is set toward God we must not be discouraged though the emotion often fail us.

We judge the direction of a stream not from its shallows but by its current, not by its eddies, but by that deep and steady trend that bears its waters straight onward to the sea.

The Lord preserveth the strangers.

To my mind this plan of work includes all those efforts, varied and manifold, whereby White Ribbon women have merited the characterization given them by a desolate woman whose son they saved from the death trap of a village on the far frontier, the local society away yonder having been written to by the local society in her own town. She said, "What it amounts to is that as you have ten thousand local unions, every boy in this country has ten times ten thousand mothers willing to look after him and help him to the good." The temperance hotel, the temperance restaurant, the club, the Gospel temperance meeting, the homelike mass-meeting, the sociable, the red-letter days and the ingenious, witty inventions of our wise "Y" societies for the purpose of helping young men to overcome temptation—all these are specifications of that branch of our plan of work through which "He preserveth the strangers."

He relieveth the fatherless and the widow.

In our work we give a broader meaning, for we deal with those who are worse than widowed and more forlorn than if they had been fatherless. This line of effort takes us into the disintegrated, dismantled homes that are the necessary outcome of the liquor traffic. Industrial homes for boys and girls have been founded in many of the States through the efforts of our society, and ought to be in all. There is not a State or Territory in the Union in which the united efforts of the W. C. T. U. for a single year would not suffice to found such an institution. Among the happiest incidents of the twelve years that I was continually on the war-path helping to found the society, I reckon those when I have been present at the laying of the corner stone of some beneficent institution, where the trowel has been placed in the hand of the State President of the W. C. T. U. by good men who were our helpers in the legislature and outside of it, and who felt a pride in having women officiate on the occasion, because they knew these women were the real workers who had won from the powers that be the wherewithal

MISS WILLARD IN HER "DEN," REST COTTAGE, 1890.

THE POLYGLOT PETITION—SEVEN MILLION SIGNATURES

to bless tempted lives by a new institution which would put honorable bread-winning weapons in the hands of those whose home help had failed them utterly.

The way of the wicked He turneth upside down.

This is the climax, the keystone of the arch of our beautiful and holy endeavor. It means prohibition by law, prohibition by politics, prohibition by woman's ballot. In Ohio the heroic band of veterans who constitute the State W. C. T. U. have taken this passage as their motto, and they are entitled to it as the leaders of our growing host, for they have "borne and labored, and had patience," since the pentecost of God fell on them in those fifty days of the Crusade which, in the winter of 1873-74, routed the liquor traffic "horse, foot and dragoons" in two hundred and fifty towns and villages. The figure in the passage is complete, for "the way of the wicked" is to be "turned upside down"; then the traffic is to be completely overthrown, and nothing less will ever satisfy the World's White Ribbon Host. "The Old Guard never surrenders," for while we have no harsh criticism for good people who adopt less drastic methods of reform, the White Ribbon Women will say at last, as they felt called to say at first of prohibition: "Here I stand, I can do no other, God help me. Amen." And we do this because we believe that what is physically wrong can never be morally right; what is morally wrong can never be legally right; what is legally wrong can never be politically right.

Song of Victory:

The Lord shall reign forever, even thy God, O Zion, unto all generations. Praise ye the Lord.

This is our song of victory: "The Lord shall reign forever." It is beginning to seem nearer in its fulfillment than when, twenty-one years ago, we first raised its notes in faith. The White Ribbon has already "conquered many nations." That crusade fire, kindled of God, has spread, till in more than forty countries it is burning today. The great Petition, with its seven and one-half million signatures and attestations asking for the abolition of the liquor traffic in all nations, is soon to be carried round the world. The World's Woman's Christian Temperance Union, with its glorious motto, "For God and Home and Every Land," is an assured fact — an element in the world's regeneration which can never be overlooked.

The noontide hour of prayer, like England's drum-beat, circles the globe. Everywhere and at every hour there are hearts uplifted in petition to Him who shall "reign forever." He is reigning now in the brain and heart of those who are consecrated to Him in the service of humanity. He to whom one day is a thousand years, and a thousand years as one day; He who sees the end from the beginning and the beginning from the end, looks down upon the earth, and there is not a saloon, a gambling house, a haunt of infamy anywhere to be found, so that from God's point of view all that we see has already come to pass and it is for us to behold the same picture in the outlook of our Christian faith, and to make true, so far as in us lies, on the plane of material cause and effect in the everyday world, that which, in our faith-filled moments, we have beheld on the Mount of Vision.

> "Faith, mighty faith, the promise sees
>   And looks to that alone;
> Laughs at impossibilities
>   And cries, It shall be done."

CHAPTER IX

FOUNDER OF THE WORLD'S WOMAN'S CHRISTIAN TEMPERANCE UNION

FRANCES E. WILLARD was a patriot of patriots. Love for her fatherland, breathed into her as a child, waxed stronger as the years passed by until it became a passion, and her home-loving heart turned more and more to her "ain countrie." But she could never be a patriot in the sense in which love for one's own excludes love for all other countries, and as her affection for her native land deepened and broadened, it included all other lands until she exultantly heralded the coming day when Humanity will recognize its brotherhood not in word only, but in deed — when "the parliament of man, the federation of the world" shall be more than a poet's dream — a gloriously established fact.

Miss Willard's first public mention of her aspiration toward a world-wide organization of Christian women was made in 1875, in *Our Union*, then the official organ of the National W. C. T. U. But the time was evidently not ripe for such a movement. Seven years later, in 1883, Miss Willard wrote: "On an organizing trip to the Pacific Coast and the Puget Sound region we visited the famous 'Chinatown' of San Francisco, saw the opium den in all its loathsome completeness standing next door to the house of shame. Reputable Chinese women were not allowed to accompany their husbands to California, but here were Chinese girls, one in each of many small cabins with sliding doors and windows on the street, constituting the most flagrantly flaunted temptation that we had ever witnessed. In presence of these two object lessons, the result of occidental avarice and oriental degradation, there came to me a distinct illumination resulting in this solemn decision:

'But for the intrusion of the sea, the shores of China and the far East would be part and parcel of our land. We are one world of tempted humanity. The mission of the White Ribbon women is to organize the motherhood of the world for the peace and purity, the protection and exaltation of its homes. We must send forth a clear call to our sisters yonder, and our brothers, too. We must be no longer hedged about by the artificial boundaries of states and nations; we must utter, as women, what good and great men long ago declared as their watchword: "The whole world is my parish and to do good my religion."

"In my Annual Address the next autumn at Detroit, this, which I believe to be one of those revelations from God that come to us all in hours of special spiritual uplift, was frankly placed before my comrades who, although they had no special enthusiasm, agreed to have the five General Officers constitute a committee to see what could be done. Two months later, Mrs. Mary Clement Leavitt, of Boston, Massachusetts, who was already one of our National Organizers, and who was on her way to the Pacific Coast when the sights of San Francisco had burned themselves into my brain, had accepted a commission to make a tour of reconnoissance around the world. . . . . A year after Mrs. Leavitt's departure, while following her in my thought, I read a book on the opium trade in India and China, and under the impulse of its unspeakable recitals I wrote the Polyglot Petition, feeling that she must have not only the Crusade story to tell, with its sober second thought of organization under the W. C. T. U., the plan of organization to describe, the white ribbon to pin above ten thousand faithful women's hearts, the noon hour of prayer to impress upon their spirits the sense of that divine impulse which alone can give an enduring enthusiasm in any cause — but she must speak to them of something to be done, and to be done at once, in which all could alike engage in England, America, the Oriental nations, the islands of the sea and, so far as possible, in the continent of Europe, whose great wine-growing countries render it the least and last of all in Temperance reform. A petition against the liquor traffic and the opium trade asking that the statutes of the world should be lifted to the level of Christian morals realized to my thought 'the tie that binds' thousands of hearts and hands in one common work, for the uplift of humanity, and included that 'White Life for Two,' which has since become an integral part of our work."

The Round-the-World White Ribbon Missionaries who have since gone out under the banner of the World's W. C. T. U. are Miss Jessie Ackermann, of California, who honeycombed Australasia with local Unions, federating them into a National W. C. T. U. of their own, of which she became President; she also traversed all the Oriental countries, and in her seven years of journeying covered a distance nearly equal to seven times round the world; Mrs. Elizabeth Wheeler Andrew and Dr. Kate C. Bushnell, of Evanston, Illinois, whose work resulted in the breaking down of the system of legalized vice in the Indian Empire and brought to light the hidden things of darkness in the opium trade of India and China; Miss Mary Allen West, of Illinois, who fell at her post in far-away Japan after a few weeks of heroic exertion, leaving a memory hallowed by all good people in the beautiful Empire; Miss Clara Parrish, the first missionary who has gone out from the ranks of the young women and who has taken up the work where Miss West laid it down; Miss Alice Palmer, who remained nearly three years in South Africa, placing the W. C. T. U. of that great country on a firm and enduring basis; and Mrs. J. K. Barney, of Rhode Island, who has just returned from a trip to the Hawaiian Islands, Australasia, Ceylon and the Holy Land. Several others are under appointment, and the world's Union is now organized in fifty nations — in America (North and South), Europe, Asia, Africa, Australia, and many islands of the sea.

Our leader, to whom belonged from first to last the inspiration and the plan of this great society, was long ago described in the words of the apostle, "Always [she was] looking for and hastening unto the coming of the day of our Lord."

The Polyglot Petition is a notable instance of her power to pierce the future and her ability to plan for generations yet unborn.

Miss Willard named this document "The Polyglot Petition for Home Protection," and addressed it, "To the Governments of the World (Collectively and Severally.)" The following is its text:

"*Honored Rulers, Representatives, and Brothers:*

"We, your petitioners, although belonging to the physically weaker sex, are strong of heart to love our homes, our native land, and the world's family of nations. We know that clear brains and pure hearts make honest lives and happy homes, and that by these the nations prosper and the time is brought nearer when the world shall be at peace. We know that indulgence in alcohol and opium, and in other vices which disgrace our social life, makes misery for all the world, and most of all for us and for our children. We know that stimulants and opiates are sold under legal guarantees which make the governments partners in the traffic by accepting as revenue a portion of the profits, and we know with shame that they are often forced by treaty upon populations either ignorant or unwilling. We know that the law might do much now left undone to raise the moral tone of society and render vice difficult. We have no power to prevent these great iniquities, beneath which the whole world groans, but you have power to redeem the honor of the nations from an indefensible complicity. We, therefore, come to you with the united voices of representative women of every land, beseeching you to raise the standard of the law to that of Christian morals, to strip away the safeguards and sanctions of the State from the drink traffic and the opium trade, and to protect our homes by the total prohibition of these curses of civilization throughout all the territory over which your Government extends."

This petition, written in Miss Willard's workshop in Evanston in the year 1884, was first presented to a convention by Mrs. Mary Bannister Willard, at the International Temperance Congress in Antwerp, Belgium, September 12, 1885. At the first convention of the world's W. C. T. U., its significant folds draped the walls of historic Faneuil Hall, Boston, and in Tremont Temple during the session of the National Convention immediately following. Its first public presentation was in Washington, D. C., February 15, 1895, where it decorated the great Convention Hall holding seven thousand persons. Miss Willard's masterly address on that occasion, which embodies a complete history of the petition up to that time, is here largely reproduced:

"Home protection is the keyword of woman's work. Manufacturers seek the tariff for the purpose of protection to industries, adult and infant; trades unions are founded to protect the wage-earners from the aggressions of capital, and corporations and monopolies to protect from the encroachment of competition; but ten thousand groups of loyal-hearted mothers and wives, sisters and daughters have been formed for the purpose of acting in an organized capacity as protectors of their homes, as guardians for innocent childhood and tempted youth. For this cause 'there are bands of ribbon white around the world,' and this Polyglot Petition is but our prayer that 'tells out' a purpose of our hearts and heads wrought into a plea before the nations of the world. It is the protest of the world's wifehood and motherhood, its sisterhood and daughterhood — a protest 'in sorrow, not in anger.'

"We expect to present this petition to representatives of every civilized government. This cannot be done in the usual form, because when once received this Magna Charta of the home would become the property of the various legislatures and parliaments, and our plan requires that it be conveyed from one to another. We are also aware that in a legal and technical sense no government accepts the signatures of those outside its own boundaries. We have therefore preferred to make our petition a great popular testimonial against the enemies of the home, but we expect that its presentation will give an added impetus to progressive legislation against the liquor traffic, the opium trade, the gambling den, and the house of shame. For, while the last two are not specifically named, they are so closely interwoven with the traffic in alcohol and opium that the spirit of the petition necessarily includes them all.

"The Woman's Christian Temperance Union has circulated many petitions. The number of signatures and attestations secured throughout the world to our different petitions in the last twenty years aggregates not fewer than fifteen million of names—probably twenty millions would be nearer the truth. In this estimate I include the memorials and petitions for Scientific Temperance Education in the public schools; also for laws raising the age of consent and otherwise involving the better protection of women, not to speak of the anti-cigarette crusade and numberless local petitions circulated by the faithful hands of White Ribbon women. We are, therefore, veterans in our knowledge of petition work, and for this reason are perfectly aware that the best outcome of such undertakings is the agitation and consequent education that comes to those who affix their signatures, or who by resolution make the prayer of the petition their own. For example, in the State of Illinois, in 1878, we circulated a 'Home Protection Petition,' asking that 'since woman is the born conservator of home, and the nearest natural protector of her children, she should have a voice in the decision by which the dramshop is opened or is closed over against her home.' Two hundred thousand names were secured in a few weeks, some of us traveling from town to town for this purpose, and remaining for months at Springfield, the capital, in the hope that the Legislature would adopt the 'Hinds bill,' based upon this righteous plea.

"I need not say that we were wholly unsuccessful with that Legislature. Not for that end was it born; not for that cause did it sit in the great Statehouse among the cornfields of the Prairie State and near the tomb of the immortal Abraham Lincoln. On the contrary, it was a Legislature chosen for no other purpose so explicitly as to legislate in the interest of the Peoria distillery, the Chicago brewery, and the Illinois saloons in which the 'middle men' of those great monopolies dealt out their deadly product. But the reflex influence of the petition work upon the home-folk of Illinois was such that under our local option law, in six hundred out of eight hundred towns, the popular vote that year was registered against the dramshop, a larger percentage of temperance votes, I grieve to add, than my State had ever cast before or has cast since up to this day.

"We prize the Polyglot Petition work because it has afforded a nucleus around which women may rally. It has furnished immediate work to new and distant societies which was essential to their success. The petition has also been the peg upon which have been hung paragraphs and presentation speeches, sermons and songs in every part of Christendom — and the end is not yet; nay, the beginning is hardly here. Because we are patriots we have come to the capital of our native land to present this petition, first of all, in the country in which it originated, and which has sent out all the White Ribbon missionaries who have secured its circulation in foreign countries. The greatest number of names, indorsements, and attestations has been secured in our own country, and next to ours in Great Britain. Miss Gwellian Morgan, of Wales, has superintended this work in the mother country, under the untiring and efficient leadership of the President.

"We greatly regret that none of our Round-the-World missionaries could be present on this occasion, toward which they and we have looked forward so long, and which their faithful work has alone made possible. . . . .

"Time would fail me to tell of the earnest women who have circulated this petition in every nation. We could not have secured signatures in Oriental countries, but for the co-operation of the denominational missionaries, who have been most faithful and devoted.

"The labor of sending out blank petitions for signatures was largely carried on by our lamented Mrs. Mary A. Woodbridge, of Chicago, Corresponding Secretary of the World's and National W. C. T. U. They were gathered in and acknowledged by Miss Alice E. Briggs, for years the Office Secretary of the World's W. C. T. U., at the Temple, Chicago, and were mounted on white muslin by Mrs. Rebecca C. Shuman, of Evanston, Illinois, the seat of Northwestern University. The dimensions of the task which Mrs. Shuman undertook may be imagined from the fact that the aggregate of time she has already spent amounts to about two years of steady work. The signatures came to hand in fifty languages; they were of all sorts and sizes, and were to be trimmed and prepared for mounting as compactly as possible on interminable webs of muslin, one-half yard in width, one edge of which is bound with red, the other with blue ribbon — red, white and blue being the prevalent colors of the flags of all nations and the symbolic badges of the great temperance movement of modern times.

"The names are necessarily mounted somewhat irregularly, but they average four columns abreast, making, in reality, a quadruple petition, with about one hundred names to the yard in each column. Mrs. Shuman has now mounted 1,928 yards, or over one mile of canvas — making five miles of names written solidly, one under the other — 771,200 in all. This is exclusive of about 350,000 names that came from Great Britain already mounted, making the total of 1,121,200 actual names on the document that will be submitted to President Cleveland. Besides these, there are hundreds of thousands of names yet waiting to be added to the long roll. Nor will we ever rest until we have 2,000,000 actual names, besides the present 5,000,000 additional signers by attestation.

"It must be remembered that the signatures to this petition are of three kinds. First, the names of women; second, the written indorsements of men; third, the attestations of officers of societies which have indorsed the petition by resolution or otherwise. The document has been circulated in fifty nations, and in the three ways stated has received over 7,000,000 signatures. The total number of actual signers from outside the United States is 480,000. Great Britain, with Lady Henry Somerset's name at the head, leads the procession with its 350,000. Canada comes next with 67,000. Burmah with 32,000, and Ceylon, Australia, Denmark, China, India and Mexico follow, with all the others coming after.

"Though this is a woman's petition, it should be noted that it is indorsed by perhaps 1,000,000 men — some by personal signatures, but the greater number by the attestation of the officers of societies to which they belong. Even from far-off Ceylon, which we are accustomed to think of as a small island of dusky savages, come the signatures of 27,000 men who call for the cessation of the liquor and opium traffic. The following are the countries represented by this Petition:

United States. — Forty-four States, five Territories and Alaska.
Canada. — Nova Scotia, New Brunswick, Prince Edward Island, Quebec, Ontario, Manitoba, British Columbia.
Newfoundland.
Mexico.
Jamaica.
Bahamas.
Madeira.
South America. — Brazil, Chile, Uruguay.
Europe. — England, Scotland, Ireland, Wales, France, Holland, Belgium, Denmark, Norway, Sweden, Spain, Russia, Finland, Turkey, Bulgaria.
Asia. — China, Japan, India, Burmah, Siam, Corea, Ceylon.
Africa. — Egypt, Congo Free State, Transvaal, West and South Africa, Angola.
Madagascar.
Mozambique.
Australia. — Victoria, South Australia, Queensland, New South Wales.
Tasmania.
New Zealand.
Micronesia.
Hawaiian Islands.

"To enumerate the languages in whose characters the beliefs of women have been recorded in this far-reaching document, would be to make a list of almost every tongue that has survived the confusion of Babel. There are columns of Chinese women's signatures that look like houses that Jack built. There is a list of Burmese signatures resembling bunches of 'tangled worms.' The thousands upon thousands from the spicy Isle of Ceylon are enough to make a shorthand man shudder; the incomprehensible but liquid vowels of the Hawaiian Kanaka jostle the proud names of English ladies of high degree; the Spanish of haughty senoras of Madrid makes the same plea as the 'her mark' of the converted woman of the Congo. There are Spanish names from Mexico and the South American Republics, French from Martinique, Dutch from Natal and English from New Zealand, besides the great home petition from the greater nations. The total, counting men's and women's signatures, indorsements and attestations, aggregates seven and one-half millions.

"In making this petition, we claim we are entirely constitutional, inasmuch as the right to sign 'has not been denied or abridged on account of race, color, or previous condition of servitude.' Perhaps this is the reason why we have secured many names of reformed men, and why Catholic, Protestant and pagan have all been represented.

"It would be invidious to mention the names of signers, but they represent every grade of human life, and the great procession is headed by the name of Neal Dow, the father of prohibitory law, who signed when over ninety years of age, and who is hale and hearty, and would be with us tonight but for the severity of the weather in his own piney woods of Maine. Scientists teach that every signature involves some touch of personality, not only in the appearance of the autograph itself, but by the impartation of individual particles that surround everyone, and which project themselves into every deed that we perform. That this is true is more than likely, so that when we consider that every nation, tribe and people of the earth, almost, is represented; when we reflect that these infinitely varied autographs representing persons born and bred under equally varying conditions have found in this petition against the greatest curses of the world their focusing point, there is reason to believe that by God's good providence we have in the Polyglot Petition the promise and potency of the better time when by the personal interdict of a higher intelligence and the conclusive law of social custom the sale of intoxicating drinks and opium shall be banned and banished from the world. In that day the laws for which the great petition asks and which we believe must be enacted as the most cogent means of education for the people, will no longer be required, but every human being will enact in the legislature of his own intellect a prohibitory law for one and enforce that law by the executive of his own will.

"'It will come by and by, when the race out of childhood has grown.'

"It is more than ten years since the petition was written; if I had to rewrite it I should assuredly include the enfranchisement of women among the requisites it specifies, for I believe that our Heavenly Father will not suffer men alone to work out the great redemption of the race from the bewilderment of drink, the hallucination of opium and the brutal delirium of impurity. Hand in hand we have traversed the Sahara of ignorance and escaped from the City of Destruction; hand in hand let us mount the heights of knowledge, purity and peace."

The personal presentation of the petition to President Cleveland at the White House was made on the afternoon of February 19, the General Officers of the World's and National W. C. T. U. with the President of the White Ribboners of the District of Columbia being granted an interview at the Executive Mansion. Miss Willard spoke as follows:

"Mr. President: The Polyglot Petition, addressed to the governments of the world, and calling for the prohibition of the traffic in alcoholic liquors as a drink, the prohibition of the opium traffic and all forms of legalized social vice, has been signed by half a million citizens of this Republic; by means of signatures, indorsements and attestations it includes seven and a half million adherents in fifty different nationalities. This petition has been circulated by the World's Woman's Christian Temperance Union, and will be presented to all the leading governments. Inasmuch as the petition originated and has been most largely signed in the United States, it is hereby respectfully brought to your attention, not on any legal ground, but because it is addressed to the governments of the world, and you are the executive chief of this Government."

After placing a copy of the petition in the President's hands, the Recording Secretary of the National W. C. T. U. read the document with remarkable impressiveness, and Miss Willard resumed:

"Mr. President: We are aware that the petition just read in your hearing cannot come before you as a legal document, but rather as an expression of the opinion and sentiment of a great multitude of your countrywomen who believe that if its prayer were granted the better protection of the home would be secured. Knowing how difficult it was for you to grant us this hearing at a time when you are even more than usually weighted with great responsibilities, we have foreborne to bring the Great Petition to the White House. Permit me to hand you this attested copy and to thank you on behalf of this delegation, representing the Woman's Christian Temperance Union in this and other lands, for the kind reception you have given to our delegation."

In the following spring the petition was taken to London and was the central feature of the Third Biennial Convention of the World's W. C. T. U. In Prince Albert Hall, where the monster demonstration meeting was held, its countless folds encircled galleries and platform like a huge white ribbon into which had been woven the symbolic badges of the great host of women who in every land are publishing the tidings of purity and total abstinence. Lady Henry Somerset presented to Her Majesty, Queen Victoria, two richly bound and illuminated volumes containing the text of the petition with the signatures of such of her royal subjects as were among its signers.

In 1897 the great rolls crossed the ocean again to adorn Massey Music Hall, Toronto, on the occasion of the Fourth World's W. C. T. U. Convention. It was Miss Willard's earnest desire to assist in presenting the petition to the Canadian Government, and one of her last dictated messages during her illness in New York City concerned its future destiny. She has left it as a precious legacy to her White Ribbon sisters as well as an object lesson to the world of the marvelous dimensions to which an idea may attain. The Convention at Toronto was our leader's last active work for the World's Union. Her faith in the ultimate outcome of twenty-four years of heroic struggle shone with undimmed luster, and never was it more clearly apparent that she held in her little hand both ends of the white ribbon that belts the globe.

Following Miss Willard's "Summing up of the whole matter" concerning the "Organized Mother-Love" of the World's W. C. T. U., we publish her last message to her White Ribbon sisters the world around — the address which, as President of the Society, she delivered before the Fourth Biennial Convention in Toronto on the morning of October 23, 1897.

"THE SUMMING-UP OF THE WHOLE MATTER."

Humanly speaking, such a success as the Woman's Christian Temperance Union has attained has resulted from the following policy and methods:

1. The simplicity and unity of the organization. The local union is a miniature of the national, having similar officiary and plan of work. It is a military company carefully mustered, officered, and drilled. The county union is but an aggregation of the local, and the districts of the counties, while each State is a regiment, and the national itself is womanhood's Grand Army of the Home.

2. Individual responsibility is everywhere urged. "Committees" are obsolete with us, and each distinct line of work has one person, called a superintendent, who is responsible for its success. She may secure such lieutenants as she likes, but the Union looks to her for results, and holds her accountable for failures.

3. The quick and cordial recognition of talent is another secret of W. C. T. U. success. Women, young or old, who can speak, write, conduct meetings, organize, keep accounts, interest

children, talk with the drinking man, get up entertainments, or carry flowers to the sick or imprisoned, are all pressed into the service.

There has been also in our work an immense amount of digging in the earth to find one's own buried talent, to rub off the rust, and to put it out at interest. Perhaps this is, after all, its most significant feature, considered as a movement.

4. Subordination of the financial phase has helped, not hindered us. Lack of funds has not barred out even the poorest from our sisterhood. A penny per week is the general basis of membership, of which a fraction goes to state, national and world's unions.

Money has been, and I hope may be, a consideration altogether secondary. Of wealth we have had incomputable stores; indeed, I question if there exists a richer corporation today than ours — wealth of faith, of enthusiasm, of experience, of brain, of speech, of common sense. This is a capital stock that can never depreciate, needs no insurance, requires no combination lock or bonded custodian, and puts us under no temptation to tack our course or trim our sails.

There are two indirect results of this organized work among women, concerning which I wish to speak:

First: It is a very strong nationalizing influence. Its method and spirit differ very little, whether you study them in Boston or Bombay. In South Africa and South Carolina White Ribbon women speak the same vernacular; tell of their Gospel meetings and petitions; discuss the *Union Signal* editorials, and wonder "what will be the action of our next Convention."

Almost all of the other groups of women workers who dot the continent are circumscribed by denominational lines, and act largely under the advice of ecclesiastical leaders. The W. C. T. U. feels no such limitation.

Second: Our W. C. T. U. is a school, not founded in that thought, or for that purpose, but sure to fit us for the duties of patriots in the realm that lies beyond the horizon of the coming century.

Here we try our wings that yonder our flight may be strong and steady. Here we prove our capacity for great deeds; there we shall perform them. Here we make our experience and pass our novitiate, that yonder we may calmly take our places and prove to the world that what it needed most was "two heads in counsel" as well as "two beside the hearth." When that has come the nation shall no longer miss as now the influence of half its wisdom, more than half its purity, and nearly all its gentleness, in courts of justice and halls of legislation. Then shall one code of morals — and that the highest — govern both men and women; then shall the Sabbath be respected, the rights of the poor be recognized, the liquor traffic banished, and the home protected from all its foes.

Born of such a visitation of God's Spirit as the world has not known since tongues of fire sat upon the wondering group at Pentecost, cradled in a faith high as the heart of a saint, and deep as the depths of a drunkard's despair, and baptized in the beauty of holiness, the Crusade determined the ultimate goal of its teachable child, the Woman's Christian Temperance Union, which has one steadfast aim, and that none other than the regnancy of Christ, not in form, but in fact; not in substance, but in essence; not ecclesiastically, but truly in the hearts of men. To this end its methods are varied, changing, manifold, but its unwavering faith these words express: "Not by might, nor by power, but by My Spirit, saith the Lord of Hosts."

When I consider the work already accomplished by the World's White Ribboners, the sacred meaning of our society is a thought well-nigh overwhelming. Your kind hands that I feign would clasp, have been placed on the heads of little children of whom we have half a million in our Loyal Temperance Legions; they have given out total abstinence pledges to a million tempted men; they have pinned the ribbon white, as the talisman of purity, above the hearts of ten thousand tempted prodigals; they have carried bread to the hungry, and broken the bread of life to those who were most hungry of all for that, although they knew it not. These hands have carried petitions for the protection of the home, for the preservation of the Sabbath, for the purification of the law, and during twenty-one years of such honest, hard work, as was rarely, if ever, equaled, they have gathered not fewer than twenty million names to these petitions. Your friendly faces have bent over the bedsides of the dying, for whose souls no one seemed to care; they have illumined with the light that never shone on sea or shore many a dark tenement house in attic and cellar; they have gleamed like stars of hope in the darkest slums of our great cities. Your voices have sung songs of deliverance to the prisoners in ten thousand jails and almshouses; they have brought a breath of cheer into police courts, bridewells and houses of detention all around the world.

Your willing feet are more familiar with rough than with smooth pavements. You know the byways better than the highways. If all your errands could be set in order they would read like the litany of God's deliverance to those bound in the chains of temptation, sorrow and sin. Some touch of all that you have seen and done chastens each forehead and hallows every face. God has helped you to build better than you knew. If White Ribbon women had their way — and they intend to have it — the taint of alcohol and nicotine would not be on any lip, or in any atmosphere of city, town or village on this globe. If they had their way — and they intend to have it — no gambler could with impunity pursue his vile vocation. If they had their way, the haunts of shame that are the zero mark of degradation would be crusaded out of existence before sundown, and the industrial status of women would be so independent that the recruiting officers of perdition would seek in vain for victims. If you could have your way, the keeper of the dramshop would become in every state and nation, as, thank God, he is already in so many, a legal outcast, a political Ishmaelite, a social pariah on the face of the earth, for you do not seek the regulation of the traffic, nor its prohibition, even, but its annihilation.

Among the reflex influences by which this temperance work has broadened my own outlook and enriched my hopes, I must speak of the sweet and tender lessons of White Ribbon homes that have sheltered me. I have learned how such solemn vicissitudes as come into the lives of women only, help to confirm your faith in the world invisible. The breath of eternity falls on your foreheads like baptismal dew in those hours of unutterable pain and danger when a little child is born into your home. Your steps lie along the border-land of this closely curtained world.

"And palpitates the veil between
With breathings almost heard."

Into your eyes fall the first mystic glances of innocent and trusting souls. Tender little hands folded in prayer, and winsome voices saying,

"Gentle Jesus, meek and mild,
Look upon a little child,"

have done more than all traditional restraints to keep your hearts loving and unworldly. Always this will be so; always from manhood's more exterior view of life's significance you are separated by the deepest and most sacred experiences which human hearts may know. That anchor holds. But God has given the mother-heart for purposes of wider blessing to humanity than it has dreamed as yet. Let us go gently forward until that loving, faithful heart shall be enthroned in the places of power; until the queens of home are queens indeed.

And, best of all, the hand of Him whose Gospel has lifted us up into the heavenly places in Christ Jesus, of Him who was a brother to the Marys, and who, in His hour of mortal agony, did not forget His mother — that pierced hand points the way.

GREETING.

Beloved Comrades from Many Lands:

Nothing more pleasant can be said by old friends as they recount cherished scenes of long ago than the warm-hearted phrase of explanation, "We were brought up together." Thinking of you more often than you know, seeing your illumined faces in the golden glow of fancy, feeling the clasp of your warm hands, and inspired by the good cheer of your genuine tones, I have said to myself again and again, in anticipation of this happy scene, "*We were brought up together.*"

I knew that you were gathering from near and from far; that every continent would be represented in this meeting of which we have all thought so long ; that Iceland and New Zealand would meet in this bright auditorium, made fair with flags from many lands. I knew that Oregon and Armenia — brave Oregon, sacred Armenia — would here sit side by side. I knew that the mighty Empire whose center is London, "heart of the world," would be nobly represented, and the blessed Republic, dear to me as the beating of this glad heart, would send its big contingent ; that a few prophetic ones from the great wine and beer drinking continent of Europe would learn a new optimism from the cheery Australasian delegates ; and that here in the Dominion that has prepared for us with so much beautiful forethought, we should meet this day and feel in our inmost hearts that "We were brought up *together.*" For there is one book that lies, well-worn, upon the table at home, one that you have carried with you, no matter what you may have left behind — one at sight of which, upon your father's knee, you were wont to gather in that most hallowed circle that the world can show, the group at family prayer ; and I know you kept, as I do, in some sacred place, untouched save by reverent and loving hands, the little Testament whose worn pages were once turned by fevered fingers that are dust ; and so, though you lived in land of palm and I in land of pine, though Christmas came in midsummer where you dwelt or the sun for three months shone not on your habitation ; though the equator divided us until now and the salt sea's brine had risen up to keep us severed — still, by all that is most holy and endearing, "We were brought up together."

If I should start the hymn, "Jesus, lover of my soul," you who learned it in Japan would sing it with me who heard it first on a Wisconsin prairie in the hallowed precincts of a pioneer's home. If some of you should give us the keynote to "There are bands of ribbon white around the world," there is no voice among us but would join that song of hope. We have all been trained alike to love the wonder of the world, the splendor of the midnight heavens, the glory of the newborn day ; brought up together in the ultimate and great endeavor to say with fond hearts fervently, "O universe, what thou desirest I desire."

This globe was a great unknown area once ; the seas separated us then, they join us now. We can send messages by telegraph, and have an answer from almost any point on the round earth in a few hours. When the Siberian and Alaskan railways are finished, at the beginning of the next century, only three years from hence, one can go around the world in a little more than thirty days. But we do not need to wait for that, we are never far apart ; the thoughts of our hearts are always the same, and mutual thought gives mutual presence. If some one stood up here and spoke to you in Hebrew, only those who knew that sacred tongue would make reply. Our crusade mothers brought to the world the home protection tongue, and it has spread so fast and far that we who learned and loved it, we who believe that the tabernacle of God is in the home, and that nothing that hurts or destroys should be permitted entrance to that holy place; we who believe that love and law must go together, man and woman work side by side in the world's larger home that we will help to make; wherever we may have lived, wherever we may have learned this tongue or cherished this love, we women of the white ribbon, the home's fireside, the nation's safety, the world's brotherhood and sisterhood, *we* were "brought up together"!

It is related by an eye-witness that in one of the New England regiments of the Civil War, every member was a professed Christian, and that this even included the brass band. They had regimental prayer meetings led by this inspiring orchestra. But theirs was one of the first regiments to feel the fire of the enemy, and the men retreated into the forest, whereupon the Colonel called on the band to play one of their favorite hymns, beloved in boyhood days at home, "My faith looks up to Thee." At this they rallied and fought again, but a second time they were overcome by superior forces, and in the midst of the forest, with shot and shell hissing around them, those devoted men heard the notes of that inspiring hymn —

"A charge to keep I have,
A God to glorify."

At this the regiment rallied once more, and proved itself to be one of the bravest in the undying records of the battle of Seven Pines.

These men had been recruited from many different towns and cities, but in the deep things of the heart they proved in those hours of unequaled bewilderment and danger, that their hearts had been attuned to the same inspirations at the sacred altar of their homes. And so it is with us, by joy and grief, by faithful fireside teaching, by mother's love and father's loyalty, by sister's tenderness and brother's generous good will, by hearts touched into flame for the cause of temperance, purity, and peace, we were "brought up together." Thank God for the holy ties that bind our hearts in Christian love.

TORONTO.

We meet in the most reputable city of the English-speaking race; no saloon-keeper can be a member of the City Council; the police force is declared to be largely composed of temperance men. Listen to that, ye dwellers in San Francisco and St. Louis, Chicago and New York! The result of this is, that public drunkenness and idle loafing are practically unknown. Although the city, with a population of 200,000, has as many saloons as it has churches, and that is well-nigh 200, they are carefully watched, are obliged to close every night at 11 o'clock, and all day Sunday, also on that Sunday of the patriot, Election Day. Intoxicating liquors are banished from all the public functions of the City Council in entertaining guests at exhibitions, etc. It is the law of the Province of Ontario, that no liquor seller is eligible for election to a municipal council. Selling to youths under twenty-one years of age is illegal. The city has no Sunday papers, and until recently not a street car moved a wheel on Sabbath Day. When the plebiscite was taken, which resulted in 81,469 majority for Prohibition in the Province of Ontario, Toronto's majority was 2,463. I hardly need point out the large proportion of women's votes that were sound on the question — 6 to 1. In the Dominion the total vote was 132,918, counting all the provinces except New Brunswick, whose legislature has, however, voted unanimously for Prohibition.

All children under fourteen years of age are obliged to attend school, and the law is efficiently carried out by a faithful truant officer. The number of these children is 28,000, and the students at universities and colleges, 6,000. Scientific temperance instruction is a department of White Ribbon work in Toronto as well as throughout the Dominion, and I have the word of one of the best teachers in the city that the subject is most carefully and enthusiastically taught by a majority of the public school instructors, many of whom are members with us, and have helped in the arrangements for this convention. We are to have a chorus of a thousand public school children, who will favor us with patriotic and temperance music on one of the evenings of this convention, on which occasion the Toronto Public School Board will give their patronage.

We are in a city beautiful for situation and magnificent in architecture, its educational institutions being models both without and within. It is so near to Niagara, which every American thinks he owns, and every Canadian knows he does, that the sound of its eternal hymn can almost be heard from where we are gathered today. Doubtless it will not be long until the lighting, heating and locomotion of Toronto will be obtained by harnessing that mighty force so long allowed to go to waste. And this reminds me that the cataract of women's sympathy and tears is already turning the mill of public life to some extent on this side of the water, where a limited franchise for women has been granted. God hasten the time when we can say as much for every State in the Republic, and every nation represented here today.

THE CANADIAN PLEBISCITE.

Canada leads the world today in the great Prohibition struggle, and it leads with cheering prospects of success. The country is homogeneous, it has not that great foreign population to contend with by which we, of the States, are almost fatally handicapped; its people are serious-minded and practical; its average standard of morals and religion is higher than ours; as I have said, it has put itself on record by a popular plebiscite in which prohibition triumphed; it has survived the horrors of the Royal Commission to investigate the liquor traffic, and is on the eve of another popular vote in which, although it must contend against the united power of the alcohol trade in all countries which will be brought to bear upon its politicians and its people, we have faith to believe (and we go largely by sight as well, because this thing has been done once) that "Our Lady of the Snows" is going to pluck from the heaven of purity and plant on her own fair brow the bright star of Prohibition, which means happy homes to her people and a harbinger of peace to all the world.

. . . .

We all rejoice that the great Polyglot Petition, presented already in the United States and Great Britain, has been sent over by Lady Henry Somerset and is here today — the grandest object lesson of the Cause. We rejoice, too, that it is going to Ottawa to be presented to your government in the interest of the home plebiscite (as I like to call it), which is to be the most important ever taken in the country of the Maple Leaf.

THE DIAMOND JUBILEE.

It has been well said that the greatest landmark that will remain of the Victorian age is the mighty reform in law. Women have profited most by this redemption. When Victoria came to the throne, marriage transferred from wife to husband her property, her earnings, and the control and transferring of any children that might result from the alliance; but now a woman is the independent proprietor, after marriage, of whatever was her own before, including what is most sacred of all, the independent custody of her own person, and there is no corner of the British Empire, so far as it is under British law, where a father can will away his unborn child, as he still has power to do in the grand old commonwealth of Massachusetts.

We cannot doubt that the long and prosperous reign of a woman sovereign has done more to open a larger life to all English-speaking women than any other single cause, but back of it all is Christianity, which made it possible for Victoria to be a queen by permission of Anglo-Saxon men, and rendered her a ruler who has compelled the respect of the world.

It should be remembered that the new territory acquired during the present reign extends over eleven millions of square miles, covers twenty-one per cent of the land of the globe, and supports a population of above four millions of people. When the Queen assumed her title, the United Kingdom contained twenty-six millions of people, now it has practically forty millions; the United States had but seventeen millions, now it has seventy. Australia's population was then about 350,000, now it has over 3,300,000, and its trade exceeds that of Great Britain when the Queen came to the throne. One-third of Africa, which was then a *terra incognita*, has been brought under English civilization; railroads and telegraph lines are intersecting all the rich parts of the continent, and within two generations it will be as thoroughly settled by the white race as Australia is now.

Slavery was everywhere recognized sixty years ago; now it is practically unknown. Thirteen crimes were punishable with death when the Queen began to reign; now there are but two — high treason and willful murder, while the death penalty has been abolished in several American and European States.

Doubtless the most significant fact of the Queen's reign (though I have not seen it anywhere included in the list) is the invention of Professor Langley, of the Smithsonian Institute, Washington, of a flying machine that has already made repeated journeys of from a quarter to half a mile in a horizontal line. Dirigible balloons, which we have reason to believe will be as much domesticated twenty-five years hence as bicycles are now, will put a premium upon a perfectly poised brain and steady nerves such as the world has never seen, and will some day be the death of "brewing interests," to say nothing of "the product of distilleries in bond."

No colleges were open to women when Victoria was crowned; now all but about fifty in English-speaking countries are at their service.

Then there were not more than a hundred total abstainers among the ministers of all denominations in the United Kingdom, not one bishop and less than a dozen members of the medical profession; there are now two archbishops, fourteen bishops of English dioceses, thousands of clergymen of every denomination, and eighteen hundred physicians who are teetotalers, while one man in every three in the army is an abstainer.

Then public houses were allowed to remain open twenty-four hours in the day; now they are open sixteen in the rural districts and seventeen in the towns. Sunday-closing for Scotland, Ireland (with the exception of five cities) and in Wales has been obtained, and it is the general opinion that it has proved an unqualified success.

At the great dinner to the poor in London little or no intoxicating liquor was given out, and the offer of liquor merchants to furnish their product free was declined. The Lord Mayor of London was offered wine by wine merchants for the dinner, but he answered, "On one point we must be absolutely unanimous, and that is we should give no money to the outcasts and no drink." He knew that if they had money it would probably be promptly exchanged for alcoholics.

The processions at the Jubilee of Queen Victoria, and the inauguration of our President, were almost wholly military; there was no exhibition of trades or inventions, but only one long parade of uniformed men. Surely we have reached an age which has for its true emblems the arts of peace rather than those of war.

I cannot think that in the great jubilees of the future, soldiers and weapons of war will be the chief features of the pageantry, but that those wonderful inventions whereby man is making a home for himself through an understanding of the beneficent possibilities of nature and the beautiful insignia of philanthropy, poetry and art, whereby that home is elevated and embellished, will be at the front of every procession that seeks to symbolize the civilization of the New Testament.

THE POLYGLOT PETITION.

It is well known that our intention is to carry the Polygot Petition to all the English-speaking countries, to the Orient and to the various European countries as they become better acquainted with our society, and the specific plans of the present convention will be to develop the women's temperance movement on the continent.

You are all aware that two costly volumes, representing the signatures secured within the British Empire, were sent to the Queen in July last (1896), she having signified through her secretary her willingness to receive them. We are indebted to our generous comrade, Lady Henry Somerset, for rendering possible this lodgment of the great petition in the palace of the great Queen.

Under a Government which has declared by the mouth of Lord Salisbury its determination to do nothing for the temperance people, it was not to be expected that the petition would have had any such reception as its representative character and unequaled number of signatures should have demanded. It was our hope that the Liberal Government would receive the petition, and we fully expected to present it the week following the last Biennial Convention (London, June 16-24, 1895). It was stated by certain London correspondents that the great demonstrations held by the Woman's Christian Temperance Union, the presence and exhibition of the Polyglot Petition, and the stirring appeals of our representative women, had much to do with forcing the governmental crisis that was attributed to another, and as it seemed, a wholly inadequate cause, namely, a vote expressing lack of confidence in the "powers that were," because there was not enough ammunition in store in a time of universal peace!

When the Polyglot Petition went to Balmoral to the Queen a vision came to me of one, lonely, untiring and intrepid, who for nine years carried that petition and presented it to forty different nations. Her record is imperishable, and nothing can blot out its luster in the annals of the organized crusade. You all know that I refer to our first round-the-world missionary, Mrs. Mary Clement Leavitt, of Boston, Massachusetts, who went out not knowing whither she went, and who changed the World's W. C. T. U. from a purpose and a hope into a living reality.

THE OUTLOOK.

I will not anticipate the report of our Secretary, Miss Agnes Slack, which will pass our entire work in review, but this much may be said: The last two years have been among the most fruitful since the World's W. C. T. U. was organized in 1883. There has been more reaching out into new fields, systematizing of departments, securing better laws, helping on the enfranchisement of woman. In our great auxiliary, the British Woman's Temperance Association, the salient features of this year have been the testimony of Lady Henry Somerset before the Royal Commission on License, and the growth and expansion of the Duxhurst Industrial Farm Home for Inebriate Women. Ireland, Mexico and Iceland have been reached, Japan and Scandinavia are looming up, and there are no retrogressive countries anywhere.

The first National Convention of Japanese women was held in April last, and marks the most significant temperance epoch in that wonderful new land, which is oldest of all. I had hoped to conduct this convention; it had been one of the cherished dreams of many years, but it is better that a younger woman from our Western prairies had the honor and inspiration of a task so holy, and we all know that one more worthy could not have been chosen than that typical representative of the "Y," Miss Clara Parrish, of Illinois. We hear nothing but good of that loyal heart from natives or from missionaries, and have intrusted to her the development of the home cause in that trying but most inspiring field.

. . . . .

Miss Jessie Ackermann, Miss Ruth Shaffner and Miss Pratt went to Iceland to organize the W. C. T. U. soon after our last convention, and the presence of Miss Johannsdottir, president of the W. C. T. U. of that island, and its leading woman worker, testifies to the success of their visit.

Since April, Mrs. J. K. Barney, of Providence, Rhode Island, who has been more than thirty years engaged in prison work, and whose department of Penal, Charitable and Reformatory Work is one of the most ably maintained in all our list, has been making a most successful trip to the Hawaiian Islands, New Zealand, Australia, Tasmania, and she will probably go to Egypt and other Eastern countries before her return.

The disappointment that I have felt in the inability of our dear Lady Henry Somerset and myself to go to Australia as we had planned, made me doubly desirous to send a fitting representative, and when Mrs. Barney responded to the call I knew that the spirit of loving kindness, mingled with firm adherence to our principles, would characterize her every word, and of this we have received ample tokens in the unanimous expressions of warm appreciation that have come from our sisters of the youngest continent.

Mrs. Mary H. Hunt has returned in good health and heart from the Sixth International Congress against the abuse of alcoholic drinks, held in Brussels, August 30 to September 3, under the patronage of Leopold II., King of Belgium, the prime minister, M. le Jeune, presiding. The topics considered were:

(1) Alcoholic Legislation, Sociology and Political Economy. (2) Education and Instruction. (3) Alcohol in Medicine and Hygiene. (4) Women in the Battle Against Alcohol. The importance of the work of the National W. C. T. U. was evinced by the appointment of Mrs. Hunt as First Vice-President of this Congress. Dr. Destrees, a professor in the University of Brussels, gave a detailed account of experiments showing the effects of alcohol on the body. Dr. Forel, Professor in Zurich University, spoke on the corruption of civilization by alcoholism, and many other learned professors, publicists and statesmen discussed different aspects of the question. Every paper given, representing scientific investigation, taught total abstinence in the most convincing manner. Baron Plessen, Lord Chamberlain of Denmark, who was one of the delegates, said: "No one could attend the sessions of this priceless Congress as I have done and not be convinced that total abstinence is the only safe rule for individual life." His friend, Dr. Combe, from Switzerland, said that alcohol found few advocates in the section of the Congress devoted to medicine, while a delegate from Germany reported a Medical Temperance Association in that country, with a membership of 180 total abstaining physicians. A delightful reception was given in the Hotel de Ville, one of the most beautiful buildings in Europe, and the exercises closed with a sumptuous banquet. The announcement made from the platform, that "this will be a total abstinence banquet," was received with cheers. As Mrs. Hunt has well said, "The existence of this Congress is positive proof that the use of the so-called lighter drinks is no bar to drunkenness, for the representative men and a few women amply qualified to testify concerning the conditions in their representative countries, had met here for the express purpose of considering how the curse of alcoholism could be removed from the people of their wine and beer drinking countries."

Mrs. Helen M. Stoddard, President of Texas, attended, by my request, the Assembly of the Evangelical Societies of Mexico, which met in Mexico City, January 27, 1897. Mrs. Stoddard went as a fraternal delegate from the World's W. C. T. U., and was warmly received by the missionaries of all denominations. She organized a society in the City of Mexico, and by invitation has made another trip, even more successful than the first, the people gathering in large numbers to hear her delightful lantern lectures, given through an interpreter.

. . . . .

OUR DEBT TO CHRISTIAN MISSIONARIES.

The World's W. C. T. U. could never have been established but for the co-operation of Christian missionaries, who are undoubtedly the best exponents of the Gospel that the Church has to show. It is the fashion nowadays to speak lightly of them, but "may my right hand forget its cunning" when it ceases to indite their praise. It is a good thing to find out all that is helpful in the beliefs of Oriental nations, but they will strive in vain to give us any record of Christ-like deeds that is at all comparable to that made by our brothers and sisters, who, leaving home and friends, have consecrated their lives to making known in these same countries the unsearchable riches of Christ, among which the hallowed home of purity and peace stands first of all.

Julian Hawthorne, whose reports on the famine of India are regarded as unrivaled in point of accuracy, declares that "the only persons who know what is actually going on in that land of misery are the missionaries, for they go about quietly everywhere, see everything, and cannot be deceived or put off the scent by the native subordinates. . . . . . It was my great good fortune to be thrown with the missionaries from the start, and I was able to compare their methods and knowledge with those of the government people." He says that eight million people have perished by the plague.

The following testimony by Charles Darwin, the greatest scientist of the century, ought to be committed to memory by all our speakers and reprinted in all our papers: "The lesson of the missionary is the enchanter's wand. . . . Human sacrifices, the power of an idolatrous priesthood, infanticide, profligacy, bloody wars, where neither women nor children were spared — all these have been abolished by Christianity. Where now is the car of Juggernaut? It is only a relic exhibited to the gaze of the curious. What of suttee, of infanticide, of the cruel and devilish festivals of Hinduism? They are all gone before the power of Christ." As a matter of fact, the direct and indirect results of missionary work all over the world have been enormous.

ARMENIA.

The Sultan ordered the word "Armenia" to be cut out of every geography and blotted from every map used by the missionaries, but he has engraved that word on human hearts the world around. Such words as "liberty," "progress" and "brotherhood" were erased from every text-book by his order, but perhaps it is not too much to say that an angel could hardly have done more to emblazon those words with light and charm than by contrast the Sultan of Turkey has done within the last three years.

Industrial relief is the only way to help the women of Armenia. We must first teach them handwork of some kind and then provide a market for the product. The organization thus far effected in Constantinople is this — the committee communicates with the various places where work is done, as Oorfa, Van, etc., and receives the finished work. Salesrooms are opened in Constantinople and other seaport towns, for tourists and people in the city itself; these are supplied with work by the Constantinople committee. Orders are also sent for work to be sold in the various centers all over Europe. London, Edinburgh, Geneva, Frankfort, Wurtemberg, Munich and Paris have now each their own bureau, committees and centers for sale. It is astonishing to know how much the work is liked, and how large orders are sent to Constantinople. One order of £1,000 has been received from Edinburgh. In three weeks, 1,000 francs' worth was sold in Constantinople itself, and the work has supported over 1,500 people in Oorfa alone the past year.

GREECE.

A small part of our Armenian fund was used in helping to send nurses to the Greek army, on the basis that nothing better could happen the Armenians than for the Greeks to succeed, but that success was not written in the book of destiny, and today, as a result of the prestige of his victory over this nation, for which our sympathies are so sincere, the Sultan is once more in the saddle with prosperity for his ally, and it has been proved to the world that Germany's money investments in Turkey and her contribution of skilled officers for the army of the Sultan, are decisive factors in restoring to the Great Assassin the power that had well-nigh slipped from his grasp. This is a spectacle that might make angels weep and mortals give up hope, did we not know that the disintegrating power of Christian education is steadily at work under the dastardly empire of the Turk, which means that God's hand is under it, and we have no more doubt that the accursed empire will be ground so fine that no vestige of it will remain, than we have that the steam engine has displaced the stage coach, or that the common school is a later evolution than the senseless jargon of Turkish boys repeating the Koran in the Mosque of Saint Sophia.

HOMES FOR INEBRIATES.

One of the reasons why we have many departments in the W. C. T. U. is that different minds are attracted to different lines of work, and by arranging our plans under many subdivisions we win the allegiance and help of a much larger group of good women than we could by any other method. To some it is given to work for the fallen, others have a passion for preventing the fall; some believe in persuasive, others in legal forces, but no group of workers is more germane to the Crusade idea than that which devotes its gentle energies to the reformation of the fallen. No attempt of this kind has impressed me so deeply as that of Duxhurst, founded by the British Woman's Temperance Association, and by them placed under the care of Lady Henry Somerset. It is a farm village about thirty miles from London, and four miles from Lady Henry's home at the Priory, Reigate. Simple but attractive cottages have been provided, in each of which six women find a home, of which they take all the care, and invest the remainder of their time in gardening, dairy work, or any one of several avocations for which arrangements have been made. Each cottage is under the supervision of a young woman who has received special religious and medical training for her work, and the whole are supervised by a sister of remarkable ability and experience. The women take their meals together, and meet daily in the recreation hall, where exercises interesting and amusing are arranged. They have also temperance and gospel meetings every week, and there is a church as well as a hospital near by. These women are consigned to this farm colony chiefly by police justices, who, instead of condemning them to work out sentences, deem it wiser to give them into the care of the Duxhurst temperance women, who at once bring to bear upon them the saving education of home life and congenial occupation, with a loving unsectarian religious influence. One of the most successful efforts to brighten the lot of these women is the establishing of a children's home in connection with the village, where little waifs from London come for an outing, the constant presence and needs of the little people making an appeal to what is best in the nature of these friendless ones.

There seems to be but one rule, and that is, if a woman leaves this lovely retreat she shall not be allowed to come back; but she is not likely to leave unless the dreadful thirst drives her to it, or she has in some way outraged the kindness and good will with which she is surrounded. In point of fact, the women seldom run away; they are too glad to get into this happy place, and a large proportion go from it clothed with new purposes and right-minded toward the temptation whose slaves they have been in the past.

It is said by prison experts in England that this better method of caring for those who have laid themselves liable to the law is shedding a flood of light upon the possibilities of prison reform, and as an object lesson to the whole Empire its teaching is invaluable. I wish we might see a similar colony in each country to which our work has extended, because we have been from the first devoted to the idea of an improvement in the condition of prisoners.

Our dear Mrs. Barney, now in Australia, and from whose work there come to us only tidings of good, has been longer at work for this cause than any other of our experts. In Lady Henry Somerset, Mrs. Barney and Mrs. Maud Ballington Booth, of the American Volunteers, we have a trio of prison reformers whose work is of international significance.

We are not without homes for inebriate women in this country; the Martha Washington Home (Chicago), founded in 1882, had sheltered in 1896 a total of 620 patients. It is conducted by a Board of Directors, and has made for itself an excellent record. The treasurer's report shows over $40,000 received and disbursed in 1895.

I think we should give notice, and I hereby do so, of the intention to add to our present list a department of work for the reformation of women inebriates, and I hope the work already being done in the two homes I have mentioned may be carefully studied and its best features incorporated into the plans that we announce next year.

NOTE.—The Washingtonian Home, Chicago, is a retreat for men inebriates, and provides for their reformation and restoration to their homes. Its work extends over a third of a century, and in 1896, 655 patients were admitted.

HABITUAL DRUNKARDS.

A student of the temperance reform finds no more significant change in public sentiment than that which proposes to deal with the drunkard as one who commits a crime against society. The drunkard maker has long been regarded in that light by temperance people, but they have been perhaps too lenient toward the "finished product" of the liquor business. The studies of Sir Benjamin Ward Richardson and other famous experts have proved that alcoholism is a disease, while the studies of religious and ethical experts have proved it a crime against both natural and spiritual laws. Now comes the statesman, and his position is that the drunkard is an enemy of society and an unmitigated nuisance and a danger in the home. He, therefore, proposes that the State shall found industrial homes in which drunkards shall be detained by order of the Court.

England has already gone a long way toward securing such a law. It has passed the House of Commons, and the next Parliament will undoubtedly place the subject before its members.

The Austrian Government is about to introduce a bill which proposes to treat the drunkard as a person mentally incapable and likely to inflict injury upon the community, not only by actual violence but by example, and to provide for him a term of detention, which is to be two years, with power to extend or diminish the time according to results. For ourselves we believe in the "Do Everything Policy" for the drunkard. We favor the Keeley Cure, the Christian Home for inebriate men, the Gospel meeting, the temperance pledge. All of these are helps that should be gratefully recognized by those who are trying to deliver men from bondage. We hold, as we have always held, to the Gospel cure as the only complete deliverance, and we believe this view to be founded on a philosophical basis, which has perhaps never been better expressed than by Dr. Horace Bushnell in his well-known phrase, "The expulsive power of a new affection"; for when the love of God dwells at the center of a man's being, it works out through all his senses, habits and manner of life, uplifting, purifying and cleansing all. But we confidently believe that a house of detention where men might "sober up" would help them to perceive more clearly the infinite power of a Christian life to take them out of bondage. We also believe that to arrest the drunkard, no matter what his social position, and to place him in custody, would greatly deter the ignorant and thoughtless from looking lightly upon such a brutalized condition, and would thus be of incalculable service in stamping the drunkard with the displeasure of the community in which he moves about as a perpetual danger.

Holding these views, we shall never cease to urge upon the women of the W. C. T. U. their duty to use their utmost power to induce the legislatures of our respective States to pass these laws of detention under the name of the "Habitual Drunkards' Act."

HEROIC EXAMPLES.

The daily press should have its columns perpetually clothed in black, so heartrending are the recitals that it brings of bloody deeds. Perhaps the pessimism of the age finds much of its explanation in the universal newspaper reading, that in its totality must leave a painful impact on the brain. If only a single daily paper would undertake to give us better tidings! Who will start *The Good News, The Brotherly World, The Helpful Journal, The Merry Mail, The Glad Gazette?* Who will take as the motto of his paper that of our press department: "Let us so tell the story of the world today that the world's story shall be happier tomorrow"?

Many rills of pure influence have been flowing into the turbid stream of daily journalism from the White Ribbon homemakers in the past year. Is it becoming an instinct with us to send every bit of hopeful news we know to our friend, the editor?

Until journalism gives us better cheer, we must go back to those radiant illustrations of what humanity has done to prove its kinship to our heavenly Father. I think of the little girl in Kansas City, whom the cyclone hurled into the basement of the great schoolhouse full of studious children; when one of our own workers approached to try to lift the little creature from under the beam where her soft limbs were crushed, she moved her white lips and said with her dying voice, "Help Willie first, he is smaller than I."

I think of the poor factory girl at Pemberton Mills, whose sweet notes as she sang in the village choir had endeared her to the people, and who, in her last hours, as the flames gathered around her when the desperate efforts to rescue had all failed, was heard singing high above the roaring of the flames, "I'm going home to die no more." I think of the men who, when the Oregon was thought to be sinking, stood quietly back and made way for the women and children to be lowered into the boats. I think of General Gordon at Khartoum, steadily facing death and watching for the troops that never came, while his great manhood never lost its equipoise and his dauntless soul held its steady upward lift toward God. I think of Wilson's troopers on the far-away Shangani strand, when, overwhelmed by hopeless numbers, their little group stood together and sang, as they died, "God Save the Queen."

I think of Lord Shaftesbury, disavowed by his peers, but forging steadily on to secure laws that should protect the hapless little workers in the mines of Britain; and of the barefoot newsboy who, standing at the window of a picture-shop and seeing Shaftesbury's face, pointed his comrade proudly to it, saying, "He is our Earl."

I think of Agnes Weston, "the mother of the bluejackets," who, having neither home nor child, has by a life of uttermost devotion made for herself a home in the warm hearts of the British tars. I think of Lady Henry Somerset, speaking to the hoppickers in Herefordshire, the miners in Wales, the inebriate women at Duxhurst, and who, foregoing a life of ease and pleasure, has set before the women of her order in the Queen's empire an object lesson of helpful service that has exalted every home and made more helpful every heart. I think of Helen Keller, the wonderful girl who has from earliest remembrance lost every sense but that of touch, and yet through the immeasurable patience of the rare young woman who is her teacher, having become so intelligent that she has passed the examinations to enter Ratcliffe College, and who, on being recently asked by her teacher for a definition of love, eagerly spelled out with her expert little fingers, " Love is that which everybody feels for everybody else."

Surely with such examples of the exaltation, of the tenderness and purity to which humanity may be lifted upon Christ's cross of sacrifice, we will take heart of hope and move steadily forward, hand in hand, with faces lifted that the Spirit's light may fall upon them from above.

WOMEN'S ENFRANCHISEMENT.

It would seem that the heavenly fiat has gone forth and no large advances are to be made hereafter by men alone in the great realms of Church and State, from which their laws have debarred those loving and sagacious advisers who, as the best of them are free to admit, have been to them the strength and joy of life.

One of our poets represents America as saying :

> " Bring me men to match my mountains,
> Bring me men to match my plains;
> Men with empires in their purpose
> And new eras in their brains."

This prayer is being answered in the West, in New Zealand, and in some of our Australian provinces, but man-made government is bearing fruit in English diplomacy at Constantinople and Athens; in the mock trial of Cecil Rhodes of South Africa; the C. D. Acts of India; in the mutterings of Germany and France, the despotism of Spain, the prostration of Cuba; all showing forth the decadence of an out-worn *régime*.

As is well known, Norway has called in the help of women in its efforts to solve the drink problem, all above twenty-five years of age having been made voters on the temperance question. In 1895, of twelve towns voting, ten voted down the government saloon; in 1896, seven other towns voted, and five of them voted it down; this year eleven have voted, but we have not as yet the result, and next year twelve will vote under the local option law, so that by the united efforts of temperance men and women it looks as if the Gothenburg system will disappear and prohibition will be the law of Norway.

It is probable that we have never had a more comprehensive argument for woman suffrage than that priceless sentence from Abraham Lincoln, who said, "No person is good enough to govern another without his consent."

One of the best results of the ballot for women will be the greater willingness of men to vote. The stay-at-home vote constantly increases, and the Boston *Arena* vouches for the statement that in some cities less than thirty per cent of the voters cast the ballot, and in twenty-four of our largest cities barely half the voters go to the polls. But it is observed that in cities where women have the ballot a much larger proportion of men exercise the liberty of the franchise.

Temperance and woman's ballot will be helped by women in business. Being in business they will not be so much in haste to marry, thus seeking a support; they will be better able to select, and they will not select men who are under the influence of bad habits, therefore men will have to brush up a bit. Again, the fact that men and women meet constantly in business will cause men to improve their habits; unconsciously they will feel that they wish to be more presentable, and the purity of the woman's habits will have its effect upon them, just as it does in our coeducational schools, while the presence of men will make women less petty and personal in their topics of discourse, will broaden their outlook and give them a clearer judgment in all their business affairs and a "calm view" of everyday annoyances.

The press is always alert to thrust in a javelin when it has or can make an opportunity. In pursuance of this object we had Associated Press dispatches immediately following this year's election in New Zealand, with startling headlines to the effect that women had voted against prohibition. Feeling sure this was not true, I wrote Miss Powell, the Corresponding Secretary of the W. C. T. U. of New Zealand, and it seems worth while to give her answer in full:

"By a resolution of the Convention just held in Christ Church, I was requested to send an official reply to your letter of December 14, 1896, supplementing that of our beloved New Zealand President. We are constantly receiving fresh light upon the recent local option poll, and as time goes on are more and more encouraged as to our own position, and more and more sorrowful at the deceit and corruption which are brought to light. We are fully convinced that we never shall know the strength of our vote, which was much greater than it appears, though even the 98,372 no-license votes with which we are officially credited, as against 48,993 in 1894, give great cause for thankfulness. To have more than doubled our votes in two years and nine months is surely a good record, and if during the next three years we can add another fifty thousand the victory will be ours. The votes in different districts seem to have been counted in as many different ways as was possible; but it is a remarkable fact that all the mistakes and blunders seem to have favored the drink party. I have not heard of a single vote for continuance being counted to no-license, though in numberless instances the reverse has been true.

"By way of explanation, let me say that the voting papers read as follows:
'I vote that the present number of licenses be continued.'
'I vote that the present number of licenses be reduced.'
'I vote that no licenses be granted.'

"As each elector can vote on two issues, we were advised by the Prohibition League to strike out the top line, when, if no-license failed to be carried, our votes would also stand for reduction, and a hymn called 'Strike out the top line' was sung at all our meetings, up and down the country. This helped to fix the instructions in our memory, and hundreds of us voted thus, only to find subsequently that in certain districts such votes were either discarded as informal or counted only for reduction. One feature of the struggle was the marked way in which all temperance bodies throughout the Colony acted in concert with the Prohibition League. We are highly favored in this land in our grand leaders, the Isill brothers, to whom all are affectionately loyal. The prevailing feeling now is one of thankfulness for past successes, coupled with an earnest determination to work still harder for the next local option poll. At the same time, we shall insist upon fresh legislation whereby past mistakes may be rendered impossible.

"We have had a most successful Convention, marked specially by Christ's own spirit of love."

ECCLESIASTICAL EMANCIPATION.

Ecclesiastically there is a great awakening; the voice of Christ rings in our ears saying, as of old, "In vain do ye worship me, teaching for doctrines the commandments of men."

Whether in Church or State, the human intellect has developed to the point of perceiving that men are nothing but men, and that infallibility is absolutely absent from their proceedings; that their creeds, whether in Church or State, whether of political economy in commerce or of co-ordination of power in the home, are merely the opinions held at a given time, and in the order of nature must give place to the more reasonable opinions that successive generations form as the outcome of a longer experience, and from a more acute perception of their relation to their ever-changing environment.

At one of the congresses connected with the World's Fair in 1893, a Catholic bishop prayed at the opening of a Council of Jewish women, they having invited his presence and co-operation. No more significant sign of the times could be cited than this. We all perceive that unless religion is converted into terms of conduct that holy thing becomes a mockery; doubtless the motto of the age to come will be those words of Christ: "Why call ye me Lord, Lord, but do not the things that I say?"

Happy are we who live in an age when "Names and creeds and altars fall, and our Christ is all and all." For He and He alone brought to the world emancipating truth; He is the universal solvent; the Searchlight of the mind and the dynamo of that Love which is the only inexorable force of which we are aware.

PEACE AND ARBITRATION.

"Thicker than water in one rill,
Through centuries of story,
Our Saxon blood has flowed, and still
We share with you the good and ill,
The shadow and the glory."

The greatest practical advantage of arbitration is that men may deliberately choose when they are not angry with each other a method by which, should they become angry, they could settle their dispute without resorting to blows. By this means they invoke clear-eyed reason instead of leaving their lives to hang on the thread of sudden passion. It is the highest instinct of self-preservation and protection for the individual, the family and State that has ever been thought out, and could occur to the mind of no nation until it had long been saturated with the Gospel of Christ.

The cause of peace has won great victories this year. The Arbitration Treaty with our Mother Country is only lying over; already we have reason to believe that through the influence of the President, arrangements are being made for the presentation of another treaty of wider scope, and it is not improbable that we may soon be saying, "How good it was to reject the less valuable that we might gain a greater, even a universal treaty of peace."

The Storthing of Norway has appointed a committee of nine to consider the question of forming arbitration treaties with foreign nations, and to submit proposals to that end. It is well known that France is moving in the same direction, and the recent declarations of the Russian Czar and the Emperor of Germany are unmistakably in favor of pacific measures, while the treaty between Turkey and Greece, recently promulgated by the Powers, is a peace triumph, even though it registers the subserviency of Christian nations to the great Moslem hierarchy.

PURITY.

"Whoever sounds the highest moral note does the most for his country."

"If I forget thee, O Jerusalem" (and to me, humanity's Jerusalem is evermore the home), "may my right hand forget her cunning, and my tongue cleave to the roof of my mouth." By God's grace, I will always stand with you, my comrades, for those holy principles of action that build strong defences around the sanctuary where two have united their dearest earthly destinies, and where the hallowed light of a child's face is to them, even as it is to us, the beacon of a better world.

Wendell Phillips declared a great principle when he said, "Plant only the tiniest seed of concession; you know not how many and how tall branches of mischief shall grow therefrom."

The Faculty of the University of Christiana has recently put forward a statement on the subject of "Continence and Health," that ought to be reproduced throughout the press. I quote in part: "The recent declarations of certain persons that a chaste life and continence are injurious to health, are, in our view, wholly false. We know of no disease or of any weakness which can be said to be the result of a perfectly pure, chaste life. On the other hand, we have a number of diseases which follow in the wake of licentiousness. If we could imagine prostitution abolished, we could imagine the prompt eradication of these scourges. Without its abolition, we cannot. Those who believe that its legal control (in itself a sociological chimera) can prevent the dissemination of infection, occupy an unscientific ground, one which is not assumed in reference to any other infectious disease."

For there is a higher law: "Thou shalt not commit adultery"; second, "Thou shalt love thy neighbor as thyself." Whatever degrades the women of India puts the stamp of deterioration upon all women. To this it will be replied that they have degraded themselves, and the means proposed are only to mitigate the consequences; but it makes all the difference in the world to us whether their degradation came about through any forces that we have set in motion either before or after the facts. By parity of reasoning, we might say the saloon is here, and here it will remain; let us do all we can to make it less degraded. But this is not the point; our *attitude* toward the saloon, first, last and always, is an attitude of utter hostility, and it makes all the difference between right and wrong whether its presence among us is in spite of our protest and work, or whether we have taken measures that render its continuance probable. Besides this, we must remember that although military officers may not think so, the moral contamination of the future husbands and fathers of England is a calamity immeasurably greater than their physical deterioration. The foundation and the keystone in the arch of heathenism is the sacrifice of woman's purity on the altar of man's sensuality; and if there is one monstrous thing which above another represents the Antichrist, it is that fact. In oriental countries women are helpless in the hands of men, as they have been through the dark centuries; and the depths of degradation to which this utter dependence has reduced them, are beyond all power of western comprehension.

The English law in the Straits Settlements is said to be "for the protection of Chinese girls"; none are allowed to register as prostitutes except of "their own free will," and "with the consent of their mothers." But women physicians among the missionaries testify that they have treated little Chinese girls, four and five years of age, who had been bought in north China and taken south to be raised for vile purposes, and who, when they were made to register, would never dare to say the woman with which each one was living was not her "mother." As for "her own free will," none of these poor creatures ever had a free will, or ever will have. And this is the protection that England affords to Chinese girls. It is well known that the moral tone of army life is very low in oriental countries, and to expect that military men would ever subject their soldiers to examination and registration because they had visited these women whom they have provided, is to cherish an idle hope.

It need hardly be said that Lady Henry Somerset has never dreamed of applying the method she advocates outside the British Army in India, and the mistake she made (for we all think it a grievous mistake, much as we love her) was in advocating a measure whereby the "equality of men and women" in an act that degrades both, and strikes at the very foundation of the integrity of home, comes to be an equality that levels down instead of up, that blurs the moral sense of those who administer hardly less than of those who engage in it, and will no doubt prove as difficult of execution as the plain, clear-cut, "Thou shalt not," which is the only edict pronounced in God's laws of nature or of grace.

We hold that it was not right to cut down the proportion of married soldiers in India from 33 to 6 per cent; that it was not right to leave them without specific moral instruction and helpful recreation; that it was not right, and never will be right, to arrange for them to have the services of the State Church and the services of "the poor little women of India" in the same cantonment.

We cannot check an immoral disease by measures which recognize the sin as something to be regulated rather than prohibited. This is the crux of the situation. We believe that the moral injury to the soldier, resulting from any possible provision for the dishonor that he works upon himself and a poor, ignorant and debased woman, is unworthy that Christian Empire whose Queen declares that the Bible is the foundation of her government. And we believe there is no blot upon her throne so deep and indelible as that these wretched little beings, provided for the soldiers of India by its Government, universally bear the name of "the Queen's women."

We rejoice that Sir George White, Commander-in-Chief of the Forces in India, has made a manly and outspoken deliverance at the present crisis; he points out "that the majority of the venereal cases are found within a narrow circle of men, who are admitted to the hospital again and again, and thus the numbers of admission are swelled." He holds that the only reasonable way to deal with such men is to punish them, and declares that they are fitting subjects for all the discipline that can be imposed upon them, as they habitually render themselves unfit to fulfill the engagements they have entered into with the State, and throw upon their more self-respecting comrades the burden of their own duty."

The defense of the down-trodden often comes from unexpected quarters, and the warning uttered by Mrs. Steel, the famous novelist, who has lived in India many years, may yet be heeded by her countrymen in time to prevent the re-introduction of those C. D. Acts to which our British leader has declared herself as much opposed as we are. Mrs. Steel says:

"Knowing the women of India as I do, I feel it would be cowardly to keep silence in the face of what is being done against them. The proposed legislation is most unwise at such a time as the present, when, to my eyes, all that is needed to change ignorant dissatisfaction to ignorant defiance is some common cause, such as unscrupulous agitators found forty years ago in the 'greased cartridge.' I only venture to remind those in power that men are always ready to fight for their gods or their women; and that knowing, as I do, the vast credulity of the masses in India, I do not see how any new legislation regarding women can be other than a weapon of calamity given into our enemies' hands at a most critical time."

But let us hear the conclusion of the whole matter as it appears to us. No provision shall ever be tolerated by us for the illicit gratification of any man's desire, and the only word we have for the English soldier in India and his poor little sisters of an abject race, is the word, not of Holy Writ, for that might have little weight with him; not of the White Ribbon women, for that would be received with jeers and anger, but the word of a great physician than whom none has deserved more profound respect from his contemporaries, Sir Benjamin Ward Richardson, who, in commenting on the most loathsome disease that impurity causes, has left on record these golden words:

"Every kind of remedy has been proposed for this disease, every kind of means has been carried out for its prevention except one, and that is PURITY."

But there are two kinds of mind: one flies, the other walks; one looks up, the other on; one says, "the best shall be," the other says, "the possible shall be"; one is called "an idealist," the other "a practical character." These two join hands in reform and philanthropic work, because they both seek the Godward side of things, they both purpose to leave the world better than they found it by the sum total of that increment of power that they by nature or by culture have obtained; but while they have a thousandfold more in common than the apathetic, the sensual, the base, there is just difference enough in their keynote to make discord possible. Out of this grow some of the greatest difficulties of philanthropy, for not to agree in one's own group is a more potent source of disintegration than to be pressed upon by those ponderous forces from outside that do not make for righteousness. But these inevitable internal difficulties would be vastly diminished if the two classes of minds would but recognize their points of difference, and treat each other with forbearance instead of cudgelling with epithets and laying low with illustrations, one side saying, "Alas, for those idealists, with their castles in the air," and the other crying out, "Alas, for those materialists, with their plantigrade step, they drag our standards in the dust." Meanwhile the great gainsaying world drones on with its favorite phrase, "Behold how these Christians love one another"; while the cynic wags his worthless head and shoots forth the lip of scorn, exclaiming, "These women serve the Lord like the very devil." "By these means is the cause wounded in the house of its friends, but God loves them both," the idealist and the materialist; the one who moves "toward the far-off divine event," and the other who plods on along the dusty road doing what he thinks will mitigate the present distress. Whatever anybody else may think, I firmly believe that our beloved comrade who leads the happy host of one hundred thousand British women, honestly thought that her plan of dealing with unchaste soldiers in India would have better practical results than any yet proposed. She thought that by subjecting them to a medical examination whenever they were known to break the law of continence, and ceasing to classify them as "exemplary" when their relations to women were impure (thus making their chances of promotion dependent on their wholesomeness of life in this particular) the most thorough safeguards would be provided. She believed that by this means the little women of India, who sell themselves for purposes of shame, would be less debased because less patronized, and that by means of the medical examination, in their case to be conducted by a woman physician, and in the case of men to be as explicit as in that of women, the best possible protection that is practicable as yet would be supplied.

In Lady Henry Somerset's address before the National Executive Committee of the British Woman's Temperance Association, July 28, 1897, she has stated her position in these words:

"It is not that there is any divergence of principle between us, I must steadily maintain, but rather the outcome of the theory as to what is the greatest deterrent from wrong, between myself and those who differ from me on the Cantonments Acts in this Association. If there is anyone who would for a moment believe that in principle I could have changed my outlook; that I for one single moment would wish to make vice easy, or to encourage a laxness of morals among men, or a loose idea as to how sin is to be met in our army — let me at once state that they are absolutely mistaken. Nothing can or ought ever to be attempted or done that should in the slightest degree give rise to the idea that sin is not grievous, entailing serious and lamentable consequences, and that all in authority are not bound to condemn it; that to deter from evil is the fundamental principle on which all law is based. There is no sin of any kind that is a necessity. We are living in a world full of evil, the result, probably, of the long trend of ideas that has gone before; the shaping of communities in past times; and the cultivation of thought. But not one of these reasons can stay us for one moment in our unalterable determination to do away with evil and to uphold good. I am not going to argue here as to the merits or non-merits of my plan, which is a question for experts, but I do insist that no one dare say it is immoral. It may be mistaken; it may be misconceived, but when Mrs. Butler, in her pamphlet, says 'truth before everything,' she has hit the real nail on the head while trying to make an argument against me."

Speaking of my proposal she says:

"I have seen something of the worst side of humanity. I have encountered men who were more demons than men. I have been forced to fathom the depths of human corruption; yet, I thank God, my faith is as strong as ever in the recoverability of the most abject of human beings, and in the spark of divine light which lingers even in those who are generally believed to be hopeless. I refuse to believe that our poor young soldiers in India, at the age of from eighteen to twenty-five, have reached such a depth of degradation as to accept or to cease to revolt against such rules as the above, and that it will ever be possible to drill them in debauchery so perfectly as to induce them to practice it with the order and precision with which they might attend a concert or a lecture, having their names entered, with the date, the circumstances, the number of the room visited, etc. None but the coarsest, the most stupidly animal and shameless of the men would consent to perform their acts of impurity thus openly, under the eyes of the military police and the whole camp."

It is precisely because it would have the effect of being considered degrading that it would be in the end eminently successful in proving the strongest deterrent from vice that you can find.

What Lady Henry wanted was a quarantine system, and not a license system, and she wished to label those men who called themselves incapable of continence, and to have the facts concerning their condition included in the papers which are made the basis of promotion, and which now bear the word "exemplary," irrespective of those degrading relations which a proportion of them sustain to the servile women of India, who sell themselves for a price.

Now, while we White Ribboners will not give an atom of our influence in favor of any high-license movement, or in favor of the use of beer instead of the fiery drinks, it remains true that all these tokens show that men are obliged to think about temperance and are trying to climb up some other way, proving that there is today a very different attitude of the public mind from that of half a century ago. And to follow out the analogy, who believes that twenty-five years ago it would have been soberly considered by military men to examine the men as well as the women who frequent houses of shame? From our point of view it is a lower plane, but from the point of view of military men it is a higher plane, and these things we must not forget.

The plan differed from the C. D. Acts that disgraced England's legislation in this, that it was not simply seeking to supply a demand and to make sin more safe for impure men, but was meant to hold them back by motives of shame and the desire of promotion, from the illicit indulgence of propensities intensified by the tropical climate and lowered moral tone of their new environment. But to this view White Ribbon women oppose two considerations which they deem vital. First, they hold the opinion, universally so far as I have learned, that the plan I have outlined will never be pursued by military men. They could not if they would subject the soldiers to the examination proposed, and their standards, largely derived from military doctors, a majority of whom hold that indulgence, whether illicit or otherwise, is necessary to young men, are diametrically opposed to the enforcement of any such provision as our comrade has set forth. Secondly, White Ribbon women are idealists; they work for what they believe to be the holy, unchangeable right; their vocabulary has no place for the word "regulation"; it has once and forever been replaced by the word "abolition." What little strength they have is being used to hold up God's standards, to preach His gospel for this evil time. They believe that a man's ability to control himself is chiefly based on the mental attitude that he holds toward his physical nature; they believe that, like St. Paul, he must "keep his body under," and that it is the business of women in gentle and reasonable ways evermore to put before him the vision of the heights. We hold that there is but one standard of purity for men and women, and that they are equally capable of living up to it; we steadfastly believe that all law should set forth the ideal, that it should beckon men to the summit rather than provide for them, under no matter what restrictions, those indulgences in alcoholic liquors, opium and social vice whereby they live in the dark valleys of sin. Our beloved comrade has hoped to reach the same result by regulation that we propose to attain by prohibition or not at all. But while we differ so completely as to methods, we repudiate any personal attack upon or severity of language toward the woman, who, at the risk of personal violence, publicly repudiated the candidacy of an impure politician for parliament and dared the fierce criticism of the press in her attack on the living pictures of the London music halls; who forwarded by every means in her power the heroic work of Doctor Bushnell and Mrs. Andrew; who has personally reformed more unfortunate women and girls than any one of us; whose zeal has been that of a flaming herald, whose devotion is a household word among White Ribboners, and whose untiring work in these long years, carried forward under conditions more difficult than any that have hedged up the path of any reformer whom I have ever known, have bound her to our hearts with cords that never can be broken. We admire and trust and love her; we believe that when she sees that her plan is not adopted in the Indian army, she (who has been silent under many rebukes) will frankly admit that although she put it forward because she thought it "practical," it partook far too much in its severity of the "impracticability" attributed to our own ideas, and she will stand with us, shoulder to shoulder, heart to heart, as she has done so long and bravely. God bless and comfort her in these hours of anxiety and pain — our loyal sister, Lady Henry Somerset.

TOTAL ABSTINENCE.

Whoever in this audience, or city, or nation or world, has within the last hour had the greatest number of serene and helpful thoughts is the person who best illustrates the purpose of God in his creation, and it is because the use of intoxicants diminishes the power of the user to think with beneficent serenity, that we are here assembled.

The novelist and poet make much of wine, but the "*Cup of cold water*" has been hallowed by the words of lips divine and sacrificed by David from a sentiment of loyalty to his brave comrades; by Alexander when he declined to drink lest his soldiers seeing him would grow more thirsty; by Randolph of Hapsburg, who thrust the cup of blessing from his parched lips, saying, "I thirst not for myself, but for my whole army," and by Sir Philip Sydney who gave the cup for which he longed to a poor soldier with the immortal words, "Thy need is yet greater than mine."

Cold water wins its widening way, without haste, without rest. The wineless dinner table is becoming cosmopolitan.

Cold water was declared to be "the best beverage ever brewed" by Abraham Lincoln when he offered it to the committee of leaders who brought him news of his nomination to the presidency; it was apotheosized by John B. Gough in his most famous passage listened to by eight millions of delighted men and women during the great advocate's "Forty Years' Fight with the Drink Demon"; its pledge was given to millions more by gentle Father Mathew, and the little folk are singing our Anna Gordon's chorus throughout Christendom —

"We are all cold water children,
 Won't that help the cause along?"

This is our position: That the crown of creation, so far as we know, is the domelike head carried on human shoulders; that this is the universe in miniature, and the nearest to God of anything of which we are aware; that forth from it has come all that makes the earth different from a den of beasts; that water is the brain's natural restorer and lubricant, and that any material sold or used which produces its deterioration beyond the degree that any other material does or can, shall not be made or sold under the guarantees and safeguards of the State.

The great battle is now against moderate drinking; drunkenness is outlawed save among the human sediment of parlor and purlieus. But the man who is on the way to this same degradation, as science steadily holds, will not believe it, this being the most painful part of his hallucination.

In this great fight for a clear brain some of our good friends counsel us to give up the word temperance, but it is a word too grand and far-reaching to be sacrificed. Let us all diligently teach that temperance is the moderate use of all things harmless, and total abstinence from all things harmful. Some persons have the sanguine temperament, others the bilious, others the lymphatic, others the nervous, but now and then we come upon a favored one who so combines all these that it may be said of him, he has the tempered temperament; he is made up of every creature's best. So it is with the temperance reform — all the best things of life are in it; no other word so fully represents that self-control which makes man great; none so combines conserving powers with progressive possibilities. A temperance man looks upon his body as the temple of the Holy Ghost; a temperance man is chaste, teetotal, anti-tobacco, anti-gambling; he is for home protection, the emancipation of women, the lifting of labor to every opportunity that life can yield; his eye is clear, his hand untrembling, and when you meet him you have met one of whom the Arabs would say in their beautiful phrase, "He is a brother of girls."

The supreme duty of the hour is to convince the moderate drinker that he is doing himself harm. If only this belief were general, men would soon become a law unto themselves, to such a degree that statutory enactments would be but the outward expression of an inward grace. Upon the sullen fortress of moderate drinking the artillery of the temperance reform must concentrate in future years. It has been an incalculable gain to make drunkenness a disgrace instead of an amiable peculiarity as it was a hundred years ago, or a pardonable peccadillo as it was in the memory of the oldest inhabitant, or a necessary evil as it was a generation back. The forces that have worked to this end are precisely the same that must now be directed against so-called "moderation." We must stoutly maintain the position that there is no moderation in the use of what is harmful. Happily, in taking this position we have "great allies," of which the greatest is the dictum of the modern sciences. These declarations of standard authorities are now being taught to the children in the public schools, not only of America, but to a great extent throughout the English-speaking world; and their introduction is being urged in France, and has to some extent penetrated Japan. It is in the nature of poetic justice that Germany, the greatest beer-drinking country in the world, should have furnished the scholars who are perhaps doing most to undermine the fallacy that intoxicating liquors (*i. e.*, poisonous liquors) taken "in moderation," are either harmless or helpful in the physical economy of life.

"TOO MUCH."

There is hardly a form of expression more frequent than, "He took *too much.*" We hear it even from the lips of the temperance mother who believes that any at all is too much when it is a question of using intoxicating liquors as a drink. When a drunken Mexican recently assaulted President Diaz "with intent to kill," our papers with one accord declared that the would-be murderer had

had "too much pulque." But no person of intelligence would touch this national poisoned drink that has so long degraded the Mexican people, and no intelligent patriot and Christian who has studied the causes of misery in our own favored land, would fail to regard any alcoholic liquor as "too much" if the reasons for so doing were presented to him with adequate considerateness and wisdom.

The effects of alcohol are thus treated of by Prof. C. F. Hodge, of Clark University, Worcester, Massachusetts, writing in the *Popular Science Monthly*. He says: "Helmholtz has said, in describing his methods of work, that slight indulgence in alcoholic drinks dispelled instantly his best ideas. Professor Gaule once told the writer that, as an experiment, during the strain of his 'Staatsexamen,' he suddenly stopped his wine and beer, and was surprised to find how much better he could work. An eminent professor in Leipsic has stated that the German students could do 'twice the amount of work' if they would let beer alone. Dr. August Smith has found that moderate non-intoxicant doses of alcohol (forty to eighty cubic centimeters daily) lowered psychic ability to memorize as much as seventy per cent."

Rev. Dr. Stuckenburg, whose philosophical books are well known to the intelligent, makes a statement that I wish might be copied out by our press superintendents. It is as follows: "For the encouragement of temperance workers there comes from German and other continental professors of physiology, physicians, directors of prisons and insane asylums — the very ones formerly thought to advocate moderate drinking — a scientific literature of unsurpassed excellence in favor of total abstinence. It is not less convincing because based so exclusively on thoroughly scientific investigations of physiological laws. These scientists demand total abstinence in order that the fearful devastations which are destroying the nation may be checked.

Buchner, the great authority on bees, declares that robbery and murder become their trade if brandy is mixed with the honey on which the larvæ feed. The naturalist says it makes them act just as men do under similar conditions.

When Victoria was crowned Queen of England, over 20,000 gallons of wine were consumed by the people of London. Now, at the celebration of the sixtieth year of her reign, the committee having the arrangements in charge announces that it has "courteously declined to accept five pipes of port wine offered by wine merchants."

The President of the United States does not have wine at his table, nor serve it at his Cabinet dinners. The Governor of New York does not serve liquor of any kind to guests in the executive mansion at Albany. The Archbishop of Canterbury, primate of the English State Church, does not offer wine at Lambeth Palace.

Society daily becomes more clearly founded on the principle of the greatest number's greatest good. We enforce sanitary arrangements, enter people's houses and tell them what they may and may not do; but to banish intoxicating drinks is a sanitary measure, the most important of which we can conceive. The great steamship companies do not permit the officers on their lines to drink, because the smallest amount might deflect the judgment at a critical point and endanger or destroy the lives of passengers, and, what means more to the ship-owners, sink the millions of dollars they have invested in this floating palace. The railroad company forbids the men who handle its trains to use intoxicants or to gamble, because either of these vices renders them less clear-headed for their work. It is a matter of dollars and cents with the capitalist. But what shall we say of society itself, for the sake of which all other things exist? What shall we say of that great company of men, women and children who are too wise to use strong drink, but who are at the mercy of those who do? We forbid the cyclist to invade the sidewalk because collisions might occur, and sooner than our opponents think we shall forbid the man with the jug to walk with us the crowded thoroughfares of life. There will then be no more talk of "personal liberty," but the watch-cry will be personal protection, home protection, national protection from the worm of the still and the sodden beverage brewed from golden grain and fragrant hops by the prostitution of honest labor and expert skill.

At the last General Assembly of the Presbyterian Church, only one Presbytery of the United States reported a majority of its churches as still using fermented wine at the sacramental table.

This simple statement seems natural enough, but what an avalanche of work it indicates to those behind the scenes. Let me give a single illustration: One Sunday morning the President of the W. C. T. U. in a leading Western State went to the Presbyterian Church of which she was among the most helpful members, and distributed in the pews, before anybody had arrived, a leaflet containing keen arguments and affectionate persuasions against the use of alcoholic wine at the Communion, all of these having been written by scholarly clergymen of the Presbyterian Church.

If these points had been made by our White Ribbon women they might have stirred up strife, but even the conservative could not object to having their pure minds stirred up by leaders of their own flock.

This quiet work carried on for more than twenty years as a part of the varied and vigorous propaganda conducted by temperance pastors and workers within and without the Church has won the day. But we can only reap where we have sown.

PROHIBITION.

Public sentiment is, in man's mental world, what steam and electricity are in the world of things mechanical. We must not only know why the times are out of joint, and what will put them where they ought to be, but we must harness the forces that will do it to the car of reform. In short, we must "hitch our wagon to a star." When coal in the mine but not in the grate will warm you; when flour in the barrel but not in the loaf will feed you; when wool on a sheep's back but not woven or spun will clothe you, then the public sentiment lying dormant in every sane mind but not aroused, condensed and brought to bear through the electric battery of the ballot box, will put the liquor traffic under ban of law.

There is no doubt but that the right to prohibit the sale of intoxicating liquors for drinking purposes will, in the future, be largely based on the harm they bring to the people who never drink them. For the liquor traffic is an assault upon the non-drinker. This claim, always virtually put forth by temperance people, needs the emphasis of constant reiteration, and I beg our superintendents of literature to take note of it and show it forth in brief and pungent paragraphs. For even yet it is not generally known that we hold that it is the harm that drinking does to the man who does not drink which gives the non-drinker the right to prevent the drinker from doing him that harm. Prohibition is self-protection, and is based on the elementary rights of civilized man.

The State control of the liquor traffic is now the favorite method of those who would like to see the political power of the saloon broken, but are not ready for Prohibition. This constitutes a large and intelligent group of good men who are as much convinced from their point of view as we are from ours, and it is but reasonable to admit that State control, as conducted in Norway, with power given to the people to prohibit the trade in any town or city that can muster the necessary majority and with the votes of women included in that electorate, has thus far worked wonderfully well, because, in most instances when the time arrived for the voting, it resulted in local Prohibition. If such a law prevailed today throughout the United States, except in those happy Commonwealths already under Prohibition, I am confident it would be a blow that the liquor traffic would not long survive. Men and women in Norway do not vote until they are twenty-five years of age, and if all our population who have reached that figure could vote tomorrow on the question, I am confident there is enough public sentiment against the Curse to vote it out; but because we believe that it is our work to educate toward Prohibition and that alone, whether it be prohibition of the liquor traffic, the gambling house or the strange woman's habitation, we can never favor any of these milder movements, though we can think and speak with the highest esteem and good will of those earnest-hearted men who look upon us as fanatics, and hope the day will come when we shall "cease to be dreamers and wake up to do practical work."

The bill introduced by Hon. Elijah A. Morse, of Massachusetts, Chairman of the House Committee on the Alcoholic Liquor Traffic, prohibiting the sale of intoxicating liquors in the Capitol in Washington, was passed by the House with a vote of 104 to 7, but the United States Senate, which has made a painfully bad record in the past year, prevented the bill from coming to a vote, that typical Democratic senator, David B. Hill, talking against temperance in the interest of the liquor dealers until the opportunity was lost.

The House of Commons in Canada is in a similar plight, having closed the bar in their end of the parliamentary buildings, but the bar in the Senate end remains open. Meanwhile Sir Wilfrid Lawson has vainly tried to banish intoxicants from the British House of Commons, and his merciless raillery seems to have driven the Government to "an access of nerves," which nothing brings so readily upon them as a proposal to interfere with the presence of their favorite tipple at all times and in all places.

The general aim of all good people ought to be to leave the world better for their progeny than their progenitors left it for them. The plebiscite soon to be placed before our Canadian comrades puts them in the strategic storm center of the temperance movement, and we are persuaded that the manhood of its homes will give a good account of themselves upon that day of days, as we know the women will. If only the mothers could drop in a ballot the majority would be already sure. I sometimes ask myself, "Could unwisdom farther go than to disfranchise the class who, by glorious discipline and blessed sorrow, are most naturally inclined to Home Protection and saloon destruction?"

It is well known that Lord Salisbury is the merciless enemy of temperance reform, and has the bad preëminence of having stated officially that he will do nothing for this cause, and having in his usual relentless manner, reintroduced the C. D. Acts in India without requiring the examination of men as one penalty, and as another making their promotion dependent upon the decency of their personal relations with women. But while we grievously lament these acts of retrogression, we get a crumb of comfort out of the news from the old home country that the advance in temperance sentiment is shown by the general refusal of magistrates to grant new licenses at the recent "Brewster Sessions."

We have got our politics down to so fine a point "over the line," that without the knowledge of either Senate or House, the Committee of Conference on the tariff can "get in" the famous ten per cent "discriminating clause." Heaven grant that some such sleight-of-hand be not practiced upon you in the anticipated plebiscite.

A Spanish wit was explaining to an English gentleman in Madrid the difference between the two great political parties of that country. He said: "The Liberals are assassins and great robbers; the Conservatives are robbers and great assassins."

So far as we can discover, this is the definition of the two great political parties of our own, and indeed of every country, in the present turbulent and

LADY HENRY SOMERSET—1890.

"SAINT COURAGEOUS," HER DAUGHTER FRANCES
AND ANNA A. GORDON.

seething condition of public affairs. But I believe that Richard Cobden's rule, which Gladstone has followed all his life, is the only one worthy of us, namely, "Never assume that the motives of the man who is opposed to you in policy or argument are one whit less pure and disinterested than your own." For nobody is wholly good and nobody is wholly bad. But alas, it is our custom to consider that wisdom will die with us, and that truthfulness first had its being when we were born; while the facts are, speaking broadly, that being subject to a certain pressure of education, certain great masses of men look upon public matters in one way, and other great masses look upon them in another, and nothing short of that universal argumentation which politics furnishes will enable both groups to reach at last an equilibrium of thought by leavening the entire lump with the two different kinds of education, so that one view shall modify the other.

CHRISTIAN CITIZENSHIP.

We have lost this year one of the most God-smitten spirits that has come to the planet in our country, Prof. Henry Drummond, the intellectual mediator between science and religion, between theory and practice. No utterance that I have seen so completely condenses the significance of that great movement toward Christian citizenship in the midst of which we are, as the following from his pen, that seemed dipped in light. It is a bugle blast for every man who has a vote, and every woman. To take life in the practical way which our great brother, whom we have lost so lately, has put it before us, is indeed to be a true disciple of Him who went about doing good:

"To move among the people on the common street; to meet them in the market-place on equal terms; to live among them, not as saint or monk, but as a brother man with brother men; to serve God, not with form or ritual, but in the free impulse of a soul; to bear the burden of society and relieve its needs; to carry on its multitudinous activities of the city — social, commercial, political, philanthropic: this is the religion of the Son of Man and the only fitness for Heaven which has much reality in it. . . . . Traveler to God's last city, be thankful that you are alive. Be thankful for the city at your doors and for the chance to build its walls a little higher before you go. Pray for yet a little while to redeem the wasted years. And week by week, as you go forth from worship, and day by day, as you awake to face this great and needy world, learn to 'seek a city' here, and in the service of its neediest citizen to find a Heaven."

WOMEN AT FUNERALS.

I have been much pleased with the attention given to an article in the *Union Signal* on this subject, the gist of which was that under the head of the Flower Mission might be included an effort to increase the participation of women in the exercises pertaining to funeral rites. The W. C. T. U. has already done more to bring this about than any other influence. In almost all the funerals of our promoted comrades their associates have been honorary bearers, have walked in the procession, occupied seats together in the church, and had some part in the exercises at the grave. What could be more appropriate than that she who sits beside the cradle should follow those to whom she gave birth and being even to the cradle of their last repose? With this effort at a change in the conducting of funerals, whereby they shall become less conventional, would naturally go suggestions to make the home more bright and cheery in these days when the loved form is lying there after the soul's release. The white ribbon rather than the black as an emblem telling of the event to passer-by, the opening rather than the closing of blinds, the lighting up of the home at night, the moderate use of flowers as the sweetest tokens of affection, the solemn entreaty to good people not to dress in black when they believe their friends have entered into eternal radiance—all these and many more helps toward brightening those days usually so dark and dreary would be in harmony with the spirit of our work and might help to bring about the needed reform.

Nearly all these tokens were apparent at the recent funeral of Neal Dow, a fact that will encourage many others to adopt less lugubrious methods, let us hope.

IN MEMORIAM.

"WHILE WE MAY."

The hands are such dear hands;
They are so full; they turn at our demands
   So often; they reach out,
   With trifles scarcely thought about,
So many times; they do
So many things for me, for you—
   If their fond wills mistake,
   We may well bend, not break.

They are such fond, frail lips
That speak to us. Pray, if love strips
   Them of discretion many times,
   Or if they speak too slow or quick, such crimes
We may pass by; for we may see
*Days not far off when those small words may be
   Held not as slow, or quick, or out of place, but dear
   Because the lips that spoke are no more here.*

They are such dear, familiar feet that go
Along the path with ours—feet fast or slow,
   And trying to keep pace—if they mistake
   Or tread upon some flower that we would take
Upon our breast, or bruise some reed,
Or crush poor Hope until it bleed,

We may be mute,
   Not turning quickly to impute
Grave fault; for they and we
Have such a little way to go — can be
   Together such a little while along the way,
   We will be patient while we may.

So many little faults we find.
We see them; for not blind
   Is love. We see them; but if you and I
   Perhaps remember them some by and by,
They will not be
Faults then — grave faults — to you and me,
   But just odd ways — mistakes, or even less —
   Remembrances to bless.
Days change so many things — yes, hours;
We see so differently in suns and showers.
   Mistaken words tonight
   May be so cherished by tomorrow's light.
We will be patient, for we know
There's such a little way to go.

"Why, she talks about herself as if she were dead!" exclaimed one of our wittiest workers, speaking of another whose weakness it is not "to let her works praise her in the gates," but to serve in the capacity of her own trumpeter. Well would it be if we talked of others as we would if they were dead; but such is the perversity of temperament in those who are "built that way," that they will speak and write of their living associates in terms of pitiless severity, when if the sacred seal were on the foreheads of these same comrades, no one would crown them with more fragrant flowers. My sisters, these things ought not so to be, and I fervently hope that the effect of this memorial service may be to soften every heart toward every other, as we remember that "There is such a little way to go." What we say here will neither make nor mar the record of those whom we have lost in 1897. They are beyond the words of praise that all of us are glad to speak, but we cannot afford to pass lightly over the great fact that they are gone, nor to ignore its lessons. The scientist tells us that even while the sap of spring ascends to the highest twig on the tree, it carries in solution from the soil mineral materials which, being deposited at the place where the young leaf joins the wood, will accumulate until enough sap cannot get through to keep the leaf alive, so that in the very substance of its nutrition there is an explicit provision for its death, and the same is true of man, as the deposits from his food diminish the size of the sluiceways of vitality. The knowledge of these facts, and countless others like them, reveals death to us in a totally new aspect, and proves that it is provided for as carefully as breath, and that the one could not exist without the other. It is replacing in the common mind the fancies of the past, and we face the future with a confident belief that the mysteries concerning the genesis and exodus of man upon this planet will be as clearly understood in some future age, and that not a distant one, as the sources of the Nile and the laws of electricity are becoming known to the thinkers of today. They have passed onward, that is all, beyond our sight, above our ken — the choice spirits who were withdrawn from the procession of progressive philanthrophy in 1897. Time would fail me to repeat our Roll of Honor, to be read while we stand in reverent silence on memorial day. But there are five, Gen. Neal Dow, of Maine; Sir Benjamin Ward Richardson, James H. Raper, Dr. Frederick R. Lees, of England, and Letitia Youmans, of Canada, than whom we had no greater ones to lose. The father of Prohibition, the greatest scientist who ever espoused the cause of temperance, the chief popular temperance orator of England, its best equipped scholar, and our Canadian Deborah who, called out by the Woman's Crusade of 1873, went forth as a burning herald of temperance reform throughout the great Dominion, had among us no superiors. Alas, how long it will take the younger ones, who must carry this holy cause to its completeness, to win the public ear and enshrine themselves in the people's heart, as these have done!

Among our own White Ribboners we think first of that untiring spirit now happily released after long suffering, Mrs. Letitia Youmans, fittingly named the "Deborah of the Dominion"; a woman who, at a greater sacrifice of physical comfort than was submitted to by any other I have ever known, organized the W. C. T. U. in every Province of Canada, and after fourteen years of devoted and productive toil, endured with Christian fortitude eight years of pain before she was released into the larger life.

Mrs. Youmans received her first inspiration at the memorable meeting in Chautauqua, in August, 1874, when Mrs. Fowler-Willing conducted the preliminary organization. On her return home she organized a local union in her own town (Picton) according to the plans outlined at the Chautauqua Assembly. Previous to this, a union had been organized in Owen Sound, so that Mrs. Youmans organized the second. She traversed Canada in every part, and the Republic everywhere but in the South. What this meant to one of her age and size can never be adequately estimated by us. She had great power of speech, and had she been a man, the halls of Parliament would have echoed her voice. She had a massive brain and happy wit. A woman of her remarkable abilities could not fail to feel defrauded that by the laws of her country she was debarred from taking a statesman's part in its affairs. She knew this would not be so always, and was outspoken in favor of the full and equal participation of all men and women of adult age in the making and administration of the laws by which they were to be governed.

Nor do we by any means forget the founder of the British Woman's Temperance Association, Mrs. Margaret Parker, of Dundee, who although for many years unable to engage actively in our work, early made for herself a record that will be imperishable.

GEN. NEAL DOW.

Never to the mansions where the mighty rest
Since their foundation came a nobler guest.

On the 2d of October, 1897, we lost the great character who for fifty years has been the foremost leader of the Prohibition forces of all lands. He is the banyan tree in the forest of public opinion; the bright consummate blossom on the century plant of temperance reform; his character gleams like a white shaft at the end of the nineteenth century's long vista —

" As some tall cliff that lifts its awful form
High from the vale and midway cleaves the storm;
Though round its base the gathering clouds may spread,
Eternal sunshine settles on its head."

We may safely declare that no public man has made a better record. As a boy he was studious and brave; he saved the life of a schoolmate, he improved every intellectual opportunity. As a youth he was foremost in athletic exercises, a protector of the weak, and a terror to them that did evil. As a husband and father his record is ideal; as a business man, connected with large enterprises, he preserved the universal confidence; as a patriot he raised a regiment and a battery, and went to war at sixty years of age, and after leading his troops in one of the most heroic battles, in which he was twice wounded, he was taken prisoner and spent nine months in Libby Prison.

His work in England, where he invested three years and gave two hundred addresses on Prohibition without fee or reward, led to the founding of the United Temperance Alliance with Sir Wilfrid Lawson, our great parliamentary champion, at its head.

When the Prohibition party was in its youth, he shared the obloquy of carrying its standard in the presidential campaign of 1880. Still later, he became convinced that the vote of women was essential to the triumph of temperance reform, and from that day he was the most honored friend and brother of the W. C. T. U.

The sorrow of a wife and mother, whose natural protector was lying unconscious in a Portland saloon, led him in his sturdy young manhood to cross its threshold for the first and last time. The saloonkeeper ordered him out, and when Neal Dow asked him to sell no more liquor to the ruined young husband and father who lay there in his drunken dream, its keeper, pointing to his license, said: " I shall sell so long as the State gives me a legal right, and the man has money to pay for his drinks." Then came the immortal reply —" Heaven helping me, I will see if I cannot change all that." God had found a new soldier, humanity a trusty leader, and the Prohibition fight began.

Not until he had completed more than half of his ninety-fourth year did he once say, "I am weary — I long to be free." What wonder that he, whose dauntless soul had drooped in its darkening prisonhouse, longed like a caged eagle for the brightness of the upper air? But an imperious question remains with us, Who shall grasp the white banner upheld by Gen. Neal Dow throughout one of the most beneficent lives that the American Republic has given to the world?

I wish the delegates of this Convention might rise as one, and stand in silence for a moment to thank God for that great leader and his white life; for that hallowed home where a pure and noble wife consoled and strengthened him, and to pray for those happy children whose father's name shall be a heritage greater than the name of king or potentate.

> "For he is Fortune's now, and Fame's;
> One of the few, the immortal names
> That were not born to die."

And as we stand here together for a moment, let our prayers ascend for that true heart, present with us today, his daughter, Cornelia Dow, whom he so greatly loved, and who, in these long and heavy months of his slowly waning strength, has been the constant nurse and guardian, helping him on through the valley of his ninety-fourth year as none other could; listening to him as he said, "I have no ill-feeling toward any being that lives"; grieving with tears she bravely hid when once he said, just at the last, "It is the end, and it is all right"; and watching, as only a devoted daughter could, when, from his sweet sleep that great soul was translated to the world "into which shall enter nothing that defileth, neither whatsoever loveth and maketh a lie."

Some years ago two noble women in Norway determined that the W. C. T. U. should become a recognized institution in that heroic land. One of them was Ida, Countess Wedel Jarlsberg, a maid of honor to the Queen of Sweden and Norway; the other was Miss Esmark. They were devoted Christians, of remarkable character and culture, and were warm friends; and they buckled on their armor — no, it would be truer to say they submitted their necks to the yoke. The result was a strong society that has done immeasurable good in the brave, beautiful country of poets, explorers and philanthropists. We shall never forget the cable that came from Trondheim when the National Society met there in 1893. The hearty good will of such a noble band swept down from those heights like a waft of good cheer. But Birgithe Esmark, the right hand of the Countess, whose bright personality had deeply impressed us through her letters, has in the last year endured a slow and painful passage from her good life here to the better life beyond. Her release came on the 2d of April last. It would be useless to try to express the chastened sorrow of the dear Countess and White Ribbon band in Norway, or to give adequate expression to the sense of loss felt by the officers of the World's W. C. T. U. Our prayers are theirs, and, like them, we lift up our hearts, asking, Who shall come to the kingdom for such a time as this, and lift the white banner for God and home and native land that our Sister Birgithe held so steadily aloft? Who will answer — for the time is short?

The temperance reform has hardly produced a more remarkable character than James H. Raper, whom we lost this year. He became an abstainer in 1837. He remembered the time when England owned six hundred thousand slaves, but he lived on with the glow of health in his noble face until the reform to which he had given his life had become the stalwart of the century. He was one of the finest popular orators that any movement has produced. When he came to America, in 1876, and I heard him in the Academy of Music, in Philadelphia, I knew he was a master; and twenty years later, in London, in the church of Rev. F. B. Meyer, where I spoke with him just before sailing for home, a year ago, I said to myself, "His bow abides in strength." He invested fifty years of devoted work for the temperance reform, and, with hardly a day's illness, slipped away into the better life. He told us that he "never traveled alone, for grace, mercy and peace were always with him." To hear him was an education and an inspiration both. Whenever he appeared on the platform the people rose up to greet him with that warmth of applause in which the English excel all other nations. I wish to put on record his personal kindness to White Ribboners who went to England. Our dear Miss Ames told me when she returned what I can say as truly, that he was always willing to go anywhere in London sightseeing with her, and was better than any book she could have carried, so familiar was his knowledge of the historic wonders of that city. When I went with him to City Road Chapel he had me stand in Wesley's pulpit, and together we sang that famous old Methodist hymn:

"Oh, how happy are they who their Saviour obey,
And have laid up their treasure above."

He told me then that he used to get up at five o'clock in the morning to attend class meeting in that building when he was a youth. He took me to the room in which those undying words were uttered by the dying founder of the church I loved, "The best of all is, God is with us"; and then, as he put me into a cab after we had thoroughly viewed the old cemetery where lie the remains of so many world-known heroes and heroines, I thanked him as I said good-by, when, with beaming face, he waved adieu, saying, "*Pass it on.*" That was the motto of his life, and no one was more intent to "pass on" everything that was good and comforting than our gifted brother who is gone.

In the swifter pace of these last years, set to the key of the telegraph's click and the typewriter's chorus, we linger not so long at the graveside of those who leave us; the rising waves that we must meet each day seem to absorb what force we have, and few things have grieved me more than to note the lengthening roll of honor of our promoted ones who drop from the ranks of an army that marches at a quick step. But I like to believe that they, in their heavenly individuality, are even busier than we in the beatitude of faculties that do not weary, and that with some bright knowledge of us, and helpful influence sent out to us according to our need, they happily pursue their vocations with an infinite freedom and joy.

I wish we might hold the names "writ large" upon our records in more vivid remembrance by attaching them to our enlarging work. It seems to me that we should thus remember a comrade so serenely active as was our first treasurer, Mrs. Ella C. Williams, of Montreal, who, although suffering under a most painful disease, was writing up her books and sending checks almost up to the day she left us. I, therefore, venture to propose that we institute a fund for our Round-the-World Missionaries, enabling them to go forth with a sense of independence, because they know there is help specially provided and to which they can turn in time of need; and that this be named the "Ella Williams Fund," in perpetual memory of a woman loved and honored by our Crusade sisters and throughout the ranks of the World's W. C. T. U., to which she freely gave those winsome services in which a sister's love was mingled with the business acumen of a master of finance.

> Vainly we weep and wrestle with our sorrow—
> We cannot see His roads, they lie so broad;
> But His eternal day knows no tomorrow,
> *And life and death are all the same with God.*

. . . .

"POOR RICH."

Many of us have heard Lady Henry Somerset relate with her inimitable drollery the following incident: She was present in a Salvation Army meeting in the slums of London, at which the presiding officer in his bright uniform was vehemently "laying it off" in a denunciation of the rich. Near her a poor inebriate Irish woman was seated, who to her natural geniality of disposition added the garrulity of her condition, and as the Salvation Army brother grew more and more excited as he depicted the contrast between the West End and the East End of London, the old woman wagged her head, and in a seeming soliloquy she said in her warm-hearted Irish tones, *"Poor rich! they've a dale to contind aginst!"* Lady Henry said she greatly appreciated the remark, and thought it as true as it was kindly. White Ribbon women hold the same opinion; they strongly feel that the growing distance between rich and poor in this and other countries is not so much the fault of anybody as it is the necessary result of that process of development which no class can greatly help or hinder. We rejoice in the unnumbered tokens of a conscientious use of property on the part of men and women who are Christians not in name but in fact. We sometimes wonder that these good people do not help us more, for our treasurer's reports show that no society so large and influential has received so little help from those who have full pocketbooks and generous bank accounts. But we remember that it has been our painful duty to antagonize the politics and to some extent the customs of those who have property, and that, after all, it may be best for reformers to find themselves hedged in by financial disabilities. Therefore, let it be understood that when we speak out against the rich, it is not because we have any harsh feeling toward these brothers and sisters of ours as a class, but only that we believe it is our duty to cry aloud and spare not against the inequality of condition that the present economic system cannot help involving.

OUR DISAPPOINTMENT.

Two comrades upon whose presence we had greatly counted cannot be with us. To miss their winsome presence, ready wit and gifts of speech and sympathy is a loss that we all deeply feel. I refer to Lady Henry Somerset and Lady Windeyer. And we are the more grieved because the reasons that have prevented their union with us at this happy feast suggest to our chastened hearts life's pain and loss. Sir William Windeyer, ex-Chancellor of the University of Sydney, New South Wales, and barrister-at-law, died suddenly a few weeks ago while on his way with his daughters from Switzerland to England, and Lady Windeyer, who was expecting soon to sail for this country as one of our delegates, was obliged to return to Australia. I need not say that she and her family have the sisterly sympathy of this entire Convention, which will be expressed at the memorial service and by letters that you will authorize.

Lady Henry Somerset has not been well for months, and Sir James Sawyer, one of England's stanchest teetotal physicians, has declared that it would be hazardous for her to attempt the sea voyage. Lady Henry is resting quietly at Eastnor Castle, whence she has sent us messages of affection from the loving heart that we know so well and cherish so warmly. I hope to see her before long, and shall bear to her the assurance of your devoted sympathy.

LIVES THAT LIVE ON.

One day a young nobleman on horseback rode impatiently up and down the streets of a village in Cornwall. He was seeking for a public house where he could get a glass of that concerning which our Shakespeare said, "Alas, that men should put an enemy in their mouths to steal away their brains." But his search was vain, and coming upon a white-haired peasant on his way home after a day of toil, the young man said with rising anger, "Why is it that I cannot get a glass of liquor in this wretched little village?" The old man recognized to whom he was to speak, and taking off his cap made his humble obeisance and replied, "My lord, about a hundred years ago a man named John Wesley came to these parts"—and the old peasant walked on. "A hundred years," and he was living still, that dauntless, devoted disciple of our Lord! Cornwall has never been the same since John Wesley went there to preach the Gospel of a clear brain and a consecrated heart. Of whom will such great words be spoken when a century has passed in those dear countries of the English-speaking race, from which most of us have come? Who doubts but that in Maine some good man going to his safe and happy home will be saying in answer to some unfriendly wight, vexed because he cannot get his dram, "A hundred years ago a man named Neal Dow came to these parts"? Who does not believe that in Canada some loyal voice will give the explanation, "A hundred years ago Letitia Youmans came to these parts"? Verily, comrades, we are building better than we know. It is a holy thing, this influence that reaches on and away into illimitable distance; this coming to be one of the wheels within the wheels that are the wheels of God. For it is said, "The wheels were full of eyes," and these eyes are on us when we know it not; they see us when we wake and when we sleep.

The following letter written by Lady Henry Somerset to Lord George Hamilton gave Miss Willard great joy and was a fulfillment of the belief which she expressed in her Toronto address concerning our beloved English leader:

EASTNOR CASTLE, LEDBURY, ENG.
January 28, 1898.

DEAR LORD GEORGE HAMILTON,—Your lordship invited me two months ago to give you my view of the dispatch that had been addressed to the government of India on the health of the army, and in a letter in which I did so I ventured to suggest some methods, moral and disciplinary, which seemed to me the only ones likely to succeed, because they had at least the merit of being logical.* I was lead to do so by two considerations. First, the dispatch in question seemed to imply that the government would give encouragement to any form of elevating agency, and so emphasize the altered spirit in which the subject was approached, and that such suggested supervision would only affect an incorrigible minimum; and second, that the system I had in mind would be so drastic and penal in its nature as to make state interference odious and finally impossible.

That was ten months ago, and in that time nothing has been done of which

---

*This refers to the position taken by Lady Henry Somerset that if regulations were introduced, there should be no discrimination in the examination of the sexes.

the public has heard to strengthen the forces that make for moral improvement. What has been done — namely, the repeal of the Indian acts of 1895, which prohibited inspection — has been in a direction exactly opposite. It seems to have been the object of the government to obtain the maximum of impunity with the minimum of protest from those who desire to see the state shape its actions according to Christian views of ethics.

I need not tell your lordship I am not writing to say how strongly I am still opposed to the course which the government has taken, but I find that my letter to your lordship of last year has been taken by many to mean that I am on the side of the accepted view of state regulation, and I am from time to time quoted as a sympathizer with such views.

I am therefore writing to withdraw any proposals made in that letter, for the reason that the events of the past year have convinced me of the inadvisability and extreme danger of the system that in April last I thought might be instituted. The absence of any serious effort by the government to bring about a higher standard in the army is a final proof to me that as long as regulation of any kind can be resorted to as a remedy it will always be regarded as the one and only panacea. My view was that it would be instituted as an odious, but possibly effective, auxiliary to moral efforts. I find it will always be accepted as a convenient substitute.

I take the liberty of addressing this explicit withdrawal or an indorsement, of whatever form, of the principle of regulation, because it was in a letter to your lordship that I originally incurred the responsibility. I trust, therefore, to your lordship's indulgence to forgive me troubling you further with the matter.

    I remain, my lord,
      Yours very truly,
        Isabel Somerset.

CHAPTER X

A GREAT MOTHER

"SOME are born great, some achieve greatness, some have greatness thrust upon them." "Of my blessed mother," writes Miss Willard, "all these affirmations are true. There are not many men, and as yet but few women, of whom when you think or speak it occurs to you that they are great. What is the line that could mark such a sphere? To my mind it must include this trinity — greatness of thought, of heart, of will. There have been men and women concerning whose greatness of intellect none disputed, but they were poverty-stricken in the region of the affections, or they were Liliputians in the realm of will. There have been mighty hearts, beating strong and full as a ship's engine, but they were mated to a 'straightened forehead.' There have been Napoleonic wills, but unbalanced by strong power of thought and sentiment — they were like a cyclone or a wandering star. It takes force centrifugal and force centripetal to balance and hold a character to the ellipse of a true orbit.

"My mother, my Saint Courageous, was great in the sense of this majestic symmetry. The classic writer who said, 'I am human, and whatever touches humanity touches me,' could not have been more worthy to utter the words than was this Methodist cosmopolite who spoke them to me within a few days of her ascent to heaven. She had no pettiness. It was the habit of her mind to study subjects from the point of harmony. She did not say, 'Wherein does this Baptist or this Presbyterian differ from the creed in which I have been reared?' But it was as natural to her as it is to a rose to give forth fragrance to say to herself and others:

'Wherein does this Presbyterian or Baptist harmonize with the views that are dear to me?' Then she dwelt upon that harmony, and through it brought those about her into oneness of sympathy with herself. She was occupied with great themes. I never heard a word of gossip from her lips. She had no time for it. Her life illustrated the poet's line:

'There is no finer flower on this green earth than courage.'

"My mother had courage of intellect and heart, and physical courage as well, beyond any other woman that I have known. 'We are saved by hope,' was the motto of her life. 'This is our part, and all the part we have,' she used to say. 'The existence and love of God are the pulse of our being whether we live or die.'

"Some characters have a great and varied landscape, and a light like that of Raphael's pictures; others show forth some strong, single feature in a light like that of Rembrandt; some have headlands and capes, bays and skies, meadows and prairies and seas; the more scenery there is in a character, the greater it is—the more it ranges from the amusing to the sublime. My mother's nature had in it perspective, atmosphere, landscape of earth and sky.

"She was not given to introspection, which is so often the worm in the bud of genius. 'They are not great who counsel with their fears.' Applied Christianity was the track along which the energy of her nature was driven by the Divine Spirit. She would have been just as great whether the world had ever learned of it or not. 'Mute Miltons' are not all 'inglorious,' and however small the circle might have been in which she spent her days, she whom we loved and for awhile have lost, would inevitably have been recognized as one adequate to the ruling of a state or a nation with mild and masterly sway. The fortunes of the great White Ribbon cause gave her a pedestal to stand upon. She had been, in her beautiful home, a mother so beloved that she drew all her household toward her as the sun does the planets round about him, but she became a mother to our whole army. She came to the kingdom for a sorrowful time, when homes were shadowed over all the land and her motherly nature found a circle as wide as the shadow cast upon the Republic by the nation's dark eclipse. Perhaps, until then, she had not been a radical so pronounced as she became in these later battle years, but what she saw and learned and suffered, out in the cross-currents of society and the great world, made her as strong a believer in the emancipation of woman as any person whom I have ever met. She had no harsh word for anybody; no criticism on the past. She recognized the present situation as the inevitable outcome of the age of force, but her great soul was suffused to its last fiber with the enthusiasm for woman. She believed in her sex; she had pride in it; she regarded its capacities of mental and moral improvement as illimitable, but at the same time she was a devoted friend to men. How could she be otherwise with a husband true and loyal and with a loving and genial son? All her ideas upon the woman question were but a commentary upon her devotion to that larger human question which is the great circle of which the woman question is but an arc. Oftentimes I have said to myself, 'If this temperance movement had come to women in her day what a great magnetic leader she would have been. How wholly she would have given herself to the Woman's Christian Temperance Union, seeing in it the outcome of all her hopes and prophecies, for the protection of the home and the regnancy of "two heads in counsel, two beside the hearth."'"

The following reference to Madam Willard's charming methods of child culture is given by her daughter:

"She never expected us to be bad children. I never heard her refer to total depravity as our inevitable heritage; she always said when we were cross, 'Where is my bright little girl that is so pleasant to have about? Somebody must have taken her away and left this little creature here who has a scowl upon her face.' She always expected us to do well; and after a long and beautiful life, when she was sitting in sunshine calm and sweet at eighty-seven years of age, she said to one who asked what she would have done differently as a mother if she had her life to live over again,

'I should blame less and praise more.' She used to say that a little child is a figure of pathos. Without volition of its own it finds itself in a most difficult scene; it looks around on every side for help, and we who are grown way-wise should make it feel at all times tenderly welcome, and nourish it in the fruitful atmosphere of love, trust and approbation.

"With such a mother my home life was full of inspiration; she encouraged every out-branching thought and purpose. When I wished to play out-of-doors with my brother, and do the things he did, she never said, 'Oh, that is not for girls!' but encouraged him to let me be his little comrade; by which means he became the most considerate, chivalric boy I ever knew, for mother taught him that nothing could be more for her happiness and his than that he should be good to 'little sister.' By this means I spent a great deal of time in the open air, and learned the pleasant sports by which boys store up vigor for the years to come. She used to take me on her knee and teach me the poems of which she was most fond, explaining what the poet meant, so that even at an early age I could understand much that was dear to her. Then she would place me — a fragile little figure — on a chair or table, and have me repeat these poems, 'suiting the action to the word.' Once when a neighbor came in and told her that Frankie was standing on the gatepost making a speech, and warned her that she must curb my curious taste, mother ran out delighted, took me in her arms, and without criticising me for having chosen such a public pedestal, told me she thought I would better say 'my pieces' to her rather than to anyone who might be passing by, because she understood them better and could help me to speak them right." Thus, without reproof, but by substituting the more excellent way, she had the rare and happy art of securing obedience without seeming to seek for it. "To my mind," says her daughter, "the jewel of her character and method with her children was that she knew how without effort to keep an open way always between her inmost heart and theirs; they wanted no other comforter; everybody seemed less desirable than mother. If something very pleasant happened to us when we were out playing with other children, or spending an afternoon at a neighbor's, we would scamper home as fast as our little feet would carry us, because we did not feel as if we had gained the full happiness from anything that came to us until mother knew it."

Sir Walter Scott tells a story of a brave young knight in whose soul burned the Crusader's passion to rescue from the infidels' defiling hands the tomb of his hero-Christ. Girding on shield and buckler and sword, he knelt before the woman who through the years had given her life to him in lavishment of mother-love and claimed her mother-blessing on his eager heart's desire. With never a falter of voice or a sob to betray her anguish of grief and fear, with never a tremble in the hand that touched his bright young head, with only courage in tender tone and touch she sent him forth, inspired by her blessing under the banner of her love. In his garments she hid her jewels against his hour of need, and with the promise that she would stay at home and guard for him his castle and his lands, she bade him depart, remembering that his glory was to redress human wrongs, to keep a spotless sword and soul.

When many years had come and gone and the youth returned crowned with victories won on many a field where he had vanquished wrong, he found his castle and his lands better cared for than when he left, his people taught to reverence his name and to love him for his knightly deeds.

This beautiful picture of the Scottish novelist but faintly sets forth the work of that noble mother, "Saint Courageous," who, when the daughter went forth the "Knight of a New Chivalry," kept the fires of love burning brightly upon her hearth, kept the light in the window for the brave daughter who went forth on her crusade pilgrimages, not to save an empty tomb, but to rescue the living Christ in human hearts from the enemies that defile the temple of God.

To the music of the Traveler's Psalm (121st), accompanied by the strong, tender voice of commending prayer, Mother Willard sent forth her apostle of sweetness and purity and light, even as of

FRANCES E. WILLARD
FROM PHOTOGRAPH BY ALICE HUGHES, LONDON

Interior Views – Eastnor Castle – Ancestral Home of Lady Henry Somerset

old that English mother commended her young knight to the guidance of Him who had promised victory to all who war against iniquity and sin. And to that heart and home the gentle conqueror hastened back less like a victor to claim her own than like a bird to its sheltering nest. Here one month at least of every year was given to her mother, that the springs of love and hope and inspiration might be refilled. Sitting by the fire with clasped hands, the mother would give to her daughter reminiscences of her early life, telling of the beautiful Christian traits of her father and mother; recalling to mind the older home in Vermont; describing the noble hills upon which her windows looked; recounting the way she spent her days, the morning hours given to books and study, the afternoons to weaving, spinning and household cares, the evenings spent again about the fireside, until when 9 o'clock struck, the entire household assembled while her father read from the dear old Bible and, by the force of fervent prayer, drew them all within the circle of divine protection and love. Often the household saint would break forth into words of gratitude for the long life that had been so rich in opportunity, so blessed with friendships and affection. Often she rejoiced in the good gift of the uninterrupted strength that enabled her to fill all the years with toil. Neither mother nor daughter were ever able to brook the thought of invalidism; they could not bear to think of rivers that die away in the sand before their force is spent. They wished rather to resemble those streams which run full-breasted to the sea, and bear to the ocean upon their bosoms fleets of prosperity and of peace.

"I must keep well for the sake of my daughter and the work God has given her to do," would say this sympathetic mother, who in her seventieth year led the W. C. T. U. of her own town. If the daughter encircled the world with the white ribbon of love and sympathy, the threads of that shining strand were surely spun in the warp and woof of her mother's loving care.

Each passing season as the years sped on found her more and more the child of happiness and hope. Pilgrims from the noble army of workers who turned from life's fret and fever to seek an hour apart in Rest Cottage will remember the sunny upper room which all looked upon as the chamber of peace. Its tranquillity was the atmosphere exhaled by the sweet spirit of this woman of courage and of buoyant optimism, this self-sustained soul, whose quietness and assurance were her strength.

In that chamber bright with her presence one always found Madam Willard with a serene smile upon her face and a word of good cheer trembling on her lips. On the tables around her were grouped her favorite authors, scrapbooks upon which she was working, letters and documents intended to further the beloved cause of reform. During her daughter's long absences Madam Willard was lovingly ministered to by the White Ribbon sisters who for many years made a home for themselves in the addition to Rest Cottage, built and formerly occupied by Mrs. Mary B. Willard.

Recalling her first visit to Rest Cottage in October, 1891, Lady Henry Somerset, whom Mrs. Willard fondly called her "English daughter," writes: "When I came to your shores a stranger a year ago, the name of Frances Willard was as familiar to me as it is to women all over the world who are in any way associated with works of philanthopy or the upbuilding of the home. I had read her life and had some knowledge of her work, and with that work of course her mother's name was closely associated. But only when I crossed the threshold of Rest Cottage could I realize what a factor that mother had been in her great career. I have mingled with those who are called noble because of hereditary descent; I have talked with empresses and queens, with princesses and princes, but when I took the hand of Madam Willard and she welcomed me to her heart and home, I knew instantly and instinctively that here was one of the world's great women. A lady of such fine, delicate instinct, with a mind so cultivated and purified by continued aspiration toward the good and true; with a face serene and full of all that inherent worth which came to her through her spotless ancestry and her own natural purity and refinement, I at once classed with all the greatest and noblest that I had ever met. I need not dwell here upon the way in which that home circle impressed me, but as I turn the pages of my Bible, I find a note entered there which I wrote the first night in which I came beneath that roof: 'October 28, 1891 — A day to be remembered in thanksgiving. Rest Cottage, Evanston.'"

Mrs. Willard's mind was stored with much of the best English prose and verse of which in her rhythmic expressive voice she would often recite her favorite stanzas.

Sitting at the head of the table on the morning of her eighty-seventh birthday, she quoted the following lines:

> "Never, my heart, shalt thou grow old;
> My hair is white, my blood runs cold,
> And one by one my powers depart,
> But youth sits smiling in my heart."

Her daughter writes: A volume of household words might readily be made from my recollections of mother's quotations from poets and philosophers. Her motto, " It is better farther on," was taken from "The Song of Hope," and the memory of her low sustained voice, as she used to repeat it, will forever linger in the hearts of those who heard.

> "A soft sweet voice from Eden stealing,
> Such as but to angels known,
> Hope's cheering song is ever thrilling,
> It is better farther on.
>
> "I hear hope singing, sweetly singing,
> Softly in an undertone;
> And singing as if God had taught it,
> It is better farther on.
>
> "Still farther on, oh, how much farther?
> Count the milestones one by one?
> No! No! no counting! Only trusting
> It is better farther on."

Two of her favorite preachers were George McDonald and Phillips Brooks. From the first she often quoted this sentiment: "Age is not all decay, it is the ripening, the swelling of the fresh life within that withers and bursts the husks." And from the second she quoted the question: "Why cannot we, slipping our hands into His each day, walk trustingly over the day's appointed path, thorny or flowery, crooked or straight, knowing that evening will bring us sweet peace and home?"

She was wont to watch the children of the neighborhood as they passed Rest Cottage on their way to school. She would speak of them in a voice of infinite tenderness and sympathy, hoping and praying that they might have friends in their youth and inexperience, that they might make their way nobly and well along the intricate path of life and into a safer and a better world. Indeed, the only note that was not jubilant in all the many keys that her varied conversation struck was when she talked of the pitiful little child let loose in this great grinding mill of a world.

At eighty-five she wrote a charming bit of verse which has been recited all over the world by the little soldiers newly mustered in, to fight the army of temptation and of sin:

"LITTLE PEOPLE.

" The world will be what you make it,
    Little people;
It will be as you shape it,
    Little people.
Then be studious and brave,
And your country help to save,
    Little people.

" When we walk into the gray,
And you into the day,
    Little people,
We will beckon you along
With a very tender song,
    Little people.

" If war is in the air,
When we make our final prayer,
    Little people,
We will pass along to you
All the work we tried to do,
    Little people."

In Madam Willard's journal of her last year we find these entries:

> "I am not I until that morning breaks,
> Not I until my consciousness eternal wakes."

And again these words of Victor Hugo: "I am rising, I know, toward the skies; the sunshine is on my head; the nearer I approach the end the plainer I hear around me the immortal symphonies of the worlds which invite me."

The last time she led in the home service of prayer her faith was thus expressed: "We walk out into the mystery fearless because we trust in Thee; we face the great emergency with our hearts full of vital questions that cannot here be answered; we leave them all with Thee, knowing that Thou wilt cherish our wistful aspirations toward Him who lived and has redeemed us. We would know many things that Thou hast not revealed, but we can only love and trust and wait."

During the last weeks of her life the solar heavenly look was ever on the countenance of Saint Courageous. Those who stood closest to her will never forget the sweet joy and the boundless anticipation with which she looked forward to the hour when she would enter into immortal life. She and her daughter Frances talked together of the great change that was approaching. Without a single fear or tear she looked forward to the day when she should pass from earth's twilight into heaven's morn and meet again those whom she had "loved and lost awhile," lending them to God. In one of those hours her daughter thus stated her belief as to the problem "Does death end all?"

"Suppose a man should build a ship and freight it with the rarest works of art, and in the very building and the freighting should plan to convey the ship out into midocean and there scuttle it with all its contents! And here is the human body, in itself an admirable piece of mechanism, the most delicate and wonderful of which we know; it is like a splendid ship, but its cargo incomparably outruns the value of itself, for it is made up of love, hope, veneration, imagination and all the largess of man's unconquerable mind. Why should its Maker scuttle such a ship with such a freightage? He who believes that this is done is capable of a credulity that far outruns the compass of our faith. Death cannot be an evil for it is universal. It must be good to those that do good because it crowns man's evolution on the planet earth. 'Lord, we can trust Thee for our holy dead.'"

If for Mother Willard the years had been full of storm and tumult, these contrasts and adversities had also been full of culture. Unconsciously she was herself the fulfillment of the thought of one of her favorite authors: "The most beautiful thing that lives on this earth is not the child in the cradle, sweet as it is. It is not ample enough. It has not had history enough. It is all prophesy. Let me see one who has walked through life; let me see a great nature that has gone through sorrow, through fire, through the flood, through the thunder of life's battle, ripening, sweetening, enlarging and growing finer and finer and gentler and gentler, that fineness and gentleness being the result of great strength and great knowledge accumulated through a long life — let me see such a one stand at the end of life, as the sun stands on a summer afternoon just before it goes down. Is there anything on earth so beautiful as a rich, ripe, large, growing and glorious Christian heart? No, there is nothing."

It was the going from life of such a mother that made earth empty and the heart of the daughter forever bereaved. Ever after her spirit drooped; a part of Miss Willard's deeper spiritual self reached out toward that universe to which from the moment of her mother's departure she felt she too belonged. In her journal we find the ever-recurring eloquent question, "Where is my mother?" A question that was to persistently reiterate itself until like a tired child she had been restored to her mother's arms. Not otherwise than Monica and Saint Augustine did these two, Saint Courageous and her daughter Frances, sit in the open window and gaze into the open sky into which the mother was soon to take her flight: they saw the heavens open and those who once had dwelt within their home, standing by the throne of God. If in the supreme hour of entrance upon the life with God the mother ascending sent benediction down upon her daughter and upon all the world, the daughter gazing into the open sky cried out, "I give thee joy, my mother! All hail, but not farewell. Our faces are set the same way, blessed mother: I shall follow after — it will not be long."

CHAPTER XI

IN THE MOTHER COUNTRY

"The many make the household,
But only one the home."

IN the sunset years of her mother's life Miss Willard had centralized her work in the dear home now adorned by countless kindnesses of comrades and friends. Picturing the busy hours in the cozy "Den" when shut in with that serene and benignant being "Saint Courageous," Miss Willard was lifted above her former toilsome life, we are reminded of her journal note, written when as a young teacher in Kankakee, she mused on the home faces of her "Four":

"I thank God for my mother as for no other gift of His bestowing. My nature is so woven into hers that I almost think it would be death for me to have the bond severed and one so much myself gone over the river. She does not know, they do not any of them, the 'Four,' how much my mother is to me, for, as I verily believe, I cling to her more than ever did any other of her children. Perhaps because I am to need her more."

Surely she who could bear and train such a daughter was worthy to be what she always remained — her inspiration and her ideal.

Now that Frances Willard was motherless, Rest Cottage only "a dumb dwelling," hundreds of loyal hearts and lovely homes longed to shelter and console her, but God had opened an English home, a gracious, queenly heart, and the last six years of Miss Willard's life were to be equally divided between the "mother country" and the home land. The origin of this notable friendship, which was to mean much to both women personally as well as to the cause they represented and to womanhood in England and America, is thus described in Lady Henry Somerset's own words:

"It was on a rainy Sunday some twelve years ago that I went down, as I was wont to do when alone at Eastnor Castle, to have tea with my capable and faithful housekeeper. We often spent an hour or two on Sunday afternoons discussing the affairs of the village and the wants of the tenants, among whom she conducted mothers' meetings and kept the accounts of the women's savings clubs. I saw on her table that day a little blue book, and taking it up, read for the first time the title, 'Nineteen Beautiful Years.' Sitting down by the fire, I soon became so engrossed in reading that my housekeeper could get no further response from me that day, nor did I move from my place until I had finished the little volume.

"To me it was an idyl of home life — fresh, peaceful and tender — while its culmination in the passing of that pure soul was a revelation of childlike faith that left me 'nearer heaven.' The name of Frances Willard was but a vague outline in my mind until that day. The Temperance Reform was only then beginning to unfold its lessons, and I was in the infant class of its great world school; but from the hour I read the tribute that this broken-hearted girl of twenty-two had laid in tears and loneliness upon her sister's grave, I felt the spell of that personality which has meant so much to women the world over. The simplicity, the quaint candor, and the delicate touches of humor and pathos with which the book abounds, brought into living relief the character of one who has since become so nearly allied to me in our mutual work for the home and for humanity. Who of us can tell the unseen influences that guide the lives of those who stand in the forefront of the battle, and who may know the counsels that determine when those bound in heart shall clasp hands in high endeavor? Perhaps it was the gentle angel who, watching over the destinies of her loved sister, sealed the friendship that unites in so close a bond the great band of women in two continents who 'wage their peaceful war for God, and home and every land.'"

Mrs. Hannah Whitall Smith, author of "The Christian's Secret of a Happy Life," seems to have been the connecting link between Lady Henry Somerset and the British Women's Temperance Association. They had never met when Mrs. Smith went to Ledbury, the seat of Eastnor Castle, to give a series of Bible readings; Lady Henry attended the meetings and invited her to her home. Here they communed concerning the things of the kingdom, and after Mrs. Smith's return to London, as she sat with the committee that was discussing the difficult question of a President of the British Women's Temperance Association, to succeed Mrs. Margaret Bright Lucas (sister of John Bright), there came to her the conviction that Lady Henry Somerset was the God-ordained woman for the place. She announced her inspiration. Few had faith that she would accept the position, and at first Lady Henry positively declined, but Mrs. Smith presented unanswerable arguments, and together they earnestly prayed for guidance from God. Lady Henry then promised to accept the leadership of the society should it be offered her. When the Association met in annual council a few weeks later, her ladyship was unanimously elected, and in response to a telegram came to the convention and accepted the honors conferred upon her.

Miss Willard, whose vision embraced the English-speaking world as her field, presaged at once the progressive spirit that this valiant and exceptionally equipped president of the British Women's Temperance Association was to bring to the White Ribbon cause. From that hour the desire of these leaders to meet was mutual, and the centripetal impulse of a first World's Convention in 1891 brought together the two who were already one in the new concept of Christ's Gospel in action.

America, New England and Boston first (where the meeting was held) did honor to the noble English guest, so distinguished in all the progressive philanthropy of her own country. After the convention Lady Henry Somerset went west to the prairies of

Illinois, and in Rest Cottage received the benediction of "Saint Courageous," who "farther on," as she saw the lights in her Heavenly Father's Home, tenderly said, "My English daughter has lighted up the whole world for me in her affection for my child."

In August, 1892, three weeks after Miss Willard lost the earthly presence of her mother, she sailed for England to be met by sympathy, thoughtfulness, a sustaining love and care which were to help prolong her own heroic and compassionate life. "The tears would just well up," she writes from Eastnor Castle in the first weeks of her grief. This heart that had brooded over the sorrows of so many was realizing the supreme experience of the daily longing for the most intimate of her life's companionships.

On the first birthday anniversary without her mother, September 28, 1893, the British Women's Temperance Association, through Lady Henry, sent an offering of flowers and this testimonial:

"To Frances E. Willard, President of the World's Woman's Christian Temperance Union:

"Beloved President,—The sadness that enshrouds your coming to our country forbids any demonstration of national welcome; yours is a loss in which each of us have a share; with you we mourn a mother who by a long life of courage and triumphant entry into Eternity has taught us that it is 'always better farther on.'

"We cannot, however, refrain on this, the anniversary of your birth, tenderly to wish you many years rich and full of useful labor. In approaching you with our congratulations it is on no commonplace errand of courtesy that we come, nor do our good wishes spring solely from our love and gratitude. We lay this tribute in your hands because from you we have received the message of women's greatness; because, looking back on the story of the past, we see none other to whom her fellow-women should confess so large a debt; because we know that life and strength to you will ever mean priceless and unflinching toil in the cause which seeks to bring humanity nearer its divine ideal. Your great heart, which knows no limitations of creed, class, or nation, but beats only with the pulsations of humanity, has thrown out the life line of the White Ribbon, and today it girds the world, fit emblem of the white light of truth that called it into radiant existence. You have stood for the forces which level up and not down; your life shall chant itself in its own beatitudes after your own life's service, for you have understood the divine motherhood that has made the world your family."

In another letter from Miss Willard we have the picture of the tranquil days passed at Eastnor Castle in retirement and work for the annual convention at home. . . . . "We are keeping very quiet here at the Castle, seeing no one. We are receiving shoals of letters that come to us from all parts of the Kingdom as well as from 'Home, sweet home.' . . . . For myself I am not very vigorous, but am grinding away at my annual address, though with but little enthusiasm since mother is not here."

Two months later Miss Willard was again on American soil in attendance upon the National W. C. T. U. Convention at Denver, Colorado, where a memorial service for her mother welded anew the hearts of her loyal constituents. Lady Henry accompanied her guest, Miss Willard returning with her to England in November. The succeeding weeks, which were filled with public work, were marked by a great welcome meeting at Exeter Hall in honor of the Founder and President of the World's Woman's Christian Temperance Union. Lady Henry Somerset, as vice-president of this organization and hostess of Miss Willard, had issued invitations far and wide, calling upon all, irrespective of creed or sex, to come and do honor to her beloved friend, and in response a remarkable gathering assembled. Five thousand people united in this welcome; not only leaders of the principal English humanitarian organizations of the day, members of Parliament and London County Councilors, but a homogeneous company of representatives of missions, leagues, unions, societies and guilds, over fifty of these groups being represented. Miss Willard was greeted with an ovation, the "audience and platform rising en masse, waving handkerchiefs, and giving three British cheers in a manner which, with all their enthusiasm, no American audience has as yet mastered, for it takes the burly form and the broad chest of John Bull to cheer in the lusty fashion of our Saxon and Viking ancestry." Lady Henry presided, and in an eloquent address of welcome presented the woman and the work they had gathered to honor. She said:

"It is fitting that this historic hall should have been chosen as the scene of a welcome to one who above all other titles deserves that of Reformer. Wherever the temperance cause has a champion, wherever the cause of social purity has an exponent, wherever the labor movement lifts up its voice, wherever woman with the sunlight of the glad new day upon her face stretches forth her hands to God, there is the name of Frances Willard loved, cherished and revered. Tried by a jury of her peers—even amid the clashing opinions of this transition age where the old is unwilling to die, and the new seems hardly ready to be born—there would still come the verdict, she is a fair opponent, she is a kindly comrade; as Lincoln said, she has 'firmness in the right as God gives her to see the right, and moves along her chosen path with malice toward none and charity for all.' From that more august and perhaps impartial jury, beyond the circle of reform, comes the verdict prophetic of that which history shall one day record—she made the world wider for women and happier for humanity.

"We know that America owes her greatness to the sterling worth of those intrepid Puritan pioneers who were the best gift of the old world to the new; so Frances Willard, who has in her veins that pure New England blood, owes to her ancestry much of the strength and courage that must ever be the basis of a reformer's character.

"If no other work had been accomplished, one of the greatest achievements of Frances Willard's life has been her mission of reconciliation to the women of the South while yet the scars of war throbbed in their breasts, and new-made graves stretched wide between sections that had learned the misery of hatred. It was the white ribbon taken by her tender hands that bound these wounds and gently drew the noble-hearted women of that sunny land into the hospitable home circle of the Woman's Christian Temperance Union.

"'Sacrifice is the foundation of all real success,' and it was a crucial moment in Miss Willard's life when she deliberately relinquished the brilliant position of dean of the first woman's college connected with a university in America, to go out penniless, alone and unheralded, because her spirit had caught the rhythm of the women's footsteps as they bridged the distance between the home and the saloon in the Pentecostal days of the temperance crusade. She has relinquished that which women hold the dearest — the sacred, sheltered life of home. For her no children wait around the Christmas hearth, but she has lost that life only to find it again ten thousand fold. She has understood the mystery of the wider circle of love and loyalty, and the world is her home as truly as John Wesley said it was his parish. She has understood the divine motherhood that claims the orphaned hearts of humanity for her heritage, and a chorus of children's voices around the world hail her as mother, for organized mother-love is the best definition of the Woman's Christian Temperance Union.

"'Live and take comfort; thou wilt leave behind
 Powers that will work for thee —
 Air, earth and skies.
There's not a breathing of the common wind
 That will forget thee; thou hast great allies;
 Thy friends are exultations, agonies,
And love and man's unconquerable mind.'

"In honor of such a guest we have gathered our choicest flowers of rhetoric and birds of song, for it is good and true to pour out the fragrance of our affection and our praise, and place our tribute in the warm clasp of living hands rather than lay it on the cold marble of the tomb."

Before resuming her seat the chairman called upon the Rev. Canon Wilberforce to give the first greeting to Miss Willard because he knew something of the work she has accomplished, and his visit to America had given him an insight into the power and strength of women's work there, and Canon Wilberforce then dashed into an earnest temperance appeal and offered Miss Willard a hearty welcome in the name of the Church of England Temperance Reformers.

The crowd driven back from the doors had flocked down the staircase and filled to overflowing a small hall capable of holding some fifteen hundred people. Here the eloquent Canon, followed quickly by Madame Antoinette Stirling, retired to keep them in patience until Miss Willard and Lady Henry Somerset had completed their duties upstairs.

After nearly a score of welcome speeches, at half-past nine Miss Willard rose, and in swift, generous utterance responded to the sincere British enthusiasm expressed in genial phrases: "The English," she said, "as individuals are reticent, but as an audience they bloom at you like a garden bed." In the glow of this sympathy her sensitive spirit was at once at home, and she took into her heart for aye her English audiences. "I do not know," she said, "that I was ever more pleased than I am tonight that I can trace my undiluted ancestry back nine generations to an honest yeoman of Kent. 'Brave hearts from Severn and from Clyde and from the banks of Shannon,' I come to you from the Mississippi valley, and in that 'whispering corn' of which my beloved friend and our great leader has spoken, I used to sit on my little four-legged wooden cricket, hidden away that nobody should know, reading out of poets and philosophers things that caused me to believe more than I knew, and I do it yet. I do not know that Prohibition will capture old England, and salt it down with the 'inviolate sea' as a boundary — but I believe it will. I do not know that the strong hand of labor will ever grasp the helm of State — but I believe it will. I do not know that the double standard in the habitudes of life for men and women will be exchanged for a white life for two on the part of the Anglo-Saxon race — but I believe it will. I do not know that women will bless and brighten every place they enter, and that they will enter every place — but I believe they will. [Cheers.] The welcome of their presence and their power is to be the touchstone.

. . . . . .

"On a green hill far away was the great scene of history where, on a wide-armed cross, was lifted up that Figure whose radiant love, shining out through all the generations since, has brought you and me together; given us our blessed temperance reform; is lifting labor to its throne of power; has made men so mild that they are willing to let women share the world along with them. And that reminds me that I wanted to speak a word about the gentle Czar. Have you ever heard of him — the gentle Czar? This one of whom I speak had at one time absolute power. He dwelt in his own world, woman was his vassal; she could not help herself, and had not wit enough perhaps to want to do so. But behold, the Czar said: 'Since woman has a brain, it is God's token that she should sit down with her brother at the banquet of Minerva.' So you invited us to school and then we came tripping along like singing birds after a thunderstorm. No vote except that of this hydra-headed Czar ever opened a school for women to get their brains nurtured and cultured. I read that in Edinburgh (which classic city I hope to visit in a week or two), the trustees had, by order of this Czar, invited women to join the College of Arts, and instead of the young men being crusty about it they were received with loud huzzas. In my own country, in some of the States and towns, the women have the municipal ballot; they have it under restriction in England. Who gave it to them? The gentle Czar. The Barons at Runnymede had to force their charter from King John, but the baronesses of this age have but to say: 'Would not you like to come and help us?' and the gentle Czar extends his scepter, when lo! the doors are opened wide. So I have no quarrel with men, and I have two reasons for thinking that they have been full of wisdom in letting us into the kingdom,

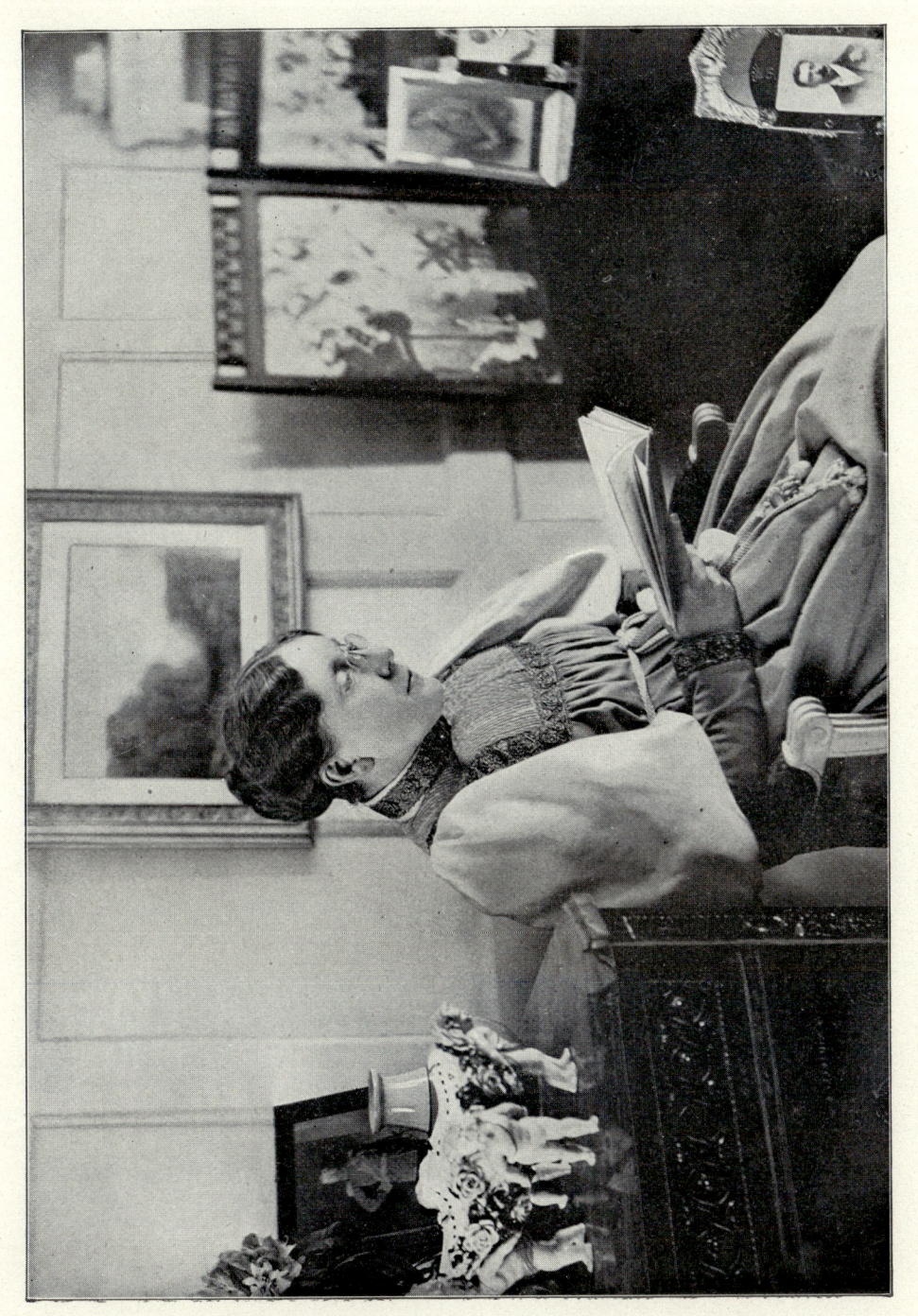

MISS WILLARD IN THE DRAWING ROOM, THE COTTAGE, REIGATE, ENGLAND, 1895.

"EAGLE'S NEST," THE CATSKILLS, N. Y.   EASTNOR CASTLE, REDBURY, ENGLAND.
REST COTTAGE, EVANSTON, ILL.
REST COTTAGE, GARDEN VIEW.   THE PRIORY, REIGATE, ENGLAND.

for we want a fair division of the world into two equal parts. Please take notice, an undivided half is what the women want; they do not want to go off and set up for themselves and take their half, but to let it remain for evermore an undivided half. I believe men have let us into the kingdom because they have had six thousand years of experience, and consider themselves tolerably capable of taking care of number one. [Cheers.] In the second place, I think that they are well assured in their own spirits that nobody living is quite so interested to do them justice, and to look after them in a very motherly way as these very women folk! There is between us but one great river of blood, one great battery of brain — our interests are forever indivisible, for every woman that I ever knew was some man's daughter and every man I ever saw was some woman's son, and most of the men that I have been associated with in Christian work were 'mother's boys,' That is the best kind of a boy, whether he belongs to the children of a greater growth or whether he is still in the bewildered period of the first and second decades.

. . . . .

"Some people have said that the 'Do Everything' policy is a 'scatteration' policy; but I am willing to sink or swim, live or die, survive or perish under the working of the 'Do Everything' policy. By this we mean what they did at the Battle of the Boyne — 'Whenever you see a head hit it.' Wherever the liquor traffic is intrenched, there put in an appearance and send out the ammunition of your Gatling gun rattling its fires along the entire field. That has been our method from the beginning. The liquor traffic is intrenched in the customs of society — go out after it, then, with the pledge of total abstinence for others' sake. The liquor traffic is protected by the people's ignorance — go after it into the Sunday schools and public schools with a 'Thus saith Nature, thus saith Reason, thus saith the Lord.' The liquor traffic is safeguarded by the law — go after it into legislature and parliament, and give them no rest for the soles of their feet till they give you better law than you have yet achieved. But laws are made by men, not by abstractions, and men are elected by parties. Then do not be the least afraid, but go out among the parties and see which of them will take up your cause and then stick to that one. Parties are built up from units of humanity, and they need a stronger contingent of moral power. Let us, then, bring that contingent to the front; bring up the home guards and add them to the army. There are two serpents, intemperance and impurity, that have inclosed and are struggling with the infant Hercules of Christian civilization, Let us strike at both, for purity and total abstinence must go together: the two must rise or fall together; and when we find that the Siamese twins of civilization are purity and total abstinence, when we find that we must foster both, or each will die, then we shall have widened our cause as God wants to see it widened.

. . . . . .

"Alcoholized brains are like colored glass. We cannot transmit the light of the truth unless we are under the power of that holy habit — sobriety. May every home that you love be the home of peace; may every life that you cherish escape the curse of drink; may every child that you left tonight when coming to this meeting grow up sweet and pure and true. May every man that has lent to us his attention at this hour belong to the great army of the gentle Czar who is willing to welcome women even to the throne room of government.

" 'Strike, till the last armed foe expires,
Strike for your altars and your fires!
Strike for the green graves of your sires!
God and your native land!' "

[Loud cheers.]

Quaint, humorous, reminiscent and prophetic, Miss Willard, with womanly tenderness, took her listeners back into her sacred home life, pregnant with association and inspiration, and with statesmanlike vigor out into the universal life of human need and aspiration.

Lady Henry Somerset then addressed Miss Willard, saying:

"We cannot detain you to listen to all the telegrams from individuals and from the branches of the British Women's Temperance Association by which Old England greets New England's daughter. Three hundred branches of the British Women's Temperance Association have sent their greetings; every post has brought their loyal welcome, and their names are recorded upon this testimonial which the British women gladly present to you. This beautiful banner has been embroidered by the loyal hands of British women, and we beg your acceptance of it that it may grace the platforms of America and remind you there of your English sisters."

The London *Times* devoted considerable space to a report of what it was forced to admit was a "remarkable spectacle"; while the *Daily News*, organ of the Liberal party, said: "Miss Willard has perfect command of eloquence which is unadorned, and her quaint Americanisms, homely practicability and quiet earnestness have a wonderful effect upon the audience. She established sympathetic relations with them at once and her response was a wonderful combination of dry humor and common sense. The demonstration, from first to last, was a magnificent success."

The Exeter Hall meeting awoke England from Ramsgate to the Isle of the Dogs, and countless invitations poured in urging Miss Willard to meet great audiences and illustrious statesmen. The cities of England seemed to unite in the request that she should visit each of them. It would be but a repetition of occasions similar to that of Exeter Hall if we were to follow her from city to city as she was welcomed at great meetings and enthusiastic receptions. Already the physicians who had been consulted in regard to her physical condition insisted that absolute rest was imperative for the restoration of her strength, and slowly there was wrought in the quiet and beauty of Lady Henry's own home a marvelous change. Beautiful and invigorating days were spent in Switzerland in the Engardine. The air and altitude were a delight to Miss Willard's spirit and brought with each day increased buoyancy of mind and body.

During the World's Fair in 1893 Lady Henry Somerset came

to America, assuming heavy burdens connected with the World's and National Conventions in Chicago, in order that Miss Willard might recuperate in the restfulness of retired English life. The American leader was meanwhile the guest of Mrs. Hannah Whitall Smith at Haslemere, and writes to the *Union Signal:*

"DEAR SISTERS,— During the absence of Lady Henry Somerset and Anna Gordon, I am most kindly cared for by my long-time friends, Robert and Hannah Smith, and am penciling this letter 'up a tree.'

"We know that when Buddha made 'the great renunciation,' he went alone and sat under a 'Bo tree' until he entered into the Nirvana of complete renunciation of the world.

"So when my host, with thoughts of quiet hours in the evening of his life, sought separation from the bustle of a large household, he selected a great oak tree in the front of the upper portion of the woods at his country seat in Surrey, and building spiral rustic stairs around its trunk, he made, about twenty-five feet up in the tree, a 'House in the Garden' and called the oak a 'Bo tree.' This retreat from the world is eight by sixteen feet, faced all around and on top with glass, and floored with boards arranged like an opened fan, with the tree trunk as a center. Here are rustic chairs and a fur-covered lounge, and I am writing, this beautiful sunny October day, before the large open window, looking over the tops of the trees extending for a mile down into the valley, and beyond this a finely wooded, beautiful country to the 'downs' or hills, twenty miles away, which overlook the English Channel.

"Goethe well said, 'In the tops of the trees there is rest,' and rest more perfect, more complete, could scarcely be found or conceived of in any earthly outward surroundings. It is the glory of Scripture that its words have so many meanings, deeper and deeper as we are able to see more, our 'views' being merely what we, at this point of our experience, are able to see; and here has been given me a deeper meaning of the words, 'And when he *had come to himself.*' Is it not true that even in our work for the Master, amid all our activities, we come to many things before we can say,

'I have come to *myself*.' Whichever of many varying meanings this may have to my comrades, when it is true to them inwardly they, like their 'elder sister,' will each one exclaim with a new and deeper meaning, 'I will arise and go unto my Father.'

"In this soothing, inspiring sunshine, sitting all alone, beholding the delectable mountains, the varying shadows of the light clouds chasing each other over the hills, and the miles of calm tree tops beneath my window, the morning passes, then the lunch bell rings; then comes my daily three hours' drive, my faithful little stenographer, Edith Goode, my dinner, and — can you believe it? at the early hour of eight — my bed. I believe that by these days of mingled work and deep immersion in the quiet of nature I am regaining life and health for my place among the workers of my native land. With every pulse of returning health and energy my heart beats with longing to be once more among them.

"This beautiful home is named 'Friday's Hill,' a name thought to have originally been 'Freya's Hill,' the same as Ceres, the goddess of increase, and here it is supposed that in Druidical days the religious heathen gathered to their human sacrifices. We have a better altar and a better sacrifice, not of death, but of life and all it contains, to the God and Father of our Lord Jesus Christ.

"I do not need to say that my heart, hopes and prayers have been with you in the great conventions. As yet no word has come except the beautiful and loving cable messages, but we look for 'Lady Henry's ship' on Tuesday next, and Anna's but a few days later, and then we shall know all. Tender greetings from 'our Hannah.' God bless you all! FRANCES E. WILLARD.

"Haslemere, Eng., October 28, 1893."

In the months following, as her strength increased, Miss Willard not only helped the World's work and notably the British branch, but kept in close touch with the work at home, and with Lady Henry did a vast amount of public speaking in England and Scotland. We give as current history this account from the press: "Both ladies (Miss Willard and Lady Henry) are entering into the work with great zeal, and have in several of our large towns evoked an enthusiasm which has not been witnessed for many years. The temperance movement has at different times drawn to itself a great deal of public attention. On more than one occasion it has seemed to carry with it the promise of victory; but great activity has been followed by feebler effort, and by diminished zeal. At one time it has been said the movement has been too political, at another too sensational, at another that it has depended too much upon individual effort, while occasionally it has been said that the chief object has been the substantial rewards which have been reaped by those who have been the popular advocates of the cause. There can be little doubt that these charges have sometimes been unjustly made; but they have, at any rate, taught temperance workers a few lessons which are worth considering. No doubt blunders have been made, false steps have now and then been taken; but on the whole it must be admitted that good work has been done, and that in many places a decided change has been brought about in the habits of the people. At the outset, temperance reformers did not receive much help from the more educated classes, or from those who occupied good positions in society. The earliest and most successful workers were men of religious conviction and purpose. They laid the foundations of whatever measure of success has since been attained. Among the churches there were two denominations especially that gave prominence to temperance teaching more than fifty years ago: these were the Primitive Methodists, who labored chiefly in the North of England, and the Bible Christians, whose activities were chiefly confined to the southern and western counties. It is now a general thing to hold temperance meetings in connection with all church assemblies, but at the time of which I am writing this practice was confined almost entirely to the two denominations I have referred to. Lady Henry Somerset and Miss Willard are, in an important degree, leading temperance reformers back to the ground which they originally occupied. They have insisted that the aims and methods of the associations with which they are connected shall be thoroughly Christian. It must, of course, be admitted, and in this letter it is gladly acknowledged, that there have been among those who have not held the Christian faith not a few earnest temperance workers. But if appeals are to be made of the most searching and convincing character, they must be appeals founded upon Christian experience. The Bible is the temperance handbook, and those who seek to do temperance work will derive the greatest inspiration from a study of its pages. The temperance movement needs the guiding light of Christianity; it needs the enthusiasm also which alone can be kindled by a conscious fellowship with its spirit and teaching.

"Lady Henry Somerset and Miss Willard are also resolved to do battle against impurity, gambling and profanity. There is no moral condition worse than that in which a man or a woman is saved from one form of evil only to surrender the nature more fully to another. Gambling is one of the greatest evils in England at the present time. True temperance means purity in every direction, and of this Lady Henry Somerset and Miss Willard are thoroughly convinced. They are stimulating not only the temperance women of England, but the men also, to put forth their best exertions to make this country a sober and righteous nation. There remains, however, one thing which must be done, and with this all temperance reformers will agree. The law of the land, in regard to the granting of licenses and the sale of intoxicating drinks, must be altered. At the present an irresponsible body of men, called justices of the peace, have the power to thrust upon an unwilling people licensed houses which are not needed and are not asked for. And if, as has been the case in a few rare instances, the magistrates have determined to lessen the temptation to wrongdoing, and so help those who need protection, the local authority has been overruled by the chairman of Quarter Sessions. Flagrant instances of this kind have been known in the County of Lancashire, and in regard to the action of the Darwen Bench. It is high time the people made short work with an iniquity of this kind. So temperance people will have to be determined in choosing town councilors, county councilors, and above all, members of Parliament, to vote only for those candidates who are favorable to the principle of local option. Unless the people can gain their point in this matter, much labor put forth in other directions will be spent in vain. So long as public houses are kept open and licenses are granted in the way they are, will Christian and temperance efforts be again and again checked and hindered. The temperance question is now what it was in the days of Cobden, the most important social question of the hour. If temperance can be fairly grappled with and overcome, the question 'how to improve the trade of the country' will be successfully answered, and what is more, we shall then see how this nation may not only be great, but also just and true as well."

During Miss Willard's sojourn in England the suggestive and instructive points in its organizations and institutions, especially their expression in woman's life and work, vitally interested her. As the guest of Lady Henry Somerset, opportunities to study their prominent phases and characteristics were many and varied. To attend political conventions in which men and women were equally interested was to her a novel experience; English methods of election were an absorbing study, but the most inspiring phenomenon was the place of prominence given to women in political life.

With great stirring of spirit she thus describes a convention of the Woman's Liberal Federation:

"Nowhere on the face of the earth have women organized with so much strength, skill and devotion to forward beneficent *political* movements as in the mother country. Seventy-five thousand of them are banded in the Woman's Liberal Federation for the purpose of advancing the interest of that great party which has for many years been 'casting up the highway' of emancipation by which England shall pass over into the promised land of liberty, equality, fraternity. Mrs. Gladstone has been from the first president of this organization, and as an educator for women it has no rival in the island; for successes, and failures, too, are teaching the women that only when great causes are incarnated in politics and parties do they command the public mind and crystallize into those better laws that bring a section of the 'organized millennium' equally to each and all.

"No one (save duly elected delegates from the local societies and accredited representatives of the press) is allowed to be present at the annual meetings of the Woman's Liberal Federation. Fortunately for me I was chosen a delegate by the women of Newport, Wales, and though under orders not to speak, I could hardly do less than move the resolution, intrusted to me by them, condemning the placing of any further restrictions on the work of women until the opinion of the women themselves has been ascertained in each case. Physically it was an ordeal to be present as a spectator in meetings of such momentous interest, but it was the chance of a lifetime. I had prepared for it by several weeks of quiet living in the country, and hope soon to recuperate from the fatigue, while the memory will remain with me an unfailing fount of inspiration.

"To some of us, who believe in the great educational power of what may be called the æsthetic side of a movement, it would seem to be an improvement if there were more in the outward form that appealed to the imagination and engraved upon the heart great battle cries condensing argument and conviction in the form of an epigram.

"A peculiarity of English conventions (they never use that word here) is the cut-and-dried order of business, which is called an Agenda. Each resolution, motion and amendment is printed in full, with the name of the person who advocates it and the local society that he represents. As a result of this arrangement there is very little occasion for the intricacies of parliamentary usage, and there is practically no participation from the floor of the house. The women who, under this rule, spoke at the 'Woman's Liberal' (as it is called for short) were survivals of the fittest, or rather survivals of the best; they spoke from the platform, and having known for days or weeks that they were to do so, brought excellent preparation, and in almost no case was any manuscript to be seen. They were, as a rule, well heard, and what they said was full of practical good sense, often brightened by humor. There were the usual complaints in the rear of the hall that 'nobody could hear a word; nobody could hear what was going on; speak louder; there is too much whispering on the platform, as well as on the floor.' In the midst of these mildly murmured criticisms the new president, Lady Aberdeen, smiled graciously, and evidently held the confidence and good will of the assembly. She used no gavel, but rang a little bell from time to time to bring the delegates to order; they were, however, remarkably decorous, and all the arrangements combined to make them so, the popular character of the meeting being its least emphatic feature.

"While there are advantages in the strong hand of officialism and the sway of committeeism (both so dominant in all public affairs on this side of the water), I question if the greater spontaneity of individual initiative, which is the ruling factor in our American conventions, is not an advantage of still greater value in that development of character and intellectual acumen on which, in the last analysis, the success of associated effort must depend.

"Without a dissenting vote the ballot for women was indorsed as one of the objects of the 'Woman's Liberal,' to be included in its constitution. This decision created more enthusiasm than any other subject that came before the council. Home Rule was adopted as a matter of course without dissent; the same is true of the Liquor Traffic Local Control Bill; the Sunday closing of public houses; closing during polling hours for all elections, parliamentary or local; and the council 'earnestly desired that a law should be passed giving all the adult inhabitants of each locality the complete control of the liquor traffic.' This resolution was moved by Lady Henry Somerset in a brief but effective speech, and seconded by Mrs. Hugh Price Hughes. The Welsh Local Veto Bill was also unanimously indorsed, It was decided by unanimous vote that married women should stand on the same ground as spinsters and widows in the suffrage bill, and that while English women have already a municipal vote (*i. e.*, ratepayers who are spinsters or widows), they ought, without distinction of class, to have not only the municipal but the parliamentary franchise, on precisely the same basis as men.

"The bill to establish parish councils whereby local legislation shall be taken from the hands of squires and parsons and given to the people, was warmly indorsed, and it was declared that this bill should make it perfectly clear that women are equally eligible with men to elect and be elected, not only in parish councils, but in district and county councils.

"A resolution in its favor was indorsed without dissent; indeed, every legal disability of women seemed to be passed upon and declared against with practical unanimity. Eight resolutions, each of them covering some important phase of the Liberal movement as it relates to women, were adopted with enthusiasm."

The Salvation Army with its militant leaders attracted Miss Willard, and she gives this account of "General Booth in Action":

"On March 27, 1893, in a Union church — which I suppose means a Congregational in London — spacious and on the amphitheatre plan, I first saw and heard the man whom I have long been wont to call the 'old war eagle' of the Salvation Army. It was eleven o'clock on a bright spring morning when we entered, and the church was nearly full. A brass band was stationed at the right of the pulpit, and the bonnets of the sisterhood were a marked feature, not only on the platform, where one of the General's daughters was seated, but throughout the audience, while the Garibaldi shirts of the brotherhood lighted up the scene on every hand. One of the officers, who has a bassoon voice, was singing as we entered, and this was the refrain, 'He saves to the uttermost'; his voice was mellow and immense. The General put an arm over the huge shoulders of the singer and said, 'You shan't sing it unless you mean it,' upon which the gentle giant smiled, nodded his shaggy head, and all the people shouted 'Amen!'

"Having been escorted to the platform by one of the officers, I had a good opportunity to study the leader. He is, I should think, over six feet in height, and has an 'off-hand' manner in the presence of an audience, such as he probably used when disporting himself at home with his children in earlier days. He has a remarkably fine, large head, well poised; keen, dark-brown eyes; an eagle beak like the Duke of Wellington, and a long gray beard, worthy of St. Gerome. He has a fine, delicately made hand, with the wedding ring on his finger that reminds one of that great woman — 'the mother' of the Salvation Army. In her going the light of this world went out from the life of this great leader, for no two were ever more devotedly attached. He walks up and down the platform; advances with the Bible extended in both hands; pounds the pulpit; thrusts his hands through his abundant dark locks, now turning to gray; and gestures with his shoulders as well as head and hands. He was talking to the officers, who had assembled to celebrate what was announced as a 'day with God,' which means a day given up to the endeavor to realize more thoroughly the personal relations of the Salvation soldier to the Captain of the salvation of us all.

. . . . . .

"It was a moving scene, as rough men came forward crying to the altar, women with their little children, girls with worn, wan faces, which told of harder lives than they ought ever to have known. 'Thirty-four are in the Gospel net!' called out one of the brethren, going down among them to help, and we noticed that men talked with men, women with women; there was no exception to this rule, which seems worthy of imitation in all revival meetings. Among those who superintended this solemn altar service was a grandniece of Sir Fowell Buxton, the anti-slavery reformer, and a cousin of Elizabeth Fry.

"'You want white robes,' cried out the General. 'They are not the fashion now; they're scarce down here; the smoke of London seems to soil them, but they will be the fashion yonder, and God will help us carry them white and clean into the promised land.'

"It was a scene that recalled the old-time camp meetings in the far West. It had all their simplicity of heart, earnestness and devotion. Again and again the band led the great assembly as it sang: 'He saves to the uttermost.' The effect was indescribable, and moved to tears eyes not used to weeping; the pure faces of the Salvation women as they knelt beside the hapless, friendless young girls who came forward, the brotherly tones of the men as they knelt beside the horny-handed, hard-faced offenders, who were crying for deliverance; and while they prayed, the General turned to Lady Henry Somerset and me, and showed us a handful of stub pipes already given up by the men, and said: 'We get these, and lots of whisky flasks, too, and so we work for temperance.'

"A cultivated woman handed me these words, hastily written, as she looked on the scene I have described: 'In spite of all criticisms, and after all is done and said, I always ask myself, What other organization brings the people out of the abysses of sin better than the Salvation Army? I have seen it in nearly all countries of the world, and it stops my mouth when I hear something said of the Salvationists which may be true or not, for the one thing needful always remains, that the Salvation Army men and women are at it, all at it, and always at it to save the world.'

"One thing I know, that this weary scribe went out thence with tearful eyes and a more mellow mind, singing in tones unheard except in heaven:

"'Take my poor heart and let it be
Forever closed to all but Thee.'

"Doubtless this did not come to pass, but I drew a hair's-breadth 'Nearer, my God, to Thee,' because of that strange morning with the old war eagle and his devoted brood."

Nearer to Miss Willard's heart than either of these nineteenth century movements was Lady Henry Somerset's cherished enterprise, the Duxhurst Industrial Farm Home. Miss Willard's lifelike description reveals to us how at one she ever was with everything that meant help to those who thought themselves forgotten:

"To one who looks below the surface there is untold pathos in the group of pretty gray cottages that cluster in the edge of the trees, which, with the children's 'Nest' near by, the chapel and hospital, the Manor House and Hope House, make up a veritable village among the pleasant hills of Surrey, for on this spot center the affection and honest hard work of the 'British Women' and their leader, who have set themselves by God's help to give to England its most gracious object lesson in the cure of inebriety. But the real pathos of their holy endeavor is in the fact that they are working for mothers, for wives, and for little children — the three classes of human beings in whom center the most of tender thought and sacred love, and the Gospel of Christ alone renders such an institution possible. 'Neither do I condemn thee; go in peace, and sin no more,' is the word of life He spoke, and it applies not to one sin, but to all.

"Hence it was fitting that the central building of this significant and attractive group should be a church, and that its dedication should be the first public exercise ever engaged in here by the members and friends of our farm colony, and it was fitting that Canon Wilberforce, of Westminster, whose name suggests the devotion of generations to 'whatsoever things are pure' and good, and whose lifelong loyalty to the cause of temperance and his later declarations in favor of the cause of women mark him as the champion in the English Church of those reforms whereby the Christian religion incarnates itself in custom and in law. It was fitting, too, that the twentieth annual meeting of the British Woman's Temperance Association should have this dedication as its first service. Lady Henry Somerset, who has been from the first the presiding genius of the enterprise, arranged the plan, the details of which were filled in by her devoted and capable associates. The Executive Committee came down from London with other invited guests. The girls of St. Mary's Home and the children of the 'Guild of the Poor Things,' with the cottage patients, furnished the music. Tea was served in a large marquee on the grounds, and the committee had several hours in which to go over the village, most of them never having visited it until today. When the dedication was over, tea was served in Lady Henry's room, where Lady Katharine Somerset, Canon Wilberforce, his wife and daughter, Mrs. Pearsall-Smith and Miss Agnes Weston were the principal guests.

"That so much had been accomplished in so brief a space was a delightful surprise and the general theme of congratulation. No enterprise was ever more nobly served than this one has been from the first, but among the capable and faithful workers it will not be deemed invidious to mention the Sister Superintendent, a woman who is a born leader and organizer of forces on a large scale; Sister Kathleen, who is a very Madonna to the homeless little ones in the Nest; and Miss Smith, the lady gardener, whose patient skill is working out a lovely frame of green sward, flowers and vines for the picture made by these charming cottages.

"The church is modeled after one at Engelberg, Switzerland, which had attracted Lady Henry Somerset's attention when sojourning there, and of which she brought away a photograph; but the coloring, like that of the interior of all the cottages, is according to a scheme of her own, the theory being that strong masses of color help to make the walls attractive. The rafters of the church are painted a dull geranium red, and round the string-course on a gold band the Lord's Prayer encircles the building, being so arranged as to bring the words 'Our Father' directly above the altar.

"The walls are gray-blue; at the east end they are covered with a beautiful design painted on canvas, while the hangings are all rare embroidery of the fourteenth century. The ornaments of the chapel were given by Adeline, Duchess of Bedford. Yesterday the east end was beautifully decorated with lilies, palms and white hydrangeas, while the altar was wreathed with roses and large standard lilies, all from the gardens of Reigate Priory.

"Canon Wilberforce had prepared a service that was especially appropriate and tender, in the carrying out of which he was assisted by Rev. Aston L. Whitlock, rector of the parish and one of the most helpful friends of the enterprise.

"The address of Canon Wilberforce was characterized by the

well-known spiritual elevation of thought and vigor of utterance that places him in the forefront of English pulpit orators. He made the spiritual the basis of physical health, and said that it had been proved in recent scientific investigations that the sun's rays will kill out every form of microbe and bacillus. Even so the Divine beams of the Sun of Righteousness, shining into the human heart, will kill out the germs of every evil appetite. He said that though one feel as if his heart were ice, this need be no impediment. It is well known that in Sir John Franklin's expedition a lens cut from a block of ice concentrated the sun's rays so that they burned whatever combustible was placed beneath them. Even so a heart, no matter how cold, could transmit the Divine warmth, only it must be adjusted according to the laws of optics, so that it might receive those rays. This was a matter of the will, and we were responsible only for putting our wills in the attitude of loyalty to God according to our best knowledge, and He himself would answer for the rest. There could be no failure when the will, which is the central faculty of the human soul, is deliberately made over to Him who gave it. Thus the process of escaping from the bondage of any evil habit is not intricate or mysterious, but is within the apprehension of every mind, and may become the most blessed fact of every day's experience. This temple reared by loving hands for the glory of God, for the renewing of the spirit of our mind, for the coming together of groups of earnest worshipers, was the central edifice of this friendly village, this true city of refuge, but its significance would be lost if any gathered here should fail to realize that what the Master seeks is that other temple, of which He loved to speak, even the human body, soul and spirit, in which may dwell the Shekinah, whereby each of us becomes 'a temple of God through the Spirit.'

"At the close a touching procession came down the aisle, the little crippled and blind boys whom Sister Kathleen and Sister Grace are caring for at the Children's Nest — to which Countess Somers, mother of Lady Henry Somerset, has so largely contributed — that halcyon home of happy outings for little people from

"OUR ARMENIANS."
REFUGEES FROM THE CONSTANTINOPLE MASSACRE.

Hill Homestead.

Willard Home.

the London slums. They carried the Union Jack and the flag of their 'Guild of the Poor Things' (suggested by that pitiful story of Mrs. Juliana Horatio Ewing, entitled 'The Story of a Short Life'), and it bore the legend,

> "'The Son of God goes forth to war,
> A kingly crown to gain;
> His blood-red banner streams afar:
> Who follows in His train?'

"This is the chosen song of the guild, and there were tears in all eyes as the little fellows sang their hymn of conquest, all the verses of which they knew by heart. They have been taught that their crutches if used in the right spirit and in the Master's sight, are swords of victory, and this is their motto, which they repeat in cheery voices: *'Happy is my lot.'*

"It was a tender climax to the hallowed service, this song from the loyal little hearts that know what suffering means and how to overcome it 'in His Name.'

"As the audience came out to the pretty portico, there stood Lady Henry Somerset, who has consecrated such devoted toil and generous gifts to the enterprise, holding in both hands a big brass plate, and looking into every face, her smiling glance seeming to say, 'And now concerning the collection.' Many gold coins were left in her care, and Mrs. Massingberd — who but she, whose great heart makes her gifts for good continuous? — left a scrap of paper on which were penciled the words, 'In gratitude for the dedication services; a hundred pounds more from E. L. M.'

"And when it was all over, as I stood watching the long procession of brakes, filled by those noble women of the executive committee who are the special coworkers of their great leader; as I saw the little crippled fellows in their crimson blouses, shouting 'Three cheers for Canon Wilberforce' (who lifted his hat to them as his carriage swept past with as much deference as if they had been 'the Queen's Own'); as I saw the women, who are the objects of so much loving thought, going quietly to their peaceful cottages, and the gentle Sisters in uniform, who have them in their care, I wondered if there was in all this great and powerful England a spot of ground dearer to God than that on which the Farm Home Colony has raised its sacred walls."

At the farewell meeting given to White Ribbon delegates in London on the occasion of the World's Convention in June, 1895, Miss Willard introduced a novel feature, destined to become a permanent and delightful one in our great gatherings. It is thus described in the *Union Signal:*

"Exeter Hall — that historic gathering place which has resounded with the tones of voices renowned in eloquence, the hall in which the famous May meetings of reform and philanthropic societies of every description are annually held—presented a festal appearance to the large audience at the farewell meeting to the delegates, June 23. The familiar world's banner, first used at the Boston Convention, upon the organ loft, the large motto on the gallery opposite — 'We wage our peaceful war for God and Home and Every Land' — the beautiful lilies, palms, gay banners, all gave the room the appearance of a genuine W. C. T. U. gathering. Beyond the fact that Miss Willard was to preside and Madam Sterling sing, nothing was known of the character of the meeting. But no one was left long in doubt, for after the opening hymn and devotions, the chairman divulged her unique programme: 'It is well known,' she naively said, 'that the temperance women are minute women, and so I simply asked to have a list of the names of those who were to sit upon the platform, and have no other programme. Not a single woman was told she would be called upon.' The amazement of those who sat facing the audience was intensely interesting to those beyond the pale. But the result proved the correctness of the president's faith. Scintillating truths and nuggets of golden thought dropped in showers. Not a soul within reach of the chairman's keen eye escaped a call. Gems of thought were uttered in quick succession and so spontaneously that the venerable and knightly Sir George Williams, the pioneer philanthropist, founder of the Y. M. C. A. and President of the Band of Hope Union, was moved to say: 'Often have I sat in this hall, but never in my life heard so many speakers at one meeting. I never knew how beautifully a meeting could be conducted until today!' There were thirty-seven speakers in the two hours, besides the singing — a record hardly to be broken by any other organization or any other chairman in any land!"

In connection with the same convention, a gala-day for the delegates was the reception and garden fete at Reigate Priory, one of Lady Henry Somerset's charming country homes. Again we quote from the *Union Signal:*

"The quaint and beautiful English village was stormed by White Ribboners, whose processional advent along the leafy, peaceful streets was looked upon with interest by the inhabitants of Lady Henry's quiet retiring place. Two long excursion trains had rapidly borne the happy host out from the city, and to the delegates, worn somewhat with constant attendance at the great meetings and interludes of sightseeing, the sweet country air and genial sunshine of the perfect June day were as nectar to a thirsty spirit.

"The long line of women, with here and there a favored man, proceeded along the village streets, past the familiar 'Cottage' (recognized at once by many), and through the gates to the Priory, whose long, low, simple outlines gave little indication of the wealth and beauty within. At the door of the great hall, Lady Henry Somerset graciously made all feel at home, and just inside the first entrance Miss Willard, with a happy and pertinent word for each, received the guests, whose number was nearly one thousand. The fine mansion was thrown open to the visitors, who soon invaded every corner — the perfectly decorated, pale green silk-hung drawing-room; the library in white and gold, with its hundreds of rare volumes; the dining room, with its dark wainscotings and handsome red tapestry hangings; the dainty reception room, and others rich in rare furniture, portraits, armor and bric-a-brac. But the chief points of interest were the 'dens'— Miss Willard's, with its artistic furnishings, at once recognized by 'mother's' picture over the mantel and the familiar traveling hand bag with its initials, F. E. W., lying upon the desk; and Lady Henry's room, which appeared very thought-inviting. The familiar face of the beloved Quaker poet looked down upon the temperance workers of many lands who peeped into this sanctum of the reform leader.

"Out upon the lawn and in the garden the scene was a festive one. Under a magnificent willow tree a band (appropriately of women) played lively melodies. At the long tables beneath the canvas tent and at many smaller tables near, the guests were being served in true English fashion. It was a social, friendly company, for no other introduction was needed than the significant knot of white. Armenian and Scandinavian, Indian and South African, German, Swedish and French delegates mingled with those of English-speaking countries in unhedged social converse, giving the gathering a real cosmopolitan character. Of course, with such a company speechmaking could not be omitted, so a platform was improvised, and those who could get within hearing distance doubtless heard much that was witty and wise. The occasion was honored by the presence of the Countess Somers, Lady Henry's mother, vying with her daughter in youthful looks. Countess Somers is greatly interested in the reform work of her noble daughter, reading the *Union Signal* and following the progress of the great reform.

"So much had the weather, the occasion and the surroundings delighted the happy guests that it was with regret they heard the sweet bells of the Priory clock announce the hour of departure. It will be long before the tourists 'forget that day in June' which took them into the sunshine of Lady Henry Somerset's lavish hospitality."

But this workaday world of speaking, writing and sociological sympathies was irradiated by charming recreation, excursions to historic places, short visits to the seaside and rare glimpses of delightful English homes. We know how congenial was the touch of spirits akin to her own on an intellectual plane, and she has told us in her own incisive way of her love of the companionship of the wise and good:

"If I were to ask of every person I met, the question of all others pertaining to this world that I would like to ask, it would be this: Who and how many among the great characters of our time have you personally known, and what can you tell me about them? . . . . . . I confess that everything about elect souls has a personal interest for me; their letters I preserve; their pictures, in simple heliotype, fresco my walls; their photographs crowd my ever-growing 'collections'; their autographs are sedulously cherished, and every word, allusion, or anecdote which brings them out into clearer perspective is of zestful interest always. For I think there is much in the theory of an 'aura' surrounding every one of them, the veiled effluence of the spiritual body, perhaps, by which something of absolute personality goes with the handwriting and passes into the photographed face. This may be wholly fanciful, but it is a most pleasant fancy to me and peoples my little room with presences noble, gracious and inspiring."

First among the personalities toward whom Miss Willard was drawn in England was Her Majesty the Queen. She gives us this picture of the true and noble woman who is first in the hearts of all English-speaking people as she saw her in London at the opening of the Imperial Institute:

"We were on hand at ten o'clock although we knew the Queen would not arrive until after noon. The grand stands with their thirty thousand occupants were filled a little after ten. Opera glass in hand, we watched the gradual rally of what is technically known in these parts as 'the aristocracy,' preceded by their gorgeously attired guardians and variegated flunkies. The cheering is but slight as many great ones come, for the waiting thousands are all watching for the Queen. Punctuality is the politeness of royalty, and though famous for this quality, and promised to the crowd at fifteen minutes after twelve, such is the throng through which she has to pass, that the Queen does not arrive till half-past twelve.

"'Is it not curious,' says an American White-Ribboner whose field glass is faithfully directed toward the distance whence the Queen is to emerge, 'that I can be thinking of all this pageantry, the like of which I never saw before and shall not see again, and yet away down in my heart I am observing "the noontide hour" of the White-Ribboners?'

"'So am I,' was the answer, and no more is said till the flash of spears is seen, the passing of half a dozen carriages containing the lesser lights of the royal household, and then a carriage drawn by six cream-colored horses from Hanover, each gorgeously caparisoned in red and gold, the manes being entirely covered by tassels of bright color; a plump postillion mounted on the left-hand horse of each pair, besides a gentleman in scarlet who leads each separate horse; two handsome Highlanders in a high seat perched up behind; two fair, attractive young Englishwomen, Princess Christian and Princess Beatrice, on the front seat, and all alone in the middle of the back seat a somewhat stout, short figure dressed in black, without a jewel, without a ribbon, just a kindly, quiet, dignified lady that anybody would have been glad to call his mother or his grandmother. At a foot pace the carriage passed, amid loud hurrahs, while a bright flag bearing the harp of Erin, the Cross of St. Andrew and the Lions of England was suddenly flung out into the sunshine from the top of the tower and bands of music played 'God Save the Queen.' Victoria and her daughters bowed quietly to the right and left, the Queen simply inclining her head with a most intelligent and kindly expression; and one stalwart republican from the New World looked at her with dimmed vision as she thought that here and now came to a focus all that is best in man's achievement during all the centuries; and that a woman was the chief figure in all that gorgeous pageantry — a woman who has been true to the sacred duties of wife, mother and friend, true to the magnificent powers reposed in her as Queen.

"I remembered that when at sixteen years of age she was told that she was to rule over this mighty Empire, there was no exultation in look or tone, but with clasped hands she faltered out, 'God help me to be good.' I remembered her tender love and loyalty to that pure, noble man to whom she gave her heart in early youth, and that when asked the explanation of England's greatness, she said, 'It is the Bible and Christianity. I knew that England did not live up to its high standard, but believed she would some day; and that this great reign — so rich in triumphs of literature and art, in the spirit of civilization, in the uplift of the people, in the emancipation of women — has contributed more than any other reign the world has known to bring about the realization of universal brotherhood. I knew that no human being on the globe concentrates in her history and influence so many thoughts; that this quiet woman is the cynosure of civilization; presidents and princes come and go, but she goes on and on until it seems as if her reign is likely to be the longest, as well as the most beneficent, of which history makes mention.

"We waited an hour while the Queen, leaning on an ebony cane, disappeared with her children into the great temple of industry and achievement, and we knew that she had made her speech when the chime of bells in the beautiful tower told that the inauguration ceremony was complete. We knew that Sir Arthur Sullivan had conducted the orchestra, that Madame Albani had led the audience in singing 'God Save the Queen'; and that the chimes were to tell us all of the joy — that the climax had come.

"A few minutes later the whole procession passed us on its return to Buckingham Palace, and it was a touch of nature pleasant indeed to see, when the Queen's sons with their wives and children — Wales, Edinburgh, and Connaught with his blithe young princess beside him — walked along the pavement to meet the carriage of the Queen, and to salute Her Majesty, who smiled on them with the simple kindness of a mother.

"Meanwhile the chime of bells rang merrily, each bell named after one of the Queen's children, and the chime christened Alexandra for the Princess of Wales. To me as I gazed at the vanishing figure that was the center of all this pomp and circumstance, and knew that I should never see again the Queen of England and Empress of India, the music of the bells seemed to be saying those matchless words of Tennyson:

"'The love of all thy sons encompass thee,
The love of all thy daughters cherish thee,
The love of all thy people comfort thee —
Till God's love set thee at *his* side again.'

Describing "An English election from an American point of view," Miss Willard writes:

No object lesson that I have ever seen has so deeply impressed me with the importance of woman's franchise to the well-being of everybody as the elections just over in the mother country. Lady Henry Somerset and I have participated in the campaign, speaking for Sir Wilfrid Lawson and other temperance candidates of the Liberal party, and have never addressed audiences so much to my liking — I mean political audiences. They reminded me most of all of the Constitutional Amendment campaigns of other years, only these are even more homelike in their character. Many of the political meetings here are held in churches and presided over by the ministers, who make the opening speech; others are held in schoolhouses, others in halls and opera houses. They are attended indiscriminately by women and men, youths and maidens, boys and girls. When a speaker who is especially liked comes forward the whole audience arises and gives three cheers, repeating this action at the close. If he makes points all along through his speech, they are caught with great rapidity, and applauded with cheers and "Hear, hear," so that a speaker is likely to do much better than before the comparatively silent audiences in our own country. I have heard the candidate, after an uproarious reception, proceed to read off a list of those whom he wishes to especially thank, and it is curious enough to note that this list was usually made up of the names of different committees of women; the British Women's Temperance Association usually coming in next to the "Women's Liberal," that being the political tender to the express train of the Liberal party throughout Great Britain, for the canvassing from house to house to see if the registration has been carried out; and the electioneering is done chiefly by women. In one of the large meetings a devoted mother stood forward and made an impassioned plea for her son, a fine young fellow, who was the Liberal candidate. She described his qualities, his training, his home life, school and college life, and his career since then. She told the electors that they could not vote for a candidate of whom it could be said more truly that he "had always been a good boy." When his father and mother, sister and brothers came upon the platform they were received with cheers, and the speech that I have mentioned was followed with a regular three times three round of cheering "for the mother."

Women have been out speaking during this campaign, and the Conservative high-born dames, who are most exclusive, have not hesitated to throw themselves heartily into the canvassing. It is said that Henry M. Stanley, the great explorer, owes the seat he has just won (and which he lost at the last election) to the constant "wooing of the electorate" since then by his accomplished wife, Mrs. Dorothy Tennant Stanley.

I have never seen an election so homelike in every sense of the word, for women are everywhere, and, alas! in this country they are in the saloons and public bars serving out liquor on the election day! The development of athletic sports is so tremendous in this country among women that it has become literally true that you can hardly mention any recreation — including politics — in which men and women do not go forward side by side.

The downfall of the local option measure is greatly deplored by our temperance workers, and, oddly enough, it is attributed by many to the great White Ribbon demonstrations that, it is said, "alarmed the wageworker lest he should lose his beer and his place of recreation by the closing of the public houses." At any rate, the election has turned on the temperance question, and while the Conservatives will not do all that we wish, they are pretty sure to bring in some measure that will help to ameliorate the present situation. Mr. Arthur J. Balfour, the leader of the Conservative party in the House of Commons, has made the following declaration since the election:

"But we have not in this country sunk so low," he said, indignantly, "that our constituencies are to be manipulated at the will of any interest, however powerful; and depend upon it, it does not rest with publicans and brewers — be their merits or be their demerits what they may — to determine who it is shall govern the destinies of this Empire."

What we need is woman's full participation in the franchise, and then the temperance and purity questions, the wage questions, and that of old-age pensions will be handled with the wisdom and mercy of the combined heads of the home and the human family at large. Because I believe this I am not so downcast over the recent rout of the party to which every American must belong — that is the Liberal party — as I should be were not my faith in the future based on "that Power not of ourselves that makes for righteousness."

Reigate Priory, England, July 24.

Even an outline record of the six years of alternate life at home and abroad would be incomplete without an allusion to a happy summer with Lady Henry Somerset in "Eagle's Nest," at Twilight Park, the Catskills — that skyey, woodsy, delicious hiding place, made downy and soft by White Ribboner's hands, and alive with the artistic sense of its beloved inspirator. There were farewell meetings on the English side the sea; there were glad welcomes on the American shore; and in Berlin, Germany, a "ten-days' wonder of an Easter outing" which is thus described by Miss Willard in one of her home letters to the *Union Signal*:

"To be able once more to send a lead-pencil letter 'en route' to 'our folks,' is a token of improved physical condition that brings me into happy harmony with the tender fields of green and skies of blue, and that about me and above. We have had a ten-days' wonder of an Easter outing, all of which, except the two twenty-seven-hour journeys from 'The Cottage, Reigate,' to the German capital and back, we have invested with Mrs. Mary B. Willard and her children. Lady Henry went to Paris with her son, and, having remained quiet all winter, I thought to try my wings preparatory to the home flight in June, and am delighted to find that, though ill by reason of a cold in the early days of my sojourn, I have been able to go about somewhat the last two, revisiting the scenes I had known in 1868, when in Berlin as a student.

"But while I met many distinguished men and women (of whom more anon), the most delightful episode was an evening in the large drawing-room of my sister's 'American Home School,' with herself, my nieces Katharine and Mary, my nephew Frank, and the pupils from many States, including California and Colorado. We agreed to give each other of our best, and talked of the life of God in the soul of man, and that life of man in the soul of his brother, which together make up all true work and worship. We sang dear hymns of home and sanctuary, enshrining memories the most tender and hopes that 'lay hold on immortality.' Among them were the Church of England's beautiful 'Hymn for Those at Sea' as there are almost always those in the group whose loved ones have 'gone down to the sea in ships.' We spoke of Matthew Arnold's definition of 'culture' as a 'knowledge of the best that has been said and done in the world' (a free rendering this, from memory); whereupon we incited each other to quote from the poets, and the choice morsels were like honey in the honeycomb. 'From grave to gay, from lively to severe,' we ranged, like bees in a posy garden, and if I could write here one-tenth of the good things garnered from years of reading by that score of aspiring Americans, that inspired French teacher, and the accomplished young Japanese (a student in the university who quoted from his native poets), it would make one whole appetizing number of the White Ribbon woman's own pet paper.

"But I shall not attempt it, for the spirit of that halcyon hour can no more be adequately reproduced than the song of a shell or the tint of a rose leaf. Of the practical outcome, however, I wish to say a word: We then and there resolved, unanimously, that it was every one's duty and privilege to quote at least one couplet — so far as possible the best — from each leading poet of all times, and especially from each leading poet of England and America. We then declared that as the big quotation books are costly, unwieldly and impracticable for people generally, we would proceed to compile a little pocket handbook which, were one familiar with its contents, would make him (or her) master of one priceless thought from each of the electest minds, especially those whose language-drapery was after fashions English or American. We then appointed a committee, in good, orthodox fashion, and any who are interested may look out for our booklet in time for the next holidays. 'Can you quote from Spenser? From Dryden? Schiller? Hugo?' will be questions then answered in the affirmative by many who must now be silent — at least that is our notion.

"When the happy, helpful evening was over, we all made a 'ring, round rosy,' holding hands (as I told the girls was our custom at the close of W. C. T. U. conventions, and repeated together after singing 'Auld Lang Syne,' our White Ribbon farewell: 'The Lord bless thee and keep thee.'

"So good-by, gentle readers, and 'God bless us, every one.'
"FRANCES E. WILLARD.
"On the cars in Holland, en route to London."

Miss Willard's bright setting forth of "A Day with Lady Henry Somerset," is our last touch on the picture of life in the Mother Country, a rich and glowing experience which at some future time must be painted by the artistic hand of the friend whose lavish love made it possible:

"The natural likings of Lady Henry Somerset are remarkable for their simplicity. While she is notably æsthetic by nature and cultivation, her surroundings always being strikingly harmonious in form and color, and her dress remarkably attractive, it was perhaps the most salient feature of her life in America, in the simple flat she rented in Chicago; also at Rest Cottage, and in my primitive Eagle's Nest chalet in the Catskills, that Lady Henry was one of the least exigent of guests and housekeepers. In the Cottage at Reigate, twenty miles from London, where she lived seven years, she seemed more happy than in the palatial halls of Eastnor Castle, or the rich garniture of the Priory.

"But the coming of age of her son, and his marriage to a duke's daughter, have involved a return to the luxurious modes in which she always lived until she became a reformer. As a matter of course, this adds to the complexity of a daily routine already difficult.

"To sit down to dinner at eight or nine o'clock, to breakfast at ten, lunch at two, and have tea at five o'clock, cannot conduce to the success of her philanthropic plans; but such is the versatility of this thorough woman of society and the world, who has become a devoted White-Ribboner and all-around reformer, that she moves on among the intricacies of her environment without altering the substantial quality of her work.

"As a matter of course she does not rise early; it is the well-known European custom to take coffee and rolls before leaving one's room, and to this Lady Henry adds the mental breakfast of the London morning papers and a mail made up of anywhere from seventy-five to two hundred letters, besides papers innumerable from all parts of the world, and press clippings on any subjects concerning which she wishes to be specially informed. This voluminous report from the great world is looked over in a general way and then carried to the office of her secretary, Mrs. Ward Poole, a remarkably quick-minded and genial lady, who examines it with care, dealing with the painful reiteration of requests for help, and giving out much of the work to stenographers.

"Lady Henry's maid (a devoted young woman who was scnoolmistress at Eastnor, and signed the pledge when she did) brings in the letters and assists in her ladyship's toilet, after which the Priory bell rings, and the household gathers in a pretty chapel under the trees, where Lady Henry conducts morning prayers after the manner of the Church of England.

"Then comes breakfast in the beautiful dining room, embellished with carvings, paintings, and furniture, all from Venice, and looking out on a velvet lawn shaded by ancestral elms. Lady Henry then retires to her 'den,' an exquisite room, which, perhaps more than any other in the house, bears the impress of her personality. Over her writing desk are busts of Dante, Whittier, and John Wesley — a fit indication of her wide hospitality of thought. On an inlaid cabinet near by is a bronze statuette of Joan of Arc when, as a girl of sixteen, she led the armies of France. In one of the bright windows stands a group of the Madonna and Child; over the fireplace is an inlaid carving illustrative of temperance; the alcoves on either side are full of choice books in several languages, and ranging over an almost unbelievable variety of subjects; in another window, under glass, are some rare chrysalids and butterflies, sent her from India, whose evolution the mistress of the establishment watches with intense interest.

"Pictures and photographs cover the walls. They are not what you would see elsewhere, probably none have ever greeted your eyes before; many of them are the work of famous artists, and none are finer than the oil painting by Earl Somers, Lady Henry's gifted father, who made a study of the Greek monasteries and transferred the most picturesque to canvas.

"Lady Henry is very fond of pets. One could write a charming article about her horses, sacred cattle from India, Egyptian gazelles, donkeys, ponies, birds, dogs and cats. While she is at work she likes to have the most attractive of them all, Maggie, her Scotch collie, beside her, and they make a charming picture, the bright, winsome activity of the mistress and the intense devotion of the beautiful dog.

"By the time Lady Henry is ready to meet the public many are waiting to see her. Perhaps one is her business factotum, Captain P. (formerly an officer in the royal navy), her steward, butler, housekeeper, gardener, the superintendent of the Duxhurst Industrial Colony for inebriate women, four miles distant (from which three thousand have been turned away this year for want of room), or the matron of St. Mary's Home for Friendless Children, an institution erected by Lady Henry in memory of her father. All these, and many others, are likely to be waiting for a word; or the housekeeper from the cottage, hardly a stone's throw distant, where guests are always staying; or philanthropists of various degrees, who have come from London by appointment, and who wish to make known to her the very best way of conducting her enterprises or to enlist her in their own; or the steward of Eastnor Castle, or some other of its officials, perhaps the rector or curate, have come over one hundred miles to see her on important business; or it may be that the general officers of the British Women's Temperance Association, of which she is president, or of the World's Woman's Christian Temperance Union, of which she is vice-president-at-large, have come to hold with her a consultation in the 'den' or the great 'Holbein hall' of the Priory, or under the beautiful elms, where I have seen a hundred women gathered in council on a soft spring day, and where the Rope Workers' Union of working women, or a Liberal Club from Westminster, or the Ladies' Cycling Association, or the public schools of Reigate, or the guild of the 'Poor Things,' or the Duchess of Sutherland's Home for Boys, or the children of the Catholic Total Abstinence Society, or any one of a hundred different charitable groups, have permission to come for a day's outing.

"Meanwhile the little yellow-covered envelope denoting a telegram is brought into the 'den' anywhere from ten to twenty times a day, and in the midst of dictating to her skillful special stenographer, Miss Edith Goode, her ladyship replies to these messages, steps out on the lawn and speaks a few minutes to the different groups which are gathered, perhaps some quite at a distance from the Priory, away by the pond or near the 'Bo tree,' a lovely little room perched nearly sixty feet from the ground in a great elm, which a friend of Lady Henry's built for her in the fond fancy that she might find retirement there, and in memory of Buddha's tree told of in 'The Light of Asia'; or the guests may be in the courtyards or shrubberies, for the grounds are so extensive that it takes a two-mile walk to compass them — conservatories, kitchen gardens, and all.

"Stenography has been the salvation of Lady Henry, as it is of all those who are helping forward movements involving many people. She has half a dozen young women at her command for this work, and her dictation covers not only addresses, but editorials for her paper, the *White Ribbon Signal*, New Year and other occasional letters to the hundred thousand enrolled women, of whom she is the leader in her own country, leaflets on our different lines of work, Gospel addresses, Bible readings, pleas for the Armenians, for the homes she has helped to build up, and an enormous private correspondence. Her work constantly increases, and her friends greatly fear that the present manner of life may undermine her health.

"Were she not obliged to divide her attention in a hundred ways, Lady Henry would become a well-known writer of books. She has put forth but one thus far — a little volume of her experience of working in the slums, entitled 'Studies in Black and White.' Of this book some of the most critical papers in London declare that it proves her ability, had she the time, to take high rank among the writers of short stories.

"Not infrequently her ladyship is called to the telephone to communicate with the headquarters of the White Ribbon movement of Great Britain, which are delightfully located in the Albany buildings, Victoria street, London. About four days in the week she goes to London, often being driven over to Redhill, two miles away, and thus getting about all the out-of-door air that she is to have until her return, which is rarely before six, seven or eight in the evening. When she has an unusually quiet day at home, which is as 'rare as a day in June,' she avails herself (if there are not too many guests) of half an hour's exercise in a gymnasium which she has had fitted up after the Swedish manner. Here Miss Maxwell, founder of the St. Botolph Gymnasium, in Boston, was with us for two summers, an expert of undoubted

EARLIEST PORTRAIT—8 YEARS. STUDENT—18 YEARS.
LATEST PORTRAIT—58 YEARS.
PRECEPTRESS LIMA SEMINARY—28 YEARS. DEAN WOMAN'S COLLEGE—34 YEARS.
PRESIDENT W. C. T. U.—48 YEARS.

THE EMPIRE HOTEL, NEW YORK CITY.

skill, and, with her usual generosity, Lady Henry opened the gymnasium without charge to the young lady employes in the shops (or 'stores,' as we should say); also to the friendless little ones in the Home, besides other groups of women who greatly needed systematic exercise.

"Indeed, if I were to mention what has impressed me most in the steady ongoing of this noble life, it would be that, besides the public giving in which she is constantly engaged, there are a thousand quiet charities, helps afforded to individuals, lifting hands stretched out to young people striving to start in the world, assistance to families who wish to join their friends in other parts of the Empire; there is aid to young authors and artists who wish to sell a drawing or a manuscript, or to poor women who offer a bit of lace, a knitted shawl, or some other little product of their industry, and a thousand other loving deeds of a like nature. But all these things take time; and although the private secretary is the almoner of her bounty, and the capable maid keeps all the personal accounts, the results must be looked over by their principal.

"I have not written of the 'house parties,' at which from twenty to thirty guests with their servants are entertained at the Priory or Castle, often including names in literature, art and politics, in Church and State, that are known the world around. Of the endless lecture trips, the committee meetings whose name is legion, the corner-stone layings, the fountain unveilings, the bazaar openings, of which she is the central figure. With all these cares, the day speeds on so rapidly that one of her most frequent expressions is, 'I have hardly got my papers in order, and behold, the day is done!' A turn on the bicycle in the shady evening paths, a long, ceremonious dinner, coffee afterward in the Holbein hall, and an evening of bright conversation in which Lady Henry's is always the most musical voice and hers the sparkling wit and comprehensive statesmanship of conversation to which the others like to listen, and her difficult day 'is rounded with sleep.'"

CHAPTER XII

ANSWERING ARMENIA'S CRY

BEFORE 1892, people had but vaguely known there was such a thing as an Armenian Question. They knew that somewhere beyond the mountains in Eastern Turkey, in the land that looks toward Ararat and the rising sun, a war was going on — a religious war — in which those that suffered bore the name of Christians. And yet the term "War" implies the possession of weapons on both sides and at least a fighting chance for the weaker to sell life dearly. Here the weapons were all on one side, the other having nothing to oppose to them save unmailed breasts, clenched fists, attempted flight, and hard endurance of the inevitable. There was not much chance for even individual cases of fierce vengeance. In this terrible plight were men, women and children. Even the unborn babe was snatched into the world to draw its first breath in a shriek of agony, and die. Turks were the aggressors, Armenians the sufferers, in this strange war, and thus it bore something of the character of a race conflict.

The name Christian stood for honor to marriage vows which gave to Armenian women respect for themselves and reverential loyalty to their husbands, to Armenian men exceptional uprightness in domestic relations, and if some bearing the name of Christians knew little of Christianity vitally, they yet held it to the death as a symbol of their national life. When, in the fifth century, a Persian king tried to force them to exchange the Bible and the name Christian for fire worship, they answered: "You have your sword, and we have our necks. We are not better than those who have gone before us, who gave up their goods and their lives for this faith."

For generation after generation the Armenians continued a people apart, oppressed, plunder for the Turk and the freebooting mountaineer Kurds, who fed from their harvests, feasted on their sheep, and carried away their wives and daughters, while they were forbidden the arms necessary for defense.

No marvel that the Bible became a sealed book. There were only Moslem schools to teach boys to read the Koran. When the American missionaries first printed the Bible in a cheap form for the people and established schools in which they could learn to read it, the common people "heard the Word gladly," and many voluntarily impoverished themselves to the last degree to possess a copy of the sacred book.

Matters came to a crisis a few years ago. The Great Powers, partly for reasons of their own, made Armenia an "issue." Turkey went wild with the craze of greed and pride and domination under the name of religion. The madness of the Turkish government had method in it. It was a good time to end Christian Armenia. So long as it remained it was a possible menace, and it was rich plunder. The first step was to enlist the Kurds in the Turkish army, and set them to police the same Armenian fields which they had plundered for three hundred years. The victims had not much with which to resist, but now and then the dead body of a Kurdish ravisher and thief caused the report of a great revolt. Then the order went out from the Sultan, and forty villages in their fertile fields were burned. Men, women and children died with such bravery, refusing life at the price of apostasy, that the far, faint sound of their martyrdom stirred Europe to shame.

So they perished — fifty thousand in one year — helpless, weaponless. Massacre after massacre occurred; men, women and children were penned together as prisoners and slaughtered. Crops were carried off, homes burned, shops looted. They died anywhere, everywhere, with additional details of tortures too horrible for words. And all this went on like a slaughter behind closed doors, from which a cry, heard now and then, was unnoticed, unrealized, by the passers-by.

In 1896, certain of the Armenian victims escaped in a friendly ship to Marseilles — with their lives, but maimed forever, bearing within and without tokens of suffering, and of hideous memories. Here was a young bride whose husband had been slaughtered in the night, and the pieces of his body piled at her feet; here a man whose aged father had been sought out in his own home and slain; here an old woman, with a fine, firm, furrowed face, who, alone with her little grandson, had escaped. The day following, having hidden the little one, as she watched for some chance of escape, a neighbor, a trusted man, though a Turk, approached. He told her the slayers were again seeking the child, and if she wished to save him, she must trust the boy to his care, for they would not search a Moslem house. In her anxiety she brought the child and intrusted him to the false friend, only to see him led into the courtyard and killed. Here was a poor creature burned nearly to death, the Kurds having saturated his clothing with kerosene and set it on fire. True maids and faithful wives wept continually, hiding their faces from sight, for from behind closed doors of torture and death, poor wretches, mad with fear, covered with blood and wounds, rushed into the open street, and fell with a helpless appeal among the passers-by.

In the summer of 1896, five hundred victims escaped from the Turkish shambles to Marseilles. The French government was perplexed. It feared "international complications," and the poor refugees, penned in an open barn by the local authorities, were given a few cents each every day or two, with which to buy bread.

Some one saw in the situation material for an interesting letter, which was afterward published by the London and Paris newspapers. This reached the eyes of Miss Willard and Lady Henry Somerset, just as they were starting on a brief bicycle tour through Normandy, seeking much-needed change and recuperation before the long winter of work began. They were weary and worn almost to the point of exhaustion, but determined to go at once to Marseilles.

They promptly opened communication with General Booth, of the Salvation Army, and the grand old General, from whom they received cordial help, at once sent an army officer to Marseilles. They besieged the local authorities until part of a charity hospital was turned over to their use. It was three hundred years old, damp and musty, but there were great stone troughs of running water in the courtyard. Miss Willard and Lady Henry Somerset, with a young missionary lady from Turkey, who providentially was able to assist them, put things into some degree of comfortable readiness, and there the Armenians were brought.

Their first problem was to procure suitable and sufficient food, and soon they were making soup by huge kettlefuls, meat and onions and red peppers bubbling together, and for each a whole pound of good bread was provided. The appetizing odor penetrated the bare, long halls, and those of the weary creatures who could not assist gathered about the doors and eagerly waited. When all was ready, great bowls were set in rows along the floor. "Surely," said an aged priest, "this is the kitchen of Jesus Christ"; and calling a young lad to him, laid his old hands upon the youth's head, and bade him say grace. The boy repeated the Lord's Prayer, and all the people chanted "Amen."

The building was soon humming like a hive with hope and life and mutual helpfulness. The young men were washing clothes and scrubbing the floors; those who could were cobbling the shoes of the entire party, and the women were cutting and sewing needful garments from cloth furnished by Miss Willard and Lady Henry Somerset.

Then arose the problem of permanent provision for these victims of man's indifference to man. How to find for them places of useful service to others and support to themselves was the serious question. Arrangements were made for distributing two hundred on the Continent; one hundred Lady Henry Somerset took to London, leaving the Refuge Hospital in the hands of the Salvation Army. Many begged to be sent to America, which was "the Lord's home for the oppressed," they said, thinking of the American missionaries. Two hundred Miss Willard brought to this country through the co-operation of noble and leading White Ribboners, some of whom became personally responsible to the United States Government for twenty-five refugees each until they could become self-supporting.

Miss Willard now appealed to America in behalf of Armenia. To the country at large, as a nation just, brave and generous; to women as the molders of public opinion, reverencing the name of Christ and sympathetic with the downtrodden and oppressed; to the women of the W. C. T. U. especially, as sisters loved and faithful, co-laborers with her for years in every form of endeavor; to Christian ministers, urging them to devote a Sunday evening service to the Armenian question, and to secure the passage of resolutions of protest — to all these the cry went out. The general officers of the National W. C. T. U., under Miss Willard's leadership, sent the following earnest petition to Congress:

"We, the officers of the National Woman's Christian Temperance Union, representing a membership and following of not fewer than a million people, who believe that the protection of the home is the supreme duty of statesmen, do hereby most earnestly and solemnly beseech you to take such action as shall put our home-loving Republic on record as having used its moral and material influence for the relief of Armenia, the martyr nation, in the time of its supreme distress. We respectfully urge that our country should no longer remain a silent spectator of the agony and outrage inflicted by Moslem savages upon our brother and sister Christians, whose only fault is their devotion to Christ and their loyalty to a pure home.

"We beg you, therefore, as the legally constituted representatives of the wives and mothers of our nation, to give heed to our devoted prayer and aspiration that America may, through her highest legislative authorities, give expression to all the world of her abhorrence of the atrocities in Armenia, and may make an appropriation from the people's money for the relief of our brothers and sisters who have been driven to the last extremity by the fatal fanaticism of the Sultan and his soldiers."

These appeals have hardly been equaled in effect in the annals of the world. "Sisters, countrymen," she cried, "our fellow-worshippers perish because they will not apostatize. An ancient nation is being slaughtered on the plains of old Bible story. Fifty thousand victims slain under God's sky in the slow-moving circle of a year! Women suffering indignity and death; children tossed on the bayonets of Turkish soldiery; villages burned; starvation the common lot. Now, even now, while the sun is shining on our own safe homes, on the white spires of our churches, on our living children in our arms, these tortures, these martyrdoms continue.

"And, behold! Europe, that promised so much and so sincerely — Europe, with seven million soldiers, and statesmen and diplomats clever as money-lenders — has neither statesman, diplomat nor soldier able to save a single helpless life, protect a single helpless child, or give a single loaf of bread to the starving mouths. The Turk is a savage; our statesmen are — over-civilized! The Turk follows his will; we follow our interests. His part is the less ignoble of the two."

The practical power of Miss Willard; the cool level-headedness which no indignation, pity, or scorn could disturb; the quiet judgment as to what could be accomplished; the careful choice of means to an end, was never better shown than in the general "field order" to her own women of the W. C. T. U. which followed. "I call upon you to organize meetings in every locality, urging our government to co-operate with England in putting a stop to the massacre and giving protection thenceforth to Armenian homes. Let these meetings be addressed by the pastors, business men and most capable women. Let money be raised by systematic visitation as well as by collection."

To the women all over the land she said: "May God so deal with us at last as we deal with our Armenian sisters and brothers, and their little ones, in this hour of their overwhelming calamity." Appeals like these through the aid of the Armenian Committee in New York City went out by the hundred thousand in every mail. "Angry?" Yes! "Full of indignant grief?" Yea, verily! As Mark Twain said, "I should be ashamed not to be angry." These appeals were also full of good sense, and they were effective. Clergymen gave a Sunday to Armenia. A million Christians united in petition. Money poured in. The *Christian Herald*, of New York, rallied grandly to the rescue, most generously supporting the cause. Business men gave. Above all were heaped the offerings of the women, and the Christian Endeavor and other young people's societies. They were hearing "the cry of the world," and nobly they responded, filling full the hands of Clara Barton, who sailed for Turkey, under the sacred protection of the Red Cross flag, bearing seed corn for the fallow fields, food for the starving, garments for the unclothed, and hope and help for all whom hope and help could reach.

Of the results that will live in history it is not yet time to tell. The work, in many of its aspects, is still going on. There is abundant testimony in confirmation of Miss Willard's judgment in respect to those who were sent to this country, for they are proving themselves honest, intelligent citizens, of the kind which America may well be proud to own. It is needless to say that this work endeared Miss Willard to their hearts as nothing else could have done. As one of her coworkers stood by the landing-stage waiting to greet a party of the immigrants from Marseilles arriving in Portland, Maine, a young man among them, seeing her white ribbon, sprang forward, touched it, and bending low to kiss the hand that was extended in greeting, eagerly repeated the one word of English that they knew — "Willard."

From one of those welcomed to Massachusetts comes this touching tribute:

"I sympathize with the Woman's Christian Temperance Union for the saddest and most unexpected flight of Miss Frances E. Willard, the *Lady* of ladies. We read in newspapers and wept so much, but in vain. She passed away, having performed her duty. She will not come back again. But we may turn to her. This is the lament of my heart for her:

> "O! the single *angel* on earth,
> How quick you passed away from us!
> O sweet *Willard*, the only *Seraph*,
> You sowed the seeds of kindness everywhere!

> "O tender-hearted maiden of the Lord,
> You were a virtuous and blessed *Virgin*,
> Who embodied *Jesus* in her active life,
> Who vibrated the strains of the hearts of sisters equally.
> O the great heart, the *heart of hearts*, the *lady of ladies!*
> Who reached the ends of the wide world,
> To uplift the fallen humanity to its *Home Paradise*.
> You did not spare your last ability, energy, and even your *precious* life.
> Your whole life has been a *sweet prayer, a charming melody, an inspiration!*
> The body, the *earthly tabernacle*, failed at last, while the soul endured to the end
> And passed away for *largest spheres of services*.
> O Jesu, bestow in us the *double spirit of hers*,
> That we may accomplish our best to keep on
> What she began through *Thy power* on high
> To hasten Thy kingdom, O the King of kings, the Lord of Lords!"
>
> D. H. SISLIAM, *for H. Hagopian.*

P. S.—God be with you till we all meet again in yonder. "How sweet and beautiful it is to be with God."

Very cordially yours,
THE SAME.

The weeks spent in Marseilles were followed by days of great weariness for Miss Willard, and reaching America in time for the National Convention in St. Louis in November, 1896, she came before her beloved constituency with an annual message unwritten save on the "red tablets of her heart."

But she talked out of that great heart as never before, and in closing an address resistless in its compact force she said:

"I had begun to dictate little slips of my address when all of a sudden the savages of the Sultan put the knife to the throat and the big bludgeon to the head of the Armenians in Constantinople, and soon after we heard of the refugees in Marseilles, without shelter or food. Then something said to me, 'Why, those Armenians stand for your ideas, the White Ribbon ideas; the sanctity of home life, the faithful loyalty of one man to one woman; and they have illustrated this like no other nation on the face of the earth; they lived it centuries before Mohammed had ever conceived his vile religion which degrades manhood, puts lust instead of love, and makes woman a bond-slave of man in the harem to which he has consigned her.' And so I said: 'Yes, these are they whom I would like most of all to help; they love the Gospel of our Lord and they have laid their lives upon the altar for Christ.'

"And then our missionaries told me how women had leaped into the rivers rather than have the Turk pounce with his heavy hand upon them; they told me of members of their schools, sweet young girls, who had thrown themselves into the flames of the Christian church at Sassoun because the Turkish officers pursued the youngest and fairest of them to take them away. They told me things not lawful to utter of what young husbands suffered in the presence of the young wives who were true to them and who with them endured a double death in the open streets. And I said in my heart, 'That is God's nation, and I am going to Marseilles to help.' [Applause.]

"Now I only want to say one thing more, though I kept it as a little secret, but you do not know what waves and storms I came over to get here. Some of the friends of Armenia in the dear old mother country urged me to go to Jerusalem and see the patriarch, whom the Sultan has dismissed, to see if I could not bring him to England to stand up in his patriarchal robes and tell his story to the people.

"There was another plan to go to the help of the Catholicus, who is at the head of the whole Armenian church, and who has an army of refugees around him; or to Cyprus, where it is proposed to found a colony for the women and children. Oh, it all looked so heavenly to do; but I said, 'There are older ties; there is a deep, throbbing chord between me and the White Ribbon women of my country, and though I could not leave England until I knew whether my native land would welcome the Armenians, I came to you with a glad heart, although there was work — a holy work — and a great-hearted comrade whom I left behind. [Applause.]

"And now, beloved ones, with your kind, familiar, responsive faces, I want to tell you why our beloved Lady Henry is not here. It is because she is going to work for the Armenians in the ways I have described and many more. It is because she and the British White-Ribboners have established a farm village for inebriate women; because she is now holding her executive committee, one hundred strong, in Edinburgh; it is because she is devoted to work for the Armenians that this year she could not come, but she said, 'If I have the breath of life I shall come to America next year to attend the National and Dominion Conventions and the World's Convention.' [Applause.] I want to hold you just a moment to speak of the Polyglot Petition, which has been presented to the Queen in the most magnificent volumes I ever saw, with engrossed covers in delicate, artistic coloring, by the finest artists in London, with every British name photographed, embellished with our monogram, a white ribbon trailing across outside; and each volume is so big that I could hardly lift it, and Lady Henry had these made herself. She said, 'The petition shall go to the Queen of all the British Empire in such a way that she will know what the White Ribbon movement means.'"

Miss Willard's extempore address at this convention occupied nearly an hour. Her great audience of eager listeners cheered her on with responsive enthusiasm and a hush fell on their tender hearts as her closing words graphically described the awful accident in connection with the coronation of the young "Czar of all the Russias."

Two scenes have stamped themselves indelibly on the brain of the world: First, the Czar, blazing with diamonds, guarded by soldiers standing so closely together that they were practically visible for the whole length of the road from St. Petersburg to Moscow, four hundred miles away; not the smallest detail forgotten that could guard him from danger, not the least token of self-prostration that humanity could exhibit lacking from the amazing and to thoughtful minds the shocking spectacle of his "apotheosis." Second, the great plain outside Moscow, where half a million peasant people gathered, brimming with ignorance and loyalty, to receive a pewter mug and a piece of cake in memory of the pageant they had watched from afar.

But human life is cheap where Emperors reign; for it is a natural law that the artificial aggrandizement of one is in exact proportion to the minimizing of the mass. What the one gets the mass misses; and so for the mass on the plains there were no guardians, no police, no disciplined host to hold them in order. If they had been cattle their value would have led to a careful distribution of drovers who would have taken care that they did each other no harm; but they were only peasants — and to the number of these Russia adds a million a year; so they were left to themselves; and lacking the power of self-protection, at first the inertia, and afterward the momentum of their vast bulk forced them literally to walk on one another. As one peasant said: "When I reached my hand to take the cup I knew I was standing on the soft body of a woman." Six thousand were trampled to death, and six thousand more were wounded. What an offering this to the Czar!

Journalists who describe the catastrophe say that there was no screaming or demonstration of any kind, but all through that mass of humanity could be noted an undertone of unspeakable agony too terrible to hear, like the wail of the waves on the shore. It was the voiceless heartbreak of the oppressed. It has surged out through the nations; it is borne on breezes to the West; it was the cry of ignorance that might have been knowledge; weakness that might have been power; misery that might have been happiness; and — most heart-breaking of all — it was the wail of faith that had failed and loyalty that had been crushed under the heel of the most massive despotism that still remains to curse the world.

We are told that Russia is the strongest of all governments, and she has proved it by her power to trample on the great host of her subjects, not on the wide plain near Moscow, but across the great empire, from Siberia to the Baltic. We are not inveighing against the young Czar; he is but the puppet of his predecessors; he cannot do other than carry out the traditions of his nation; indeed, we are kindly disposed toward him and his young consort, and have tender hopes that this calamity may touch their hearts, already kind, to greater devotion toward their people, so loyal and distressed; and we pray that the martyred Armenians may yet find outstretched, for their deliverance, the iron arm of the "White Czar" in his character of "Little Father," as the faithful peasants love to call him.

CHAPTER XIII

OLD HAUNTS AND HOMES REVISITED

. . . . . .

"'Tis not in battles that from youth we train
    The governor who must be wise and good,
And temper with the sternness of the brain
    Thoughts motherly, and meet as womanhood.
Wisdom doth live with children round her knees:
    Books, leisure, perfect freedom, and the talk
Man holds with week-day man in the hourly walk
Of the mind's business: these are the degrees
    By which true Sway doth mount; this is the stalk
True Power doth grow on; and her rights are these."

WORDSWORTH'S sonnet, the last words Miss Willard committed to memory, gives her ideal of home. "Thoughts motherly, and meet as womanhood," blessed her childhood, and a woman she went out to bless the homes of all the world. The sanctities of motherhood were not denied her, since she made sweeter the sleep and safer the steps of every little child. She was a fireside being and found a place by a hundred hearths, consecrating and quickening the flame that was kindled on each, while she loved her own home with all the purity and enthusiasm of her nature.

When we remember the child in her daily frolics and rambles and tender twilight dreamings at Forest Home, the young woman planting trees with her father in Evanston and noting all the magic play of nature, we comprehend that home was not a platitude but a plenitude to this woman of ideals. In its quintessence of intimacy, endearment and sympathy it comforted her, but as a type of universal kindness it warmed her imagination. Her soul builded ever "more stately mansions," but it never forgot its primitive surroundings, its growing-cells. Nature, Humanity, God, became her "dwelling place," through which she passed right graciously to her last home, yet loving to linger at each dear stopping place, each tenement of all the way. Fast outgrowing the earthly garment of the flesh, Miss Willard turned in these last months with all her tenacious purpose toward revisiting those places which had sheltered her as child, maiden and woman, shutting her away, in their sweet restfulness, from the world to which she belonged.

In the mother country she had gone through quiet fields and flowery byways to the village of Horsmonden, in Kent, where lived those stanch English lives that bequeathed such resistless courage and unspent energy to their descendants. In the registry of the parish church she saw the name of Simon Willard, with the date of his baptism, and under the spell of by-gone years, standing in the high-perched pulpit, she recited Mrs. Hemans' hymn:

> "The breaking waves dashed high
>   On a stern and rockbound coast,
> And the woods against a stormy sky
>   Their giant branches tossed;
>
> "And the heavy night hung dark
>   The hills and waters o'er,
> When a band of exiles moored their bark
>   On the wild New England shore."

It was the first home revisited, a mystic and sentient hour for our leader, a realization of those primal unities which make America one with England. The old Horsmonden church now holds a commemorative tablet presented by Miss Willard as an expression of her gratitude for the inheritance of "a good great name."

After the St. Louis Convention in November, 1896, Castile, New York, was selected as a winter residence and became a genuine home through the constant thoughtfulness and gracious personality of the presiding genius of its sanitarium, Dr. Cordelia A. Greene, whom Miss Willard was wont to describe as the essence of strength and gentleness in combination, a chemical amalgam of scientist and saint. The home group that drew about Miss Willard in pretty "Daily Cottage" included a blessed mother and her trio of daughters, and was the circle closest to her whose practical thought and genial fancy directed and beautified the winter.

Of Castile Miss Willard writes: "I wish you could see this little Western village on top of its hill and under its ice and snow. It abounds in fine tall elms and maples, although they do not console one very much these days! But its evergreens are a real comfort, a protection when we sit out 'breathing deeply' on these cold wintry mornings, and sometimes when the heavens are brilliant and the angle of vision just right *I can see the flush of leaves that are to be* in the top of a lovely willow that lifts its symmetrical proportions just across the street."

This sensitiveness to the charms of nature gave vividness and pathos to every phase of Miss Willard's home life, even when she made home of transient tarrying places where she stopped but a day. Her acute acquisitive spirit attracted to itself immediately the distinguishing qualities of the landscape. The mind that saw "the flush of leaves that are to be" naturally saw infinite things besides, and the fragile form accentuated the mystery and variety of the soul's expression.

A delightful interruption to the usual routine was Miss Susan B. Anthony's visit, the experience of which Miss Willard shared with her comrades in a letter to the *Union Signal:* "It was a bright sunny day in this upland town, fifteen hundred feet above the sea level. I cleared my writing room for our dear friend, and A—— went to the station to meet her. We gathered in a group at the door as they drew up, it being my intention to 'help Susan out.' But I saw that anybody less swift of foot than a football expert need make no such attempt. Forth stepped Miss Anthony, seventy-seven years of age, with traveling bag and umbrella, her movements as balanced and agile as they were a half century ago, her face lighting up with smiles and the cheery 'How are you?' as she walked in, bringing a breeziness that seemed perennial. As a

KATHARINE WILLARD BALDWIN

LILLIAN M. N. STEVENS
MISS WILLARD'S SUCCESSOR AS PRESIDENT OF THE NATIONAL W. C. T. U.

matter of course, we sat down for a talk, which continued with slight interruption until the afternoon of the next day, each one 'getting in a word' as opportunity offered, and very likely each saying to herself, 'There, she has stopped to breathe, now comes my chance.'"

This picture of Miss Willard as a hostess will be widely recognized. Outgoing, inclusive, comprehensive, instantly *en rapport* with her guest, feeling with electric rapidity the subtle combination of the forces to be met, she rose to every occasion and adapted herself perfectly to the varying phases of thought and feeling in other minds.

It was at Castile as she sped her parting guest, Mrs. J. K. Barney, of Rhode Island, just starting for Australia as our White Ribbon missionary, that Miss Willard gave utterance to such vigorous words of faith in the work and the worker as sent her forth like an officer in the great army inspired by the commands of a general.

Never did Miss Willard's working power seem more creative. Editorials, articles for the newspapers; plans for a birthday celebration for Neal Dow; eager sympathy and effort for Armenia; "A Woman's Plea for the Purification of the Press"; plans for the "W. C. T. U. New Year," made during visits from a number of temperance experts; a "lift" for the local union when dearly loved White-Ribboners spoke under its auspices; an evening of fun for the Sanitarium patients — all these entered into the winter's activity.

With spring's coming she drooped; the physical energy that had been gained by unfailing response to her wise physician's behests slowly ebbed away and it was believed a stay at Atlantic City would refresh the weary worker. With deep concern it was seen that ocean breeze and varied seaside life failed to bring the wished-for strength. For three weeks she was in the open air, much of the time in her rolling chair, looking out over the wide expanse of ocean dictating correspondence and articles, letting the tides of human life and the sea make fuller her spirit's vigor, while the body gained only small treasure of strength, and the pathetic whiteness of her face told its own sad story. During the stay in Atlantic City an excursion was made to Washington, D. C., where Miss Willard spent a memorable Sunday as a guest at Cedar Hill, the home of Mrs. Frederick Douglass. Returning to the seashore, she welcomed Miss Jackson, then on her way to Germany, and a week of reminiscence and prophecy was given to these friends of "Auld Lang Syne." It was fitting that this their last visit together should take place in New Jersey near the hospitable Jackson home from which the young friends years ago had set out upon their European travels.

On May sixth Miss Willard spoke in Broadway Tabernacle, New York City, fulfilling a long deferred promise that an address should be given by the National President to the State securing the largest number of new members during the year, and a similar promise was redeemed for New Jersey by an address at Jersey City five evenings later.

Then for five weeks in the shadow of Cambridge University she rested by a congenial fireside and enjoyed in her hostess a woman of rare culture and most entertaining originality. Whoever knows Cambridge needs no description of its richness of romance and erudition, and the rare charm of its gracious hospitality. Miss Willard took daily drives behind a gentle, slow-paced Norwegian pony lent her by the poet Longfellow's daughter "Laughing Allegra." "How little I thought," said the guest, "when a child in my linsey-woolsey gown on a Wisconsin farm, that 'Laughing Allegra' would ever lend me her pony, but so it was to be. It was probably because I knew and loved them long ago that I am near them now." Here in the quiet family life, ministered to by devoted friends, Miss Willard became stronger, and in June she started northward toward the hills, settling for the summer months at Hotel Ponemah, in Milford Springs, eight hundred feet above the sleepy little village of Amherst, New Hampshire, noble in situation with a restful prospect of farm lands and hills filling the wide western horizon. In the weeks that followed, Nature sought her child, and she lent her ear and eye to all the tender, coaxing sights and signs about her. Laying her tired head upon that tireless heart, breathing deep fragrant inhalations, she heard those well-known chirpings and whisperings, the speech of insect and leaf that had wooed her in her girlhood. On a drive between the hotel and Milford, she counted seventy varieties of trees and shrubs and recorded them for her pleasure. Noting intently every passing expression of summer — that last sweet summer of her earthly life — she dwelt with childlike joy on every fern and flower and singing bird. Her love of birds was more than a fondness, it was an affinity. As a girl she had dreamed of all things free, and her last verse was to celebrate that longing for flight she shared with every winged thing.

But even into this summer idyl would break the human love, the longing for distant friends or the ever-present mindfulness of whatever by her side might creep or cling, and we note this memorandum carefully fastened to her dressing table and as carefully carried out: "August 17 — Go to see the ninety-five year old lady; also the paralyzed woman who lives at the foot of the hill. Take to each of them some magazine, or picture book, or something."

The village of Chesham, once a part of Dublin, New Hampshire, is but a few miles west of Milford Springs, and there, toward the last of the season, Miss Willard spent a happy holiday at Brookside Farm with the descendants of her great-great-grandfather, Elder Elijah Willard, who for forty years preached in the Baptist church of the village. Over shady roads reminding her of English lanes she drove through sloping farm country in sight of Mount Monadnock, recounting the adventures of "that trip with father" forty years before, when she went east to take "Nineteen Beautiful Years" for publication, and when all the relatives were visited and the first mountain seen by the prairie-girl traveler. Sunday morning she sat in the old church that had been but little changed in the changing years, and at the Young People's service of praise in the evening she spoke tender words of recollection and cheer. She drove up the steep hills to the low-studded homestead in which Elder Willard lived and died, and standing on the quaint porch, shading her eyes with her delicate hand, she drank her fill of majestic Monadnock, and turning to Mount Willard on her right remarked: "Yes, these are the old haunts from which I received my original fibers."

Monday morning, after a chat with an aged farmer who had known the Elder well and who every few minutes would say with strong emphasis, "Yes, Elder Willard was a *beautiful* man," Miss Willard drove to her ancestor's grave and placed there a bunch of water lilies, the floral emblem of the World's W. C. T. U. Many calls were made on those related by ties of kindred and affection to the pastor beloved, many stories of his progressive views and sound judgment were enjoyed, and Miss Willard was like a happy child, her overflowing spirits communicating themselves to all about her.

August seventh found her in Ogunquit, the guest of near and dear friends summering there. These days on the rugged Maine coast had in them the true witchery of the sea. A thoroughgoing clambake, a ride on the white smooth beach on her bicycle, dictating daily from a rock if not a rocking-chair, exulting in the sunlight and the sunsets, the days went on full of thought for the conventions soon to meet. Portland was close at hand, and for a few days she was a guest in that city while earnest convention plans were made with her closest coadjutors in National and World's work. Touching, in the light of days to be, was her last interview at this time with Gen. Neal Dow; a talk keyed to the harmony of heaven between two associated in lifework and so soon to enter upon eternal endeavor.

With the last days of August she said good-by to the sea "down in the haven," and felt again the impulse of the hill country as she started to visit the homes of her father and mother in Vermont. They were a hill-born race and acquired among that uplifted company their wide-eyed vision. Eleven miles only separated the lad and lassie Josiah and Mary. The girl grew on the breezy plateau of Danville, with its distant sky-line curved with mountains and its hushed pasture lands — a far-seeing place — and she did not know the boy who from the heights above Wheelock Hollow was looking out on the same magnificent range of the White Mountains. Nature was in her most imperial mood that August thirtieth when she stood on the spot where her revered mother had been given to the world, and planted a fragrant balsam and a sturdy pine, symbols of the two lives that had meant the most to her. There, surrounded by home-folk who claimed her as a daughter, a sister, a mother beloved, Miss Willard made one of those speeches which search out the heart. Old men and women wept like children, and one man summed it up in a sentence as the most "homey talk" he had ever heard. Oh, the blessed memory of that day! Writes one who was present: "Do you remember how with almost girlish glee she threw the earth over the roots of the trees and dashed the water on?" As she drove from the village, followed by the love and "God bless you" of the country folk, there were two stopping places on the way — one to visit the quiet graveyard where she lovingly placed flowers on the hillock that marked the resting place of "mother's deskmate in the long ago," the other to enter the home of an invalid White-Ribboner and to leave with her bright blossoms before the hand that eagerly grasped them should be still forever. From Danville she drove to Wheelock, planted snowball bushes at her uncle's grave, visited the Willard Farm — her father's birthplace — and was loath to leave the "sugar bush," whose kingly maples were the boys' most worshiped sylvan divinities.

Once more in Milford Springs she reveled in Shakespeare's plays, English and American history, and held "quiz classes" in the twilight hours under the trees, catching the first notes of autumn's melody, the soft low strain of Nature's lullaby. She took a lingering farewell of loving mother earth. Can we picture it? — this slight figure with its pathetic movements of weariness and occasional buoyant gestures of life and expectancy? Here the sisters, Mary (from Germany) and Frances, spent that day together, of which Mrs. Willard writes: "Frances could not talk fast enough. She wanted me to know so many things, old secrets, new hopes and plans. How heavenly she was even then! Out in the morning sunshine on the veranda she threw open her arms to the sky and exclaimed, 'O universe, what thou desirest I desire!' So at one was she with the divine of heaven and earth, so heavenly, at the same time never so human. I have rarely seen her in a more tender, loving attitude toward every friend of now and then. Her very last whisper in my ear at the station was one that breathed love of kin and fellowship with all of us who are left to mourn her."

The poetry of friendship and nature were but a part of those halcyon days. During the hours bounded by the sunrise and sunset, thought at its intensest stretch kept pace with time, and it was her spirit that got through the work. Yet her strength seemed largely regained, and she went bravely forward with preparations for the convention — that yearly home-coming she loved the best of all. The vacation over, a soft September day was spent in Still River, Massachusetts, on her way to Skaneateles, New York. Still River held the attraction of a home built by Henry Willard, great-grandfather of Miss Willard's great-grandfather, and a gifted relative, a true Willard, who with his two maiden sisters entertained her with spicy conversation, not forgetting more substantial delicacies. In a Quaker home at Skaneateles, a home full of memory's pictures, the charming colonial country seat of one very dear, Miss Willard completed her addresses for Toronto and Buffalo, and all too soon came the hour for stepping out into the great world that awaited her.

In Toronto, in October, Miss Willard, in a foreign yet a home land, presented the crowning message of her life. She was strong in her beauty, and never had she seemed so lifted up in the sweep of her thought and the brilliancy of her leadership.

On "Children's Night," in Massey Music Hall, when she stood a graceful figure, her face aglow with light and love against a background of one thousand little people waving to her their enthusiastic welcome, many hearts said she will never look nearer to heaven than she does tonight, no matter how many years of her pilgrimage remain.

At Buffalo, in the convention that followed, some who "saw" tell us they detected already the look of change upon her face, that expression which separates mortals about to become immortal. Certainly when in an hour of transcendent renunciation she was ready to give home and the new year of her life upon which she had just entered to the lifting of a material burden far out-measuring her fragile health, her friends felt something of the limitless strength of her spirit. One picture of those days will be forever treasured, when, behind the flower-laden desk, the president, still directing the thousand women before her, bent to write a message to a college girl whose heart was breaking with her first sorrow, and in the midst of all the queenly homage of the hour "forgot herself" as ever in the sweet consideration of another life. It was a typical moment in the career of the beautiful crowned womanhood whose boundless spiritual affluence could plan for humanity, or touch with a mother's pity the grief of the tenderest human thing.

At the close of the Buffalo convention Miss Willard went to Churchville, New York, her birthplace, for a Sunday with beloved relatives. The morning was spent with the only surviving relative of her mother's generation, "Aunt Sarah," and in the afternoon she met the White-Ribboners in the Methodist church. After the service, two by two they walked to the house where Miss Willard was born. Seeking out the very room into which the little stranger came, standing closely about their leader, they heard her talk of motherhood and of the great home to which she was looking, now that her mother's ear would never again hear her returning footsteps.

It was in that room the mother-love had hung over the cradle of the child Frances as the star hung over the babe in the manger of Bethlehem. It was her coming that called forth these words of Mother Willard in the last year of her earthly life:

"Motherhood is life's richest and most delicious romance. And sitting now in the sunshine calm and sweet with all my precious ones on the other side save only the daughter who so faithfully cherishes me here, I thank God that he ever said to me 'Bring up this child for me in the love of humanity and the expectation of immortal life.' My life could not have held more joy, if some white-robed messenger of the skies had come to me and said 'I will send a spiritual being into your arms and home. It is a momentous charge, potent for good or evil, but I will help you. Do not fear. Therefore, mother, step softly. Joy shall be the accepted creed of this young immortal in all the coming years. This child shall herald your example and counsels when you are resting from your labors.'"

After a fond good-by to Aunt Sarah and her kindred beloved, Miss Willard, repeating the first journey of her life, went westward to Oberlin, where Mary was born. Here again in the old home she received greetings from friends and relatives, held glad converse with her first Forest Home teacher, addressed a W. C. T. U. gathering in the afternoon and a public meeting later where the children of the Loyal Temperance Legion flocked in; attended prayers in the college chapel with memories of President Finney and the illustrious Christian manhood and womanhood his influence had helped to form.

She tarried but a day amid these dear scenes, and reaching Chicago was the warmly welcomed guest — nay — beloved member of the family, in the artistic home of her cousin Hattie. There she received all that a tender, unselfish and sisterly heart could devise to upbuild her physically and to shelter her from the various engagements and demands that came whenever she returned to her home city. Frequent visits to Evanston were more significant than any home-goings. The hours in the "rifted nest," as she now styled Rest Cottage, had pathetic moments, while even the thoughtful kindness of friends old and new who entertained her and the genial circle of Evanston neighbors could not break the sense of homelessness more poignant here than anywhere else in the world. She had loved this roof-tree as only those can who turn to it from other quarters, who rest in it after many wanderings.

It is pleasant to think of the cheery social events in which

Miss Willard was able to take part in Chicago and Evanston, though never did she work more untiringly for White Ribbon interests. It was particularly gratifying to her to address the students of the Northwestern and the Chicago Universities, the quaintness and sweetness of her words and her lovely presence drawing to her the hearts of her younger brothers and sisters, and her evident physical frailness arousing their chivalric sympathy.

In the circle of home with her kindred on Thanksgiving Day and at Christmas time, she was full of merry playfulness, or with an instant change of thought would say grace at table, bringing the divine realities so near as to move all to tears. Her jubilant alto voice joined in all the songs with only a tremolo in "Home, Sweet Home," which was sung around the children's Christmas tree. How varied and sparkling was her table talk while the precious body took less of nourishment than the mind gave out to others! The story of those hours when the vase-like purity of her being was so sheer a screen for the flame of her soul cannot be told. Reminiscence and suggestion will not give again the countless intimations of ethereal beauty which she shed about her.

New Year's Day was to see again at Janesville, Wisconsin, the woman of ripe years, of grand achievement and of gentle perfected womanhood, as it had seen her go out a mere maiden long ago. Here her last public address was given in the Congregational church, with the friends of her childhood days meeting the glance of her tender eyes as she spoke words of life and love concerning the sanctity of the home, and said with hand lifted in blessing as she left the pulpit, "Good-by, dear friends of my loved childhood's home, good-by—perhaps forever—and if forever, may we meet in our home in heaven." With her cousins she revisited Forest Home, stood on the old veranda, talked with the bright-faced teacher and children in the schoolhouse near by. This home more than any other had been inwrought into her life and must have given her the conviction that "homes are as immortal as folks, and in their essence will be of us in the real and better and oncoming life."

CHAPTER XIV

NEARING THE HEAVENLY HOME

"And so to the land's
Last limit I came —
And can no longer,
But die rejoicing,
For through the Magic
Of Him the Mighty,
Who taught me in childhood,
There on the border
Of boundless Ocean,
And all but in Heaven
Hovers the Gleam."

"THERE is such a little way to go," Miss Willard had said to her comrades in the memorial service at our Toronto Convention in October.

Tenderly she had plead with us always to talk about others as we would were the sacred seal of death already on their foreheads. Oh, beloved friend! The light of heaven was always in her true, far-seeing, kindly eyes — she long ago caught the sweet spirit of saints redeemed; her charity was never aught but God-like! What wonder that we failed to think her words prophetic! As we traveled swiftly toward the cosmopolitan city that links our great republic with every other land, how could we dream that after all these happy and eventful years of travel by land and by sea we were taking our last journey together?

Many letters were written on the way; there was rich converse of nature, of science, of God, sometimes suggested by her own deep thoughts when persuaded to rest awhile, or called out by paragraphs in the daily papers, and many were the plans proposed for the weeks to be invested in work before crossing the ocean to spend the summer months with Lady Henry Somerset, and look again into the faces of dear comrades in the annual council of the British Women's Temperance Association.

Just before leaving Chicago Miss Willard had received a telegram which brought tears to her eyes and a quiver to her lips as she said, "This is something quite unusual; such kindness from a stranger touches me deeply. The telegram read:

"To have as a guest at the Hotel Empire the author of so much good will more than recompense us; there will be no charge for your apartments.
"W. JOHNSON QUINN."

Dear friends had called at the Hotel Empire with the thought it would be a pleasant home for us while in New York, but the prices were found to be far beyond our possibilities. The hotel was delightfully located near Central Park and Riverside Drive, not thickly surrounded by business blocks or homes, and therefore in the best atmosphere. After an interchange of letters it was decided that even the generous terms offered by the proprietor were more than a reformer's income could meet and we had planned to take rooms in a quiet boarding house down town, when this message made us the grateful guests of Mr. and Mrs. Quinn, in a sunny suite of apartments on the first floor of this homelike hotel.

During the first two weeks of our stay we drove for an hour every pleasant day in the Park, or up the beautiful Riverside Drive as far as the tomb of Gen. Grant, and late in that first week we spent an afternoon in the charming home of Miss Willard's niece, Mrs. Katharine Willard Baldwin, seeing for the first time the little grandnephew, Summerfield. When Mr. Quinn called upon us, Miss Willard was deeply impressed with his brotherly good will and his sincere wish that we should remain at the hotel just as long as we desired. "Why," said Miss Willard, "I thought we ought not to stay beyond a week," only to receive the reply, "You could not do me a greater kindness than to stay a year if you cared to, and any time in the future if you are in the city I want you to feel that you, and whoever is with you, will be welcome to the best rooms at my disposal."

About two weeks after our arrival Miss Willard complained of great weariness and unnatural languor, but kept bravely at work notwithstanding our pleading that she should allow herself a few days of absolute physical repose. Then gradually the hours of work were shortened, while the nights grew strangely long, and many of their wakeful hours were solaced by a repetition of the poems and psalms she loved, and which I had long ago memorized. Soon she was really ill, and when, at her own suggestion, the tired head was pillowed during the day, our hopeful hearts said a few weeks of rest and our loved one will be herself again. Dr. Alfred K. Hills, who had been Miss Willard's physician during the summer months, and under whose treatment she had been well-nigh restored to her old-time vigor, assured us that although she was suffering from a marked case of influenza, there were no symptoms that need give us alarm. Desiring that our precious charge should have skillful as well as loving care, the assistance of a trained nurse was at once secured, whose tender devotion to Miss Willard could not have been exceeded.

From the first of her illness Miss Willard felt she might not recover, but as a similar impression had often characterized her when ill, it gave us less apprehension. Her physician assured her she would soon be sitting up, and we endeavored throughout those long days of enforced quietness to make her believe her earthly work was not done. It was physical quietness only, for brain and heart were never more busy. Reading aloud from her favorite books I would often be interrupted by the question, asked with irresistible charm, "Could I dictate to little Mamie (our faithful stenographer, Mary Powderly), just one very important letter?" or, "I think, dear, you will have to get a paper and pencil and let me put something down that *must* be done, and don't you forget it!" Oh, those hours of retrospect and of hopeful outlook, whose deep, rich thoughts might all have been known but for our constant endeavor to conserve the precious strength all too slender for the strain it had to bear.

Her last "memorandum" was given me one week before her home-going. "Don't fail to put it down," she began, "that I have always recognized the splendid work done in 1874 by the women of Washington Court House, and that while I regard Hillsboro as the cradle, Washington Court House is the crown of the Crusade," and she added, "Fredonia must always be remembered as the home of the first local W. C. T. U. If I don't get well you must send some souvenir and a message of special remembrance to Mother Thompson, to Mother Stewart, and to Mrs. Zerelda Wallace" (pioneers in the W. C. T. U. movement). Mrs. Dio Lewis had called the day before, and as I told Miss Willard of her visit she talked much of the early days of her acquaintance with Dr. Dio Lewis, of his part in the Crusade movement, and said she hoped that at the twenty-fifth anniversary of the Crusade the National W. C. T. U. Convention would take some action in regard to having a day for the special and grateful remembrance of the work of this early reformer. She talked of the Polyglot Petition, and her great wish that more signatures should be secured, and spoke of the hope she had cherished that she might help in its presentation to the Dominion of Canada, and thus aid the plebiscite campaign; but, she added, "I feel I shall never do it, and I want you to ask my friend, Colonel Bain, to make that speech for me."

Miss Willard had looked forward to the annual meeting of the British Women's Temperance Association, to be held a few months later, and her affection for her English sisters was apparent in the earnestness with which she bade us carry out certain plans to which she frequently alluded, and which are now a sacred obligation.

Frequently Miss Willard asked if I had remembered her request to send to *The Union Signal, The Voice*, the various officials of our society, and to the friends in Canada and in England, letters urging co-operation in the observance of Gen. Neal Dow's birthday, March 20, as Prohibition Day.

On the last Sunday afternoon (February 13), she talked much of the Temple, telling her physician of the heroic efforts of its founder, her loved and generous-hearted friend, Mrs. Carse. Speaking with emphasis and frankness of the forces that had helped and the forces that had hindered the enterprise so dear to her heart, she exclaimed: "Oh, if I only could be of help! Oh, that some one would help me in my extremity, so that success might come to the Temple. Everything about it has not been wise, but was there ever a great enterprise without faults? Yes, they should go on and help the women, and get everything into shape. It was a pity, perhaps, to make it so big. I would rather they had not; but it's grand to work for a great cause, and you musn't let it fail." She was interrupted by the doctor, who said: "If you will only get well, Miss Willard, we will create a great enthusiasm and get that Temple paid for; but to get well is the first consideration." "No, no," was the pathetic reply, "I believe you could do better if I didn't get well. Oh," she continued, "there have never been such women as our White-Ribboners; so large-minded, so generous, such patriots, such Christians. We have had a great, beautiful past, and the people don't know it; they think we are fanatics. It has been a great fight, and they'll never know what we have been through. Oh, how I want our women to have a new concept of religion; the religion of the world is a religion of love; it is a home religion; it is a religion of peace; and tell them — tell them not to forget it is a religion of patriotism. We have set up to be patriots, we White-Ribboners, and we have fought amidst much ostracism. Tell our White-Ribboners to study the New Testament; I love the New Testament. No human being has ever conceived as he should what the New Testament means by loyalty to Christ."

Later, when alone with this precious friend, she pointed to a picture of the Christ, a life-size drawing from Hoffman's painting, in which Christ and the sinful woman are the central figures. This was a Christmas gift from Lady Henry Somerset, and as Miss Willard looked lovingly toward it she said: "He can do everything for us." Then she talked about her beloved friend in terms of the most tender endearment, saying, "You must carry that picture to Lady Henry as my parting gift." "Oh, no," I replied, "you are going to get well, and you know we shall sail just as soon as you are strong enough, and you must take it to her yourself." "No, no, when I take that picture to England cosmos will have become chaos. You must take it to her, and you must have, in pretty letters that she would like, up at the top, the words, Only the Golden Rule of Christ can bring the Golden Age of Man, and underneath you must put what Christ said to the woman, 'Neither do I condemn thee; go, and sin no more'; then don't forget to put the word Hoffman down in the right-hand corner, so that everybody will know he painted this beautiful picture."

She asked lovingly about her comrades at the Temple, and her associates in White Ribbon work. "Do they know how ill I am?" "Yes," I said, one of the very last sad days, "they do know, and they are all so sorry," and, mentioning each name at Headquarters, and many others, I added, "They are sending you such beautiful letters and telegrams every day, all of them." "How good," said the faint, tender voice; "give each of them my love; but, oh, they'll be sadder before they are gladder."

On the 14th, Miss Willard remembered that it was Saint Valentine's day, and that on the previous day my dear mother had celebrated her birthday, and, thinking of one whom she had lovingly called "mother" since her own Saint Courageous went away, she said, "Give my dearest love to Mother Gordon and to your sisters."

In the evening a friend sent an illuminated card bearing the text, "Unto you which believe He is precious." In the shaded light of the room I thought Miss Willard could not distinguish the words, but as I held the card near her she slowly read them, and said, "Thank dear Fannie, and tell her it is the loveliest valentine I ever had in all my life."

The next day Miss Willard became extremely restless, and

piteously begged us to take her to the home of her friend, Mary Lathbury, in the suburbs of the city. "I could rest there," she moaned, "and perhaps I should get well." She spoke of Rev. John M. Scott, author of a devotional book, "Kindly Light in Prayer and Praise," which she had greatly enjoyed reading, and wished he might come to see her. So earnest was this desire that we at once sent word to him, but by the time he reached the hotel Miss Willard's condition was so critical that her physician felt the interview should be postponed.

That morning Mrs. Baldwin came, bringing lilies of the valley to her aunt, and saying, as she placed them in her hand, "Here are some of grandma's flowers for you, dear Aunt Frank." Beds of these fragrant lilies used to nestle close to Rest Cottage and were Mrs. Willard's pride and delight. When Katherine's sister Mary was a wee tot she was asked by her grandmother one Sunday morning what the minister had preached about. It was early spring, the beautiful lilies were in full bloom, and the sweet child responded, "Why, grandma, he talked about the lily of the valley of the shadow." As our best beloved held the flowers, her face brightened, and she murmured, "Lilies — of the valley — of the shadow." Then, though we little dreamed it, came the last talk with one of her own kindred, which included loving messages to her sister, Mrs. Mary B. Willard, in Berlin, and to each of the nephews, and to her niece, Mary Bannister Willard. This conversation reminded Miss Willard of Evanston days, and later I was given commissions regarding her neighbors and friends in the old home, and a special message to her dear and long-time friend, Miss Katherine A. Jackson. Miss Willard lived over the Janesville days at "Forest Home," and talked of Rock River and her happy childhood, alluding also in loving terms to relatives in her birthplace, Churchville, New York, while the poor, weary head tossed incessantly from side to side. Night came, and we vainly tried to quiet her to sleep, and as I knelt beside her she said, "sing 'Hush, My Babe,' perhaps that would put me to sleep." I sang it over and over until I heard her say, "How strange it is; I should think that would make me sleep, you sing it so sweetly. Suppose you try, 'Gently, Lord.'" In Rest Cottage days that was a favorite hymn at family prayers, and one morning, long ago, she had changed the second line, which reads "Through this gloomy vale of tears," to one more consonant with her concept of life, "Through this vale of smiles and tears," and thus I sang it to her now. On reaching the last two lines I could not recall the words. She quickly prompted me by saying, "'Till, by angel bands," and thinking only of her I finished the hymn:

>"'Till, by angel bands attended,
>I awake among the blest.''

"Oh, no, not I; it's we, it's always we; Christianity is we, not I; you know it's *our* Father; *don't* forget that. Now sing it again, please, and sing it *we*."

Morning dawned, but no rest beyond a few moments' unconsciousness had come to soothe or to restore. The awful pain in our hearts grew more intense; how often we had heard her say when some great purpose illumined her soul, "Here in the body pent." "Mother, Sissy's dress aches," she had moaned as a child, on the long overland journey by carriage from Churchville to Oberlin, during every mile of which her mother held the little one. Was Saint Courageous near her now to hear the same pitiful plaint applied to the dress of mortality in which she had journeyed so fast and far during these fifty-eight years of unparalleled activity? Could it be that this great soul was soon to be set free to enter upon the unwearied work of the life immortal? No, no, we said in our human selfishness and overwhelming agony, God cannot, *will not take her now*. We thought of that dearest of friends across the sea whose daily messages were a benediction to our patient sufferer, who watched for them with loving eagerness, and our aching hearts refused to believe that these two friends were not to meet again on earth.

Our physicians did not conceal from us the anxiety they now felt, but assured us there still was hope. Devoted comrades everywhere were pleading with strong crying and tears for the life of their brave and beloved leader. A general call to prayer was sent out from Headquarters in Chicago, and at the noon hour Willard Hall was filled with a vast audience, the cry of every heart being, "Spare her, O God, if it is Thy will."

Mrs. Stevens, of Maine, had come to us several days before in response to my earnest request, and early this morning she sat for a few moments by the side of her beloved friend and comrade in the battles of the Lord. As Miss Willard felt the hand laid tenderly upon her own she looked earnestly into "Stevie's" face, saying, "I felt sure that you would come"; then, with characteristic thoughtfulness, she inquired for each member of Mrs. Stevens' family, for Miss Cornelia Dow and for her warm friend, Miss Agnes Slack, in England.

There were friends endeared to Miss Willard by years of association and tender love who longed to minister to her during these anxious days, but her physician felt that with a brain so active and a body so weak there must be the utmost quiet. By telegram and letter came anxious inquiries, and that room from which she was soon to pass to heaven, became the center of thought and prayerful solicitude for thousands. Many relatives and friends were daily informed of our hopes and fears through the unwearied kindness of my sister and others whose helpfulness will never be forgotten. Flowers constantly cheered our uncomplaining invalid — one day delicate orchids gathered in a private conservatory and sent with heartfelt love; another, bright jonquil blossoms brought by the waiter who had served Miss Willard's meals from the dining room. Daily telegrams from the proprietor and his wife (who were in Atlantic City on account of Mrs. Quinn's ill health), expressed their deep sympathy and placed at our command every resource the hotel afforded.

Of one faithful heart I must specially speak; "dear little Mamie," who with unexampled self-sacrifice sat at her typewriter from morning until night, sending to aching hearts news of their beloved one, when she might have been in the sick room ministering to her whom she so deeply loved and for three years had devotedly served. Whenever she came quietly into the room on an errand, Miss Willard would recognize her and would say, "Why, there's dear little Mamie!" and have for her, as always, some pleasant word.

Evening came, but the terrible unrest continued, smiting our hearts — lest her prophetic words were all too true — lest this beating of her tired wings against their earthly prison-house would be followed by her flight far beyond our loving care.

Suddenly she gazed intently on the picture directly opposite her bed. Her eyes seemed to meet those of the compassionate Christ, and with the old eloquence in her voice, in the stillness of that never-to-be-forgotten night, she said:

"'I am Merlin, and I am dying,
But I'll follow the Gleam.'

I'm getting so tired, how can I follow it much longer? . . . He giveth His beloved sleep, but oh, sometimes He is a long time doing it. . . . The next time you read 'De Profundis' you will think of this day, the longest and hardest of my whole life. . . . Oh, let me go away, let me be in peace; I am so safe with Him. He has other worlds and I want to go. I have always believed in Christ; He is the incarnation of God." Speaking of Lady Henry, as she did so often that night and always, she said: "She did everything for me, and was so good."

Toward morning she whispered, "I want to speak to you quite alone," and bending near her to catch every faintly uttered word, I received this sacred message: "I want to say what Mary and I used to say to each other away back in the old days on the farm when we were going to sleep. I would say to Mary, 'I ask your pardon and I thank you,' and she would say, 'I freely forgive you and welcome,' and then we would change about with the same sweet words of forgiveness and gratitude. I want to say that to you, and to every White-Ribboner, and to everybody."

CHAPTER XV

TRANSLATION

EARLY on February 17, the last day God let us have her with us, she remembered it was time for her "letter from home," as she loved to call our official paper *The Union Signal*, and sweetly said, "Please let me sit up and let me have our beautiful *Signal*." She was soon laid back upon her pillows, when, taking Dr. Hills' hand in hers, she spoke tender, appreciative words about her friend and physician, of which the last were these, "I say, God bless him; I shall remember his loving kindness through all eternity."

A little later Mrs. Hoffman, National Recording Secretary of our society, entered the room for a moment. Miss Willard seemed to be unconscious, but as Mrs. Hoffman quietly took her hand she looked up and said, "Why, that's Clara; good Clara; Clara, I've crept in with mother, and it's the same beautiful world and the same people, remember that — it's *just the same*."

"Has my cable come?" she soon asked; "Oh, how I want it to come;" and when, a few moments later, a message of tenderest solicitude and love was received from dear Lady Henry, I placed it in her hand. "Read it, oh read it quickly — what does it say?" were her eager questions, and as I read the precious words I heard her voice, "Oh, how sweet, oh, how lovely, good — good!"

Quietly as a babe in its mother's arms she now fell asleep, and though we knew it not "the dew of eternity was soon to fall upon her forehead." "She had come to the borderland of this closely curtained world!"

Only once again did she speak to us, when about noon the little thin, white hand — that active, eloquent hand — was raised in an effort to point upward, and we listened for the last time on earth to the voice that to thousands has surpassed all others in its marvelous sweetness and magnetic power. It was like the lovely and pathetic strain from an Æolian harp on which heavenly zephyrs were breathing, and she must even then have caught some glimpse of those other worlds for which she longed as she said, in tones of utmost content, "How beautiful it is to be with God."

As twilight fell, hope died in our yearning hearts, for we saw that the full glory of another life was soon to break o'er our loved one's "earthly horizon." Kneeling about her bed, with the faithful nurses who had come to love their patient as a sister, we silently watched while the life immortal, the life more abundant, came in its fullness to this inclusive soul, whose wish, cherished from her youth, that she might go, not like a peasant to a palace, but as a child to her Father's home, was about to be fulfilled. A few friends who had come to the hotel to make inquiries, joined the silent and grief-stricken group. Slowly the hours passed with no recognition of the loved ones about her. There came an intent upward gaze of the heavenly blue eyes, a few tired sighs, and at the "noon hour" of the night Frances Willard was

> "Born into beauty
> And born into bloom,
> Victor immortal
> O'er death and the tomb."

The babe Frances could not sleep without the palm of her tiny hand laid upon her mother's cheek; the girl Frances lying upon the grass in the soft gathering stillness of summer twilight would reach up her hand beseechingly for God to touch; the woman Frances, when all her loved ones had been transplanted to the gardens of the higher life, had followed that way with sublime and childlike trust, greeting her glad proof of immortality with the grandly simple words, "How beautiful it is to be with God."

The stillness was broken only by sobs as we closed the earthly eyes of one who was always a seer, and who now beheld the King in His beauty and the land that she so often said is *not* far off.

My sister breathed out the prayer of all our hearts, "Dear Father, we give Thee back Thine own," while my desolate soul responded, "And we thank Thee for taking her so gently."

With sublime trust the broken-hearted women clasped hands and amid their tears tried to sing in unison with the great White Ribbon family in heaven and earth

> "Blest be the tie that binds
> Our hearts in Christian love
> The fellowship of kindred minds
> Is like to that above."

An hour later a smile of joy irradiated the sleeping face. She lay at the close of her life's long day of loving toil — serene, majestic, supremely beautiful. She had sown many harvests of happiness for children and youth. She had built a booth in the desert for pilgrims weary and wounded. She had lifted the cup of cold water to many smitten with life's fierce heat, had seen the signal swung out from the heavenly battlements and had made ready for her departure. There came to our thought what Bunyan said of the end of the long battle which Christian fought: "Then said Christian, 'I am going to my Father's; and though with great difficulty I am got hither, yet now I do not repent of all the trouble I have been at to arrive where I am. My sword I leave to him that shall succeed me in my pilgrimage, and my courage and skill to him that can get it. My marks and scars I carry with me, to be a witness for me that I have fought His battles who will now be my rewarder.' When the day that he must go hence was come, many accompanied him to the riverside, into which as he went he said, 'Death, where is thy sting?' and as he went down deeper, he said, 'Grave, where is thy victory?' So he passed over, and all the trumpets sounded for him on the other side."

Before the early dawn we carried the precious form of our beloved one to the home of her niece. "How radiantly beautiful she is," said all who saw her; "surely it is majestic sweetness that enthrones her brow." Victory as well as the peace of God was in her looks, and so natural seemed her sleep that Katherine's little son sweetly called to his aunt as he was lifted up to look at her, and in his baby innocence tried to awaken her that she might take his pretty rose. The young mother's heart was deeply stirred, and she said, "Aunt Frank was just a dear, sweet baby herself, besides being the greatest woman in all the world."

Thousands of hearts who read the sad tidings in the morning papers felt a sense of irreparable loss and personal bereavement. Cables, telegrams, letters and flowers came hourly to the sorrowful group at the hotel who, because of the great love they bore her, must not weep — but work.

"We know no other woman," said Mary Lowe Dickinson, "whose home-going would have left so many other women feeling as if the sun had gone. And we know no other out of all the many noble women of our land whose going would so swiftly have marshaled the thronging stars. . . . . No one could fail to feel, as that brave life drifted serenely out beyond the sunset, the overwhelming loss and gloom creeping piteously upon the great hearts that loved her and the great work that she loved. The bitter loss, the sore hurt to both, could not be told in words. Genuine grief finds refuge in silence; real heartbreak sobs itself out to God.

"But light broke upon this shadow when from East and West and North and South began to gather the brave and tender souls that through many years had shared Miss Willard's battles for humanity, standing, some lower, some higher in the ranks, yet all in heart side by side with their leader. As one by one, or in groups, their white, tear-marked faces shone out of the gloom we saw the stars arise; we knew that however human hearts might ache or break, Miss Willard's work was safe. These rallying leaders, gathering in New York at the news of their chief's departure, were representative of a great army, that would, in groups, or separately and alone, gladly have brought to their one great leader and comrade their own kind tribute of loyal and sorrowing love."

Each day quiet groups filled the hotel parlors, where tears and sobs of strong men mingled with those of White Ribbon comrades and personal friends, as they sought to comfort and counsel one another.

The room from which went home the blessed spirit of "Saint Frances," as Bishop Vincent calls her, will be forever hallowed. Friends came to it one by one as to a sanctuary. The only picture that adorned the walls was the Christ on which the closing eyes had rested, and just below this on the writing desk were grouped photographs of the dear ones "loved and lost awhile," and a miniature of Lady Henry Somerset. Bright, fragrant flowers gave a message of joy and hope, though the rain had not ceased to fall and the storm to beat against the windows since that winged soul had taken its flight.

Many a silent prayer was offered from anointed and chastened spirits. "It is well with her," they said, and praise ascended to Him who, through His own victory over death, had given their beloved an abundant entrance into the blessed Homeland.

PART II

IN MEMORIAM

CHAPTER I

THE COMMEMORATIVE SERVICES

IN the home of her loved niece, in the heart of the greatest city on the continent, in the State in which her eyes had greeted the light of earth, Frances E. Willard lay in her last sleep. Early Sunday afternoon, February 20, relatives, friends and leading White-Ribboners gathered like a family group about the beloved form. With sobs and tears that could not be suppressed the heartbroken White-Ribboners repeated the texts she loved, uttered brief, fervent prayers, and solaced their hearts with blessed memories and triumphant hope. The dear one drew us close to her as she always did in life. Surely we could fear no evil if this was death. Each heart received its own message, and to all she seemed to say, "Little children, love one another." Never was she so great, never so beautiful, as "sceptered and robed and crowned" she lay against the soft linings of her silver-gray casket, whose only ornament was the broad encircling white ribbon. She was robed in a home dress of softest white; her fair hair was arranged in the old familiar way; the "little bow of white" was not hidden by the floral heart of lilies and cape jessamine that rested, by Lady Henry Somerset's request, on the purest heart that ever went home to God, while in the dear hand which had long beckoned us onward were lilies of the valley. Every care-line had vanished from her madonna-like face, and there was over it not alone the hush of a great stillness, but the awe of an infinite wonder — the radiance of an eternal joy. The flowers of earth were all about her, and the perfume of the immortal flowers of the life beyond seemed to fill the room and pervade all our hearts. A tender hymn was sung, Mrs. Stevens led in the W. C. T. U. benediction, which was followed by the temperance doxology, and we went out from a home, made sacred forever, to the Broadway Tabernacle — the church in which the voice now hushed had last spoken in New York City.

The vast audience rose, the organ's solemn requiem found a deep response in hundreds of sorrowing hearts, as the casket, draped with her favorite white silk flag gleaming with golden stars was borne into the church and tenderly placed in a garden of heavenly bloom. The platform and chancel of the shadowy old Tabernacle had been transformed by those who loved her into a tropical bower of palms and bright flowers.

Rev. Dr. E. S. Tipple, a leading young clergyman and warm friend of Miss Willard's, conducted the simple funeral service of the Methodist Church, assisted by Rev. Dr. A. E. Kittredge, Rev. Dr. R. S. MacArthur, Rev. Frederick B. Richards, Rev. Dr. Charles L. Thompson, Rev. Dr. Charles H. Payne, and Bishop John H. Newman, who offered the following prayer:

Gracious God, Father in heaven, forgive us if we mourn today amid this general grief; but we thank Thee that we do not mourn as those without hope, for Thou hast given us hope, and we come to Thee with thanksgiving upon our lips for all Thy loving kindness unto this beloved, whom Thou hast taken unto Thyself. We praise Thee for her parentage. We thank Thee for her power, for her imperial intellect, for that vast amount of useful knowledge acquired to render her mission efficient and successful, and we thank Thee above all things for her loyalty to Jesus Christ in good report and in evil report, for her philanthropy, for her sympathy with the suffering humanity of all continents; and we bless Thee for her noble convictions, her purpose to elevate the race to sobriety and to purity. We return Thee thanks today for her, we bless Thee for our association with her in the great reforms of life, for the sweet influence she exerted upon us, for the noble example she showed before others. She was steadfast amid all trials, and we rejoice in that beautiful Christian life she lived, that noble heart, that consecration of all her powers to Thee, which made her to have but one object in view — to do Thy will on earth as the angels do it in heaven, and to glorify Thy holy Name. And we bless Thee for that quiet death that Thou didst give her, that she might peacefully fall asleep in Jesus, and her spirit ascend to Thee, her Creator and her Redeemer. Now we ask Thy blessing on all those noble enterprises in which she was engaged, that they may reach a glorious consummation. Grant, we pray Thee, that this cause of sobriety which she pleaded with such eloquence, and of personal purity, Christian purity — this cause of temperance — may become a universal fact. May the governments of the world put forth a power that shall restrain inebriety; may the legislatures of the world hasten to the redemption of humanity from all the evils that grow out of intemperance; and we pray especially that Thy blessing may rest upon these noble women, these sisters that are banded together, consecrating their hearts and their lives and their fortunes for the accomplishment of these great purposes. We thank Thee, though our departed one has passed from life, that she yet lives in thousands of lives, lives in the thoughts, the affections, the aspirations of many. We praise Thee for this corporate immortality. We pray that this organization which she represented may be under Thy guidance, under Thy heavenly inspiration until the great work shall be accomplished.

And we pray especially for that dear woman who was her traveling companion on sea and land, whose pen was the pen of a ready writer; and bless that precious woman beyond the seas, the companion of our departed one, who is today thinking of this funeral occasion. May that noble woman be sustained by Thee.

Hear and answer us, and when this brief life is done, may it be well done. May all our powers, having been consecrated to Thee, attain to a glorious consummation, and may we be more and more consecrated to those great interests that will bring about the millennium of Thy glory. May we be more and more the instruments of Thy power, so that at last when life is over we may sleep with Jesus and meet this precious woman and the thousands who have gone before, and, above all, Christ, our Lord. And unto the Father, Son and Holy Spirit shall be the glory, world without end. Amen.

In rich tones of deep emotion and earnestness, Mrs. L. M. N. Stevens, Vice-President-at-Large of the National W. C. T. U., read the Ninetieth Psalm. Mrs. Mary T. Burt, President of the New York State Society, announced and eloquently read the hymn, "Blest be the tie that binds our hearts in Christian love," reminding White-Ribboners in a few touching words of the many times at the close of National Conventions, with hand clasped in hand, this hymn had been sung with our sainted leader, and Miss Cassie Smith, National Evangelist, soothed our hearts as she carried their burden to the God of all comfort, praying:

Oh, Lord, we thank Thee today for the *privilege* of *prayer*. We thank

Thee that a part of Thy mission to this world was "to *bind up the broken-hearted.*" We represent, and bring to Thee, the sad hearts of a vast multitude on this occasion. And yet, though "sorrowful," we are "*rejoicing*," and come "into Thy courts," as Thou hast taught us, "with thanksgiving."

We praise Thee for the wonderful life of our best beloved — that she *illustrated* as well as *loved* the sentiments of this hymn —

> "To serve the present age,
> My calling to fulfill,
> Oh may it all my powers engage
> To do my Master's will."

We magnify the grace of the Lord Jesus Christ today, in that she was enabled so to endure the ordeals that came to her in her pilgrimage that they were made a blessing to herself and to others.

We praise Thee that her heart was filled with love for God and humanity, and that Thou wast her Leader in the accomplishment of her world-wide mission. We thank Thee that some of us were permitted to see her transfigured at the recent W. C. T. U. Conventions. We bless Thee, on behalf of our "White Ribbon Host" that, while our human leader has gone, our Savior remains with us. We "lift up our eyes unto the hills from whence cometh our help"; and while we praise Thee for the ministry of her life, we *plead* for the ministry of her death. We pray that *more* may be accomplished by this affliction that touches every nation of the world, than when, like her Master, she "went about doing good" among the children of men. We thank Thee that Thou didst fulfill to her Thy promise — "I will come again and receive you unto myself; that where I am there ye may be also," and that she, "of whom the world was not worthy," has heard Thee say, "It is *enough*, come up higher." Help us to "follow her as she followed Christ." Carry on Thy work through those who remain, and raise up others to take our places when we, too, shall be called home. We ask all *in Jesus' name.* Amen.

In closing the simple and fitting service in memory of a great soul, Doctor Tipple said, "The highest tribute we can pay to Frances Willard is to mention her name, sing the songs she loved, and pray to her God."

Was ever woman so beloved? was the thought of those who watched for hours the slow-moving procession of rich and poor, representing many sects, sections and races, who reverently looked for the last time upon the face of their friend, each New York White-Ribboner placing a white carnation upon the casket.

The sad journey to her home city, Chicago, was made in a special car, in which the casket was surrounded by flowers and guarded by loving hearts. Stopping briefly at Churchville, New York, Miss Willard's birthplace, in the church established by her grandfather, loving kinsfolk, neighbors and comrades of Monroe County united in a memorial service led by the brotherly pastors. Mrs. Helen M. Barker, Treasurer of the National W. C. T. U., represented the White-Ribboners in the following address:

We rejoice in this life that has been given to us and to the world; we rejoice and lift up our hearts in thanksgiving to the Giver of all good who has enabled her to accomplish so much for the world, for all those who are afflicted and oppressed, and we see in her mission the mission of Christ, for she went forth doing His work. During her last illness, in speaking of this religion of the Lord Jesus Christ, which was the secret of her power, she said, "Tell the world it is a home religion, it is a religion of peace. Tell the world it is the religion of love, tell them it is a patriotic religion." In her life she honored Christ; she did not lose her faith in Him. He was her strength and inspiration. Churchville claims her; Janesville, in Wisconsin, claims her; Chicago claims her; New York claims her; England claims her especially; the world claims her. She did not belong alone to the Woman's Christian Temperance Union. She sympathized with every organization of men and women that worked for the uplift of humanity, for the regenerating of sinful hearts. Hers was a wonderful mission, and to us who have worked with her closely for the last twenty years, who have been with her in executive counsel, with her at the altar of prayer, we who know what she was to us and to our work, realize our great loss as others cannot. All desire to honor her, and how are we to do it? These flowers are fond tributes to her memory, this gathering is a tribute to her, but, my sisters, and especially my sisters of her native State, New York, how can we honor this loved one most? I answer, not with these flowers, not by this service, which all appreciate, but by being faithful to the work she loved. Do we lack courage? Let us pray that some of the indomitable courage which she possessed may be ours. Are we inclined to criticise? Let us have her spirit of charity and love. In all my acquaintance with her, I think I never heard a disparaging word spoken of any worker that our beloved did not find some word of excuse for that one, and she would say, "Oh, we do not know, perhaps she does not look at it just as we do; perhaps she does not see it from our angle of vision."

And now my message to you, my sisters, in the words of Saint Paul, is,

"Remember my bonds," and when we are led to criticise one who does not think or speak as we do, let us remember that there may be something hidden away out of sight that binds, something in the home that cripples, something in the early education that hinders, something in the vision that handicaps, and so let us emulate that love, that sympathy, that charity that she so beautifully exhibited in all her life. We look at her beautiful form and say, "She is gone"; but, oh, she has not gone, she will continue to be our leader, and I believe from the battlements of glory she will watch our work. I believe she will still inspire, I believe she will whisper to our consciences thoughts of what we may do and what we ought to do; and, my sisters, how much we need her! But the Lord who led her is leading us today, and this may be a time of consecration, insomuch that from this day forth the Woman's Christian Temperance Union that she so loved may be a power in the world such as it has never been before. Then she shall be honored!

We say, "How brief her life, she should have lived twenty years longer"; but if we measure her life, not by days and weeks and years, but by the great work she has accomplished, by the enterprises she has inaugurated and carried on to victory, she has rounded out a grand old age, she has accomplished more in the fifty-eight years of her life than many of us would do were we to live one hundred and fifty-eight years. Into that brief span has been crowded so much of brain power, of heart love, of the burden of humanity, and how beautifully she has borne it. I say there has been crowded into this life so much, that it has been a long, grand life — a life so broad that it has reached to the extremities of civilization and Christianity; a life so deep that no poor soul had ever sunk so low that her love and sympathy could not reach it. My sisters, let us praise God this morning, that we have been permitted to come into close relationship with her beautiful spirit, and then let us honor her by going out to do the work that she would exhort us to do *faithfully*. Let us in this divine presence pledge to her, pledge to God, pledge to each other, that we will be more loving, more faithful, more self-sacrificing, more devoted, and that we will honor her by honoring the God she loved and the work to which she gave her life and which she has left to us.

At Buffalo a large delegation of White-Ribboners who four months earlier had joyfully welcomed their President and the National Convention, passed sorrowfully through the car leaving "lilies of love and loyalty" and singing with subdued and faltering voices,

"Some day, some where, we shall know."

Silently the snowflakes fell, surrounding us with a white world as we carried our dear one homeward. Honored representative

LADY HENRY SOMERSET
MISS WILLARD'S SUCCESSOR AS PRESIDENT OF THE WORLD'S W. C. T. U.

PLATFORM OF WILLARD HALL, THE TEMPLE—FEBRUARY 23, 1898.

men who had revered Miss Willard, received us at the station in Chicago, and as the casket was slowly and reverently raised to the shoulders of the bearers, and borne along the tessellated corridor of Willard Hall, which her feet had so often trod, it was preceded by a guard of honor of her own Illinois women, who through their tears triumphantly sang the old Crusade hymn,

"Rock of ages, cleft for me,
Let me hide myself in Thee."

The resting place of state in Willard Hall seemed like a plot in Paradise, so fragrant and plentiful were the floral offerings, so graceful and beautiful the decorations of purest white. Doves with their white wings outspread hovered in midair above the peaceful sleeper, and behind the palms sweet voices sang her favorite hymns. The flags of the city floated at half-mast all day, while silently the people passed to take a parting look at "their great citizen." Said *The Union Signal:* "Chicago has never seen such a spontaneous offering as the multitude laid at the feet of our chieftain, for it was an offering of love. For an hour before the procession reached the cross-surmounted portal of Willard Hall, there were crowds waiting for admission, and for another hour they patiently stood on the wet pavement with the cold wind sweeping in sleety gusts against them before they gained admittance. During the day more than thirty thousand people passed down the aisle, each one pausing a moment by the casket. There were children lifted in their parents' arms, there were decrepit men and women who leaned upon their sons or daughters for support; many hobbled in on crutches, and some looked as if they might have newly risen from a bed of sickness. Multitudes stood in line for hours, and through it all there was no evidence of morbid curiosity. The beautiful decorations were a secondary matter to the desire for a last look upon the dear face of the one who slept long and well. Particularly touching to White-Ribboners at headquarters was the entrance of the employes of the printing department of the Woman's Temperance Publishing Association, some eighty men and women, led by the business manager, Mrs. C. F.

Grow. Miss Willard always felt a peculiar interest in everyone connected with the work of the Publishing House, in whatever capacity, and had the love and loyalty of the whole force.

At the noon hour a brief service was held. Mrs. Frances J. Barnes, General Secretary of the Young Women's Branch of the World's W. C. T. U., spoke tenderly of our promoted leader; prayers were offered by Mrs. Annie O. Rutherford, President of the Canadian W. C. T. U.; Mrs. Moses Smith, a crusader; Mrs. Frances E. Beauchamp, Assistant Recording Secretary of the National W. C. T. U.; and Mrs. S. M. I. Henry, National Evangelist. Mrs. Lucy J. Thurman, Superintendent of Work among Colored Women, paid a special tribute to the greatness of heart that enabled Frances Willard to take into her active sympathies all creeds and all races. In the afternoon Miss Eva Booth, of the Salvation Army, accompanied by a number of young women on their way to the Northwest, knelt by the casket while the Commander offered a fervent prayer. As the day waned and the doors were to be closed, Bishop John H. Vincent besought our Heavenly Father's benediction, closing with these words:

We give thanks for the life of our departed sister, for her loyalty to righteousness and purity, for the sweet charity that burned in her heart, dwelt in her eyes and went forth in the sweet echoes of her voice. We pray that, inspired by her example, we may live the same strong and earnest life and do good service in the cause she loved so well.

At Evanston, where hundreds were assembled at the station, the University students acted as escort, and when the beloved one was carried into dear Rest Cottage, her young relatives softly sang "Home, Sweet Home." At the door of Rest Cottage was fastened a wreath of evergreen gathered by the W. C. T. U. and the temperance children of Oberlin, Ohio, from a hedge planted by Miss Willard's father, and in the dainty parlor hung a cluster of evergreen bearing this card: "Sweetbrier that Frank planted, Janesville, Wisconsin." Bright flowers filled the bay window, and friends who passed quietly in and out felt that the room breathed the heavenly cheer always associated with the presence of those who had been its life.

A simple home service the next morning preceded the one at the church. "How Firm a Foundation" was sung to the Southern lullaby air loved by Miss Willard. Standing beside the quiet form of her friend and leader Mrs. L. M. N. Stevens, of Maine, prayed with breaking voice:

Heavenly Father, come near and tenderly and pityingly hover over us at this hour. We thank Thee for the precious life of our beloved — so full of beauty and nobility. Help us to understand what she meant when she said, "How beautiful it is to be with God." Help us to know more of that other worldliness of which she spoke and taught. We thank Thee for all the precious memories that cluster around Rest Cottage; for the life of Saint Courageous; for all the holy influences which have gone out from this home. Wilt Thou in tender love bless the niece and nephew of our beloved and the other family members who are with us today, and the absent ones wherever they may be. Wilt Thou bless and comfort the one who has been to our promoted leader helper, companion, more than friend, who has been faithful even unto death. Wilt Thou console that great heart over the sea who is cast down by this great sorrow. Remember the White Ribbon sisterhood everywhere. Bless the world — for she loved the whole world. We humbly pray in the name of Christ whom she loved so much and served so loyally. Amen.

The sweet young voices of the quartette were again heard as the soothing words,

"Gently, Lord, oh gently lead us,"

floated once more through the home, and the benediction was pronounced by the venerable Professor Emerson of Beloit, Wisconsin, in these words:

Now may the blessing of the loving Father who has called the dear daughter home, and of the loving Brother who has led the dear sister to the Father's house, and of the loving Holy Spirit which was the breath of her life here, and is so there, be and abide with us all, that we may be now and forever with the Lord. Amen.

Reverent, patient thousands gathered in and about the First Methodist Episcopal Church of Evanston, where old friends and dear were to speak in sacred memory of the exalted life of their own Frances E. Willard. Love had outloved itself in lavish expression of tenderness, through flower and fern and palm and draperies of symbolic white. Behind the pulpit hung a large silk flag, made entirely by women's hands and carried at the head of the dedicatory procession of the World's Columbian Exposition in 1892. The owner of the flag had affixed an inscription which read: "This flag has traveled over four thousand miles of this country, and always floats in the interest of liberty, peace and arbitration. It floated over Miss Willard in life, and we want it to float over her in death." The "religion of patriotism" also shone forth in the Stars and Stripes that floated from the organ loft and draped the speakers' chairs—our sacred flag,

"With its red for love, and its white for law,
And its blue for the hope that our fathers saw
Of a larger liberty."

At this Methodist altar Frances Willard had knelt alone in the presence of her fellow-students and dedicated her young life to the highest ideals. Now, hundreds of students filled the galleries and stood in the aisles to do honor to one who called herself their "elderly sister," and whose glorious and Godlike career they desired to emulate.

The Willard pew, held by the family for over thirty years, was draped with white and filled with floral offerings.

The words of the solemn processional were read by Rev. Dr. Frank M. Bristol, pastor of the church. Following him came the faculty of the Northwestern University, President Henry Wade Rogers at their head, and the pastors of the Evanston churches. The casket was borne by six students of the college. Honorary pallbearers, General Officers of the National W. C. T. U., the White Ribbon Guard of Honor, relatives and closest friends came slowly after, Miss Willard's nearest relatives present being Mrs. Katherine Willard Baldwin, of New York, and Robert A. Willard, of Florida, daughter and son of her brother Oliver.

"I wonder if she knows?" was the tender, unspoken question of many a heart, as the casket was placed before the altar, amid such a scene of beauty as even the one to whom it was consecrated had rarely seen in life. The casket rested on a rug of roses and violets, and forming a radiant arch over the beloved sleeper was a rainbow of spring's blossoms — violets, the tender blue of hyacinths, the living green of smilax, pale-yellow daffodils and the deeper glory of the crimson-touched tulip — a bow of promise shining through the clouds. She has gone beyond the glory of the rainbow, but the "everlasting covenant" remains. Beneath the rainbow, and caught away from the casket by a hovering dove, was a broad white ribbon bearing in silver letters these words, the last spoken on earth, and, may it not be, the first enraptured cry of the soul set free from mortality: *"How beautiful it is to be with God."*

Bishop Bowman offered prayer and the choir sang Tennyson's immortal ode, "Crossing the Bar."

President Rogers was the first speaker, taking for his theme

MISS WILLARD AS A UNIVERSITY WOMAN AND AN EDUCATOR.

We of the University honored and loved Frances Willard. Once she was dean of what was then known as the Woman's College, was a member of our faculty, and in these later years, of our Board of Trustees. She loved the University and was proud of what it had become. A few years ago she wrote of it, "It greatly outranks any other west of Lake Michigan, and richly deserves the name of 'The Northwestern,' in the modern sense of that great and comprehensive designation. Steadily may its star climb toward the zenith, growing clearer and more bright with each succeeding year." The last speech she made in this town, which she delighted to call "The Methodist Cambridge of the prairies," her "ain familiar town," was an address to the students delivered in the college chapel only a few weeks ago. How little we thought she was so soon to pass beyond the veil! But had she known then that her life was fast passing on toward the twilight, so ready was she to go, she might even have said to it:

> "Then steal away, give little warning,
> Chose thine own time,
> Say not good-night — but in some brighter clime
> Bid me good-morning."

We mourn that she has been taken, but we do not forget that she was given. She has done a great work, grown weary and fallen on sleep. May the beautiful spirit which dominated her life inspire us all to nobler things!

In February, 1871, she was elected president of the Evanston College for Ladies. At that time the institution had no connection with the University. She was the first woman to be elected president of a college. It is due to her labors that the town authorities gave as a site for the new college what was then one of the chief parks of Evanston. Upon that site was built what is now known as the Woman's Hall. She, with others, made the canvass for the money with which it is erected, and brick by brick she watched its walls as they climbed high above the trees. It was in her thoughts by day and by night, and she was fond of it. She said of it, "It is my sister Mary's that died, and it is mine."

In June, 1873, the institution was incorporated with the University under conditions largely dictated by her, and she became dean of the Woman's College and Professor of Æsthetics in the Faculty of Liberal Arts. As professor and dean she had her trials. She taught the classes in English, and met them in the president's room in University Hall. It was a new experience for college men to recite to a woman teacher. They tried her mettle only to find that she understood herself and them. They admired and respected her. She was popular and inspiring, and in every way a successful teacher. It is an ambition worthy of the immortals to build one's own life into the lives of others, and this she was able to do to a remarkable degree.

On June 13, 1874, she resigned her office as dean and at the same time her professorship in the University. Speaking of it years after she declared that this severance of her University relations was the greatest sacrifice her life had known and ever could know. It has been said that she left her work in the University to devote herself to the cause which she afterward espoused and with which her name is henceforth to be forever identified. That she did not do so is known to all who have read her "Glimpses of Fifty Years," in which she wrote: "It grieves me that I cannot truthfully say I left the deanship of a college and a professor's chair in one of America's best universities on purpose to take up temperance work." But it is true that having left the University she determined upon temperance work in the face of tempting offers to teach elsewhere, and that she held to that work though attractive positions in other fields were open to her all along the years had she cared to occupy them. It is no secret that she voluntarily withdrew from the University because she did not approve of the policy which the faculty had at that time adopted respecting certain questions of administration. "There's a divinity that shapes our ends, rough hew them how we will." There were other kingdoms awaiting her of which she knew not. This was an hour of disappointment. But Ruskin tells us that in the secret of disappointment, as in the twilight so beloved by Titian, we may see the colors of things with deeper truth than in the most dazzling sunshine. And who shall deny that as she sat in the shadow of her disappointment it was revealed to her what her mission was to be. She could say,

> "My bark is wafted to the strand
> By breath divine,
> And on the helm there rests a Hand
> Other than mine."

The story of the severance of her relations with the University reveals that gentleness of her nature which so impressed us all. The world needs nothing so much as gentleness and kindness, and these attributes our friend possessed in an eminent degree. "Thy gentleness hath made me great," says the Psalmist. It made Frances Willard great, too, and you may gain an insight into the beauty of her character and the greatness of her soul from the facts she has told us of this crisis of her life.

On the night she resigned as dean of the Woman's College she shut herself out of sight in her suite of rooms at the college and with agony of tears gave way to her anguish. Let me tell the pathetic story of what transpired as she has written it, for it reveals the tenderness and nobility of her nature as no words of mine can do:

"At last everything grew still and sweet and holy, while far into the night the deep June sky bent over me with a beauty that was akin to tenderness. The storm in my soul ebbed away slowly, the sobs ceased, the long sighs were less frequent. As dies the wave along the shore, so died away forevermore my sorrow to lose the beautiful college that my heart had loved as other women's hearts love their sweet and sacred homes. In the long hours that followed, the peace that passeth understanding settled down upon my soul. God was revealed to me as a great, brooding, motherly spirit, and all of us who tried to carry on the University, while He carried on the universe, seemed like little boys and girls, who meant well, but who didn't always understand each other. The figure was of children playing in a nursery, and one little boy had more vigor than the rest of us, and, naturally, wanted us to play his way, while a little girl, whom I thought I could identify, said: 'No; my way is best!' Then a deep voice declared, 'This is the interpretation — good to forgive, best to forget.' And then the happiness that mocketh speech flowed, like the blessed, tranquil river of dear old Forest Home, all through my soul, and overflowed its banks with quiet, happy tears." Soon thereafter she went to the president, and, extending her hand, begged pardon for everything she had ever done and said that was not right, and assured him that she desired to be at peace with God and every human soul, and from that hour on they were the best of friends.

It was this spirit that made it possible for her to say that she did not know a reason why any human being should hesitate to speak to her with cordiality and kindness, or why any middle wall of partition should exist between her spirit and any other human spirit that God had made. Had she not sat at the feet of the

Prophet Micah, and heard from him what it was that the Lord required of her, that she was to do justly, and to love mercy, and to walk humbly with her God!

She was one of the early advocates of the higher education for women. This was to her a sacred cause. She believed, too, in the co-education of the sexes, and was wont to impress upon her women students that the experiment of co-education was on trial, and that in some degree its future rested with them. "God help you to be good!" she said to them. She believed, too, in the principle of self-government, and many a time rejoiced as she thought how true and self-respecting a set of girls she had around her. One who disapproved her government said: "The trouble is, these girls are quite too loyal; they make a hobby of it."

It is difficult to overestimate what the influence of her noble nature and magnetic personality would have been upon thousands of students during all these years if her work had continued in educational lines, what inspiration for high and noble living, what pure ambitions to love and serve humanity, what strong endeavors for high scholarship and great achievement would have been born in the souls of the students coming into close touch with her great soul. She was eminently fitted to be a great teacher. One who has the power of kindling another mind with the fire which burns in his own, who can bring his soul into such close and loving contact with his students that they are stirred by his impulses and fired with his enthusiasms, has in the highest sense the teaching power, and is described as the ideal teacher. This rare gift our friend possessed, and in high degree.

The nations of Europe seek to kindle the patriotic ardor of their subjects by putting on speaking canvas the immortal deeds of their great men. And in our own country a grateful public or generous friends enshrine in marble or bronze or on canvas the memory of those whose lives have been a blessing to humanity. It is a gratifying reflection at this hour, that one of our own generous citizens will soon place in the keeping of the University the face of this woman whose life was a ministry of love, and whose death leaves the world bereaved. Generations of students, as they look upon that marble, will be moved to noble living by the memory of her unselfish services, and they will find in it a noble stimulus to purity of life, and to a consecration of their powers to the cause of humanity.

The winning personality of Frances Willard and her charm of soul made it possible for her to impress herself upon her students in a manner given to the few. She exerted upon them a far-reaching influence, not only by the thoughts she expressed in her classroom, but by her views of life and duty, which she revealed to them in her personal and private relations with them. A quarter of a century has almost passed since she retired from the faculty, but those who were associated with her in those days have preserved pleasant recollections of the winsomeness of her personality, and the attractiveness of her spirit. We can ask no better thing today than that the benign influence of this refined, devoted, noble woman and teacher may abide in the life of this University for years to come.

We lay upon her casket here today this tribute of our love and admiration. She has entered within the gate. She has been transfigured, and it has been granted her that she should be arrayed in fine linen, which is the righteousness of saints. On her head was placed a golden crown, and she was girded with a golden girdle. All the bells of that great city, the holy Jerusalem, have rung with joy, and it has been said unto her, "Well done, good and faithful servant, enter thou into the joy of thy Lord."

Mrs. Louise S. Rounds, President of the Illinois W. C. T. U., spoke of

MISS WILLARD AS A PATRIOT.

The White Ribbon women of Illinois feel keenly the death of our peerless leader, Frances E. Willard! Especially are we bereaved, for in a very sacred sense she belonged to this great State.

As a Christian, Miss Willard gathered help and spiritual power from all denominations and creeds, always finding the best in the various beliefs; but "like the bees which return to their home-cells laden with their gathered sweets, so she brought all her religious treasures back to the altar of her own cherished church," to which she was always a loyal, devoted, consecrated member.

She was accustomed to pivot her broad faith and generous charity upon this formula, to which her whole life bore never-failing testimony: "No word of faith in God or love toward man is alien to my sympathy." With such a spirit she was fit to become a great traveler, and all countries contributed to broaden her love for humanity and increase her faith in God. It mattered not how far away she wandered, nor under what flag she found temporary protection, she always returned to her native land and to the flag she loved above all others with renewed feelings of loyalty and patriotism. The Stars and Stripes were to her an emblem of broader freedom than other countries knew, and thus indicated her own great and grand spirit.

How painfully sad it is that the flag which is displayed from the platform on this sad occasion — this flag which she loved so much to have draped in convention halls where she presided — how unspeakably sad that this flag should today wave over and protect the legalized liquor system! How pitiable that the curse for the extinction of which she gave her life, should find protection and defense in the laws of our land! He only is a true patriot who is true to the highest and noblest interests of his native land, and we who weep today over her cold, pale face will cherish her parting message: "Tell the women not to forget their patriotism." And we will not give up the conflict until the Stars and Stripes shall cease to float over a legalized saloon!

Not only was she an American in its noblest sense, but the State of Illinois was loved by her as perhaps no other State in the Union. In New York she was born and in New York she died, but in Illinois she lived the longest and did her grandest work.

There is wonderful significance in the fact that the ashes of Abraham Lincoln, the grandest man, and the ashes of Frances E. Willard, the greatest woman in American history, have been committed to the soil of this beautiful Prairie State, here to rest until the resurrection morn shall summon all lands and even the sea to give up their dead.

How beautiful, as we think of her work, and in what harmony with her life, are these words which dropped like dew from her pen many years ago: "Lord Jesus, receive my spirit. That is the deepest voice out of my soul. Receive it every instant, voluntarily given back to Thyself, and receive it in the hour when I drop this earthly mantle and pass onward to the world invisible, but doubtless not far off."

Rev. Dr. Bristol read the Crusade Psalm, and never did its anthem of praise and prophecy seem more harmonious with events. The congregation sang — as best it could, for voices choked with tears — the Crusade Hymn,

> "Give to the winds thy fears,
> Hope and be undismayed."

Then Mrs. Clara C. Hoffman, in tender speech, bore witness to

MISS WILLARD AS A LEADER.

We have not come here to weep and lament and cry out in our pain. We have come to rejoice. Love is unselfish and must rejoice in the bliss and happiness of its beloved, and we will rejoice though with falling tears and breaking hearts.

For Frances Willard is no longer the "uncrowned queen of America," but crowned a queen in Heaven — no more to droop and break under burdens all too heavy to bear; no more to suffer contradiction of tongues; no more to have pain and weariness of a body all too fragile to keep pace with a spirit so eager, so alert and intense, and with a mind of such marvelous versatility and power. The fetters of flesh drop to earth, the glad soul rises and revels in the realms of light and love and labor without weariness. Aye, we will rejoice!

Our beloved was a great leader because within her little hand she held the hearts of all who followed, and with irresistible charm she drew those who lacked the courage to follow. All loved her, because she loved all. All trusted her because she trusted all.

She recognized the best in each, and each reached out and up, and made endeavor because its best was recognized. She had faith in humanity, and humanity believed in Frances Willard. She did not seek her own, but with all her might she sought the greatest good for all.

She had that within herself which awoke the very highest and noblest in others. She was honored by men, and loved by women with a fervor and a constancy unparalleled in history; and this not alone in the New World, but around the globe. Women of the Orient, the Occident and the islands of the sea lovingly gave allegiance to Francis Willard, and with glad willingness followed where she led. By heroic righteousness of word and deed she drew thousands after her who never looked upon her face, or felt the charm of her gentle, gracious presence.

It has been said that women hold no lasting friendships for each other; yet for more than a score of years one of New England's truest daughters gave the devotion of sister, daughter and lover, which made it possible for Frances Willard to achieve the very best for womanhood, and the strongest, highest type of leadership.

Across the seas a gifted, pure-hearted woman of nobility is stricken in soul today, because with us she followed hand in hand — with us she loves and is loved.

Transparently frank and openly ingenuous, our leader never stopped to scheme and intrigue; never swerved one jot or tittle from the straight line of righteous principle. Ever gentlest to those most opposed, she won all true hearts by the power of love. By this sign she conquered.

When the temperance reform shall emerge from the twilight valleys of unpopularity and *assumed* impracticability to the sunlit hilltops of assured victory — and this hour *will come* — then, bright and glorious among all who have dared and achieved for humanity, in golden letters of light, will stand the name of Frances Willard — our beloved Frances! Multitudes will repeat her words, cherish her memory, emulate her gracious gentleness, follow in her footsteps. In thousands of homes, in millions of hearts she is enshrined forever. Manhood is nobler, womanhood truer, childhood safer because Frances Willard has lived. Her voice calls ever onward through duty, upward to God.

"Ah! she is not dead,
Who in her record yet the earth doth tread,
With God's fair aureole gleaming round her head."

All hail to thee, sister beloved, friend, comrade, brave and trusted! All hail, adored leader! We shall meet again, beyond the smiling and the weeping. Ah, beloved, beloved, farewell, farewell!

The Rev. Dr. J. F. Loba, pastor of the Evanston Congregational Church, followed with a fervent prayer, in which all hearts united. He thanked God "for the benediction of this life, which in the midst of perplexity and doubt, saw clearly that the only way of salvation for the home, the city, the state, the country and the world is the path of purity and righteousness and temperance, and that she was enabled to patiently and steadfastly walk therein."

Mrs. Katharine Lente Stevenson fittingly spoke of

MISS WILLARD AS A FRIEND.

My sisters have paid their tribute to our best beloved as patriot and as leader. It is left for me in these brief moments to speak of her in the special sense in which she was to thousands and tens of thousands a friend and an inspirer of all that is noblest and best. Frances Willard knew how to be a friend. It is not an easy thing to be a friend in the true sense of that word. It requires rare traits of character. There must be truth and tact, courage and patience, love and helpfulness. She possessed all these qualities in the fullest degree. Hers was the seer's vision to look beneath the apparent real and discover the ideal, which after all is the only true real. Hers, too, was the prophet's function to arouse in every heart the longing and the will to actualize that ideal until it should become the apparent real. How she loved we know. How she loved, thousands know all over our land today as they sit in sore anguish counting over her tender words and deeds, as the rapt saint counts the beads upon her rosary. We call her the friend of humanity, and she was that in the broadest possible sense, but she was the friend of humanity because she was first, last and always the friend of the individual human unit. With her the masses were never allowed to absorb the individual. She loved humanity in the abstract, but her love for humanity in the abstract was born and nurtured of her love for humanity in the concrete. People were her life, friendship was her native air; she radiated friendliness; she took all the world by the hand, and showed to each one with whom she came in contact her throbbing heart-beats of good will.

I have many times tried to analyze the elements which entered into this rare friendliness, to discover how it differed from that which we meet in the majority of people all about us. I have asked myself during these sad days, when I with others have been following this loved form on that weary journey which began in

New York and will end in Rosehill, what it all meant. What did that concourse of people yesterday in Willard Hall mean? The crowds that stood for hours in the storm waiting to catch once more a glimpse of that loved face? What do the flowers mean that today surround that soft gray coffin? What do the tears mean which fall from every eye? Simply this, that the one thing the heart of humanity is hungering for is friendship; that kindness and gentleness are the most priceless of all gifts that we can give one another on this earth; and that this woman stands in the thought of the world today as the living embodiment of peace and good will toward all mankind.

To my thought, the first thing noticeable in her friendship, which after all is only another word for her character, was its reality. She was the most real person I have ever known. There was absolutely no guile in her. She showed forth her inmost heart with a sweet frankness which seemed to take the whole human family into confidence, saying to them, "I feel all this for you, and I believe you feel the same for me." Then she was brave in her friendships; she dared to tell her friends their faults. Who of us that have come closest to her does not remember that quaint, pretty way in which she would say, "I think I have a case against thee, dear," and then she would tell out the case without sparing and yet with such sweetness that no sting was left to rankle in one's mind. She of all others could tell one a fault because she was so constantly telling of virtues. She found them everywhere because her beautiful charity magnified the virtue and discovered ground for praise where others might not have dreamed of its existence. She lived in the "sunshine of commendation" as no one else I have ever known has lived, not the commendation which was showered upon her, but that which radiated from her to others.

Her friendship was marked, too, by almost infinite tact. No one would have dared to do the brave things she did, or, if he had dared, he would have been unsuccessful in the doing, if he had had less tact than she. She compassed things which were necessarily disagreeable in such a way that one hardly discovered how disagreeable they had been until they were accomplished. She never unnecessarily antagonized, and therefore she won her way by her sweet, gracious tactfulness through many obstacles and over mountains of difficulty which would have rendered impossible the progress of one less divinely gifted. Nothing impressed me more in her friendship than its capacity for gratitude. Indeed, her mind was made up on a different order from that of most human beings in that she always remembered kindnesses and forgot injuries. I have in thought at this moment a little incident that occurred when I was with her last summer in Vermont: Just as we were getting into the carriage to leave beautiful St. Johnsbury, a lady came to her whom she had not met for years, but she remembered her and greeted her as cordially as if they had parted but yesterday, inquiring most tenderly after a brother of the lady's. As we drove away, she said, "That dear woman's brother was very kind to me twenty-four years ago in Chicago." I said, "You never seem to forget a kindness, Miss Willard," and she looked at me for a moment so earnestly before replying, "I should hope not; ingratitude seems to me the basest of sins." It was a sin of which she was never guilty. Indeed, she was always gathering up the kindnesses of her life and keeping them in tender, perpetual remembrance.

There was a rare simplicity about her dealings with her friends and with the world at large. Only a great woman could have been as simple as was she. She used to take her audiences into her confidence with a beautiful frankness which always disarmed prejudice. I am sure they felt as I have felt many times in hearing her speak, "Why, I have had such thoughts often; I have felt just like that about the dear old home, the father and the mother, the blessed early ties of life, but I never dared to tell them, lest people should not understand." She dared; she took it for granted that the most sacred emotions of her heart she shared in common with all humanity, and so she told out the things which were most precious to her, and by that very telling helped and strengthened other lives.

The scene I have thought of most often during these days of our terrible bereavement has been of that visit I was privileged to make with her to the birthplace of her mother, in Vermont, last September. A little schoolhouse stood upon the old lot, and the people were gathered together from all that countryside to witness the ceremonies connected with the tree planting on the very spot where the old hearthstone had been. She talked to them from the steps of that schoolhouse out of her very inmost soul; she talked of the old home, with its family altar; of the blessed ties of love and friendship which had bound the neighborhood together; she told what home meant to her, and what her work had been for the protection of the home. As she talked, tears streamed down many bronzed and furrowed cheeks, and one old farmer seemed to voice the thoughts of all when he said afterward, "That was the most homey talk I ever heard." All her talks were "homey," and, indeed, her entire life was set to the music of "Home, Sweet Home."

Faith was as truly a ruling characteristic of her friendship as of her religious nature. She believed in God; He was the most real fact in the universe to her, but she also believed in men and women as sons and daughters of God; and, because she believed in them, because she always saw the possible shining through the apparent, she raised them to a plane of belief in themselves. There are countless men and women all over the world today living useful lives, filling positions of trust and responsibility, who owe to Frances Willard all that they are, because her word first aroused their dormant powers and gave them faith in themselves. She more fully than any human being I have known obeyed George Macdonald's words, "The thing I must be when I can, love now for faith's dear sake."

IN MEMORIAM

I have often thought that the highest eulogy paid to anyone in the Bible is that passage in which Moses is spoken of as the friend of God. Standing beside the bier of Frances Willard, I am sure that without irreverence we may apply the same words to her; she was the friend of God, but how did she prove her fitness to bear that high title? Not by spending her days in rapt contemplation, but by proving herself daily, hourly, through long years, the friend of man — man made in the image of God. She always saw the Lord among His people, and recognized that her service to Him must be given in service to them. She had known how beautiful it was to be with God long before she fell upon that sweet sleep, and the heart of that beauty she had found to consist in being with men in loving, constant service. Dead! Frances Willard is not dead; she is alive forevermore, and this is the lesson which comes to us from that casket today; this is what she would say to us if she could speak from Heaven: "Serve God by serving men, love God through loving man, bring the beauty of holiness into the everyday life, and lift humanity up to its rightful plane of sonship to the Father, and brotherhood each to the other."

It was touching and peculiarly significant when Miss Johannsdottir, President of the Iceland W. C. T. U., in broken accent and with breaking heart, gave her simple testimony to our leader's love for other lands. "Through her, women all the world over are sisters," she said. "Over her grave we can stretch our hands to each other and make our life as she hoped we might make it, and so carry her work on."

Dr. Milton S. Terry, of the Garrett Biblical Institute, contributed the following exquisite poem:

TRANSFIGURED.

Is that soft light a star?
Or through the dimness of our tearful eyes
Are we descrying in the open skies
    Some lovelier sight afar?

Perhaps to us is given
Another vision of that wondrous sign
Revealed of old to St. John, the divine,
    When in the open heaven

By angels guarded round,
Was seen a woman with the sun arrayed,

The moon beneath her feet, and her fair head
    With twelve stars brightly crowned.

    I'm sure I see a light
That beckons many to a holier sphere,
And with its steady shining calm and clear
    There seems to be no night.

    'Tis the transfigured face
Of saintly gifted Prophetess serene,
Whose woman-soul could take of things unseen
    And give them sightly grace.

    To her God's love assigned,
Amid the rush of human cares and fears,
Nigh threescore beautiful and hallowed years
    To honor womankind.

    Say not "She is not here";
Methinks her eye beams with a brighter ray,
And never mightier, sweeter than today
    Was her voice, far or near.

    And woman's rights and wrongs,
And mortal sorrows, and the drunkard's woes,
And virtue's claims, by her life's sudden close
    Have found ten thousand tongues.

    Hushed are all envies now,
Nor breathes the soul would take away from sight
One ray of the aureole of light
    That gathers round her brow.

    O pure white life divine!
Translated into everlasting day
Thou shalt pass never from our hearts away,
    For Christ's own loves were thine.

MRS. MARY B. WILLARD AND HER DAUGHTER MARY

A GROUP OF FRANCES E. WILLARD'S NAMESAKES

IN MEMORIAM

Rev. C. J. Little, D.D., president of the Garrett Biblical Institute, made the principal address of the service on the subject of

MISS WILLARD'S PUBLIC LIFE.

Frances Willard reminded me, whenever I listened to her, of Matthew Arnold's definition of religion, "Morality touched by emotion." She was a conscience aglow with divine light.

Her departure from Northwestern University, with its attendant circumstances, caused her intense pain; the remembrance of it was never without its tinge of grief. And yet this departure was, in the old New England phrase, a divine enlargement, the breaking of the chains that held her back from destiny.

Her strong and only impulse at the time was toward the Temperance Crusade movement, then at its height. The religious fervor, the ethical purpose, the moral martyrdom and the feminine character of this movement appealed to her faith, her conscience, her courage, and her conception of woman's latent power, and so she entered it "with a heart for any fate."

Her wisest counselors dissuaded her. Even her intrepid mother advised against it. Mrs. Livermore alone of her friends commended her resolve. But wherewithal should she and her darling mother be fed and clothed? The noble women of the Woman's Christian Temperance Union of Chicago, whose president she became, would willingly have answered. But she intended to live by faith. She would trust God.

"Frank," remonstrated her brother Oliver, "your faith method is simply a challenge to the Almighty. You've put a chip on your shoulder and dared Omnipotence to knock it off." But God only smiled in His heaven and tried His child a little longer. She did not always have enough to eat, and often when weary with working and walking, she lacked the nickel for her carfare. Soon she fell sick from hardship and overwork. And thereupon her mother chided her into a wiser conception of God and a wiser method of life. She consented to accept a salary from the women of the Christian Temperance Union of Chicago, and thus the slender Wisconsin schoolmistress started out to be a teacher of the world.

All great moral careers grow out of the concurrence of conscience and of opportunity; the compulsion of the soul combines with the compulsion of circumstance, and the real life begins. Years before she had wanted to say something, *but what was it?* And now the disclosure came. All else had been a preparation for it; her maiden shyness and her maiden independence, the inspiration of her home, the revelations of nature and of books, the experiences of travel, the trials of the schoolroom, her search for God, her aspirations, her ambitions and her sorrows. The literary gift and the magic of speech were a part of her inheritance. And yet she trembled to appear in public. She had lectured in Centenary church, Chicago, in 1871. And this first public utterance contains the germ of all she said and did in after years. The sorrowful estate of women throughout the world gave her, she declared, the courage to become a public speaker. It gave her more. It gave her the vision of the woman of the future for whose coming she thought and wrote and planned and prayed. But not until 1874 did she begin to speak with all her might, for then came to her the sign by which she was to conquer, "FOR GOD, AND HOME, AND NATIVE LAND."

Frances Willard had the gift of eloquence. She was a subtle, thoughtful, thrilling talker. Her presence was not imposing, yet it was always tranquilizing at the beginning, and afterward full of sweet surprises. Her voice was clear and melodious and strong, with a peculiar quality of blended defiance and deference, of tenderness and intrepidity that gave it an indescribable ring. Her diction was studiously simple; her reasoning luminous and homely; her illustrations full of poetry and humor; her pathos as natural as tears to a child. She was wholly unaffected, taking her audience so deftly into her confidence that she conquered them, as Christ conquers, by self-revelation.

There was sometimes a lyric rapture in her utterance that wrought her hearers into a delirium of anticipation. The New Jerusalem of the twentieth century, the transfigured homes of a new commonwealth, seemed to be so near and so real. And there was always when she talked to women and to men such a sublime confidence in their latent nobility and their ultimate righteousness that for a time, at least, they became in their own eyes the beings that she pictured them, and sat enchanted with the revelation. This blending of prophetic ecstasy with practical shrewdness, of rapture with woman's wit, gave to her tongue the accent of both worlds. The note of gladness with which she mentioned Christ (and she did it often) lifted her auditors into the presence of her divine Companion, and then the childlike mockery with which she pelted some feminine folly or some masculine stupidity dissolved the splendor again into ripples of human merriment that brought her listeners safely back to mother earth. Webster was majestic; in the days of his grandeur men trembled at his godlike flashes. Beecher was superbly human, conquering and controlling multitudes by his rich and robust and royal manhood. Wendell Phillips was demonic, casting his auditors into chains, and arousing within them all the elemental passions. But Frances Willard attracted and enchanted; she spake as never man spake, and yet with the charm of Him who conquered the grave in order to restore the shattered home at Bethany.

The Willard children had a genius for organization; they played at forming clubs and making societies. Frances developed this skill during her years of teaching. She managed her pupils with rare tact, choosing for them both the direction and the method of activity. But the fullness of this power never revealed itself until she became the president of the National Woman's Christian Temperance Union in 1879. She stood for a liberal and a radical policy, and was indeed the incarnation and the inspiration of it. Of the multiplied energies that began to cluster around her fertile brain and nimble fingers I have no time to tell. They proved too many for her at the last, exacting as they did a superhuman strength of mind and will, and pulling at her heartstrings all the time.

Miss Willard has been criticised severely for her transformation of the Woman's Christian Temperance Union into a political organization, and just as severely for her blending with the cause of temperance the cause of woman suffrage and various projects of social reform. But it must not be forgotten that from her point of view this was logical and inevitable. She was an idealist and not an opportunist. They misjudge her who suppose that any merely negative movement could have absorbed her wholly. Her famous motto lays bare her inmost thought. The excitement of the Crusade had revealed to her an opportunity and started her upon a great career. But her intellect was too strong and too sagacious not to perceive that temperance was after all not the chief question. The chief question was the home. Whether men should drink or not, affected women so profoundly, because their drinking polluted domestic life, destroyed the family, corrupted the blood of unborn children and perpetuated the barbarisms of masculine law and masculine tradition. She perceived that the ideal home which was denied to her personally, but which hovered constantly before her as the prize and perfection of the future, must be held up before her sisters and her brothers as the real goal of human effort. This involved, however, the lifting of women to another plane — the plane of political equality with men. It involved also the lifting of the masculine standard of morality to that agreed upon for all true women, so that the movement for purity blended itself inevitably with the movement for prohibition. Nor could she fail to see, when she studied the problem deeply, that the cause of drunkenness and domestic misery among the poorer classes was largely economic. This created a sympathy with labor movements and labor organizations which urged her quite rapidly toward the newer social ideas that alternately attract and repel the modern mind.

It was natural for Mr. Gough to confine his philanthropic efforts to the temperance work and to the principle of total abstinence; it was equally natural for Henry George to expect the regeneration of society from purely economic change. But Frances Willard's mind was at once too broad and too deep, and her conception of woman's place in society too exalted for her to grasp the temperance problem or the economic problem in this one-sided fashion. "Society," she rightly said, "needed mothering." She was indeed a preacher of temperance and of a new commonwealth; but she was also the soul of chastity, heralding a nobler maternity than the world had dared to dream of hitherto;

and therefore the herald of a nobler manhood, a nobler society, and a nobler humanity.

Like all idealists in the history of social progress, she took little account of time, so that the results of future centuries seemed as the stars do to the children of transparent skies, just above her head. And this immediateness of the heavenly vision made it possible for her to work and to tarry for it. She knew that it would surely come.

"The benefactors of humanity," writes Amiel, "are those who have thought great thoughts about it." For the human race needs heartening always; ideas must be translated into hopes in order that faith may overcome the world. And Frances Willard translated her ideas of home and of society into a great hope, with which she thrilled the women that surrounded her. As this great hope transfigured her, old prejudices lost power. She stretched forth her loving hands to the women of all creeds and of all sections, to the women of the South and the women of England; the past was forgotten in the rapture of a great expectation. The daughter of the abolitionist embraced the daughter of the slaveholder; the child of the American democrat found her last great sister in the child of the English nobleman; the daughter of the Puritan knelt beside the Catholic mother who prayed to Mary as she prayed to God.

Among the precious relics of her latest days is a little scrap of paper containing these beautiful words of T. P. O'Connor: "Why should we talk of the futility of life and lose ourselves in vain regrets as if dreams and mere personal longings were all we had to live for? Life is futile to those only who seek for its fruits in self-gratification. To those who see in it an ever-enduring conflict for others it is ever fresh and full, a joy and an inspiration and a hope. Ring out, then, ye Sunday bells! I awake from my selfish dreams. I am a worker, a fighter and a man again!"

On the margin of this scrap of paper is written in trembling characters the following simple words: "As the outcome of a life's experience I rejoice in these brotherly words of T. P. O'Connor. Frances E. Willard, New York, January 29, 1898."

"The outcome of life's experience!" She knew it then! The Sunday bells were ringing her a welcome home! She had done what she could! She had given her life to the poor and had followed Jesus Christ. She was going to Rest Cottage and to her heavenly wages and to the great white throne.

Did she die too early? God must answer that, not we. She might have lived longer, if she had learned to spare herself, but then she might have lived less. Her fifty-eight years were rich in experience and in thought, in grief and in aspiration, in affection and admiration and achievement. They were indeed more than centuries of common life. They were for her "years of enduring conflict for others"; for she was a worker, a fighter, a woman. And the shock of her death reveals the weight of her influence. She is no longer a voice and a corporeal enchantment weaving about us the spell of a luminous conscience and a pure heart. She has taken her place in the choir invisible — the choir audible forever to God and to humanity. Whatever may be the future of the methods from which she expected such political and social transformations, her ideal of home will not perish from the earth. The strong and serious women of the future will be her daughters, and as they bow the more to reason and to conscience, her image and her voice will guide them from the shadows of ancient bondage to a companionship with men in which the perfect interchange of thought and the perfect harmony of action will reshape the heavens and the earth, and establish beneath new stars a whiter and a happier commonwealth.

Rev. Charles F. Bradley, D.D., Professor of New Testament Exegesis of the Garrett Biblical Institute, in the closing address spoke of

MISS WILLARD AS A WOMAN AND A FRIEND.

It was thought fitting that the tributes to Miss Willard as a public leader should be followed by a few words concerning her as a woman and a friend.

Yet it is impossible to mark here a well-defined separation. In a rare degree she threw her whole self into all her work. It was as a woman and a friend that she taught, wrote, spoke, organized vast forces and led them in the war for righteousness. In public as in private life she was ever womanly and always friendly. The wealth of her regnant nature, the fruits of her varied culture, the consecration of her devoted life — all these she carried, with her simple graciousness, into the intimacies of private life. The mourning of millions today is over the loss from our midst of a great woman and a friend of mankind such as the world has seldom known. A certain Roman Catholic sisterhood bears the affecting title of "Little Sisters of the Poor." Of Miss Willard it may be truly said that she was the sister of everyone, rich or poor. Everywhere she went she met people with a winning smile and a cordially extended hand. She believed profoundly that God is our Father and that we are all brothers and sisters. These beliefs were to her more than articles of an accepted creed; far more than beautiful sentiments. They were the controlling principles of her daily life. Beyond any woman of her age, and, so far as I know, of any age, she has a right to the title of the Sister of Man. Everything which that name can signify of wise, strong and loving helpfulness, that she was in purpose and, according to the measure of her strength, in fact to all.

Yet, speaking of friendship in its ordinary sense, it is difficult to conceive the extent of her circle of friends; to estimate the numbers of those in England and America and in other lands, who have the right to say of her, "She was my friend." It was out of a wide experience that she framed the new beatitude, "Blessed are the inclusive, for they shall be included." One who knew her well has said: "In nothing is she more marked than in her lavish kindness and truth to friends. It would be impossible to say how many lives which have touched hers have been inspired to nobler purposes; have realized the balm of her sympathy in sorrow and the help of her wisdom in perplexity; have proved that even her wounds are the faithfulness of a friend whose very loyalty was demanding of them their best."

But Miss Willard's life has not only been marked by a universal friendliness and blessed by a liberal host of friends, to each of whom she gave her affection in rich measure; it has also been distinguished by a few extraordinary friendships. It is not the least of the sorrows of this hour that those who alone could speak adequately of the deepest things are unable to speak at all. Miss Willard's love for her own family was most intense. The close intimacies in this circle were with her sister, her mother and her brother's wife. The providences which ended these close associations opened the way to two others. One of these began in New England twenty-one years ago. Through all these years, amid many vicissitudes, it has never failed to deepen and strengthen. It is worthy a place among the few great friendships of history. The other friendship belongs to Old England, and is associated with scenes of romantic beauty. It united women of most diverse training, but alike in rare talents of mind and one in their active sympathies for the fallen and the oppressed. When we consider the labors, the sacrifices and the sorrows which Miss Willard endured, it is comforting to consider the sources of light and joy she had in these two radiant friendships. In both there was that absolute confidence, unfailing affection and utter self-bestowal which make such devotion between man and man, or woman and woman, shine with a radiance little less than divine.

The circumference of Miss Willard's friendly sympathy has been truly said to have included the human race. Its center and source are to be found in Jesus Christ. Her whole life shows this.

The greatness of Miss Willard's powers and the clear call which ordained her to eminent public leadership often interfered greatly with the privileges of home and social life. She frequently expressed her sense of this loss, and her Evanston friends have sadly missed her during her long and many absences. But we could never doubt the loyalty of her affection and we have never failed to love and honor her. "When I go home to Heaven," she said in her quaint way, "I wish to register from Evanston." That, too, was our wish for her. This was her home. The most sacred memories of her family life centered here. The most potent forces in her education were brought to bear upon her here. At this altar she took the vows she kept so faithfully. Here she received her call from Heaven and went forth to raise the fallen, to strengthen the weak, to relieve the oppressed. We gave her to the country and to the world. She has fought a good fight; she has finished her course; she has won her crown. Her victory the world knows. And the world, as if on waves of honor and grateful affection, brings back as a sacred trust to this city, to Rest Cottage, to this altar, to our hearts, the dear form which was the temple of so much power and goodness and love.

A prayer of benediction by the pastor, Dr. Bristol, closed this service in memory of the last of an honored and beloved household — a home circle among the earliest to form in Evanston — and the classic town forgot all else in its desire to pay the last loving tribute of profound respect to its most gifted daughter. Many who had waited outside for hours came in at the close to say farewell. The White Ribbon star-spangled banner was draped for the last time over the casket, as it was borne by the brotherly students from the "dear home church," while fresh tears fell and hearts were baptized anew.

At the cemetery — beautiful Rosehill, its pure white covering of snow dazzling in the sunshine — the receiving vault was faced with evergreen, and branches of the same emblem of immortal life made warm and soft the pathway to the entrance. Once more we looked upon her face, again our hearts sought consolation in prayer, led by Mrs. Gulick, and we left our beautiful one until the time of the singing of the birds should come when mother and daughter, lovely in life, were to rest together in the "low green tent whose curtain never outward swings."

Those who were able to leave Rosehill with lifted faces were greeted with the glory of the setting sun. In the far sky hung a rainbow; with us there had been no storm, only the gentle rain that had fallen from sad eyes. Was that bow of promise sent to cheer and comfort? Let us take it as a message from Him and from *her* to look up, not down.

On April ninth, at Graceland cemetery, three miles distant from Rosehill, Miss Willard's wish in regard to the disposition of the "earthly house of her tabernacle" was sacredly fulfilled. Drawing near to them in confiding frankness of self-revelation, Miss Willard had told her friends and the whole world in her autobiography why she chose the luminous path of light rather than the dark, slow road of the "valley of the shadow of death," stating her personal convictions on the subject in these words:

"Holding these opinions, I have the purpose to help forward progressive movements even in my latest hours, and hence hereby decree that the earthly mantle which I shall drop ere long, when my real self passes onward into the world unseen, shall be swiftly enfolded in flames and rendered powerless harmfully to affect the health of the living. Let no friend of mine say aught to prevent the cremation of my cast-off body. The fact that the popular mind has not come to this decision renders it all the more my duty, who have seen the light, to stand for it in death as I have sincerely meant in life to stand by the great cause of poor oppressed humanity. There must be explorers along all pathways, scouts in all armies. This has been my 'call' from the beginning, by nature and by nurture; let me be true to its inspiring and cheery mandate even unto this last."

Miss Willard believed in the sacredness of the "earthly house of this tabernacle" as the "temple of the living God." She spent years in showing how human beings might keep it so free from taint of drink and every other pollution that it should be a fit dwelling for the divine spirit. She was ready, for this end, to present her own frail body a living sacrifice in toil and weariness and pain, and in death to offer it as a burnt offering on the altar of her conviction of right. She felt that He who would not suffer His Holy One to see corruption certainly could not desire it for even the least of His little ones, and that this mortal might elect to "put on immortality" by the swift road of the chariot of fire, as well as by the damp, dark path of the tomb, and strength was given for the carrying out of the promise many times made to this heroic soul who even in her last hours remembered the tomorrows of the world.

A group of nearest friends and relatives gathered in the beautiful chapel at Graceland. Rev. Dr. Milton S. Terry, of the Garrett Biblical Institute at Evanston, conducted the brief, impressive service. He read from Isaiah: "When thou passest through the waters, I will be with thee; and through the rivers, they shall not overflow thee; when thou walkest through the fire, thou shalt not be burned; neither shall the flame kindle upon thee," and other appropriate Scripture. Through the tender, comforting prayer ran an undertone of grateful praise that such a soul had dwelt among us and was living still to bless.

The friends followed the casket to the door of the little inner sanctuary below the chapel, whose white walls gleamed through a greenery of palms. "Never before was this room so beautiful," said the tender-hearted official in charge. "Foliage and flowers were placed here today to do honor to the greatest woman in the world." Nowhere about the sacred place, nor in any of the preparations, was there one dread shadow of death.

The casket was borne to its final resting place through the pathway of palms, which bent lovingly over it. "Open the door *very gently*," said the director to his assistants, as the casket was placed where no flames touched it, but where in the white inner chamber through the long hours of the day and night was wrought upon the precious form within it the change that lifted it beyond the touch of decay.

Who can doubt that through the solemn midnight and on to the Easter dawn the angels watched and waited there, though no eye saw the vision? Surely in more than one heart was heard a voice saying, "She is not here; she is risen."

On Sunday afternoon, April 10, amid the Easter sunshine, a hushed and reverent company gathered at the Willard lot in Rosehill cemetery. The grave of Miss Willard's mother was opened, the sides lined with evergreens, the mound of earth also hidden by green boughs. As the sacred ashes were literally committed to the precious dust beneath them, they mingled with white roses, above which were placed sprays of evergreen, sent from the birthplaces of Miss Willard's parents, of her brother and sister, and of herself, and from Forest Home and Rest Cottage; then all was made radiant with bright blossoms, emblems of the glorious springtime. A moss-covered box, fragrant with lilies of the valley and pansies, and which had held a precious inner box of purest white, was placed over the mother's heart. Surrounding the whole in beauty and fragrance, were the floral tributes of friends, and thus Frances Willard, that great woman who never lost her childhood, at last "crept in with mother."

The white silk banner which had draped the casket nestled close to the stone which bore the name of "Saint Courageous." The soft gray clouds drifting across the blue of an April sky, seemed to pause, hovering over that open grave. High above it swung the bough of an old oak, from which fluttered down a few brown and wrinkled leaves, as if eager to share the Easter bloom. A maple, mossy with bursting buds, and a soft wind sighing in the leaves of a solemn pine, seemed each to whisper a promise to guard the sacred spot. Upon the blessed hush broke the soft music of the hymn so often sung at Rest Cottage,

> "There is a land of pure delight,
> Where saints immortal dwell."

Rev. Dr. Waters, pastor of the Emmanuel Methodist Church, of Evanston, repeated the Twenty-third Psalm, and offered a heartfelt prayer. Then again the music rose:

> "There are lonely hearts to cherish,
> While the days are going by."

The hymn went on until

> "Let your face be like the morning,
> While the days are going by,"

floated out above the rustle of the last year's leaves and the whisper of the pines. And more than one bowed face was lifted with the look of high resolve that showed the breaking of the morning on the soul.

Rev. Dr. Terry prefaced the solemn burial service with the following appropriate address:

It has seemed fitting and beautiful to select the holy Easter day on which to discharge the last office of affection and duty to our honored dead. And inasmuch as it has pleased our Heavenly Father to take to himself the spirit of our beloved sister, we bring that which was mortal to the hallowed spot where the loved forms of her father and mother and sister and brother have been peacefully waiting for her coming. We do here recall how she told us, while she was with us in her mortal form, that since the far June day when her sister Mary went to dwell with God, the world invisible had been to her the only real world. Now has she herself passed on to see and know the things invisible.

So on this blessed day of the springtide, when the birds are singing and the flowers she loved are bursting into bloom, we bring the sacred treasure of her dust and place it by the fond mother, to whom she was wont to cling — not in childhood only at Forest Home, but also in life's serene meridian, when she was giving all her strength to repeat her sister's message to the world, and tell everybody to be good. She wandered far, and her voice has been heard by thousands of thousands in distant lands; and now at last, worn out with many toils in loyal service to the best Friend that woman ever knew, she hath lain down to sleep as if nestling once more in the bosom of the mother whom she trusted as the guardian angel of her early and her later life.

We are tearful at her tomb, but we comfort one another with the thought that our Lord Jesus wept at the grave of Lazarus, where Mary and Martha were wont to go and weep; and like all those who know the power of His resurrection, we sorrow not as others sorrow who have no hope. "For we know that if the earthly house of this tabernacle be dissolved we have a building from God, a house not made with hands, eternal in the heavens. For our light affliction, which is for the moment, worketh for us a more exceeding and eternal weight of glory; while we do not look at the things which are seen, but at the things which are not seen; for the things which are seen are temporal, but the things which are not seen are eternal."

After the Gloria Patria and the benediction, which was pronounced by Rev. Dr. Charles F. Bradley, of the Theological Seminary, Evanston, and the gentle covering of mother and daughter in the soft, warm garment of friendly earth, the friends came one by one and spread over it their gifts of flowers until the precious mound was one fragrant mantle of Easter bloom. At its foot was laid an offering of field daisies, whose white, pure faces and golden hearts reminded one of the friend now out of sight. Three stately palms, at the graves of father, brother and sister, gave them a share in welcoming to their quiet resting place the last dear member of the now unbroken family. Late and long the people lingered, as if reluctant to leave the spot where this Easter day their loved leader had silently testified to her unswerving loyalty to her own soul's view of right and given her last great lesson to the world in choosing to take the pure, white path on the way to her material rest in the bosom of mother earth. To her clear vision there was only beauty in the ideal of such a passing, and with her there was only beauty in the reality.

She who now "wears the light as a garment" still leads and loves us. Richly has she earned the joy upon which she has entered as she speeds on her errands of love unfettered by the garment of flesh. "The continent of immortality" is that insatiable spirit's only fitting home.

She had often said "When I pass onward to the world invisible please do not say, 'she is dead,' but rather remember that I have entered upon the activities that are not succeeded by weariness." Gazing up steadfastly into the heavens, longing to follow her into the "sweet, the strange Beyond," we hear her beloved voice cheering us on: "Protect the Home! Hold the Light up Higher, Higher!"

"'Help your fallen brother rise
While the days are going by.'"

Yes, poor weak mortals that we are, our holiest endeavors shall be given to her cherished plans while life shall last: then and then only shall we in some little measure be worthy to see her face again.

With a pean of praise for the Christlike life of this High Priestess of the Home, this toiler for tempted Humanity, this great-hearted, unselfish, transcendent friend, this glorified saint of God, let us reverently read her last "Confession of Faith," a message she gave us in the full belief that she was about to enter the unseen world and receive her crown of Life Everlasting:

"Concerning the Gospel of Christ, I retain to this hour the teaching of my father and mother, illuminated and enforced by their high character and noble lives. The chapter in my autobiography entitled 'God and My Heart,' is as complete a presentation of what I should like to have remembered by any who care for me as I have ever given. My great love for the natural sciences, acceptance of evolution as a working hypothesis of the universe, and favorable view of the new criticism, do not in the least disturb me in my early faith. I consider that men have mingled their views with the truth of God, they have so incrusted the temple of Christ's Gospel that it will take generations to restore it to its pristine simplicity and purity. It seems to me this age is one that should have sounded in its ears, more potently than any other voice, that splendid declaration, '*In vain they do worship me, teaching for doctrines the commandments of men*'; and this, '*Why call ye me, Lord, Lord, and do not the things which I say?*'

"To me there are but five words in the language: God, Duty, Love, Humanity and Immortality. I believe in the reign of the common people; that the earth is theirs, and everything in it belongs to them; that the kingdom of heaven is going to be here; that through the Gospel there is yet to come a warmer glow of love on the part of each human being for every other than we and the icicles that we resemble can possibly imagine. I believe that there will be no private property, no private opportunities of education and culture, but that each human being will reach a plane so high that his most devoted desire will be to have every other human being enjoy to the utmost those opportunities of comfort, development and cultivation that will make of him the utmost that can be made. Until this is the spontaneous desire and the supreme purpose of each of us we are only modified savages, but I believe that the light of the truth in the face of Jesus Christ

> "Shall shine more and more,
> 'Till its glory like noontide shall be!'"

CHAPTER II

CHARACTER STUDIES — TRIBUTES

FRANCES E. WILLARD
BY
LADY HENRY SOMERSET

LONG after the Temperance Reform has become a matter of past history, long after the "Woman Question" has brought about the equality of men and women, political, social, and financial, the name of Frances Willard will be remembered, not only as one who led a great movement, but as one who gave her life, her talent, her enthusiasm, to make the world wider for women and better for humanity.

Such a record will be associated with no particular form of philanthropy, but will stand among the landmarks of the ages that point the progress of the world along the upward way. Remarkable as a speaker, excellent as a writer, with a genius for organization, perhaps Miss Willard's rarest gift is the power of inspiring others with a belief in what they can accomplish. Many a speaker has attained oratorical fame and many a philanthropist has accomplished wonderful ends by devotion and hard work, but to few has it been given so to arouse women on every hand that on all sides captains have been called, companies have been enlisted, armies organized, and the most timid, undeveloped, and apparently commonplace individuals have been transformed, under the magic power of her enthusiasm, into untiring workers and gifted speakers. She possessed in a rare degree the quality of making others believe that they are capable, for the simple reason that she believed it herself. She saw the germs of a possibility where, to the ordinary eye, there is nothing but the arid and commonplace, but under the sun of her sympathy this germ grew into a very harvest of accomplishment. There are women in America and England who have probably brought the question of the possibilities for women as clearly before the public mind as Frances Willard, but to none belonged the honor so much as to her of having influenced the masses of the home women. It is comparatively easy to convince a thinking few of the logical position which the advocates for women's liberty bring forward; it is extraordinarily difficult to penetrate the walls of prejudice which have surrounded the average woman, which has kept her a patient prisoner under the dominion of man in Church, in home, and in State, and which has been reinforced by the misquotations and misunderstandings of religious teaching, and cemented by the traditions which have been handed down for centuries; but when the history of these times comes to be written it will be found that this is actually what Frances Willard has accomplished. It has not only been carried out by the infinite patience, iron determination, and extraordinary personal sympathy of the woman herself, who, having devoted herself to a line of work, has gone forward as unswervingly as the arrow flies from the bow, but difficulties did not daunt her, sneers did not sap her enthusiasm, fatigue and hardship did not hold her back.

Miss Willard has been depicted so often in pen and pencil, in the mezzotint of the critic and the full coloring of the admirer, that it is difficult to present an original view of such a model; but, instead of "beginning at the beginning," as the children say, I propose to present Frances Willard as she appeared to me, and, looking down the avenue of time, trace that distant horizon which has caused her to be all that she is to the world of philanthropy and reform.

In October, 1891, I stood for the first time on the platform of the railway station in the "classic town" of Evanston. I had only landed in America a few weeks, but my steps were naturally bent to the mecca of White-Ribboners. It was a sunny autumn day; the rare tints of ruby and gold that gleam as summer's funeral torches in the glad New World were flaming in brilliant beauty along the shady streets of that lovely spot on the shores of Lake Michigan.

Like all temperance women, good and true, I had placed Miss Willard's image in the inmost shrine where I pay loyal devotion to those rare spirits who lead the ranks of reform; and yet, as the train glided toward Evanston, I felt that our idols seem made but to be shattered, and this one also might possibly shortly be dashed violently to the ground. On the platform she awaited my coming— a delicate, fragile figure in a pretty blue dress, her small hand shading her eyes as she looked about attentively seeking her guest; and as she came toward me I saw a face so kind and frank that it seemed as though the peaceful simplicity of childhood had somehow remained unruffled by the chilling blasts of life. Extending her hand, she greeted me, not as a stranger, but as a sister beloved, and as one to whom her soul was linked by that strong fellowship and suffering that binds us in our "peaceful war," a holy comradeship in the common cause for the uplift of humanity. From that hour I have felt that we were friends — friends not alone to joy in each other's companionship, but in that truer sense that binds souls, only to form a new link in the lengthening chain of love and loyalty that holds humanity to God.

A few minutes later I was in Rest Cottage, as it was then in its completeness; for since that day the sun has set on that great life that was the center of the home circle. Mrs. Willard stood there then in the doorway to meet me, erect and queenly still, in spite of her eighty-seven years! She greeted me with that gentle kindness that showed at once her innate refined and quiet dignity; and as we sat round the supper table that night, amid the dainty, bright, yet simple surroundings of that charming home, and, later, gathered round the open hearth in Miss Willard's "den," or walked next day on the pretty lawn with its trees and flowers, grape arbor, and rustic dovecote, I felt that in all my wanderings up and down the world, I had never found a more harmonious home — a spot which seemed to combine the breezy atmosphere wafted from the great wide world with the fragrant family life which remained unruffled in its holy calm.

A few days later I went to Boston to attend the World's and National Conventions of the Woman's Christian Temperance Union. It was the most remarkable gathering I ever witnessed.

During the convention the crowds assembled were so immense that the great hall could not accommodate them. Six overflow meetings were held daily in different churches. Nothing is more significant than the fact that on the Sundays during these memorable days sixty pulpits were occupied in the city and suburban churches by women. The convention itself was a sight never to be forgotten. Philanthropic work of every description was represented, notably evangelistic, educational, preventive, and reform in all its branches — religious, legal and social — classified into forty departments. The consecrated power of America's womanhood had united to redeem the country and the home.

On the crowded platform there stood the slender figure of the woman who led that convention with a master hand. We are told that when Sir Michael Costa, the greatest conductor we have ever known, wielded the baton and gave the signal for the mighty orchestra to commence, as the great harmony filled the air with a burst of melodious sound, the violins leading in plaintive refrain, supported by the volume of a hundred instruments, on a sudden the great master paused, and looking up, said, "Where is the piccolo?" The magic culture of his sensitive ear missed that one small sound in the harmonious whole. Miss Willard, with the same infinitely fine perception, knew each note that should be struck, each tone that should vibrate in the great White Ribbon chorus. Her marvelous power of calling forth the best arose perhaps chiefly from the fact that she expected the best, and each one wished to meet the standard by which she was measured by her leader.

Such a gathering of women, such perfect command of the situation, are not mere chances. It is not often that rare talent is given to one woman by which she can bring so much to pass. Nothing *happens* in this world; "it is the toil of a life woven into the warp of womanhood," was the thought that crossed my mind as I watched this scene; and as I noted the delicate lines that had been drawn by the chisel of time on the pale face of the President, I knew that she was among those who had laid down her life to find it again in the women whom she was creating for the twentieth century and the glad good times she was helping to bring to the world.

Capacity for work, untiring and unremitting, is one of the great characteristics which the close friendship of these years has revealed; and, save when sleeping, I have never seen her idle. She knew no days of leisure; on the cars, out walking or driving, her hand was always busy making notes, or her brain planning, thinking, devising some new method to help forward the welfare of all the various enterprises with which she was connected.

The secret of her success has perhaps lain in this — that she set herself toward her aim, and nothing would tempt her from that goal. The most glorious mountain scenery would not deter her from accomplishing the allotted task she had in mind. She wrote a convention address with her back to the White Mountains, determined to see nothing but her work. On the Hudson, one glorious day, sooner than not accomplish her task when all were rejoicing in the radiant beauty of that most wonderful scene, Frances Willard sat below because she "had work to do" for a coming Chautauqua meeting. She was among those who accomplish because she understood how to deny herself, and it was this constant habit that molded her mind and made her work ring true.

During these past years this indomitable energy has been turned to pioneer work, and Miss Willard, having set herself the herculean task, or "stint," as she called it, in remembrance of the old farm days, of visiting every city of 10,000 inhabitants, and generally those that had but 5,000, accomplished in a few years a work that it would have taken many women a lifetime to build up. During those long days of travel her faithful and devoted companion, Anna Gordon, has told me of the ceaseless letters, articles, leaflets, that flew from her busy hand. Often she arrived after a weary day's journey only in time to go to the platform and face that great pitiless public which, in spite of its kindness and good nature, so little understands the vitality that is poured out when the speaker gives up himself and lays his best at its feet. It requires an energy as superabundant as Miss Willard's to carry on the multiplicity of interests that surrounded her life, the details of organization and the responsibility of that vast association that has grown under her hand. "You have a fatal versatility," said a friend to her; and, with a little sad smile, she often repeated the remark, for with her nature it has required a real consecration to consent so far to sacrifice her ambition as to be obliged to limit her powers to do the thing in hand less well than it could be accomplished, because it was to the interest of the work to limit the time allotted to any one department.

As a speaker Miss Willard was in her way unique, with a wonderful combination of eloquence, pathos, and humor, a sense of proportion and an understanding of her audience that made her utterance always harmonious with her requirements. It is probably this power of "rapport" with other souls that was her greatest talent — the quick understanding that always seizes the perspective of every circumstance from another's angle of vision, and the intense humanness of the woman. The most difficult crises have been often averted by the gentle touch and the whispered explanation, "See here, Honey!" and who could fail to feel that ill-humor, bitterness and carping must be laid aside, and that larger-souled charity reign which seemed to radiate from the heart of the President till the darkest corners lurking in the human mind were touched by its warmth and genial glow! "She is ambitious" was the worst condemnation of her enemies, but surely if there was a noble, a pure, a true ambition it was that of Frances Willard. For she, forsaking a career as brilliant as any that ever opened to a young woman, deliberately adopted a vocation that promised not one penny of money, consecrated herself to the most unpopular reform of her time, and devoted her best years to the most arduous and often apparently thankless tasks.

An army of women the world over can testify to the unselfish interest with which she ever placed those who worked by her side in positions of prominence, and labored for their advancement with greater eagerness than she ever sought her own.

Among those characteristics which have often struck me I may mention her utter absence of self-assertion. I have sometimes smiled when I have listened to conversations between her and younger workers. They would tell her all they had done, their opinion on questions to the consideration of which she had given her life, and no word would ever escape her either of all she had accomplished or all she knew upon the subject. The gentle question would draw on the eager talker, who too often took most literally the aphorism that it "is more blessed to give than to receive."

A great surrender is the price paid for all real success. Frances Willard was early called to choose between the pleasant path of culture and self-advancement and the dusty highway of a reformer. In 1871 she was elected the first President of the Woman's College in Evanston. Her great capacity for leadership soon showed itself, and the extraordinary influence she obtained over the minds of her pupils was manifest in that development of individual character which has been her constant care. The question that was always kept before her girls was not, "What are you going to be in the world?" but "What are you going to do?" So that after six months under her tuition each of her scholars had a definite idea of a lifework.

Like many other speakers, her call to address large audiences came to her as by an accident rather than by design.

During the years 1868 to 1870 Miss Willard had enjoyed rare opportunities for travel in Europe and in the East, and at a woman's missionary meeting in Chicago she had spoken of her visions of a new chivalry — the modern crusade which the women of her country should enter upon, the chivalry of justice; the justice that gives to woman a fair chance to be all that God meant her. The next day a wealthy, well-known Methodist called on her, and entreated her to use the remarkable gift she undoubtedly possessed, and to speak out to the world all that God had put into her heart. She appealed to her mother for advice, and with characteristic courage that large-hearted woman answered: "My child, enter every open door."

And so it came about that Miss Willard addressed a great audience in Chicago, and the next day the city papers were filled with columns about the eloquence of this young woman. In 1874 a very Pentecost of God swept over the continent, and Miss Willard caught the first sound of that new language of reform which had been given to the women who had been called to join the ranks of the crusade against the liquor traffic. In that year she resolved to resign her post as president of the college. After the union of the Women's College with the University at Evanston it had become impossible for Miss Willard to carry on her work according to the principles she had laid down; and, sooner than abandon the methods she believed to be right, she gave up the position she had delighted to fill. She suffered acutely in arriving at this decision, and it seemed to her, on leaving her cherished pupils and the institution she loved so dearly, as though her lifework was broken almost before it was begun. But the scholars whom God trains learn hard tasks to fit themselves for the work that He has prepared, and Miss Willard, in the pause that followed this great decision, clearly heard the call which was to her the opening of a new existence. The woman question had long been to her of vital interest, because it formed part of the great human question. She saw that until woman participated in purifying political life the corruptions which everywhere undermine the real interests of the nation could not be swept away. Years before this thought had matured she had anticipated the movement that swept over New York in 1874–75, and on looking back over her annual addresses we find page after page devoted to the thought that the political and municipal life of America must be brought into harmony with the religious and ethical teachings of that great country. There are those who, even in these days, condemn women for taking any part in public questions; but to Miss Willard politics was part of her religion, for she believed the government of the country to be an integral part of the service demanded by God from every loyal soul. It was inconceivable to her mind that women should forever occupy the position of ambulance nurses in life's great army, without pausing to ask themselves why the sick and the wounded were strewn around them, and what was the real question at issue in dealing with the evils of the legalized liquor traffic. Almost every reformer is ahead of his age, and the message that he has brought to the world has been one of prophecy. It is only, probably, when the goal of life for him has been reached that his prediction has passed into fact, and men and women forget that the age ever existed when such teaching called forth the severest criticism of the so-called Christian world. There must unquestionably be a movement of reform in the political and municipal life of the great free country across the Atlantic, and when that history comes to be written the name of Frances Willard and the brave women who stood around her will be indissolubly linked with the crisis which made for the larger liberty of the land they loved.

In 1878, Miss Willard definitely entered the temperance ranks and was made President of the Woman's Christian Temperance Union in Illinois. The acceptance of this office was, however, coincident with a time of severe struggle for this ardent soul. She addressed at this period great gatherings of men in Chicago at midday, composed principally of the denizens of the saloon, the unemployed, and all the flotsam and jetsam of the great city. "I was glad often to think," said Miss Willard, "when I looked at their pinched faces, that I, too, knew what it was to be hungry." She had given up a remunerative position in order to "cast her bread upon the waters," and as sometimes happens, it did not seem at that time as if she would find it even after many days. Her mother shared her struggle nobly, and together they fought the grim want that seemed likely to invade their little home. By the kindness of friends the bare necessaries of life were provided for her, in order to enable her to continue her work, and by degrees, when the fame of her lectures began to spread, she was enabled by her speaking to earn a subsistence for herself and the mother whom the women of the White Ribbon Army have loved to call Saint Courageous.

In 1879, Miss Willard was elected President of the National Woman's Christian Temperance Union; and in 1881, accompanied by Miss Gordon, she made the tour of all the Southern States, and it is a remarkable fact that her extraordinary tact enabled her to speak along the most advanced lines without offending any of the conservative Southern women. There is, however, little doubt that her work accomplished more than this. As a Northerner going to the South so soon after the terrible conflict had rent the nation, she was one of the first to take the olive branch and bring home the message that "all ye are brethren" in that greater struggle for the union of souls against the enemies of mankind.

From that time onward work thickened round her. First it was the Purity Department that engaged her attention, when the nation was aroused by a cry that came from across the water, and Miss Willard dared prejudice in order to stand for women oppressed and downtrodden. Probably the greatest crucifixion of her life came to her when she felt that she must leave the Republican party, in which she had been reared and to which her father had been a stanch adherent, and throw in her lot with a political faction that took a decisive ground against the liquor traffic. Those are days the bitterness of which it would be difficult to gauge; for there is nothing so hard to bear as the criticism of friends beloved and of comrades in a good cause.

Miss Willard was, since 1892, editor-in-chief of *The Union Signal*, the official organ of the World's and the National Woman's Christian Temperance Unions, and to her belonged the honor of having conceived the first really great international scheme that was to bind women the world over. Not content only with carrying out her plans in her own country, her great soul reached out to the ideal of uniting the English-speaking nations of the world, and, indeed, women the world over, by one strong link, under the banner on which is inscribed the battle-cry of home protection. One by one she sent forth women to all parts of the world, apparently helpless, moneyless and friendless; but the promise that "according to your faith be it unto you," has been wonderfully fulfilled in the Woman's Christian Temperance Union, and as each went out she gathered around her in every part of the globe groups of women who have remained loyal and devoted, until now the international organization is a fact and not a dream. Perhaps nothing could speak more eloquently of the culmination of this work than the magnificent demonstration held in the Albert Hall, when the fifty countries in which the Woman's Christian Temperance Union exists were represented—"a great human mosaic," as Canon Wilberforce eloquently described it.

Her visit to England was the occasion of a magnificent recognition of her powers. "It is the finest speech I ever heard," was the verdict of the leader of the United Kingdom Alliance, after her great address in the Free Trade Hall, Manchester; and probably no man or woman has in our generation received from the philanthropists of this country a more generous ovation than was accorded to her in Exeter Hall when first she came to these shores. "The best-loved woman in the United States," is the saying that I have most often heard applied to her in her own country. But it would be impossible to know her and to conceive for a moment that any adulation or admiration could spoil the independence of her character. Of Puritan ancestry, tracing her descent from sturdy yeomen of a little village in Kent, where, in the crabbed handwriting of the fifteenth century, stands a record of her ancestors' births, deaths and marriages, Miss Willard has inherited from her New England mother and her worthy father that fearlessness and backbone that enabled the pioneers to found the great nation of which Americans are so justly proud. Brought up on a farm in Wisconsin, Miss Willard seems to have retained all through her life the wholesome, breezy atmosphere of those early days, when she and her sister scampered like young colts over the prairie, and yet conned their books and listened to their mother's beautiful rendering of the finest gems of literature by the old farm fireside. I have never heard of a single human being who, having admired Frances Willard on the platform or in her public work, was disappointed in her when he came to know her in her home; and this, I think, is the highest testimony that can be given to any public life. She brings to her work and to all her concepts of reform the winged spirit that must always fly above the ordinary level of the world's daily round; a soul that is ever looking upward, and that seems to expand in the conscious presence of the Spirit that guides her life and meets her aspirations. She looks upon questions of theology and reform with a wideness of vision that enables her to embrace the whole group of humanity, and yet she does not lose sight of the great horizon from which "the dayspring from on high hath visited her."

The temperance cause, in spite of the gigantic strides it has made of late years toward success, is still relegated to the shadowy land of unpopular and supposedly impracticable and visionary reform. The time, however, is at hand when it shall rise phœnix-like and triumphant, and the men and women of the future will look back over the pages of history where, written in golden letters, shall stand the names of the true patriots of this age, and none will be more clearly traced thereon than that of Frances Willard.

FRANCES E. WILLARD AS AN ORATOR
REV. FRANK W. GUNSAULUS, D.D.

We are constantly told that the art and practice of oratory are declining, and that the triumphs of eloquence which have marked the history of earlier times have not been repeated in recent years. It is an interesting fact, in the presence of such a misstatement, that Frances E. Willard's career would have been fragmentary and unproductive of much of its fairest fruitage, if, in addition to her large gifts of an administrative order, she had not possessed and exercised that congeries of varied and often dissimilar powers which are the prerequisites of true eloquence. If theatrical display and violence of enunciation, even though it be applauded by a throng of people or combined with the fortuitous enthusiasm of a great occasion, be called oratory, then surely this woman was not an orator. If ornament of expression must race with volubility of utterance in order that a speaker may produce effective speech, if brilliancy of imagery and simulated emotion must be added to these to win the triumph in such a great name as eloquence, then, indeed, Frances E. Willard secured not a single trophy for herself in this field, nor is she to be named among women conspicuous for eloquence. But if a great heart, fed by fiery streams from on high, glowing and molten with burning love for humanity, issuing forth its indignant denunciation of evil, pouring out incessant streams of argument against well-dressed error and fashionable wrong, kindling with lightning-like heat thousands of fellow-beings until they also flash to holy wrath which scathes the slayer and illumines the slain — if lifting millions of human beings from out the noise and dullness of unreason into the serene radiance of reason, so that they are willing to obey the highest ideals and to serve at any cost the noblest demands of humanity and God — if these be of the characteristics or results of eloquence, then, without doubt, Frances Willard must be considered one of the most eloquent of the orators of our time. She has told us, in her own way, of her first public address:

"One day when I was doing housework at Rest Cottage, the winter my mother, my friend Kate and I decided to have no stranger intermeddle with our lot, either in kitchen or parlor, a gray-haired gentleman, the scrupulously elegant style of whose toilet made an impression even upon one who gives but little attention to such subjects, rang our doorbell and inquired if this was the home of Frances E. Willard. Being affirmatively answered he entered, with much mingled dignity and urbanity, and addressed his remarks about equally to my mother and myself as we were all seated in the little south parlor. He discoursed somewhat on this wise: 'I have been present at several of the meetings of the Women's Foreign Missionary Society before which you have been speaking within the last few weeks concerning your observations in Egypt and the Holy Land. It seems to me you have the art of putting things, the self-possession, and many other of the necessary requisites of a good speaker. And I said to myself, I will go and see that lady; she is a good Methodist, as I am, and I will invite her to lecture in Centenary church, of which I am trustee, making this agreement, that if she will work up a good, popular lecture, I will work up a good, popular audience, will pay her a fair price for her effort, and will see that it is well represented by the press of Chicago. It occurs to me that as the result, if all goes as well as I believe it will, she will have no more difficulty in making her livelihood and broadening her opportunities of usefulness.'

"The pleasant-faced gentleman looked to me very much like a combination of Santa Claus and a horn-of-plenty as he uttered these words. Mother seemed equally delighted, and we told him he was the kindest of men to have thought of me with so much interest; that I had returned from Europe a few months before, earnestly desirous of employing my time to the best advantage for the support of my mother and myself, and for the good of those among whom I might labor; that what he had promised would suit me to a dot, as I had all my life felt a strong inclination to speak in public and had only been withheld from doing so before, because of the somewhat conservative atmosphere of the educational institutions in which I had spent the last few years and my own sensitiveness to appearing in public.

"Declaring that he had no claim upon our gratitude, the pleasant gentleman went his way, and for the next three weeks he invested a good share of his time in interviewing influential persons and in working up, with all the ingenuity of which he was a consummate master, an interest in me and in the lecture that was to be.

"For myself, I spent those three weeks in the closest kind of study, writing and committing to memory a lecture about one hour and a half long, entitled 'The New Chivalry.'

"On the evening of March 21, 1871, I appeared with my friends, Rev. Dr. Reid, editor of the *Northwestern Christian Advocate*, and his daughter Annie, at the luxurious home of the kind gentleman, where we took tea, and then went over to the handsome city church, where I was presented at the door with an elegant card, the first ticket I had ever seen about a lecture of my own. It read as follows:

MISS FRANCES E. WILLARD

WILL GIVE HER LECTURE,

"THE NEW CHIVALRY,"

In the Centenary (Dr. Fowler's) Church,

TUESDAY EVENING, MARCH 21, 1871, AT 7:30 P. M.

TICKETS, TWENTY-FIVE CENTS.

"The pleasant-faced gentleman said, as he reached his kindly hand to me, 'Turn the crank skillfully at your end of the church, and I will do so here,' for, behold, he was gathering up the tickets himself! I was gracefully introduced by Dr. Fowler, the pastor of the church, and spoke my piece, making no reference whatever to my manuscript, which lay concealed in a modest portfolio that had been previously carried in and placed upon the pulpit. My audience consisted of the *elite* of the West Side, with many from the North and South Sides, and they cheered me far beyond my merits. At the close the pleasant gentleman introduced me to a semi-circle of well-known journalists of the city, whom he had as good as coerced into being present; and, in my private opinion, he had caused to be written up at his dictation the very nice notices that the young debutante upon the platform was so fortunate as to win from the Chicago press."

More than a quarter of a century has elapsed since that audience melted away in the darkness of that evening, and at a hundred firesides there was discussed that night the old question as to whether any woman ought really to be as eloquent and powerful as was the young woman who had come to Centenary church from Evanston and captured so large an audience. In at least one home the prophecy was made that Mrs. Mary A. Livermore (of whom Miss Willard loved to say: "Everybody agrees that she is our present queen of the platform, and no American woman has a better record for patriotism and philanthropy") had already a rival in excellence of speech and nobility of endeavor in Frances E. Willard.

Miss Willard did not possess the splendid physical presence which in Mrs. Livermore—a speaker she never ceased to admire—has bent the bow of Ulysses with a superb and queenly ease. But when the bowstring twanged which her fingers had touched, an arrow sped, as sharply tipped, as finely feathered, as sure to hit the object aimed at, as though the speaker had been of enormous frame and breathed through a pair of organ-like lungs. Indeed, students of oratory will agree that the wonder of Miss Willard's physical constitution, as compared with the amount of work which she performed and the achievements she wrought as a public speaker, passed strangely out of sight when she exercised upon her audience the charm of her mellow and finely cadenced voice, attuned to the strenuous rhythm of her thought and feeling. When asked if she were a very large woman, an old toper, who was also a great lawyer, said, in describing her speech of the night before: "I should think her about eight feet high and weighing about four hundred pounds avoirdupois; but when she was wooing my heart to a better life, I thought then, and think now, that she was the sweetest little being in the world." When an audience of six thousand had assembled together and Miss Willard had serious arguments to plead and something of a prejudice to overcome by battling for a position to which even the majority of her sisters had not assented, one wished she had more of brawny stoutness. When the harp trembled and shook with emotion, as she spoke of what she meant to do by the grace of God and by force of strength that night, we feared that the strings might be worn away and the echoing harmony be heard vanishingly; but as the eye lit up with hitherto unseen fire, the finely mobile lips moved with great messages so easily, the chest expanded from slightness to largeness and strength proportionate to the richness of the outpouring truth, the most affectionate and anxious friend felt supreme confidence in the strength of her nerves and the boundlessness of her vital energy, and nothing seemed able to tire or to vanquish that combination of powers which was illuminated by the vast reserve of spiritual power attending her progress. Those who heard and saw her as she spoke knew something of that heredity and the long years of excellent breeding which was in the blood that rose into such luminous flush and communicated its rapture to a whole audience, eloquent and confident of triumph. If she had possessed such a powerful frame as would have suggested a female Mirabeau or a woman like Burke, something of the spiritual forcefulness of her presence and message must have faded. To hear her, after the massive speech of even a more ponderous brain to whom auditors gave shouts of approval, was like listening to Wendell Phillips, calm, yet fiery, alert, yet serenely sure of the truth, while yet the magnificent excitement and stalwart glory of Daniel Webster made the air tremble and burn. Her cause gained always by the fact that an auditor was perfectly certain, in her case, that it was "only a woman" after all, speaking. A perfect lady of her size must always seem to depend upon the forces that neither bear down upon wrong with prodigious material strength nor outdazzle wickedness in its flaming audacity by spasmodic brilliance. When she pleaded for womanhood, the gentleness and quietness of her demeanor, the modesty of accent and sweetness of tone, made woman's cause not less womanly than woman herself at her best. One of the boldest of the sons of Bacchus, himself an orator of no mean power, confessed that he believed "she could write a most captivating love letter."

Her voice had the harmonious swell, the exquisite flexibility, the varied richness, the height and depth which made her capable at all times of touching into response almost every string in human nature. At Baltimore, one of the greatest of our college presidents, who has made a comprehensive study of the forces of eloquence, heard her for an hour and a half, and remarked, at the close of her address: "The cause which she represents touches every interest of the human soul and body, and she has applied its persuasive appeal to every quality and concern of my personality." It was a remarkable audience — more than a thousand of her sisters in her chosen work, hundreds of restless and eager college students, scores of doubtful conservatives and unemotional educators, long serried ranks of men and women standing on their feet, who had "just come to hear a woman slash into things"; but it is doubtful if, in that hour's utterance, there was not wakened in each soul some profound sympathy, first for her who made music in each soul's particular key, and then for the cause which seemed at first to each one a personal affair, and was indeed as wide as humanity itself.

Miss Willard never needed to assume modesty — she was modesty incarnate. With such a range of power, she ought to have apologized for the first five minutes of tame and easy address when so much was expected. But the flame of usual size and intensity had not yet begun to quiver and glow; the variously toned organ had not yet shown its possibilities of music, and it was best that unarmed the peaceful opposition should be met and conquered. She has herself spoken of her own feelings on an occasion like this:

"Always, in the presence of an audience, I am saying to myself at one time or another, 'How dare I stand here, taking at least a thousand hours of time, and focalizing the attention of a thousand immortal spirits? Who am I, that so great possibilities of influence should have fallen to my lot? And I must remember that there is a stenographer always present, the stenographer of memory, and that in the white light of the world to come, not only what I utter here, but every thought I think, will stand out plain as the sun in the heavens — for every soul shall give account of himself to God.' There is something unspeakably pathetic about the life of one to whom must frequently recur the unmatched responsibility of meeting public audiences. His is a joy and sorrow with which none intermeddleth. A ring at the bell may dissipate a thought he was just catching on his pencil's tip in the preparation of a speech; a rap at the door may put to flight the outline of an address; the constant coming and going of people who really must see him, break into staccato snatches the speech that might have been flowing, deep and bright. His riches, what he has, are like Sojourner Truth's—'in his idees'—yet they are scattered right and left, as if they were of the smallest consequence, because they are impalpable, invisible, unheard. He grieves for the thousand children of the brain that might have come to light had they not been throttled in their birth. He knows the meaning of the words, 'Travail of soul.' Then he must put aside a thousand pleasant things in nature, music, books, society, for he has a certain speech to make at a certain time, and, like an engine on the track, he must go forward toward that time. True as this is on a great scale of the great speakers, it is also pathetically true of us who are the lesser lights."

With such a physical organization and with such a voice there might have been failure if her mental and spiritual machinery had not been of such a rare fashion and so exquisitely set up and finely adjusted within her personality. "Why, this woman can argue as Evarts does, and she sustains her flight of thought as Evarts cannot do without interminably long sentences," remarked one of the Judges of the Supreme Court of the United States, who presided at one of her meetings. She seemed always to think on her feet, and the unfailing continuity of her well-directed reasoning, when she had a task to perform with the intellects of men, witnessed not only to the industry and reflectiveness of her mind, but it furnished a marvelous testimony to its solidity and strength. The central stream of thought never left the stream-bed dry, nor did it meander out of sight beneath intertwining roots of tall, overhanging trees, which often prove an excellent stopping place for an audience seeking coolness and shelter, and even sleep. In an address in Plymouth church, Brooklyn, of which Mr. Beecher told the present writer as often as the name of Frances Willard came to his lips, she proved herself able to take the audience he had trained to think, and to enjoy thinking with him; and she invested her task and efforts with such radiance of humor and flashes of wit that one of his warmest admirers said of her: "She has beaten the old man on his own ground, and at the one job he has done with a success unequaled in any age."

A witty remark or a dash of humor has often proved itself so interesting to the speaker, that, for a moment, the thought has been deflected or the current of reasoning turned aside. This was never so with Miss Willard. Her humor is spoken of in another place. It enabled her to be companionable with Joel Chandler Harris; and Gough often told two of her stories, which were only a couple from the multitude which she left, like hearty laughs to ring yet in the parlors where she was entertained or in great audience rooms where she had spoken. Her wit, which never degenerated into scorn or quivered with a drop of poison, flashed and oftentimes cut deep into the heart of crowned evil or silken pretense. But neither wit nor humor betrayed her into losing the main chance of enforcing her thought and at least making the audience she addressed know the reasons why she held to certain propositions. Her will seemed to gather to itself all the powers of her personality. Eloquence is often an exhibition of brilliant weakness, because, amidst the excitement of kindled souls, no dominating will issues its high command from the throne of some imperial righteousness. The fatal difference between a fascinating speaker, possessing every desirable quality of presence, intellectual acuteness, comprehensive vision, warm emotional nature, and the true orator, oftentimes lies in this, that the former has no set and granitic purpose to which men may attach their own sympathies and convictions. Miss Willard's will came through long generations of men and women who were oftentimes thought to be a trifle stubborn, and her will was as soft as sunshine, yet as pervasive and resistless as dawn. At the height of her power, it seemed the sublime power which most identified her and her cause with the Will which controls the universe. A poetic imagination which in early years had fluted upon many reeds and filled the household with song, a remarkable memory which was never so sure or so far-reaching as when she forgot her manuscript and laid her tax upon the entire past, a clear, strong faculty for ratiocination, a passionate love of study such as rescues fluency from its disorder and converts declaiming into oratory — these were some of the possessions and qualities which she had to offer to the cause which found her.

The cause of temperance and the emancipation of woman, bound up as they are with the cause of purity, are sure to furnish a fit theme for a whole life's utterance out of such a soul and body. The cause, on the other hand, was sure to find in her all the stops and keys which were necessary for the complete expression of its many-sided appeal, its varied demand, and its world-wide hope. Every human being is more than himself when a great cause takes him, sweeps him on in his development and triumph, and calls him its own. The tenderness of Miss Willard's nature, her home-loving disposition, her deep love for humanity — a characteristic of spirit which must always belong to a great public speaker — might have become sentimental indeed if the cause for which she strove had not laid tribute, through all her oratorical genius, upon her intellectual strength and spiritual completeness.

No subject has furnished more of superficial emotion and iterant and tearful bathos than has this majestic theme, deep and dark on the one side, sunswept and blossoming on the other. "Did she cry much?" asked a cynical critic of his young son, who had left his college duties to hear her in Boston. "No," answered the young man from Harvard, "she did not cry any more about the woes of those who suffered from intemperance than Emerson would have done; no, *she* did not cry, but all the audience cried, including myself; and you would have cried about the things she spoke of if you had been there, and you would have cried just because she did *not* cry." The writer of these words remembers the honor he had of taking Wendell Phillips, when his step was infirm and his health frail, to hear Miss Willard. He was particularly struck with the "sobriety of this fiery temperance woman," and all the way home he talked of the great temperance speakers of the world. It was his amazement that such admirable gifts of administration should have been so subtly interpenetrated with so poetic an enthusiasm and so earnest an optimism. Phillips had spoken only a short time before, in the midst of the associations of culture, and before an audience most of whom were stung to anger by the old man's scorching irony and withering sarcasm. In that address he had uttered memorable statements with respect to the imperial importance of the temperance cause, and in his effort to commend that cause to fashionable scholarship he had commanded and blasted and flamed. When he was told that Miss Willard's manner — her repose of strength, the consciousness she exhibited of reserved power, her wit and wisdom, her triumphant certainty of ultimate success — brought to mind his own characteristics as a public speaker, he proceeded to say that no *man* possessing the heart to feel the fountains of tears behind Miss Willard's speech could have kept his steadiness and practiced such restraint upon his emotions. "It takes a woman to do that," he said. He laughed dryly, and said: "Ah, yes! But she is only one of the weaker vessels, as we are told."

Miss Willard always agreed with George William Curtis that the most comprehensive and philosophic utterance on the woman question which had come to her attention was the address of Wendell Phillips at Worcester. When Phillips' attention was called to this, he said: "We men do not understand the subject. I was pleading for the rights of man. I would like to hear Miss Willard ask for her own rights. But," he added, "there is neither man nor woman in Christ Jesus." No man more fully understood the remarkableness of that combination which we knew as Frances Willard than did he. The address that night seemed to the present writer not so daring, nor, indeed, so comprehensive as was usual with Miss Willard, but the old master of assemblies told me she reminded him of Theodore Weld, whom Phillips always pronounced the wisest and the truest of anti-slavery orators. "I am accused of being scornful and carrying a whole armory about with me — a combination of destructive weapons. I spent most of my life in the cause of the black man. Perhaps her cause is so much greater — certainly *she* is so much greater — that she does not need to be scornful or wrathful, as we were. Our indignation was of a pretty sound quality," he added, "but hers is the faith of the Lord God Almighty in its fullness. She is very restless under wrong, but she can wait. It is a great faith that wonderful woman has." Accosted the next day by an autograph hunter, who was held by the old man far toward the night, as he showed him relics of the abolitionists and memorials of his own labors, he was about to bid the young man good evening, when the latter, half patronizingly, said: "Mr. Phillips, I think if I had lived in your time, I would have been heroic, too." Phillips, as he stood on the doorstep, pointed to the open places of iniquity near his dwelling place, and said: "Young man, you *are* living in my time, and in God's time. Did you hear Frances Willard last night? Be assured, no man would have been heroic then who is not heroic now. Good night.'

Miss Willard has written very interestingly about Henry Ward Beecher, and she never feared the reproach of having "bowed down before the first member of this magnificent family that my eyes had yet beheld," as she said. Her mother's hero was the Plymouth preacher, and Frances' girlhood was influenced largely by the reading of Beecher's sermons, and the heroic confidence of her mother at the time of his terrible trial. Mrs. Livermore brought her into friendship with the minister and philanthropist, and soon she was speaking in Plymouth church. While they could not agree with one another in many things, each agreed that the other possessed genius.

As one reads over the affectionate words written by Miss Willard concerning Mr. Beecher, he reflects that he has only to have been favored with the preacher's opinion as a public speaker to assure the readers of her biography that he always regarded her as "an incarnate and resistless argument for the complete emancipation of woman and for everything else that was good." No one knew more truly than the eloquent preacher how difficult and marvelous is the association of commanding intellectual powers with the rich and restless emotional experiences. It was Mr. Beecher's theory that no woman in our age more truly illustrated the fact that forcefulness and influence for good can be obtained only by the alliance of a clear head with a warm heart in public than did Frances Willard. "I always feel," said he, "that she might inundate the whole assembly with tears if she were not so wise, and that she might take us to heights of reasoning where we would all freeze to death, if she were not so kind."

Such are the opinions of two of the most effective of American orators concerning the wedded strength and sweetness in Miss Willard's career as an orator. But the old Quaker poet was right when he said of her: "I always want to tell her, 'thee must know thee is great only as thy cause makes thee great. Thee might be only a lot of good qualities if thee had not been fused.'" It is true the commanding cause held her intellectual and spiritual and physical powers in unity, and actually fused them into a white heat, which, however, never left the bounds of safety save in radiance.

THE WORLD'S FRIEND

MARY LOWE DICKINSON

In a time like this it seems hardly fitting that one should speak of individual or personal bereavement. Our loss is universal, and the bereavement seems to have stirred the pulse of sorrow in the heart of the whole nation.

We know of no other instance when over the grave of any man or woman was outpoured such a flood of appreciation, of affection and regret. That flood rose until, like a sea, it has swept over the press and the pulpit and found its way into the inlets of ten thousand homes and many times ten thousand hearts. It is a privilege to be allowed to add the little drop, which is all that any one of us can offer to swell that universal tide. If on our little drop the light falls so that it reflects the image that her character has left upon our hearts, it is all that we can hope.

For many of us it is hard to think of her, as we ought first, as the world's woman and the world's friend. The instinctive claim of affection calls her "our woman" and "our friend"; and yet we must not forget that it was her great value to the world that gave her friendship its great value to individual souls.

During the great meetings of the Congress of Representative Women at the time of the Columbian Exposition, speaking of the women who formed the Woman's Christian Temperance Union, I said:

"They made a union, and that was great. They made a *Temperance* union, and that was greater. They made a *Woman's* temperance union, and that was greatest. But they made a woman's *Christian* temperance union, and that fact made the greatness of all the rest."

That which we said then of the organization through which the life of Frances Willard found its best expression, applies equally well to the woman herself. She made union. That is, she was among the first to recognize and to develop the possibilities of co-operation. In this she was great. She showed herself greater still in her power to discern and to choose the one Cause on whose success hung the welfare of the world. And she was surely greatest when she made a *Woman's* union, concentrating and combining all the highest womanly forces for the moral uplift of home and native land.

The great thought of her great heart was to gather the women of the world together and make of their outstretched arms an orphanage for the world's childhood, and of their throbbing hearts a bulwark against the world's misery and sin and shame.

Yet in all her grand conception and magnificent execution, the fact that the co-operation she sought was to be a *Christian* union was kept ever in the foreground. No matter on what field the fight for temperance and purity and patriotism was to be fought out, over every battle this Christian banner hung. Under it her own life-march went grandly heavenward. Under it the grieving ranks of the women who follow her leadership must go forward to the battles that are, as yet, unwon.

In the emphasis given to this side of her lifework lies its strength in the future. We believe that if the sealed lips spoke to us tonight from some calm height among the hills of God, that it would be to bid the women of the world to stand together to secure for the world a truer motherhood, a finer boyhood, a nobler manhood, a higher type of citizenship, and, through the help of a united Christian womanhood, homes lifted from dishonor and a land redeemed from shame.

One might easily fill a book with what could be said of this *living* and loving friend of humanity. As a child in the prairie home, as a student, as an educator — the touch of whose character was laid upon many a young life a quarter of a century ago — as an organizer, a discoverer of the undeveloped forces in womanly nature, as a leader and as an ideal Christian woman of her day, she might be brought before us as a lasting inspiration. But multiplication of words is vain. We women of her century pay her highest tribute and do her greatest honor when we learn to love humanity as she loved it, and to live under the control of such motives as dignified her life.

The following words, adapted to the sweet old tune of "Lead, Kindly Light," were written in part by Miss Willard's side as she lay in that exalted sleep under which years and pain and care faded till her face shone out upon us radiant with immortal light and calm with the unspeakable peace of God:

SLEEP WELL, BRAVE HEART.

"Sleep well, brave heart! Beloved of Christ and crowned,
    God gives thee sleep.
The wide world's love enwraps thy slumber round,
    God gives thee sleep.
His angels smile, His stricken children weep,
Yet smiles nor tears shall break thy blessed sleep.

"O, wondrous face! whose solemn, mystic grace
    O'erfloods the gloom
Till grief in all this sorrow-shadowed place
    No more finds room.
Show us, dear Lord, what sight breaks on her eyes!
Let us, too, hear the voice that bids her rise.

"Chide not our tears, so weak we are and blind,
    For she would share
Her gladness with us who are left behind,
    Heed Thou our prayer.
Not yet? Not yet? The vision tarrieth still?
Then grant us, Lord, with her, to love Thy will.

"To work Thy will, to follow where she trod,
    Without one fear;
To drink her cup, to climb the heights of God,
    Knowing her near;
To make her joy more joyful by our strife;
So may we share, e'en here, her glorious life.

"So shall our homes, our land in shame so long,
    Be cleansed from wrong;
So shall our hearts that break through love be strong;
    So shall the throng
Of suffering souls still through thy life be blessed.
Thy work rests not, brave heart. Take thou thy rest."

An address delivered at a Memorial Service at the residence of Mrs. William Dodge, New York City.

FRANCES E. WILLARD AND THE KNIGHTS OF THE NEW CHIVALRY

REV. NEWELL DWIGHT HILLIS, D.D.

Already an English, a French and an American historian have told the story of the achievements of this closing half century. From different view-points these scholars have characterized our epoch as illustrious for what it has accomplished in politics, in war and wealth, in commerce and invention. But if our century has been a proud one for all lovers of their kind, its pre-eminence does not rest upon the increase of tools releasing the multitudes from drudgery; the increase of books releasing the multitudes from ignorance; the diffusion of art releasing the multitudes from ugliness; the development of science releasing the multitudes from squalor, pain and suffering. When long time has passed by, historians will see that the crowning glory of our century has been the rise of its humanists and the development of a new order of chivalry.

For the first time in history, the material forces of society have begun to be Christianized, and literature and wealth, position and eloquence have allied themselves with the poor and the weak. No longer can rank bribe scholarship, or riches monopolize genius. In France our epoch has witnessed the rise of Victor Hugo's school, consecrating talent to the convicts and the poor of great cities. In England Charles Dickens pleads the cause of the orphan and the waif, as typified by Oliver Twist and David Copperfield, while Kingsley, Besant and Shaftesbury speak and write for the laborers in mines and factories. In our own land Harriet Beecher Stowe represents a multitude of writers who seek to ameliorate the lot of the slave and the outcast. The poets and essayists also, Lowell and Whittier, Ruskin and Carlyle; those heroic soldiers named Gordon and Lord Lawrence; intrepid discoverers like Livingstone; living philanthropists and reformers, too, there are, whose names may not be mentioned until death hath starred them — these all have counted themselves as retained by God in the interests of the weak and the downtrodden. If in former centuries a single name like Dante or Luther stands for an epoch, the hero being like a star riding solitary through the night, in our era the humanists and knights of social reform are a great multitude, like stars, indeed, for their brightness and number, and like stars also in that "God calleth them all by name."

In all ages the reformers have gone the way of contempt, obloquy and shame, having their Gethsemane. From Paul to Luther and Garrison and Gough, these men have been the best hated men of their times. In our fathers' day the very skies rained lies and cruel slander upon these abolitionists who affirmed that the fugitive slave law "was a compact with hell and a league with the devil." But if in the lifetime of the reformers the fathers stoned the prophets through the streets, covered their garments with filth, mobbed their halls and houses, the children are building monuments to the reformers and teaching their sons the pathway to the hero's tomb. "Time writes the final epitaph," said Bacon, and we now see that those who in their lifetime allied themselves with the poor and weak have supremacy over the orators and statesmen and scholars who loved position and toiled for self.

In the interests of its children and youth, what would not this nation give today if Daniel Webster and Rufus Choate and Edward Everett had only refused compromise, stood unflinchingly for principle, and marched straight to that certain defeat in life that would have meant a certain victory after death? In the Pantheon of our immortals we now behold those intrepid reformers and radicals who once vexed conservatism and annoyed the wealthy classes who loved ease, while the jurists and merchants and statesmen who sacrificed principle to selfish supremacy have received neither statue nor portrait, and have already passed into forgetfulness and obscurity.

But there in the sunlight stands, and shall stand forever, that Whittier, whose message was, indeed, sweetness and light, but who, when the fugitive slave law was passed, acted the hero's part, forged his thunderbolt, and wrote "Ichabod" across the brow of the erring statesman. And here is that elegant patrician, Wendell Phillips, the idol of Boston's most exclusive circle, the brilliant champion of purity and conservatism, with his ambition for a place in the Senate and supremacy for constitutional law, who proudly took his stand beside the slave and knew that all the doors upon the avenues had closed behind him, and, when his city jeered, hurled his polished epithets and scornful arrows upon the beautiful women and the cowardly men who once had been his companions. And here is Charles Sumner, with his knowledge of international law, his skill in diplomacy and his ambition for foreign service, who gave up all his hopes and bound his motto as a frontlet between his eyes, "Bondage must be destroyed and liberty established," and who was at last knighted by the club of a coward, who smote him in the Senate chamber and brought the statesman to honor and immortality.

And here is Garrison, serenely setting type for the *Liberator*, smiling scornfully upon the mob howling in the streets below his windows, even though destined an hour later to be dragged over the stones with a rope around his neck, and who in that hour was the only cool man in all the demoniac crowd; and here is Lowell tuning his harp to songs of liberty; and Emerson from his study flinging cold, philosophical reflections into the very teeth of slavery; and here is Beecher with his flaming torch kindling the fires of liberty all over the land; and here is Douglass with his scars speaking eloquently of the horrors of the slave market and the cotton field; and here is John Brown with smiling face and sunny heart going bravely to his martyrdom; and here also the company of noble women with their books and songs and stories, strengthening the battle line. Nor must we forget Florence Nightingale with her crusade in the hospital and prison; Horace Mann with his crusade against ignorance; Gough with his crusade against intemperance; General Booth with his crusade for the neglected poor in great cities, and Livingstone toiling unceasingly through weary years to encircle the dark continent with lighthouses for mind and heart. The time was when these reformers were despised, scoffed at and mobbed, with whose very names men would not defile their lips. But now cities are erecting their statues in the parks, and, that children and youth may emulate their virtues, building monuments in the public squares. When time hath plowed our cities into dust, the names of these reformers and heroes will survive as enduring monuments to our age and civilization.

To these reformers who sought to destroy slavery must now be added those who felt that their task had only begun when the physical fetters fell off, and so passed swiftly on to achieve liberty for each enslaved mind and heart. Our city has just buried one of its noblest daughters, whose achievements for God and home and native land were such as to rank her as one of the most famous women of this century. Only those who have lingered long over her books and essays, or have passed under the full spell of her luminous speech, or have considered her wide-reaching influence upon our education, our civic institutions, can understand why it is that two continents mourn for our prophetess of self-renunciation. When Mme. De Stael and George Eliot were borne to the tomb, it could not be said of these daughters of genius that in a thousand towns and cities the multitudes assembled in church or hall to sit with bowed heads and saddened hearts, keeping a sacred tryst with memory during that solemn hour when afar off memorial words were being spoken above the silent dead. Last Wednesday morning, midst falling snow and sleet, when the gray dawn was passing over the city, the funeral car of Frances Willard drew slowly into the station. The long sidewalks, the vast building itself, the outer squares and streets were thronged and crowded with a multitude assembled to meet the body of a woman whose life and words and spirit had helped redeem them to the higher life and made the years worth living. Then all day long the multitudes surged and thronged into the hall that bore her name until fully 30,000 people had passed in and out.

Beside that bier also stood pilgrims from Florida and from two other Southern States, people of wealth, united to this woman by no blood ties, but who in their homes of luxury felt themselves to be her debtors, and having made their way unto this clime of ice and snow that they might look for a moment upon the face of one who had increased their happiness and lessened their misery, these made their way back unto the land of fruits and flowers, where they hope again to gain their health. If titled folk of foreign cities cabled sympathy and sent wreaths and flowers, the children of poverty and suffering also crowded the streets along that line of funeral march. The death of what private individual since Abraham Lincoln's time has called forth a thousand memorial funeral services upon the afternoon of one day? The time is not yet come for the analysis of Frances Willard's character or the exhibition of her mental or moral traits. Among her divine gifts must be included a body firmly compacted and of unique endurance, yet delicately constituted as an æolian harp; a voice sweet as a flute, yet heard of thousands; rare common sense; strength of reason and memory; singular insight into human nature; intuitive knowledge of public men and measures; tact, sympathy, imagination, enthusiasm, with a genius for sacrifice and self-renunciation. Early successful as an authoress, highly honored with position or rank in the realm of higher education, she turned her back upon all offers of promotion.

She organized a work for women, through women; her brain conceiving the new thought, her heart lending it momentum, her will executing the vast conception. In the beginning she toiled without salary, until she had expended her little store, and came to such straits that for want of carfare she had to walk to and from her dark, bare office. Soon she set before herself the task of addressing the people in every city in our land that had ten thousand people. When twelve years had passed by she had stood before 4,000 audiences, a feat surpassed only by Beecher, Gough and Moody. She was largely instrumental in securing the enactment of laws in all the States of the Union save Texas, Arkansas and Virginia to introduce physiological temperance and the scientific study of stimulants and narcotics into the curriculum of the common school. For years she was misunderstood; oft was she cruelly criticised; full oft despised and scorned. But at last she has fulfilled her career. She is now with Augusta Stanley and Florence Nightingale, with Mary Lyon and Lucretia Mott and Harriet Beecher Stowe. She is with Luther and Livingstone. She has met Garrison and John Brown and Wendell Phillips. Having met them and received their approval, what cares she for our praise? It is of supreme importance to us and our children that Frances Willard should think well of us. "Whom God hath crowned," let us remember, "man may not discrown."

Not until our children's children come to write the history of the reform movement of this century can the influence of the noble women who have toiled for temperance be rightly understood. Nevertheless, if we contrast the drinking habits and customs of the former generations with those of our own era we shall obtain some conception of the enormous gains made in national sobriety. If today in Frances Willard's home in Evanston the children and youth of ninety-five homes out of each hundred have never known the taste of spirits, at the beginning of this century drunkenness was well-nigh universal. But eighty years have passed by since Lyman Beecher said: "Rum consecrates our baptisms, our weddings and our funerals. Our vices are digging the graves of our liberties." About the same time, when a prominent merchant of Philadelphia died, and his pastor went to the house to the funeral, he found the table under the trees was spread with liquor, in which the people were freely indulging. The writer affirms that on reaching the grave, save himself and the grave digger, there was not a man present who was not in danger, through intoxication, of falling into the grave. Even as late as 1826 the ministerial associations of Rhode Island and Connecticut provided wine and liquor for the annual meeting of the clergy.

And once the great temperance movement was inaugurated, it began as regulation, and not as prohibition. The earliest printed temperance pledge that has come down to us includes two clauses: 1. No member shall drink rum under penalty of 25 cents. 2. No member shall be intoxicated under penalty of 50 cents. When total abstinence was proposed men received it with scorn and jeers, and the total abstainer became almost an outcast. When one of the early founders of a temperance society in Vermont refused liquor to the neighbors who were helping him raise his new barn, his friends dropped their tools and refused their service, and although the total abstainer scoured the town for helpers he was unable to secure laborers until he furnished the usual liquors. Angry at this temperance fanatic, one old gentleman exclaimed: "How bigoted is this abstainer; unless checked such fanaticism will ruin the country, and break up the Democratic party"—which must not be interpreted as meaning that the Republicans drank less heavily. . . . . . Frances Willard was an orator as well as an organizer. Doubtless those who dwell in great cities and have only heard her speak in great halls holding two or three thousand people can have little conception of her genius for public speech. In the very nature of the case she did not have a voice like Webster or Beecher, whose tones in times of great excitement made the windows to rattle, while some said, "It thunders."

Her greatest oratorical triumphs were in villages and cities, where some hall not holding more than a thousand people was crowded with appreciative listeners. At such times she stood forth one of the most gifted speakers of this generation, achieving efforts that were truly amazing. What ease and grace of bearing! What gentleness and strength! What pathos and sympathy! How exquisitely modulated her words! If her speech did not flow as a gulf stream, if it did not beat like an ocean upon a continent, she sent her sentences forth, an arrowy flight, and each tipped with divine fire. Those students of great orators who have lingered long over the masterpieces of politics and reform are those who have most admired the oratorical method Frances Willard developed upon the platform. What a world of meaning she crowded into some of her epigrams, like, "The golden rule of Christ will bring the golden age to man." When the distinguished philanthropists and reformers and citizens of England assembled in the City Temple of London to give her a reception and heaped upon her the highest honors, those of us who listened to her response knew that her reserves of character were vast indeed. With what simplicity and modesty did she decline all praise, insisting that she received these honors simply in the name of the women of America, for whom England intended them.

In that time of strained political relations between the two nations, with what fine patriotism did she speak of her flag, saying, "I am first a Christian, then I am a Saxon, then I am an American, and when I get home to Heaven I expect to register from Evanston." To organize a great political machine that represents the Republican or Democratic party, where cities and countries and States are all related as wheel to wheel, requires the skill of tens of thousands of expert politicians, toiling ceaselessly. But beginning with nothing, in twenty years, single-handed, this woman organized the women of her country into a vast mechanism that extended to village and city and State and nation and to foreign lands, with machinery for public agitation, a system of temperance journals for children and youth, for securing instruction upon the nature of stimulants in the common schools, with more than sixty different departments and methods of activity! The measure of a career is determined by three things: First, the talent that ancestry gives; second, the opportunity that events offer; third, the movements that the mind and will conceive and compel. Doubtless for Frances Willard ancestry bestowed rare gifts, the opportunity was unique, but that which her mind and heart compelled is beyond all measurement. As in times past orators have used the names Howard and Nightingale for winging their words, for all the ages to come editors and publicists and speakers will hold up the name of Willard for the stimulus and inspiration of generations yet unborn.

FRANCES E. WILLARD

ELIZABETH STUART PHELPS WARD

My friendship with Miss Willard was not one built on many meetings, and almost always when I saw her she was under the pressure of the eternal need to "move on" beneath which a life like hers must be lived. Yet when I say that, I ask myself, Was there any other life really like hers? To the qualities shared in common with other dedicated souls she added those of a unique personality. The last winter that she spent in Boston I had the pleasure of seeing her several times under conditions when I was impressed with a side of her nature of which I had known little or nothing before. Her social quality I found brilliant and charming; and these twain are not always one. She delighted us as a guest or as a hostess; from every point of view she had the grace and the wit to have illuminated society had she chosen that narrower world. She might have decorated a salon had she not elected to honor the sturdier larger life into which the society woman cannot enter. She had a singularly childlike nature — spontaneous, appealing and sweet. Yet she had a fine tact, cultivated to the point of an inspired diplomacy.

As a reformer, Miss Willard always seemed to me a power by herself that made for righteousness in nobody's way but her own. I did not always agree with her; I could not always follow her methods; but I always honored and admired her.

As a moral power she worked like a Hebrew prophet as God bade her, or as she believed He bade her, and there was nothing to do but let her have her way — or His.

She performed a work for which remarkable is a poor adjective. She was an orator whose gift could not be questioned by her coldest critic; she was a student, a thinker, an organizer of an order which we shall rate more highly, not less so, as time prepares to classify her in its unerring catalogue.

It has always seemed to me that we have never yet sufficiently estimated Frances Willard as *an intellect*. Hers was strong and cultivated, and in proportion to its strength and culture her ethical purpose got its grip on her times. Dedication without equipment could never have done her work. Spirituality without intellectuality could not have moved the forces which obeyed the motions of her beautiful white hand. In the history of moral progress — brilliant, gentle, ever powerful, but ever womanly — she will long illustrate the value of educated consecration.

I have thought that the most memorable thing about Miss Willard's career as a reformer was its freedom from bitterness; she had extraordinary gentleness of soul toward all mankind. No evil was so black but that she credited every good quality she could to its champions; she always took her opponents at their best — they must have hung their heads for shame sometimes at the ideals of themselves which her eloquent sweetness held up before them and before the world.

A pretty story is told of her being found in conversation one day with the highest titled ecclesiastical dignitary in England, to whom she was earnestly saying, to the surprise of his Lordship and a little to the anxiety of her friends, "But my dear *brother*"—That naive gentleness was always ready for all sorts and conditions of men. The lowest rumseller was her "dear brother," and though she would ruin his devil's business if she could, she would treat him like a man who had always wanted to go into a celestial one, and had only waited for her to come along and give him the opportunity. She forgave before she struck, and blessed before she punished.

I have often thought that her work indicated a kind of study of the methods of Christ in public life far beyond that which most of us give to His mind and heart.

She was a Christian queen. She leaves a vacant throne.

MEMORIES OF FRANCES E. WILLARD
REV. THEO. L. CUYLER, D.D., LL.D.

The best-known woman in America, probably, since the death of Mrs. Harriet Beecher Stowe, was that tireless reformer and philanthropist whose busy life closed in New York, on Thursday night, the 17th of February. Miss Frances E. Willard began a career which made her known over the whole civilized world under the best auspices. She came of a goodly Puritan stock, and of a mother of such rare beauty of character that she wrote her biography under the descriptive title of "A Great Mother."

Native genius of a high order, wide and splendid culture, and a warm woman's heart were her grand outfit when she began her career as the apostle of temperance and social purity in 1874.

I first saw Miss Willard in Boston when she was the secretary of the National Woman's Christian Temperance Union, and was traveling over the land, organizing new branches of the Union, and arousing people everywhere by her electric eloquence. Mr. Moody was holding revival meetings in Boston in April, 1877, with Miss

Willard as his associate. Together they arranged an immense temperance demonstration for the 20th of that month, which which was to continue through the whole day, and be addressed by eminent speakers from all quarters. This great convention was held in the Tabernacle, and attended by over five thousand people. I never shall forget that day; the spiritual feeling was intense and the platform of that convention was kept up to white heat from ten o'clock in the morning until almost midnight. I do not now recall all the speakers, but among them were the fiery-hearted George H. Stuart, of Philadelphia; John Wanamaker, William E. Dodge, Rev. A. J. Gordon and John B. Gough, then in his full strength as the king of all temperance orators in the world. When the great meeting closed one of the other speakers said to me: "Well, the woman has beaten us all; Miss Willard's was *the* speech of the whole day."

He was right in that estimate of her arousing, incisive, trenchant, tender, evangelical and spirit-filled oration. It was Christian temperance, based on God's Word, and fired with the holy fire of Pentecost. It smote drunkenness as a sin, and the drink usages as a curse, and drink-selling as a crime, and it pleaded for the salvation of tempted souls with all the tenderness of a great woman's heart. That magnificent address was one of the master efforts of Miss Willard's life, and I have wished a thousand times that she had spent more of the remaining twenty years of her earnest and zealous life in working on the same lines that she worked that day in Boston. This nation has, of late, been hearing little else than the civil and political side of the liquor traffic; she struck deeper that day, and exposed the deadly and damning evils of the drink usages whenever and wherever found — in society as well as in the saloon.

Her grand, inspiring and unselfish career of untiring toil — with eloquent tongue and brilliant pen — for the deliverance of men from intemperance and women from impurity, has come to its glorious close. The voice of criticism is lost in the voice of grateful admiration; no differences of judgment as to the methods of promoting the reform we both loved ever disturbed the sincerity of our friendship. Over her newly opened tomb let us bespeak a closer union and a more earnest co-operation among all those who are fighting those twin curses which Frances Elizabeth Willard fought so fearlessly until she went up to her resplendent crown. Her "White Cross" is a beautiful emblem of her pure, saintly life. One of her last speeches as President of the W. C. T. U. was an appeal for a fresh campaign for total abstinence as the basal principle of our great reform. Let her beloved comrade, Lady Henry Somerset, grasp the banner that has fallen from Frances Willard's dying hand and lead the good women on both sides of the sea forward!

CHARACTER SKETCH
MARY A. LATHBURY

It is a temptation to those who have known Frances Willard in the intimacies of a personal friendship, to bring out the treasures that they have gathered from so rich a life and give them to the world. There would be no disloyalty in so doing, for Miss Willard's nature was as wide open toward all the world as it was toward heaven. With the temptation, however, there falls that restraining touch upon the spirit that makes it impossible to speak freely to others of a friend while that friend sits beside you.

I have yielded to this feeling until only a few hours remain before this book will go to press. What can I say of her whom death has not touched — who lives beside us more than ever alive, and who, with her Lord, is alive forevermore? I have no sympathy with the cult that encourages attempts at intercourse with those who have passed into the spiritual world. "He that openeth and no man shutteth, and shutteth and no man openeth," alone holds the key; but that the spiritual world lies about the natural as the air lies about the earth and lives within it as the soul lives in the body, I have no doubt.

"I think, therefore, I am a spirit," said a great preacher. Frances Willard thought she was a spirit. Men and women are trying to think after her the thoughts of love, peace and good will toward men that God had given her; and now, free from the confining walls of the body, and in closer touch with all heaven, she still thinks the thoughts of God, and by ways we need not disturb ourselves to understand. They are ours. The women who

> "Built beside her day by day,
> The fair ascents of God's highway,"

and who lovingly resolve to "do more than ever *now*," believe in their hearts that love and memory inspire the thought. Is that wholly true?

The timid soul who has always shunned publicity, and who, pausing before some great opportunity to do good, hears that clear, vibrant voice saying, "Enter every open door; that is what mother used to say," believes that it is a memory — an echo from that day on which she heard it at convention. Is it?

Miss Willard was a willing and eager recipient of life. She possessed life more abundantly than the most of us, and doubled it constantly by giving it out to others. She has left herself, as far as she was able, as a legacy to humanity. But now, set free from the limitations of the body, and serving among the heavenly forces that work for the regeneration of the world, her field has enlarged infinitely. The life that widened from that of a teacher with her girls to that of a reformer with her world has not been narrowed by passing into larger life and opportunities. She is a part of the life of today, and wherever men and women are at work building the walls of civic or national righteousness; wherever they are sowing the seed of love, peace and purity, or wherever they are together laying the foundation of the home, they may know that Frances Willard walks and works beside them, giving herself, as by a divine law she must, to the bringing in of the kingdom of Christ.

One may almost hear her low, bell-like voice repeating the

prophetic lines with which she closed a convention memorial service:

> " Forever near us, though unseen,
> The dear immortal spirits tread;
> For all the boundless universe
> Is life — *there are no dead!*"

She was — she is an immortal spirit — a cup running over with the Lord's life, and "all that life is love." Is it strange that she drops into the heart of one a desire to "do more than ever now," and stoops to whisper to another, "Enter every open door"? It would be still more strange if the soul of Frances Willard had ceased to be what she has long been — a servant of the Lord Jesus Christ.

FRANCES E. WILLARD AS A REFORMER

JOSEPH COOK

The world seems lonely without Miss Willard. One feels exposed and unprotected in the field of reform now that she is no longer on guard. Since the cessation of Mrs. Stowe's chief public activity no woman in America has been a more important leader in the moral, educational and political defense of the home and society from their chief foes than Miss Willard. A large number of vital and correlated reforms had her life-long championship. The Woman's Christian Temperance Union, of which she was president for so many years, owes chiefly to her its lofty temperance principles, its cosmopolitan range of organization, its variety and timeliness of subsidiary efforts, the courage and sometimes the audacity of its political agitation, and its pervasive and triumphant Christian spirit. The association is many sided. Like Briareus it has a hundred arms, and like Argus a hundred eyes, but in all this is only the reflex of the spirit of its chief organizer and leader.

She died as president of both the World's and the National Christian Temperance Unions, and, up to the very last, exhibited in her addresses, public letters and almost countless official communications, the same astonishing versatility and vigor which characterized her earlier career. Temperance, equal suffrage, social purity, labor reform, Turkish atrocities, Hindu widows, and whatever other topics closely touched social amelioration in any form, commanded her most zealous interest, and, through her, that of the organized host of women she led. We have heard much of Napoleon and his marshals, of Washington and his generals, and we ought to hear much of Miss Willard and her coadjutors, who have together encircled the globe with agitation for the defense of woman and the home. Some of the national superintendents of departments in the organization, as well as the round-the-world temperance missionaries, have achieved great results. Miss Willard has been criticised for entering too many departments of reform, but she has exhibited a singular sagacity in discovering leaders for these various departments and preserving their harmony and efficiency.

Her own activity has indeed been marvelous, but her capacity as an organizer of the labors of others has also been amazing. It has been well said that if any man had done in the last quarter of a century what Miss Willard has accomplished, his success would have been regarded as phenomenal, and his capacity and career among the marvels of modern times. As a lecturer, editor, preacher, author, presiding officer, correspondent, traveler, Miss Willard had brilliant qualities which were tested through a quarter of a century in the severest way and never found wanting. But perhaps her ability as an organizer and leader and inspiration of Christian aggressiveness in broadening woman's sphere was her most precious and memorable endowment.

President Willard, one of the most distinguished heads of Harvard University, was among Miss Willard's ancestors. His marble bust in the college library and hers, if placed side by side, would be seen to exhibit extraordinary similarities. They have the same highly intellectual and alert expression, the same remarkable symmetry and height of cranial contour, except that Miss Willard has the loftier coronal dome. Great spiritual genius has often been found in high heads, as in Shakespeare, Walter Scott, Tennyson, Richter, and not in low heads like those of Renan and Matthew Arnold. Whoever sees a profile view of Miss Willard's head with the hair so arranged as to show its outline will be reminded of the height and symmetry of this same region in Mrs. Browning and Mrs. Stowe and in the famous Naples bust of Plato.

In spite of the many conflicts to which her principles exposed her, she died at peace with all the world without compromise of a single one of her highest contentions and without bitterness. She had wonderfully intense attachments to personal friends and made almost a religion of family affections.

She is at home at last among her kindred, and beckons us onward, upward, heavenward. Her last words were, "How beautiful it is to be with God." And this was true in her life as well as in death and beyond death. It must be said, with devout thankfulness to Almighty Providence, that she fought a good fight and kept the faith and finished her work. In sober reality she was, in a sense very intelligible to thoughtful souls contemplating her whole career, a pillar of fire through which God looked in the morning watch of better ages to come and troubled the hosts of His enemies and took off their chariot wheels.

All just reforms are God's abode, and His eyes neither slumber nor sleep.

Newton Center, Mass.

TRIBUTES

COUNTLESS messages were received by wire and post expressing a sense of profound sorrow, and proving the unique place Miss Willard held in the hearts of the people. Each State and Territorial auxiliary of the National W. C. T. U. was represented by its President or General Officers, while the entire Board of National Superintendents, Evangelists, Organizers and Lecturers sent tender words of condolence, hundreds of District, County and local unions forwarded resolutions, and almost numberless were the heart-broken messages which came from individual White-Ribboners.

Cablegrams from Great Britain and Australia and telegrams from Canada, coming with the first daylight that dawned on a world grown suddenly dark to many hearts, were followed by letters from the entire circle of countries in the World's W. C. T. U.

From the most distant leaders came patnetic letters burdened with grief that they could never see the face of one for whose coming they had long and lovingly waited.

In addition to these official and semi-official communications, a great number of temperance, religious, philanthropic, labor, educational and business organizations paid heartfelt tributes of admiration and esteem, and expressed their grief at the loss of Frances E. Willard. Among these societies were the National Council of Women, the National Temperance Society, the National Woman's Suffrage Association, the United Society of Christian Endeavor, the International Order of the King's Daughters, the International Board of the Young Women's Christian Association, the Catholic Total Abstinence Union, the Father Mathew Total Abstinence Society, the International Supreme Lodge Independent Order of Good Templars, the National Anti-Mob and Lynch Law Association, the National Christian League for the Promotion of Social Purity, the Faculty of Chicago Theological Seminary, the Faculty of Wellesley College, the Chicago

Congregational Union, Women's Clubs and Preachers' Meetings in various cities; the Young Men's Christian Association, the Universal Peace Union, the Knights of Labor, the Council of Jewish Women, the Women's Board of Missions, the Daughters of the American Revolution, the National Society of New England Women, the Women's Relief Corps, the Association of Collegiate Alumnæ, the Order of the Maccabees of the World and the American Humane Education Society.

We append but a few of the individual messages received, selecting largely from those outside the ranks of the W. C. T. U., since the words of love of White-Ribboners alone would more than fill this memorial volume. Three hundred thousand stricken yet strong-hearted followers of Frances E. Willard form her best memorial, the truest exponent of her character; a choir ever visible, ever voicing itself in larger, deeper, more vital activities until they greet,

> "When the last deep is crossed,
> The tender face they miss but have not lost."

It is difficult to find suitable expressions for the emotions of the heart when one like our matchless leader, our true and tender friend, Frances E. Willard, is taken from our earthly vision. But we can dwell upon the elements of her character, and as we meditate upon the Beatitudes of our divine Master we may well rejoice in the fact that she so fully exemplified their possibilities.

Miss Willard's unusual qualities of mind, her gentleness of heart, her charity and her firmness of principle, together with her attractive personality, constituted her a power around which the good women of this and other lands naturally centered. The first time I had the pleasure of seeing her was at the first National Convention, in November, 1874. Knowing her high position in the educational world, and lacking a formal introduction, I hesitated to approach her; but I wished that she could realize what I felt of loving sympathy, gratitude and admiration for her position and for the consecration of her abilities to the temperance cause and the service of humanity. In view of her natural and acquired graces of mind and soul, I felt that a great power had entered our ranks.

On the second day of the convention I was invited to dine with a friend. I gladly accepted, little dreaming of the charming surprise that awaited me. Upon entering the drawing-room of my friend, Miss Willard was introduced to me. In her own sweet way she said, "I am glad of this opportunity to have a quiet talk with you about this wonderful Crusade. Let us sit right down together without formality, and talk over the Hillsboro part of it until dinner is ready."

Another charming episode in our golden chain of love and sympathy — which never had a broken link — was Miss Willard's first visit at our home. It was there that I learned her wonderful power of appreciating what interested others. I remember her expressions of pleasure in the reminiscences of my life, and of the lives of my dear parents and others.

But words are powerless to convey my appreciation of her worth. She was in most loving and sympathetic relations with me in all the joys and sorrows of my checkered life; they never seemed to pass unnoticed by this leader, friend and sister. But her crowning virtue was that humanity born from above, and akin to that of her Master, the "light of the city" where she now dwells. Her blessed influence is still felt, only on a higher and holier plane.

Hillsboro, Ohio.   ELIZA J. THOMPSON.

We old veterans claimed Frances Willard as our daughter, born of the inspiration that developed the women of the Crusade by the baptism of the Holy Ghost when the Lord called them to march the streets and pray in the saloons.

I was early impressed that our young women must be enlisted, or the ultimate hope of our work would prove futile. Where should we find a leader with sufficient social standing, mental and spiritual force to lure our great army of young women into our ranks?

The Lord was not unmindful of our need, for even then he had his hand upon one whom he was preparing, through testing discipline, to become the greatest leader of women the world has ever known.

She was a teacher of marked ability, well beloved by her students, giving every energy of her enthusiastic nature to what she believed to be her lifework, when, by a strange wrench, the bitterest experience of her life as she felt it, she found her hand empty, she knew not where to turn.

How could she know that He was taking her from the circumscribed professor's desk to the broadest, most far-reaching platform ever occupied by any woman in the world before; that He was thus leading her to her kingdom to which He had called her for such a time as these latter days.

She could not know that such trial was intended to develop the latent powers of brain and heart with which He had endowed her, but of which she was as yet unconscious. But the time came, the door was opened. On the 8th of October, 1874, she was elected President of the Chicago Union, and on the 20th she wrote me to come and help her arouse and enlist the Christian women of Chicago to take up arms against the liquor curse.

With what eagerness I responded to her call may be understood. In a few days after I was with her. I found her devoting all her time and powers to her work, drawing not only a large class of elect ladies to her side, but daily might be seen men, old and young, coming to her prayer meetings, as if fleeing to the city of refuge for protection and deliverance from their deadly enemy. In a few more days we met again at our first National Convention in Cleveland. She was made a member of the Committee on Resolutions and Plan of Work, and chosen secretary of the committee. She was elected Corresponding Secretary of our National Union at this convention.

In all the years that have followed she has proved her earnest devotion (ah, yes, even to the laying down of her life!) and wonderful powers in charming and drawing everyone to her and inspiring them with enthusiasm for our blessed work. As she said of our Prohibition hero, Would that the great space she has left empty and lonely might be peopled with forms fair and brave of our youth and maidens ready to let it be understood of them from this time forth that they are not only content, but proud that their names, as that of Frances E. Willard, are "writ in water." MOTHER STEWART.

Springfield, Ohio, April 16, 1898.

It is not easy to realize that Frances Willard has gone from us forever — nor is it possible to measure the great loss the W. C. T. U. has sustained.

My acquaintance with Miss Willard antedated her connection with the temperance reform — antedated, indeed, the organization of the W. C. T. U. Her devotion to this organization has never abated, yet she has always been prompt to join hands with all who worked for humanity, and to give her speech and influence in behalf of what she believed to be right, even when she risked her popularity in so doing. She surpassed all women of modern times as a leader, and was so magnetic and executive, so persistent and winning, that she has fused and molded the W. C. T. U. into a strong solidarity. Deeply religious, she was not a bigot, but accorded to others the same religious freedom she demanded for herself, and cared more for life and character than for creed. Possessed of splendid moral courage, she could have gone unflinchingly to death for her cause had it been demanded of her. She loved the human race with a divine affection, sorrowing over its woes, which she sought to mitigate, and rejoicing in every advance it made. She was unselfish, even to the utter neglect of her own interests, continuing to work without compensation till her friends compelled her to be more just to herself.

She was an orator who enchained thousands; a writer whose printed speech was frequently like the blast of a bugle summoning to duty; a charming personality, to whom attractive paths opened in every direction. But she gave herself to her work with all that she was, or had, or hoped to be or to have, with complete unreserve.

It does not seem possible that the heavens have "received her out of our sight," and that we shall no more behold her till we, too, lift the latch and pass into that other chamber of the King, larger than this and lovelier. It has never been so hard before to say, "Thy will be done." How can we go on without her?   MARY A. LIVERMORE.
Melrose, Mass.

In 1891 the Congress Auxiliary in connection with the Columbian Exposition began its labors preliminary to the Congresses to be held in 1893, and Miss Willard was a member of the Committee for the Congress of Representative Women. Lady Henry Somerset was visiting Miss Willard at that time and I held various conferences with them regarding speakers in Europe and also in this country, and they gave me most valuable suggestions both for the programmes and also for the speakers. I was impressed by Miss Willard's versatility; she was equally at home with the practical woman of affairs and with the idealist, and interested in both points of view. She had a perfect apprehension of the scope of the work and the results which would ensue from the broad-minded policy which was pursued by everyone connected with that great series of meetings.

Miss Willard was very simple in manner, was direct, and had a reserve power both in conversation and in public speaking which was marked. This quiet manner gave her great dignity and fitted her to be at home either on the platform or the drawing-room.

I have selected this phase of Miss Willard's character — her adaptability — to show how general were her sympathies and how eager her interest in all that tends to the advancement of mankind.

Chicago.   ELLEN M. HENROTIN,
President of the National Federation of Women's Clubs.

Miss Willard has commanded and has deserved the love and respect of millions of the women of this country. With unanimous loyalty, enthusiastic wherever they could express it, they chose her every year to be the president of their great temperance organization, whose work under her leadership has been extraordinary. Its history thus far has been the same thing as the biography of Frances Willard. That history is not simply a narrative of a noble life. It is an important illustration of wise administration. Her annual messages to her constituents are better worth reading than the messages of the President of the United States for the same time. They were messages to people she loved and who loved her, written with the enthusiasm of love letters by a woman singularly well educated, broad in her whole view of life, and, in her very heart and in every syllable which her heart prompted, brave and true.

Boston, Mass.   REV. EDWARD EVERETT HALE, D.D.

Judgment of Frances Willard was impossible when one was close to her. In that respect she was a veritable queen. Judicial process will not lie against the sovereign, and she was royal by the divinest right — the instant and persistent fealty of the people whom it was her quaint way to call "Our folks."

Absent from her, one might convict her, in his solitary thought, of errors of judgment, or even find it possible to censure her a little — much, may be. But *she herself* was not to be critically discerned, and when she slipped serenely into court the judiciary melted and the jury "packed" *itself* spontaneously. She would have been very dangerous if she had not been very good.

And now that she has been transfigured before our eyes, her presence seems even more imminent than before and a judicial temper toward her more impossible.

As to her work, there is absolutely nothing to compare it to. But it is safe to say that her quarter century of public service has been to womankind the greatest gift of any single life — save One.

Chicago.   JOHN G. WOOLLEY.

Of this blessed "daughter of The King" it might be said with Solomon: "Many daughters have done virtuously, but thou excellest them all." For intellect and eloquence she was the foremost woman of her generation. Such was the breadth of her catholicity that she recognized goodness wherever found. Her philanthropy touched suffering humanity in all lands. With the courage of an angel in her soul, she stood for the right against all forms of wrong. She was insistent for sobriety in high places and in low, and demanded the majesty of civil law against the evils of intemperance. How sublime her utterances in her vindication of the rights of womanhood against the civil and political disabilities of her sex in all lands. How persuasive her influence for the elevation of home life, wifehood and childhood wherever degraded. Her love of "native land" was only excelled by her loyal, joyous devotion to that Divine Christ whose "Golden Rule can bring to pass the Golden Age of Man." Let womanhood emulate her virtues, imitate her example, cherish her memory, till purity and temperance shall become coextensive with the business and abode of humanity.

                                             (BISHOP) JOHN P. NEWMAN.

I have heard many women — women who have achieved greatness — but never have I heard one who was so finished and eloquent as the dead leader of the great temperance movement among women. She was entitled to the palm of superiority. Her utterances were equal to those of the American Demosthenes, Wendell Phillips. There was but one Miss Willard. She inspired the motto of the Woman's Christian Temperance Union — "For God, and Home, and Native

Land"—but she worked for God, and home, and every land. Miss Willard was a leader of women. She is worthy to rank with Jefferson, for she formulated a declaration of independence for her sex.

Chicago. (BISHOP) SAMUEL FALLOWS.

Miss Willard was one of the purest and best women America has produced. She was endowed by nature with a kind heart and splendid brain. The world is better by far because of her lifework, and her name will grow brighter as the tide of time rolls on.

Lexington, Ky. GOV. W. O. BRADLEY.

While her great soul was forever expanding in gratitude to God, her great heart was ever reaching out in helpfulness to humanity. No wonder the lowly gathered about her casket to honor the woman, in the belfry of whose heart the "tender tones of sympathy" for the unfortunate were ever ringing.

Standing by her casket I looked upon as finely cut features of nobility and greatness, as touching traces of goodness and mercy as were ever portrayed upon immortal canvas.

Lexington, Ky. GEORGE W. BAIN.

On behalf of the National Division of the Sons of Temperance, I desire to express the regret we feel at the loss of Frances E. Willard. She earnestly worked early and late, wisely and well, to extend the blessings of temperance and build up the Union, world-wide in its operations and heavenly in its aims. She was a leader among women, a wise manager to smooth over minor differences and direct all efforts to bless our country and the world. Her star, like the morning one, has melted away into the brightness of heaven.

THOMAS CASWELL,
M. W. P., Sons of Temperance, Toronto, Canada.

I think it was in the winter of 1874–75 that Miss Willard made her first appearance in Philadelphia as a public speaker. I had then the honor of accompanying her on a Sabbath morning to the Green Street Methodist Church, where it had been arranged for her to occupy the pulpit. By her magnetic personality, as well as by her eloquence and the strength of her argument, she captivated her audience. As she held aloft the standard of Purity and Sobriety, it seemed to me that another Jean d'Arc had come to be our leader.

Philadelphia. JOSHUA L. BAILEY,
President National Temperance Society and Publication House.

Frances E. Willard was a brave soldier and true, a good commander, and finally and best of all, a great and gentle woman. . . . Her sympathies and interests, though most fully invested in temperance work, were not limited to it. They were enlisted in every cause of philanthropy. When the relief depot was established in Marseilles, France, for the benefit of Armenian fugitives, she performed the noble work in applying the funds provided by the *Christian Herald.* REV. DeWITT TALMAGE, D.D.

It is with profound sorrow we learn that we shall never have the pleasure of seeing again *in this world* the kind face of our friend of many years, Frances E. Willard. Her death is a great loss, not only to *the innumerable thousands* who have had the good fortune to know her, but also to the cause of humanity throughout the civilized world. "Well done, good and faithful servant, enter thou into the joy of thy Lord."
 Boston, Mass.   GEO. T. ANGELL,
         President of the American Humane Education Society.

We rejoice to live in the same day with a woman of abilities so consecrated, of life so Christlike; one in whose great heart there was no room for selfishness or resentment or bitterness, and who realized in her own character our finest ideals of all that is womanly. The eloquent voice is hushed, the inspiring presence is gone; but in spirit Frances Willard is still the loved chieftain, and we pray that the influence of this rare and noble life may move us and women everywhere to higher purposes and larger faithfulness in the work of helping to make the world better. THE FACULTY OF WELLESLEY COLLEGE,
  ELLEN HAYES, SARAH F. WHITING, ANGIE CLARA CHAPIN,
 Wellesley, Mass.   *Committee.*

The admirable proportion, the even poise of Miss Willard's powers, were most remarkable. She owed this largely to the predominance of a spiritual purpose. Her mind was full of light because she looked upon the world with a single eye. She had a clear insight into spiritual life, and made of it a ruling, harmonizing motive. This is well illustrated in the steadiness with which she pursued temperance as her primary work. She gave a large meaning to the word. She saw how much it involved. She gathered in its many accessories, but she allowed none of them to divert her from the primary purpose.
 Williamstown, Mass.   JOHN and EMMA C. BASCOM.

Our acquaintance with Miss Willard was made at an immense W. C. T. U. meeting at the Tremont Temple, Boston, in 1891. Sympathy, tact, a keen sense of humor, eloquence, and behind all a grand reserve of powerful character and intense earnestness, were all combined in the complete mastery which that sweet, gentle personality exercised over that great throng. To watch her for that one evening, and to note how the crowd was swayed by her influence, was to understand, at least to some extent, the secret of her life and power. We had the privilege of meeting her again in private life, but only on two occasions, but now and again would come one of those friendly notes, full of originality and kindliness, always giving a thought that would abide.

Ottawa, Can. THE COUNTESS OF ABERDEEN.

Frances E. Willard was a dreamer and a doer. She saw visions and wrought them into orations and devices and achievements. She was versatile and practical, intense and persistent. She swayed a scepter like a queen; and she served with willing hands like a sister. Her faith was unlimited. Her hope made the future radiant, however dark and discouraging to her friends and followers the immediate present seemed. She trusted God and her friends and the instincts of humanity. She knew how to wait, and to smile in confidence when fears filled with shadows the faces of her coworkers.

But Frances Willard's highest quality was her charity. This never wavered and never grew dim. She illustrated the grace of "perfect love" if mortal ever did. I have for years in my thought associated her with the matchless Song of Charity sung by Paul in his first letter to the Corinthians. She was full of love. Her spirit was connected with the exhaustless fountain of divine love. She has fulfilled the divine commission given to her. The Christian world will mourn her sorely. We shall do well if we follow her as she followed Christ.

Chautauqua, N. Y. (BISHOP) JOHN H. VINCENT.

Few women of her time could be so deeply missed and mourned as Frances Willard. Her whole life has been a benefaction. She has spent herself lavishly in the cause of temperance reform, and her warm, beating heart has been, like the alabaster box of old, broken at her Master's feet. Among American women no other has more generously, more faithfully, and more steadfastly wrought for the happiness of the home, the elevation of youth, and for social purity. Quiet and unostentatious, wonderfully executive, and as winsome in manner as she was strong in conviction, she was admirably fitted to be the leader of movements which have been far-reaching in their influence, and which will not cease to exert a vast and mighty power though the beautiful and loving woman who planned and led and prayed so earnestly has gone to her heavenly home.

New York City. MARGARET E. SANGSTER,
Editor Harper's Bazar.

Ontario W. C. T. U. unite with you in tenderest sympathy. John xiii, 7.

MAY R. THORNLEY,
President.

Dominion comrades mourn their chief.   ANNIE O. RUTHERFORD,
President Dominion W. C. T. U.

From the Toronto (Can.) W. C. T. U. came the following resolution:

"We rejoice that ours was the exalted privilege of having Miss Willard in our midst so recently in the great World's Convention. The memories of those hallowed, inspiring hours have endeared the work of humanity to our hearts — *love* means more to us since the irresistible power of her generous magnetic love touched our lives. We loved her as our 'Chieftain,' and think her title, 'the best loved woman in the world,' but mildly expresses the love and devotion of her subjects."

Catholic Total Abstinence Union mourns the loss of your unselfish, pure-hearted leader. No more devoted champion of Christian sobriety has sacrificed all things for God, home and humanity.

Wisconsin.   REV. J. M. CLEARY.

She encircled the whole world with the pure light of her reformatory spirit. Our city, with all its blackness and degradation, has been made whiter by her life and will be made more splendid by her monument. Her grand life is a prophecy and harbinger of the good time which has been so long on the way. Miss Willard will be mourned in all the continents. I found her name as familiar and dear in Asia as in America. Twenty years hence her name and deeds will loom up larger than even today.

Chicago.   REV. JOHN HENRY BARROWS, D.D.

Your loss is great. The breach is wide. A noble heart has ceased to beat in our midst, but the cause of temperance and purity your leader so disinterestedly and courageously championed must not suffer. The women and children of the White Ribbon and the fathers and brothers who stand by them must spring into the gap. Inspired by her spirit they must take the field and carry on the work she has left behind.

New York City.   COMMANDER AND CONSUL BOOTH-TUCKER.

We sympathize with you and Christian temperance workers in loss of a noble friend and leader.

Northfield, Mass.   MR. and MRS. DWIGHT L. MOODY.

How well I remember the day that I stood in the parlor at Rest Cottage by the casket of her dear mother, and placed on it a large palm branch, and she asked me to sing, "Psalms of victory, crowns of glory, I shall wear." It was a favorite hymn with her mother. I sang softly one verse, when she said, "Yes, Amanda, my dear mother is no more, her battle is fought, her victory is won." How glad I am for the privilege of having known her for the past twenty-five years. . . . .

Chicago. AMANDA SMITH.

I take pleasure in expressing my high appreciation of the life and work of Miss Frances E. Willard. It has been a life of devotion to humanity. Her services in the cause of temperance and good morals have been of inestimable value. Her example and influence will henceforth be a part of the forces molding the advancing civilization of our country and the world. I pay my tribute to her memory with profound respect.

Washington, D. C. JOHN D. LONG.

In her unselfish devotion to a great cause, Miss Frances E. Willard lost sight of sex, races and color, and gave her life freely to the task of making our world better. The negro race will always keep her memory green in their hearts, and will more and more strive, as the years pass by, to live by the principles that she taught.

Tuskegee, Ala. BOOKER T. WASHINGTON.

The blow has fallen. From the world has been taken another lover of humanity. There are no words to express the loss to the world and to the world's workers, and none to portray the glory into which the beautiful soul has entered.

Anacostia, D. C. HELEN DOUGLASS.
(*Mrs. Frederick Douglass.*)

That something of my words (in "Kindly Light in Prayer and Praise") comforted our beautiful sister, so tender, so true to the whole of humanity, is a very sacred thing to me. I bless God for giving her to our world. Her work by the grace of the shadow of death will increase here into an ever-greatening spiritual power.

New York City. REV. JOHN M. SCOTT.

Commanding in intellectual gifts, with rare judicial poise and far-sightedness, and the will to execute, with conscience ever regnant in her soul, Miss Willard yet won most hearts by the prodigious power of her tender womanhood. It was never hers to create and mother a home, but multitudes of homes caught her sweet womanly uplifting, and are today as if she had mothered them. That she could keep such a spirit, though thrust constantly into the high noon of this modern day, is her peculiar glory.

Chicago. REV. HERRICK JOHNSON, D.D.

It is with the profoundest sorrow that we have heard of the death of Miss Willard, the most useful as well as the most loved woman in America.

New York City.   REV. WILLIAM HAYES WARD, D.D.
Editor of the Independent.

No international bereavement has ever been as extensive among the women of the world as this for Frances Willard. We all rejoice that we have been blessed by her human preparation for the real life just commenced.

New York City.   ELIZABETH B. GRANNIS,
National Christian League for the Promotion of Social Purity.

Words fail to adequately express my appreciation of the lifework of Miss Willard. Her death is mourned in a million homes; her name will ever remain among the brightest stars in the galaxy of the world's illustrious workers in the cause of humanity. May all mankind emulate her noble example.

J. R. SOVEREIGN,
Head of the Knights of Labor.

With Frances Willard I became acquainted in 1857, when president of the Northwestern University. The friendship then commenced lasted, unbroken, throughout life. I desire to further add that in all my acquaintance with men and women, I think I never knew a mind and heart superior to Frances Willard's, or a character more beautiful. From the beginning she devoted herself absolutely to the loftiest aims — to reaching the highest ideal of character, and to realizing the largest possible usefulness.

I regard her as having attained a place among the foremost women of her time or of any time; her history is well known to all who are interested in the reforms of the past thirty years; no one could be with her for a day without feeling her power. Frances Willard's death seems premature — a great loss — but her influence will never die.

A little tribute from an old, old friend.

Dorchester, Mass.   (BISHOP) RANDOLPH S. FOSTER.

When I first met Frances E. Willard and her mother — each remarkable in her own way — Frances had just been installed as president of a girl's college; her gifts and graces were extolled on all sides. As I was their guest at Rest Cottage, I had the opportunity to appreciate their domestic as well as their public virtues, though the interests of neither were bounded by the home sphere.

I was invited there to lecture, and Frances, in a few well-chosen words, introduced me to the audience. We sat up till a late hour discussing all the vital questions of the day. We avoided the theologies, knowing that there we might have broad differences of opinion. Though twenty-five years her senior,

I felt I was talking with a woman of mature judgment, clear intellect and well digested ideas. The revelation of such a character in one so young gave me new hope in the possibilities of all women.

One of the greatest women of this generation has passed away in the prime of life, a woman of rare gifts as a writer and speaker, with great executive ability, and a sweet, gentle nature.

New York City.   ELIZABETH CADY STANTON.

Miss Willard, as I knew her, was sweet, sympathetic and approachable in private intercourse; powerful, brilliant and commanding as a public leader; and straight, fearless and faithful as a follower of the teachings of Christ. All who knew her must deeply and personally mourn her loss, and all who knew her must be inspired and helped by the memory of her life and work.

New York City.   MAUDE BALLINGTON BOOTH.

Frances E. Willard has gone! One word has stayed with me since she departed—"Of whom the world was not worthy."

I have only seen her since she left, as she *is*. I cannot make a study of her now. I can see her in the Beyond. I have seen a look at times upon her face here which helps me to see her there.

She sees the Master for whom she laid down her life, and finds it beautiful to be with God—*at rest*. But He would never be so beautiful to her now if she had not been with God in the battle on earth—it is the warrior's rest.

Frances E. Willard was a brave woman, a real daughter of The King. The word to us is, "whose *faith* follow." We may not follow, or be like her in many respects; we can follow her faith.

New York City.   MARGARET BOTTOME,
President of The King's Daughters and Sons.

Were I to speak of but one characteristic of Miss Willard, and to leave it for others to dwell upon other qualities, I would say that the quality by which I believe she will be longest remembered will be her world-wide sympathy. Most fittingly was she the president of the *World's* Woman's Christian Temperance Union, as well as of the Temperance Union of America. Her heart was never satisfied unless it took within its ample boundaries the needs and sufferings, the woes and misfortunes of the whole wide world.

Thomas à Kempis, in one of his Meditations which the world will nev willingly let die, says something of this sort: "He liveth well who loveth much, he liveth much who loveth well, and he liveth much and well who prefers the welfare of the community to his own personal gratification." These words can be spoken of our departed friend without qualification. She loved much, she did much, she lived well, because her whole life was devoted not to herself, but to the advancement and the welfare of those whom she loved better than self, the weary, the heavy-laden, the sin-burdened.

All her letters breathe this spirit, all her public utterances were of the largest and most catholic description. She never spoke a narrow, unworthy, sectarian word in her life. It was this breadth of vision, this largeness of heart, this wideness of sympathy, this catholicity of utterance which gave to her much of her power. It is no exaggeration to say, I think, that she was the first woman of America, not by accident of birth or wealth, but by her own sterling qualities of character and leadership. Never has there been a more conspicuous example in the history of our country of the fact that eminent fitness will be recognized, that genuine worth will find its own high level. In this it is a pleasure to every patriot to believe that Miss Willard was a typical American, and her conspicuous success and fitness for her task is of itself a sermon to every aspiring young person in the world.

Through her own persistent courage, her genuine regard for purity, her strong devotion to the causes which she espoused through evil and good report, her tact and loving sympathy for all, her name has been inscribed on the imperishable roll of her country's history. To have known such a woman is an inspiration, to have had her for years at the head of a great movement is a benediction not only to the cause with which she was connected, but to the nation at large. Untold millions in the future generations, I believe, will call her blessed.

Boston, Mass.   FRANCIS E. CLARK,
President International Young People's Society of Christian Endeavor.

As I sit in my study, I remember the last time I had a talk with our dear friend, Miss Willard. She came here by appointment, and we had a long discussion over mutual interests. The great work for purity and true womanhood, especially, came into our thoughts. As she told of some wonderful meetings recently held in Washington and Baltimore, her face glowed, and she showed her own glorious womanhood in every word and gesture. I count it one of the rare privileges of a busy life that I knew Miss Willard face to face. Her life has been to me an inspiration, as well as to thousands of others. While we might differ as to ways and means, we didn't differ in the great principle which we were working for. I delighted in the health of that mind, and as department after department developed in the Woman's Christian Temperance Union, I felt that the leader must have initiated them all, and to her was the praise due.

Is not her spirit still with the work, and shall not the Master allow her beautiful life still to linger in the midst of those who so loved her? Surely yes!

New York City.   GRACE H. DODGE.

I never met Miss Willard but once, but we had been the best of friends for many years through correspondence. We had a great many interests in common, and though we were both very busy women, we came to know each other quite well through the medium of the mail bag.

I had always had a dim idea that Miss Willard was a rather severe person; but when I met her I found her one of the "cosiest" women whom I had ever known. Miss Willard chaffed me a little for not being on her side of the woman question; but she was very amiable about it, and seemed sanguine that I would come round to her way of thinking in the end. I am sure that if anyone could have converted me to that side of the question, it would have been this gentle lady. We had tea out under an enormous oak, and Miss Willard was the life (or perhaps I should say the soul) of the party; when she spoke everyone listened, and with reason, for she never spoke unless she had something interesting to say.

New York City.   JEANNETTE L. GILDER.

I knew Miss Willard in her girlhood, when she was a student in school at Evanston, Illinois. She then gave evidence of the remarkable qualities of mind and character which were afterwards so thoroughly exemplified in her public career. It is useless to review, or even to allude to her work. That is on record. The instructive and encouraging thought to me is the illustration she furnishes of the power of a great personality to impress itself upon mankind. Born in comparative obscurity, she emerged, through the innate qualities of her noble mind and loving heart, into the "white light" which beats not only upon the throne, but upon those who rule the hearts of men.

Washington, D. C.   LYMAN J. GAGE.

Carlyle somewhere describes the insight of genius as "co-operation with the real tendency of the world." Among the great world tendencies of the last half century have been those toward organization, the emancipation of women, the Christianizing of reforms, and the drawing of Christians of every name into closer relations. Miss Willard had the genius to lay hold of these great strands and braid them into The Woman's Christian Temperance Union — one of the great organizations of modern times, in which woman is finding herself, and one whose Christianity is actively philanthropic, while its philanthropy is actively Christian. But few, even now, have gained the clear vision of the social mission of Christianity which Miss Willard had ten years ago. She had the genius to see, the courage to act, and the ability to accomplish. She was one of the great women of the world, and made all peoples her debtors.

New York City.   JOSIAH STRONG, D.D.,
General Secretary of the Evangelical Alliance.

Miss Willard was an ideal character, gentle yet bold, kind yet firm as adamant for the right.

The moving spirit of her life was heaven begun within, and we must wait until we see her in her heavenly home, through spiritual eyes, and in an atmosphere that casts no shadows, before we can do justice to the inner life and character of our glorified sister, Frances E. Willard. Earth has been enriched by her life and presence. The noble W. C. T. U. have lost a sister, friend, wise counsellor and brave leader. We all have lost a noble colaborer, and a sympathetic friend.

New York City. ANTHONY COMSTOCK.

I saw Miss Willard in New York about the first of February. I thought she was hovering on the brink of the Great Beyond then. She tried to appear as bright and full of energy as ever, and did not appear to realize her condition. She spoke to me of what she wished to do when she should recover. I knew her for a period of about twenty-five years, having met her shortly after her return from her first trip abroad. She was a most remarkable, a most extraordinary woman in every respect. She possessed all the attributes of a great general. She superintended every branch of her work, which included the world. She was a most masterly woman and was a representative one in every respect. She was a bunch of magnetism, possessing that occult force which all leaders must have. I never approached her but what I felt my nerves tingle from this magnetism. She had a great depth of understanding. Her brain was developed in a most wonderful manner. She seemed to have the power, so seldom possessed, to take in everything at once. The loss will be keenly felt throughout Christendom, and by every person who recognized the ability of this jewel of women.

Rochester, N. Y. SUSAN B. ANTHONY.

The characteristics which differentiated Miss Willard from every other numan being were her unique identity and sympathy with every other human being. Cicero says that, "Every man is more like every other man than he is like himself." Behind our crust of self we have a common human heart. If it can be liberated and enlarged our hearts will flow together. So the "Son of Man" is drawing all men unto Him by His self-sacrifice. The soul which takes His cross receives His power. A true soul will turn and draw to itself the best side of every other soul which will let itself be true.

So, the mystery of Miss Willard's power was its simplicity, that purity of heart which saw God and loved God with all the heart and loved neighbor as self.

But how was such a light prepared? The life of the "Great Mother" answers the question in part. We should add the influence of the strong father and of the lives of Puritan ancestry, in whom the Law and the Prophets had grown for three centuries until the time was fully come for a generation in whom the might of truth could be clothed with the grace of the Gospel to win the world. Then came the secluded education, like that of the boy at Nazareth — subject to parents and communing with nature and with God. Then at the crisis when such a gifted mind came to measure itself with other minds and with the great ranges of thought and was in peril of that pride which is the ruin of the soul, came that conversion, when in a crisis of a fever, the spirit, alone with God, resolved, "I will try to be a Christian girl." She turned and slept, and woke to a newness of life for herself, and in large measure, for her generation.

It was a generation whose best womanhood had shared the same discipline of former times and felt the same exigencies of the present. They entered into the great "Crusade" of the home against the saloon. When the enthusiasm of that Crusade reached Illinois Miss Willard had won a place among the foremost educators of the time. High positions were calling for her. But the mind and heart and soul of the best womanhood was in the movement, and the most whole-minded, whole-hearted and whole-souled of women could but be in it. Her very forgetfulness of self could but put her in the front of that larger self. By the most natural law, without effort or intent, her genius pervaded it and gave form and life to that Woman's Christian Temperance Union in which the Crusade enthusiasm found a body in which the consecrated womanhood of Illinois and our country, and the world, could unite in the labor and prayer to enlarge the walls of home to a pavilion to cover every nation and every soul — a tabernacle where God may dwell with men.

We cannot all have her gift. Can we not all seek that consecration of every gift we have by which we, too, shall win our share of all? Can we not learn that almost last word of hers to " Say *we*, not I—for is it not *our* Father?"

Beloit, Wis.   Prof. Joseph Emerson.

We cannot do otherwise than lament, for our own sake, the loss of Miss Willard's companionship and active service in the fields of her leadership; but we ought still more to rejoice over the welcome we know she has received to a higher service in a more exalted sphere. She was especially distinguished for a remarkable combination of purity, courage and strength. She was richly endowed with a genius for quickly perceiving and promptly improving opportunities for progress.

The leader of the greatest army of reform which the world has yet seen, she commanded the devoted service of her followers by her own inspiring example, and the transcendent ability with which she united forces not altogether harmonious, and removed difficulties and surmounted obstacles which would have discouraged less daring souls. In moral influence it is not too much to say that she was the foremost woman of her time. Her greatness consisted in her command of all her resources, and her readiness to act in an emergency.

Chicago.   C. C. BONNEY,
President of the Columbian Exposition Congresses.

The Council of Jewish Women, representing sixty-one cities, desire to express, through their executive officers, their heartfelt sympathy to the officers and members of the Woman's Christian Temperance Union, upon the death of their great leader, Miss Frances Willard; and to assure them that the Council of Jewish Women mourn with them the loss of a beloved sister and friend. Her name and her works will live forever as an inspiration to a nobler life.

Chicago.   H. G. SOLOMON,
President.

The death of Frances Willard deprived me of a personal friend whom I had known for thirty years. As we were for a time near neighbors in lovely Evanston, I knew her rare qualities of mind and heart as few could who had not met her amid the sanctities of the home and in the smallest circle of intimate friends. To those of us who were associated in educational work in Evanston it was a sore trial to have this gifted and accomplished woman resign the Deanship of the Woman's College and take up an untried work which was then in its infancy. It was manifestly a heavenly vision which called her and she was not disobedient. God's hand has been upon her and over her through all the years. Her gentle face is veiled from our mortal sight, but she is still here in the fragrance of undying memories, and in those invisible ministries which bind in unbroken unity "the whole family in earth and heaven."

Detroit, Mich.   (BISHOP) W. X. NINDE.

"The bravest are the tenderest,
The loving are the daring."

Such was Dr. Frances E. Willard, one of the few doctors of laws that really taught what civil laws should be, namely, translations of God's laws, and in a measure cut away, with firm but kind surgery, the cancers that human wickedness and weakness had developed in them.

Her most characteristic phrase, I think, was that word of large charity about those who opposed, or neglected, the many reforms she championed — "The arrest of thought has not come." To how many, and how sweetly, she brought that "arrest," arousing from error not only, but also from luxurious indifference, enlisting women with no higher aim than social pleasure in the grander joy of promoting social welfare.

Washington, D. C.   REV. DR. WILBUR F. CRAFTS,
Superintendent of the Reform Bureau.

Miss Willard seemed to me to express, as completely as any person I have ever known, the force of moral energy. Her whole nature was vitalized, and she seemed to utilize every ounce of her power. Her vivacity, breadth of interest and capacity for work, were evidenced by her sustained and varied activities, but her endurance can be explained only by recalling her passion for human service. This passion included not only her steady endeavor for public causes, but her constant and tireless effort to find place, room and work for others.

New York City.   HAMILTON W. MABIE

No work that Frances Willard did was small. But these two characteristics marked her service of humanity. She moved continually from the lesser to the greater, and she grew younger and fresher with the lapse of years. These two are the rarest and most potent qualities that God gives to men. The climax of a great life would have been reached if she had left the body after the establishment of the first World-Union for the world's sake and the culmination of her great work for temperance. But she was greater than this. By a new birth in her last years her vision was enlarged, her horizon was extended, and she has spoken, among her last words, her greatest message, the prophecy and the inspiration of a true social regeneration.

Boston, Mass.   BENJAMIN FAY MILLS.

Miss Willard differed from other women in her unselfishness, in her great love and tenderness to all with whom she came in contact; she never forgot any one and had the ability to call by name anyone she had ever known. A little incident comes to my mind illustrating this. In one of our Eastern cities, after one of her great speeches, when surrounded by a number of eminent people, she felt a touch on her sleeve, and looking around saw an uncouth and unkempt backwoodsman, who had known her in her girlhood days. Promptly she held out her hand, saying to those around her: "This is my old friend 'Tom,' whom I knew in the old farm days." I think she excelled other women in her consecration to duty, for which she gave up all, *even her life*. Her loving loyalty to friends, her great force of character, her personal amiability, her gentle strength, and above all, her pure womanliness, make her character stand out one by itself.

Chicago.   AMANDA B. CRANDALL.

Miss Willard possessed the scope and grasp of principles essential to statesmanship, and combined with these that delicate tact and facility in making concessions as to details, indispensable to the successful politician.

In the annals of this remarkable woman's career the historian of the civil and social life of the last half of the nineteenth century will find large materials. Her sympathy, her tenderness, her versatility, her tact, and above all, her power of generalization, compelled the slightest incidents to plead her cause, and enabled her to turn conversation which had started upon any subject whatever, to the illumination of her two great themes — the emancipation of the race from the tyranny of liquor, and the emancipation of women from political subjection.

In the course of her public career Frances E. Willard has been an honored guest in thousands of homes — homes that have included representatives of every class from cottage to palace. Every home that has sheltered her has been lifted by her presence to the dignity and the pure solemnity of a temple. Such are the temples in which will be nourished the high thoughts and lofty hopes sown by her influence.

Indianapolis, Ind.
MAY WRIGHT SEWALL,
President International Council of Women.

Through Miss Willard's efforts, thousands upon thousands of men and women have been educated up to the level of the woman suffrage movement, and have been brought to see the truth of her words — "The mother-heart must be enthroned in all places of power before its edicts will be heeded."

Boston, Mass. ALICE STONE BLACKWELL.

Love is the *greatest* thing in the world. How loving and true our dear Miss Willard was! The heart that dictated "Nineteen Beautiful Years," which so absorbed Lady Henry Somerset, was, as Lady Henry said, "Not Christly but a Christ." Miss Willard gave her life that she might "tell everybody to be good." We have gone in and out as neighbors with perfect harmony. Our entire family owe a debt of love to Miss Willard which can be paid only with love. To me she is not dead but gone forward, where they who lived on earth and now are glorified in heaven will some time greet us.

Evanston, Ill. MRS. C. P. BRAGDON.

Frances Willard was as great in her gentleness and sweetness of spirit as she was in her intellectual power, her eloquence, or her goodness. . . . Bitter and cruel things were hurled at her devoted head a thousand times. Her soul was as sensitive as the surface of a mountain lake to the kiss of the wind; but no attack from the common enemies of her cause, or from within the sisterhood she loved, ever soured her, or embittered her feelings, or robbed her of the gentleness and sweetness of her nature. . . .

Her faith in God, her devotion to Christ, her faith in humanity, were boundless. I never knew anyone who saw more clearly the possibility of good in broken and soiled human hearts and lives than did she. She lived in such harmony with the Christ that she looked upon the toilworn, the discouraged and the sinful among her brothers and sisters from the standpoint of her Lord.

Underneath the frayed and tattered garments of broken and sinful humanity she ever saw the hidden, possible Christ.

Wherever in America, or in the world, men and women fight for righteousness, and give themselves as a sacrifice to soothe the world's heartache, the name and memory of Frances Willard will be to them a comfort and an inspiration

Brooklyn, N. Y.   REV. LOUIS ALBERT BANKS, D.D.

Any words of eulogy which I write of our beloved and now sainted leader and sister, Frances Willard, whose brave life is so fully before us, seem like holding a dim lantern, that we might see more clearly the brilliant electric arc light.

No daughter of our own or any nation has labored more faithfully to show, in its true light — personal and legal — that mighty evil, the open saloon. She felt as keenly for the men, women and children who were the voluntary or innocent victims of this dire malady as though they were of her own kindred. A pity, well-nigh divine, filled her heart with almost superhuman power to work on until the fire in the soul burned out its earthly dwelling. This was the source of the untiring energy with which she strove, with tongue and pen, to comfort the suffering and reprove those who, by personal example and the almost omnipotent power of the ballot, upheld the traffic which opens the gateway to every form of vice that can be named.

Castile, N. Y.   CORDELIA A. GREENE, M.D.

Frances Willard was a woman who touched life at almost every point. She had the widest range of interests, the most all-embracing sympathies, and that charity which not only thinketh no evil, but which was so vital in its kindling love as to fairly transform evil into good, or negative faults into positive virtues. She had the most remarkable combination of power and delicacy; she carried the refined courtesy of the drawing-room into all her public life; she gave of the infinite riches of personal love and tenderness not only to near friends, but to a wide circle associated with her only in public interests; she made of even the casual acquaintance a devoted personal friend. She had a gift which can hardly be characterized as other than divination, which enabled her to immediately establish direct relations with each person she met. That lethargy of the soul, that paralyzed condition of affection and sympathy which we know as indifference, was utterly foreign to her nature. Her delicate, discriminating sympathy and keen interest and earnest good will so went out to every human being that they were as a magnetic current, lifting their object to a higher plane of living and revealing to him a truer purpose in life. She inspired one with an aim even if he had not heretofore held before himself definite ideals. Nor was this done consciously, with any attitudinizing in the rôle of counselor, but it was rather the unconscious effect of her noble personality. There was always about her an atmosphere of angelic purity, as of one a little apart from the common ways of life — not in the least an aloofness or abstraction, for her interest in everyone who came near her was greater than are even the usual friendships of social contact. The truth is that she was more alive than most people with that larger and more intense life of the spirit. No other American woman ever inspired such universal love; and still it is equally true, though it seem a paradox, that no woman has been less adequately interpreted, simply in that she was far greater than was realized. Frances Willard lived, literally, the Christ-life on earth. She was more divine than human, more spiritual than temporal, in the qualities of her character. . .

In meeting Miss Willard one could hardly fail to recall Spenser's lines:

"For of the soul the body form doth take;
For soul is form, and doth the body make."

The slender figure, the Madonna-like face with the deep blue eyes and the framing of golden-brown hair; the serene radiance and radiant serenity; the perfect refinement and gracious sweetness of her manner — that gentle, strong and illumined presence — never can that picture fade from our hearts!

Boston, Mass. LILLIAN WHITING.

A much holier war, and with weapons much diviner than all of which bloody battlefields and crimson oceans have felt the withering fury, calls for volunteers in our very land. It is the battle against the ignorance of the people and its slavery to demons that sap its virility and undermine its virtues. One heroine in this fight, a woman of light and leading, has passed to her reward. Many of us, and I among them, do not accept her manual of arms. Our strategy does not follow hers. But even we would be untrue to the best that stirs within us would we withhold from her the tribute due to her matchless devotion to high ideals. Miss Willard loved her kind with a love that passed understanding. And this love it was that sent her out a soldier to the battle. We, too, remember her among the torchbearers and the leaders.

Chicago. RABBI EMIL G. HIRSCH.

Frances E. Willard belonged to the twentieth century rather than to the nineteenth, and appreciation of her will increase as the race advances. It was not simply her brilliant intellect and splendid courage, but her genuine womanliness which enabled her to win the hearts of all. Her title to heavenly fame is the fact that she left the world better than she found it. The Ohio Wesleyan University is proud to have conferred upon her, along with William McKinley and Bishops Thoburn and Warren, the degree of LL.D. in 1894.

Delaware, Ohio. REV. J. W. BASHFORD, D.D.
Pres. Ohio Wesleyan University.

Every great leader is judged by his or her symbols and watchwords, and when Frances Willard, having fused the great world-embracing sympathies of the divinest spirits who have blessed our planet, intoned with her strangely sympathetic voice the Christlike message, "*For God, and home, and every land,*" she met a response from religionists, home-makers and patriots throughout the world — from worshipers of God and lovers of man.

Perhaps all do not recognize the mystic power of that trinity of truths, *for God, and home, and every land.* As we glimpse the enchanting vision of the new heavens and the new earth, and recognize the truth that "the little children are to lead us into the kingdom of Heaven," Miss Willard seems to be a veritable John the Baptist, and the beloved disciple, announcing the nearer approach of the message of the Madonna, as, holding the divine child aloft, the holy mother proclaims the divinity of humanity—the parenthood, not fatherhood alone, or motherhood alone, but the parenthood of the Creator and the familyhood of the created.

When a great soul comes to earth to do a special work, Infinite wisdom prepares the environment and the opportunity. Those of us who knew, loved and appreciated Madam Willard, recognize the rich heritage she bestowed upon her daughter.

Believing as we do that the Creator has chosen to manifest Himself as Wisdom, Love and Beauty, and recognizing beauty as a mighty force in the world, we were so glad to have that final message to the world, "How beautiful it is to be with God"; since through recognition of this sublime truth, is art, music, literature and education to receive its baptismal touch."

We seem to catch the vibrations of her joy, as she recognizes, with spiritual vision, the approach of a great army of wonder workers. They come, fearing no opposition to their constructive work, dreading no defeat, but conscious of complete final victory of truth and faith and love and joy. They come with a dauntless courage, an inspiring faith, a radiant hope, because they have heard the celestial harmonies of the angelic chorus, inhaled the fragrance of the lilies of the new annunciation, and felt the baptismal touch of the new name upon their foreheads.

They believe that the new day has dawned, the new age is here. Its herald is peace; its trumpeter is joy; its angels are love, wisdom and beauty; its ideals are development, opportunity, service and co-operation; while the inspiration of hope and faith, and the basis of its ministry is the organization of the inhabitants of earth into one happy, harmonious family.

Evanston, Ill.   Elizabeth Boynton Harbert.

Saint Frances was truly one of those who in life, in death, in resurrection, followed the Lord; she was the spotless sainted queen of womankind of whom we may well be proud and thank God for having raised such a mighty ruler of the World's Women's Republic. She was a miracle of Christ in this nineteenth century, for the more we see the state of women in Christless countries the more do we realize that none but Christ could have raised woman to such a high position as was occupied by her. What wisdom; what a spirit of understanding; what a power to rule not only a small body but the whole world; and, above all, what sublime Christlike love and humility did our beloved leader possess!

Under her leadership, kingdom after kingdom was conquered until the whole world was encircled with the band of love and her white standard of peace was planted in every land. Her standard shall never fall, her dynasty shall never die, and her memory shall never be wiped away from the face of the earth. The mother of Reform; the brave champion of the oppressed; the great leader and queen of womankind.

Poona, India. THE PUNDITA RAMABAI.

It is chiefly through Miss Willard's extraordinary power of leadership that the World's W. C. T. U. is the most widely established and powerful woman's organization in the world. No organization ever had a more capable leader. She possessed in an unequaled degree the power of overcoming difficulties and turning them into successes. She inspired those who worked with her with confidence and faith; ever quick to recognize all indications of general or special power in those she met, she was thus continually building up character, an essential for one who must lead a great movement. Her personal magnetism was indescribable, and to this charm were added genius, literary skill and eloquence, all in the highest degree of development. She lived high above all hate, and was always helping those who "were climbing." No woman has done as much as Frances Willard to make the world a wider place for women. She won the affection and admiration of millions in many lands.

She did not believe in keeping words of praise only to breathe them into dead, cold ears, leaving the thirsty soul to go through life unrefreshed and longing for the kind words which are so plentifully poured upon the grave.

She loved great undertakings; the World's W. C. T. U. was the greatest outcome of her life. Recently White Ribbon missionaries had been sent to Australia, Japan, Egypt and Ceylon, and her chief desire was that all our well organized countries should send more money, so that we could respond to the piteous appeals from Burmah, Chile, and some European and other countries.

The day she died, a W. C. T. U. was organized by one of our World's missionaries in Jerusalem.

Every woman has lost a friend by the death of Frances Willard. For all time her influence will live. The light of her character was more than anything she ever said. She had a Christlike personality.

White Ribbon women will now all over the world work more than ever side by side in "the world's larger home" which she helped to make.

Ripley, Derbyshire, Eng. AGNES E. SLACK,
Secretary World's W. C. T. U.

Miss Willard attained to a greatness which has been attained by no other woman of this century. What were the materials out of which this greatness was evolved? Two words contain the answer — character and genius, and the chiefest of these was character. Her genius commanded admiration, but her character compelled respect and love; and everyone who knew her, from the highest to the lowest, could but bow down before this compelling power. And herein lies the especial blessing of the legacy left us by her noble and inspiring life. Her genius we cannot have, but her character we may; and if by her death we should all learn the secret of this rare and beautiful character, she will accomplish even far more by that death than she accomplished while living, great as that was.

I have always thought, and often said, that she was the most Christlike woman I have ever met. Not that she impressed you as being what might be called "pious," which, alas! is often combined with a great deal of un-Christlikeness; but she impressed you as being good through and through, and above all, as being loved. More than any other human being I have known she fulfilled that marvelous definition of love in 1 Cor. xiii: Love suffereth long and is kind, love envieth not, seeketh not her own, is not easily provoked, thinketh no evil, rejoiceth not in iniquity but rejoiceth in the truth, beareth all things, believeth all things, hopeth all things, endureth all things, and, chiefest of all, never faileth. This was Frances Willard. It was not her friends only whom she loved in this Christlike fashion, but it was the world; not human beings only, but humanity itself. And the world she loved after this manner could not but love her in return. Although never an actual mother, she mothered humanity, and all humanity that came in contact with her rejoiced in her mothering.

She was my intimate personal friend for twenty-five years, and during all that time I can truthfully say she never once disappointed my ideal of love. With her judgment I sometimes disagreed, but with her spirit never. She seemed like a person who had, as some one expresses it, "changed eyes with Christ." She looked at everything and everybody through His eyes, and saw the good, and not the evil, in all.

The wonderful and commanding thing about her was that she did not possess her views, but they possessed her; they were herself. She was the greatest democrat I ever knew, not because she advocated any especial democratic measures, although she did this abundantly; but because she literally seemed to know no difference between human beings on account of any outward distinctions of class or money or social position. All human beings were to her the children of our one Father, and in each she recognized a sister or a brother. She was, therefore, the defender of all who were oppressed and the upholder of every forlorn hope in reform.

London, Eng.   HANNAH WHITALL SMITH.

We have come together to offer our tribute of deep, heart-felt regret for the departure of the loved and valued presence from amongst us, but also to assert that there must surely be no single shadow of anything like despondency.

There can be no despondency with those who believe; we have no cause to mourn over the ending of a noble life, over the unclasping of the sword, the resting of the Amazon after the long fight, the weary gone to God.

Miss Willard's personal influence, her platform gifts, her wonderful power of organization, her single-heartedness, her continuous communion with the Source of all power are really the reasons why that institution, the W. C. T. U., is now spread over the whole surface of the civilized world. I can remember when I was in Philadelphia, a single sentence of hers being repeated to me which made a great impression on my mind. It was during the liquor war in Texas, and whether consciously or unconsciously, she almost repeated the very language of one of her opponents. He said: "We are bound to win. We have the drinking men on our side; we have the foreigner on our side; we have money on our side — and money is a power, and don't you forget it!" A few days later she was there speaking and she ended her oration with somewhat similar words: "We are bound to win. We have the sober men on our side; we have the women on our side; we have God on our side — and God is a power, and don't you forget it!" Let us also remember "God is a power, and don't you forget it!"

Lest we forget, lest we forget. Do you not believe that somehow, not to be defined by us, there is a blending of spirit with spirit — soul to soul — mingling with a finer element than its own? Would she not give you this day that mighty word, "God is a power; don't you forget it"?

The work she leaves behind is with us, the laborer's task is done; but the lesson we should take away this afternoon is this: When a great artery is ligatured, it is the duty of all the capillaries to take on the work of the great artery; it behooves every one of us — we lesser capillaries and veins — to carry on the circulation of the truth she spread abroad, so that humanity shall not suffer. One object of this service ought to be that we each of us dedicate ourselves definitely afresh to the work to which she gave her life.

We are all assured of the irrefutable immortality of the soul of the one we loved, and know that she has reached that far world whither we are all bound.

We bless Thy holy name, O Father, for all Thy servants who have departed this life in Thy faith and fear, and especially for Thy servant, Frances Willard, beseeching Thee to give us grace that we may follow their good example, that we, too, may inherit the Heavenly Kingdom.

London, Eng. THE REV. CANON WILBERFORCE.

Miss Willard set a very noble example of self-denying labor on behalf of a great cause, and she showed how grand a work may be achieved by a single-hearted toiler, inspired by the love of God and man.

THE REV. F. W. FARRAR,
Dean of Canterbury.

Miss Willard's sudden death is a great shock, and it must be a grief to everyone who cares for the progress of good in the world. We shall feel it here almost as much as will our American friends, for of late years we had been familiarized with her splendid work and were able to some extent to appreciate it. The losses by death of our best friends within a very limited period, have of late been little less than appalling. It seems strange that they should have been called away, just when the common enemy, against which they fought so nobly, is *apparently* stronger than ever. Nevertheless, their labor and that of their colleagues have laid a sure foundation for ultimate triumph, and whether the remaining conflict be long or short, the remembrance of what they have been and done will be ever to us an abiding comfort and encouragement.

London, Eng. SIR WILFRID LAWSON, Bart., M.P.

Miss Frances Willard, whom I knew in public life, was certainly one of the most remarkable women I ever met. There was such deep earnestness, such a profound sense of the justice of her cause which she looked upon as the cause of God. She never seemed to waver as to the ultimate victory of her principle. There was also a wonderful calmness, indicating a pent reserve of silent strength. Her intellectual powers were of a high order. She grasped the bearings of great questions with remarkable power. Her oratory was of a convincing character, her speeches were apparently well prepared, and delivered without any effort or display. They were often eloquent and full of pathos. The good work she has done in the world will live after her, and her memory will be highly cherished by all those who love the truth. Her loss is irreparable. There is no one left to take her place exactly. We wait God's leisure to raise up another woman with the same deep convictions, energy and power. The world needs at this time many such, but, in the providence of God, these have never failed at the last — men and women to hold aloft the banner of truth and righteousness; and we doubt not that many arms are being strengthened for the valorous work of God in time to come.

London. REV. CANON BARKER.

It is fitting that when a good woman such as Miss Frances Willard passes to her rest her name should be held in honor. Miss Willard wielded a great influence on both sides of the Atlantic, and it was always used with whole-hearted zeal for the betterment of the masses. In the Woman's Christian Temperance Union she built up an organization which gave her an immense power in combating the evils of intemperance, and which will, let us hope, long continue to carry on the good work. As its leader and inspirer, she always acted in a broad and kindly spirit. Catholic temperance leaders in the United States, such as Archbishop Ireland, were among her warmest friends, and if Catholics were ever attacked by bigots in her presence, she did not neglect the opportunity of vindicating them. Her life was devoted to the cause which she had so earnestly at heart, and there is little doubt that her career was shortened by her devotion to it.—*Catholic Times, of Liverpool, England.*

I never had the privilege of knowing Miss Willard, nor did I ever hear her speak; but I followed her sayings and doings with the deepest interest. She seemed to me a typical representative of the New World and of the new age of womanhood. She was entirely the woman in her tenderness, her sympathy, her habit of looking at people and things in the concrete and not in the abstract; but at the same time she exhibited that freedom from all affectation and sentiment, that strength and steadiness of judgment, that power of rejection and construction which we too often claim especially for the masculine mind. Her departure is a loss to almost every good cause which makes for the welfare of humanity.

Pendleton, Manchester. REV. CANON HICKS.

Of all the women I have known, Frances Willard was unquestionably one of the very ablest as well as one of the very best. She belonged to the order of *great* women. She was great in what she did, greater in what she was. Dowered in amplest measure by nature with those faculties and capacities which specially minister to one's own enjoyment of everything beautiful in nature, in literature and in art, she nevertheless chose the somber-seeming path in life of the social reformer.

Miss Willard possessed the perspicacity to discern that to strive for social reform without solving the drink problem would be like "plowing the sand,"

Hence, she was first and chiefly a *temperance* reformer. But she was by no means a woman of one idea. Indeed, she was a woman of many ideas. For example, she had a profound and special interest in all that concerns the well-being of women. Besides, more than anyone else, she was responsible for an experiment in the carrying on of the temperance reformation which, it is true, has led to much debate and some heartburning among women's temperance associations throughout the world, but which, though still on its trial, promises well. Rightly or wrongly, she regarded the temperance question as but one of a number of closely allied social problems which are so connected that they can be most profitably treated when studied and dealt with together; and she more or less successfully urged on the societies of which she was a leader the adoption of a policy giving effect to her convictions on this subject. But, assuredly, the conception of the methods by which she impressed her own beliefs in regard to this subject on such masses of intelligent women in the United States, in Great Britain and in other parts of the world, has revealed something of the great scope and force of her intellect; while the manner in which, and the extent to which, these methods were brought into successful operation have demonstrated her to have been one of the most capable of organizers and administrators.

Manchester, Eng. JAMES WHYTE,
Secretary of the United Kingdom Alliance.

Frances Willard was a woman of fine gifts. She had the insight of a seer, the heart of a philanthropist, the courage of a crusader, the organizing ability of a trained engineer, the enthusiasm of a missionary, the pen of a journalist, the tongue of a skilled orator, and the purity of a saint. She was a typical woman worker in the completeness of her consecration to Christ; in her piercing insight into, and accurate interpretation of, the condition of the people; in the fineness of her courage and the breadth of her sympathy; in her capacity for leadership, and in the whole-hearted use she made of her life for others. She takes higher rank in the social service of mankind than Mrs. Somerville in mathematics, Jenny Lind in song, George Eliot in literature, Adelaide Anna Proctor in poetry. Surely we may say, "Many daughters have done virtuously, but thou excellest them all!"

London, Eng. REV. JOHN CLIFFORD, M.A., D.D.,
President of the National Council of Evangelical Free Churches of London.

Frances Willard stood for the capacity of women to do, to act, to plan all by their lone selves. She might have done more for temperance and other causes if she had allowed men to work in the W. C. T. U., but she would have done less for women. It was her great work — teaching women that they could do things by themselves. Women who knew, and those more numerous who felt the significance of the stand she made, felt toward her a *devotion* which no mere apostolate of temperance could have evoked.

She was an abler woman in the minutiæ of organization than was generally believed. She had great tact in managing people, in making them do what it was necessary they should do, while making them imagine they were doing it of their own free will. She was very tender-hearted and sympathetic. She had the greatest gift — a gift amounting to a perfect genius — for inspiring those who worked with her with the most absolute belief in her cause, and in her as its exponent. Those who gathered round her were women of all kinds of thought and character. But one and all believed in Miss Willard against the world. There was something that was very touching in the way in which she made you feel that God needed you. She seemed to see things so clearly herself that somehow you could not help seeing them as she did. The secret of her great hold upon her staff was not alone her personal charm, the magnetic influence; it was that she was the truth, and you could not go against her without antagonizing the truth.

That was the first secret and the greatest. The second was the same which appealed to many who never met her personally. She had a great cause. When I compare her with other women I think she is conspicuous for steadfastness. There was about her a steady determination that made you see that when the principle was touched she was iron all through. If she had not been iron she would have bent or broken; she did neither, she stood erect, and we all learned to regard her as the pillar of strength in the midst of all perils.

London, Eng.   W. T. STEAD.

I had the pleasure of meeting Miss Willard on several occasions, and she always seemed to me a woman of remarkable intellectual power, broad in her sympathies, with a warm and loving heart, and an enthusiastic devotion for all that is true and good and noble. As a speaker of the highest order, and as a worker and organizer of remarkable skill, she was a pillar of strength to the movement, and one of its brightest ornaments. It was very pleasing to learn in conversation with her, of her deep interest in temperance work among children. She recognized the truth that the training of the young in habits of sobriety and purity is the best means of raising a nation's moral standard. I think it was the last time I had the pleasure of talking to her that she said, taking my hand to say good-by, "Mr. Wakeley, you are on the right lines. If the drink traffic is to go down, we must get hold of the young."

I think all have felt that Miss Willard was essentially a steward of "five talents," all well used in the service of God and of Humanity. The words of the slothful and unprofitable servant, "I was afraid," never existed in her vocabulary. She realized that time waits neither for man nor woman, that the world is saved or lost by individuals, and so she was intensely real, intensely earnest, and intensely determined to leave the world better than she found it. Under her leadership the women's division of the army of temperance has made mighty advances, and where shall we look for a General to fill her place? May God raise up women of zeal and courage to fitly occupy the post she has vacated. The movement will not want for valiant soldiers if they are found good and wise leaders; and for the young who are pressing into the foremost ranks, no more fitting model can be presented than the leader whose loss we now mourn.

A leader indeed in temperance warfare has gone; the faithful teacher's work on earth has closed, but the loving presence and the earnest voice will still plead with her sisters who remain to work with undivided faith and courage "for God, and Home, and Every Land."

Mr. Charles Wakeley,
General Secretary of the United Kingdom Band of Hope Union.

Miss Willard has always been in my mind and heart as a saint, a veritable Ray of Love from above; and as a talker alone I have never met her equal, except John Richard Green. Her loss to the world, and to Lady Henry Somerset as President of the B. W. T. A., are two great blows to me.

London, Eng. Mrs. Haweis.

It was, I think, in 1892 that Miss Willard first made the personal acquaintance in London of many members of the Fabian Society. I remember being struck by her large-minded sympathy with the work of those who were fighting battles on lines somewhat differently drawn from those on which she had hitherto been engaged. Nor did she start back in nervous apprehension, as so many of her countrymen do at the name of Socialism. Miss Willard had fought too many hard fights for the weak and the downtrodden not to know that every good cause, from Christianity itself down to the social reform movement of today, is promptly confused by its enemies with violence, incendiarism and the breaking up of laws. She found herself in close sympathy with the principles, objects and methods of the English Socialists, as represented by the Fabian Society, and in August, 1893, she, spontaneously and unsolicited, applied for membership, signed the Society's "basis" and continued until her death to send her annual contribution to the Society's funds.

Unlike so many temperance workers, Miss Willard threw herself with equal zeal into the abolition of the sweating system or the rehousing of the poor of our great cities, for she saw that in the absence of decent homes and living wages, no amount of preaching or prohibition would put down drunkenness. The emancipation and elevation of women took a leading place in her life; but she never supposed that women could be elevated without raising the men at the same time to a higher level. What she strove for, in fact, was not personal holiness, temperance or women's rights, but the progress of humanity. However keenly she distinguished the particular trees, she always retained a perfectly clear vision of the whole forest of which they formed but insignificant parts.

London, Eng.   SIDNEY WEBB.

Ten years ago this month (March, 1898) I saw Frances Willard for the first time. It was at an immense Sunday afternoon meeting in the largest chapel in Washington, D. C., and every inch of standing room was packed with people who had come to hear one of America's greatest women speak on a great theme, namely, that of personal and social purity. I set out to hear Frances Willard because of what others told me of her wonderful speaking, but not because I admired or loved her as yet.

It was with no preconceived notions about her, either as a woman or a leader of women, that I listened to her that Sunday afternoon; and it was well for my unbiased judgment that it was so, for I have never altered the estimate of her received almost unconsciously while she was speaking.

First of all, her sweet, calm face, clear-cut and good; her dignified manner, in which there was not a trace of assumption, gave me a most cordial feeling of swift personal attraction to her. Next, the power and ease with which the opening sentences of her address were given put all the usual misgivings one feels about a speaker's nervousness or ability to hold an audience, out of court entirely; and listening by itself became an increasing pleasure as she went on. By and by I found myself crying naturally and freely over words that ran in my memory as follows: "Nay, brothers all, that poor betrayed girl thought she was stepping out along the road to Heaven, and lo! when her lover forsook her and fled she found too late it was the path to Gethsemane and the Calvary of Motherhood!"

There was no need to cover one's tears up for shame, for everyone, man or woman, was weeping and sobbing in that great audience. There was a wonderful epigrammatic finish of pregnant sentences. Now and again some quiet humorous thrust like a rapier for fineness, or a witty sally relieved the tension of long-drawn pathos, but never for an instant did it seem incongruous or hostile to the delicacy of the subject dealt with, or turn the audience from the point at issue.

We exchanged our first greetings in the vestry afterwards, and I tried in my overwhelming gratitude to thank her for the uplift she had given me. "Dear little English sister," she said, "you can't think how pleased and proud I was to see you in front of me." This little episode was typical of the greatness of soul that enabled Frances Willard so instantaneously and spontaneously to say the best thing in the best way at the best time.

"God is wider than the world," she once said to me, "and the mistake is that the folks who are not wider than their own backyard are trying so hard to cut Him down to their size!'

It will always be a source of unspeakable comfort and satisfaction to me to think of the personal fellowship realized at intervals through ten wonderful years of happiest work with this great and beautiful soul.

London, Eng. MRS. ORMISTON CHANT.

Miss Willard was a remarkable woman — more remarkable than any other temperance apostle of her time. But to describe her simply as a temperance apostle is to only mention a single feature of her many-sided work. Yet in that particular phase of work her influence in America has been immeasurably greater than that of any other woman, and not less great than that of any man, Neal Dow and John B. Gough not excepted. Just as these were unique in their spheres, she was unique in her sphere — her still wider sphere. She was a talented student — well read in all phases of the work. Starting to organize the women of the American Republic, an emotional and difficult element to organize and keep going, she gathered around her the ablest, bravest and best; and to a degree never before dreamt of, she kept them together, her wonderfully perceptive faculties enabling her to select colleagues and departmental superintendents peculiarly fitted for their particular duties. Her policy was a "Do Everything" one — a policy evoking admiration even from those who deemed it inexpedient, and a policy which only a truly great woman could have "mothered" in the way she did.

She has done more than anyone since the days of slavery to put a new soul into American politics, and to make her sex the undying enemies of the liquor traffic; and has so organized the workers that the great machinery will go rolling on almost or quite unchecked by her withdrawal — although there is no one person who can really replace her. God buries the workers, but His work goes on.

London, Eng. COUNCILLOR JOSEPH MALINS,
Chief Templar of England and Chief of the International Supreme Lodge of the Good Templar Order.

From following Miss Willard's work and reading her utterances and writings I had formed a very high opinion of the great leader of women's work for social reform. My ideas of this splendid and unique personality were more than confirmed when I had the privilege of seeing and hearing her.

Miss Willard was a gifted orator, and when she kindled into her loftiest oratorical vein, it was simply magnificent. She knew, as few speakers have done, how to feel the pulse of her audience, and how to catch the breezes of emotion that swept through it, and at such times she swayed the multitude as she pleased, and roused them to the highest pitch of enthusiasm. She had a strong and massive intellect disciplined by high culture, and in all her speaking she had something to say worth remembering. Her orations were deep, earnest thought, kindled to a white heat by a soul set on fire with the love of God.

The thing, however, which most impressed me in this noble lady was that she possessed a gift of statesmanship such as has been bestowed on very few. She constructed and controlled vast organizations, and sent her own enthusiasm vibrating through them to their very extremities. She was always ready boldly to assert her convictions, no matter how much they might be against the popular prejudices; and she had the skill to put her ideas into practical shape, and to weld others together in a union for their accomplishment. Never shall I forget the impression that was made upon me concerning Miss Willard's gifts of statesmanship when I saw her in the chair of the great assemblies of the World's Women's Christian Temperance Union in London. It has been my privilege to see the conduct in the chair of some of the most eminent and renowned chairmen. I never saw anyone excel Miss Willard. Her knowledge of the rules for the conduct of such conferences was perfect. She had them at her fingers' ends and she guided the debates, sometimes through very stormy seas, with a tact and good humor which displayed great knowledge of human nature and wonderful capacity for government. She swayed the scepter with immovable firmness, and yet, as it seemed to me, with scarcely any manifestation of the fact that she was ruling. Her expression of face, her tones, and the spirit pervading all her utterances made you feel that she was a woman of God, and that the inspiration of all her work was from on high. A true Methodist, catholicity was her watchword. Adopting John Wesley's motto, she was "the friend of all and the enemy of none." Loyal in her devotion to her own church, there was nevertheless no sectarian stamp upon her work.

London, Eng. THE REV. G. ARMSTRONG BENNETTS, B.A.,
General Secretary of the Wesleyan Methodist Temperance Committee.

It was my great privilege to have been on more than one occasion with Miss Frances E. Willard on a temperance platform, and I am therefore able to speak of the fervid eloquence which often produced an electrifying effect on the large audiences she addressed in this country. It was not merely that she had a great command of language, that her imagination was fruitful and creative, her style vigorous, original, abounding in felicities of expression and combining judgment and sensibility in a remarkable degree, which placed her in the very forefront of orators of the present day, whether among men or women; but it was the intense earnestness and religious zeal which showed her utterances came straight from the heart, which carried conviction to her hearers. She made no compromise with the evil thing, whilst at the same time she felt deeply for the wretched victim of evil. To the rescue of suffering and sinful humanity she devoted all her energies and time. As she says in that remarkable address delivered to the National W. C. T. U. at Buffalo last October, and which I received from her not very long before her death, "We shall never climb to heaven by making it our lifelong business to save ourselves. The process is too selfish; the motto of the true Christian is coming to be, 'All for each and each for all,' and in the honest purpose to realize its everyday meaning we acquire 'a heart at leisure from itself,' and in no other way." The amount of work Miss Willard managed to get through was simply amazing, and when we consider that this had been going on for nearly twenty-five years — *i. e.*, since that wonderful Women's Crusade at Hillsboro, Ohio, in 1873 — we cannot be surprised at her having overtaxed her strength and thus sacrificed her life to the great cause she ever had at heart. She lived and died the lover of her kind and the admiration of her friends. We may indeed mourn her loss, but we have the consolation of knowing that her labor has not been in vain and that she was prepared to obey the summons, "the Master has come and calleth for thee"; for these striking words occur in her last address (alluded to above). "There will come a day when we shall utter these words back again, 'Lord Jesus, receive my spirit,' and then the mystery of life, its discipline, its joys and grief, will end and the glad mystery of death will work out the transfer to other realms of the Infinite Power."

THE VERY REV. DEAN LEIGH.

The Deanery, Hereford, March 6, 1898.

I labor under the obvious disadvantage of not having heard Miss Willard speak in public. I am assured by those who have heard her that this is a very great disadvantage indeed; and I regard the assurance as a high compliment to the wisdom and eloquence of that gifted speaker. I gladly accept the invitation to write a line or two as to impressions received from her conversation, and from a perusal of some of her notable public utterances. If I were called upon to use one word, and one word only, as expressing my estimate of Miss Willard, I should chose the word "refinement," or the word "delicacy." I am well aware that such words as energetic, eloquent, masterly, and highly informed, might be used with great propriety; yet if I were driven to one word I should say that

Miss Willard was consummately and sensitively refined. Everything about her bespoke intellectual and spiritual delicacy. It would be no effort to her to be eloquent and rhythmic in public speech, but it would be an effort, altogether beyond her accomplishment, to use either careless or unbalanced language. To some speakers and writers violent expletives occur quite naturally, and are used without a proper estimate of their real roughness and almost vulgarity. Such expletives would simply never occur to a mind so high-toned and so instinct with the very spirit of accuracy as was Miss Willard's. I question whether she ever revised a speech with a view to moderating its language, because it was simply natural to her to find exquisite language for exquisite thinking. It is needless to say that Miss Willard had no talent for abuse. She never villified an opponent. Even when she wrote under the spur of pain and disappointment, her case lost nothing by unfitness of expression. Emphatically her strength was in her moderation. How pictorial she was in all her exposition and argument! Even where there was no attempt at pictorial representation, it was impossible for the mind to follow her reasoning and her illustrations without investing their development with pictorial color and expressiveness. In reading her speeches I seem to be walking over landscape of hill and dale, wood and water, and to be hearing an accompaniment of singing birds, as her fluent periods roll on with measured stateliness. The motive power of this gifted woman seemed to be the very spirit of divinest love. She did not want everybody to be happy; she wanted everybody to be good, knowing that goodness brings its own satisfaction and delight. Miss Willard was no mechanical reformer, she did not handle things from the outside; she was profoundly assured of God's love to all mankind, and she wished all mankind to realize that supreme and all-redeeming and all-stimulating fact.

No one could be long with Miss Willard either socially or in communion with her books, without being impressed by her tender womanliness. A thorough scholar, an alert politician, a well-instructed philosopher, and a commanding public advocate, she was as simple as a little child, and as womanly as a mother who lives exclusively in the affections of her children. The touch of her hand, the subdued and almost tremulous music of her voice, her benign expression of countenance, her solicitous look of wonder and of yearning, were all so many evidences of a great, warm, tender heart. Little children ran to her as if by right. Old age looked up to her with assured and eager expectancy. Her presence in the house gave the sufferer strength and courage under the sting of pain and the cloud of grief. So great an example of everything lovely and noble cannot be lost. It must live forever as one of the ministries adopted by God to assist in the regeneration and sanctification of the world. I conclude this brief reference by quoting a sonnet written by my wife which clearly expresses my feeling as to the loss of visible leadership, and personal magnetism, which the world has sustained by the death of the beautiful, gracious, unselfish and great-hearted as well as great-minded Frances Willard.

> "Frances Willard is dead! is dead! is dead!
> Ring out the woful news on every wind
> And fill with grief the bosom of mankind.
> Not for one land she lived, her love heav'n fed,
> Compassed a world! She wove a mystic thread
> Enduring, strong, from heart to heart, to bind
> Souls consecrated; then in emblem twined
> White ribbon in a knot of love, and said:
> 'I call you, oh, my sisters, by this sign:
> Live unto God, let streams of home love flood
> Lands far and near, before its power divine
> Apollyon flies! The earth on which Christ stood
> Reels in its weakness, for its aid combine,
> Dare everything in strength of Love and God!'"

The City Temple, London.   DR. JOSEPH PARKER.

I am thankful for the opportunity of sharing in the tribute to the memory of Frances E. Willard. Although I saw her only once or twice, the impression that she left was that of a beautiful soul, inspired with the loftiest aims, wholly devoted to the service of God and man, and yet with a simplicity that amounted almost to self-forgetfulness. I need not speak of the great service she has rendered the cause of total abstinence throughout the world; her memory will be a strength and inspiration to all who are engaged in the fight against the ravages of strong drink. One of the greatest distinctions of the nineteenth century is that woman has taken her place on the public platform, and has dedicated her voice to the furtherance of great moral questions. Among these there are two of whom one has come to think as almost one, whose splendid services have been preëminently blessed. Their memory will be forever associated and gratefully treasured, their work and words are immortal. Those two are Frances E. Willard and Lady Henry Somerset.   THE REV. MARK GUY PEARSE.

London, Eng.

Frances Willard's bright and blessed life has left behind a long trail of light. Truly she has passed through the world and has left it better than she found it. Thousands in England and America will bless her name. She has been an inspiration and an uplift to them in every sense. To know Frances Willard was to admire and to love her. There was a rare combination in her of power, breadth of mind and intellect, humility and love. I can see her now as she rose to speak in the Queen's Hall at the Annual Meeting of the British Women's Temperance Association in 1896. A perfect ovation met her, cheer upon cheer, and then perfect silence as she spoke in her own inimitable way, full of power, breadth and sympathy; suffering as she was at the time, pain was nothing in comparison to the deliverance of the message that she bore.

We rejoice in her happiness, and look forward to that meeting of which she used to speak when she said, "In Heaven we shall have plenty of time to talk over all these things; here we are too busy."

Royal Sailors' Rest, Portsmouth, Eng.   AGNES WESTON.

To know Frances Willard was an inspiration. I was at the first meeting which she addressed in London and she cast a spell over me which will ever remain. What a delightfully unaffected platform style she had! Indeed it was not a "platform style"; it was her own sweet, witty and winning conversation in a slightly louder but never a harsh key heard from a higher sphere. A few sentences and she had conquered every member of her audience. The listeners were her admirers for life. I was blessed with her acquaintance, and she found time in the midst of her arduous duties to write once and again to encourage when the powers of evil seemed uppermost and to cheer when the Right triumphed. She loved London and took the keenest interest in the work of its County Council. It was delightful to see how the Londoners forgave and forgot her slight American accent when listening to her racy but always uplifting addresses. It was more delightful to hear her speak in her beloved America — as I did at Boston — when standing by John Burns she pleaded the cause of the workers and praised the temperance example which the labor leader set to his fellows. No woman that I ever met conjured up such a vision of the women of the Mayflower. She seemed to step from the fresco of the lobby of the House of Commons to preach the truths for which her ancestors suffered. Of her it might truly be said,

   "When pain and anguish wring the brow,
    A ministering angel thou."

London County Council.   J. WILLIAMS BENN.

From the first time I heard of Miss Willard, on the occasion of my visit to the United States some years ago, I have always and increasingly realized that she was the most distinguished and influential woman on the other side of the Atlantic. Everyone by some irresistible impulse or instinct naturally, inevitably, gave her the first place. She was a queen among women. It is difficult to disentangle my personal reminiscences from what I have heard and read of her remarkable life. Her own delightfully written autobiography, notwithstanding her modesty and reticence, inevitably discloses a most powerful intellect and an unusually tender heart. She had extraordinary gifts and was highly cultured. Her amiability impressed and attracted everybody, her presence was always a reconciling and healing influence, she lifted everybody and everything into the highest region of thought, emotion and duty. On the lofty mountain-top where she habitually walked with Christ, narrowness and smallness and unworthy sentiment were impossible; the microbes of jealousy and rivalry, of worldly ambition and petty strife could not live on the sunlit heights where she saw God face to face.

On the few occasions when I actually met her or had correspondence with her, I was much impressed by the insight with which she intuitively seized the situation and the main point at once, by the moral courage with which she rejoiced in the most audacious Christian enterprises and by the contagious enthusiasm with which she applauded everything that was energetically progressive in all departments of human life. It was so evident that she liked strong purpose and resolute endeavor and bold advance and high ideal. The more I became familiar with her history and her character, the more deeply I realized that she was literally one of the greatest and best of her sex, capable both of grasping and of originating vast comprehensive ideas and equal to the demands of any position in which she found herself, however difficult, however exalted that position might be. I feel that we cannot sufficiently praise God for what she was and for what she did. A few more such women, a very few, would change the face of the world and achieve revolutions of righteousness that at present seem impossible, but which become promptly easy when strong and gentle souls are filled with the Spirit of God. THE REV. HUGH PRICE HUGHES,
Superintendent of the West London Mission.

Flowers more exquisite than were ever blown in my poor garden, and hands more deft than mine to weave them, are needed for her memory whom we here commemorate; but I am very glad to cast a handful of violets and forget-me-nots on the memorial tablet. We met for the first time on the deck of an Atlantic liner, on the evening before reaching Queenstown. She had been very ill and seemed as fragile and transparent as a casket of very rare china — but what a pure and intense spirit burnt within as fire. We knew of each other; she had read some things that I had written, and our souls leapt to acknowledge a kind of comradeship and kinship; then we sat down to talk and did little else for so long as her strength lasted. How merry she was that night, with her pencil in hand as we interviewed each other, I for my magazine and she for hers. But somehow her questions went strangely to my heart, and searched where only a very delicate and tender perception of the mechanism of the soul could penetrate. From that moment we became fast friends, and wherever we met, there was the glance of recognition, which those give who have entered a little way, at least, into the secrets of each other's lives. There have not been many opportunities of taking up and carrying forward that intercourse, so happily begun. Life was so full for the woman who had learnt the secret of utilizing the great stores of womanly love and skill for the healing of the open sores of the world. How to characterize her! So many qualities met and blended in her richly endowed nature. *Sensitive* as the eye to the breath of the wind, or the aspen to the breeze, she was instantly affected by her surroundings, whether of flowers, or music, or scenes of beauty, appreciation or affection; but she was *strong* as basalt in the principles of faith and conduct which underpenned her character; no persuasion or influence could make her swerve from these, when once they possessed her. A tender grace and beauty of style combined with terse and vigorous eloquence. Warm in her sympathy with the suffering, the downtrodden and sorrowful; but terrible in her denunciation of wrongdoing. Animated by purposes that engirdled the world, but strong and intense in her special and particular friendships. With the mastery of great principles, but apt to deal with small details, and an adept in the niceties of domestic management and the woman's province in the home. Witty, and if occasion required, caustic, and yet so light in her raillery and gentle in her spirit that those who elicited her retorts were not hurt or irritated. The acknowledged leader of noble women, but equally admired by the sterner sex, whom she so often addressed as Brothers.

The heart of her heart was devotion to our Lord. How well I remember the last time I saw her, at the residence of her devoted friend, Lady Henry Somerset, at Reigate. She was much overwrought, and compelled to keep her chamber. As I entered, she accosted me as the shepherd who had come to see after the sick sheep; and as I spoke or read or quoted hymns or prayed, there was such a sympathetic hearing, so instant and hearty a response. That scene is vivid with me still and will be. But she is well today; and if the first rapture of the vision of the Lord has passed, we may think of her as turning her thoughts again upon the world she loved so much; and for evermore she will be divided between her rapture of devotion to her Lord keeping her near His Person, and her yearning love to bring nearer others who have not learnt or realized so much as she. Sister, we haste to the reunion. It is but a thin veil that parts us, and heaven is even lovelier now because thou hast entered it.

London, Eng.   THE REV. F. B. MEYER.